# Teaching Primary Physical Education

# Praise for the previous edition

'Useful for the non-specialist as well as the specialist. Great to support the current priority around PE Premium.'
**Mrs Catherine Carden, Canterbury Christ Church University**

'I like this book because it views PE in the primary school in the same way that I do. It takes a holistic approach, and focusses on basic/generic skills rather than on specific games or activities. There is also an intelligent focus on pedagogy and a clear relation to learning theory. A very useful book for initial teacher education and beyond.'
**Mrs Ann Jones, York St. John University**

'A very useful and comprehensive text on an area of the curriculum in which many trainees feel anxiety.'
**Ms Ingrid Spencer, University of Leicester**

'A very useful text for those students wishing to enter primary teaching. Content is a good mix of theoretical and practical perspectives.'
**Mr Gareth Williams, Edge Hill University**

# Teaching **Primary Physical Education**

Julia Lawrence

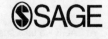

Los Angeles | London | New Delhi
Singapore | Washington DC | Melbourne

2nd Edition

Los Angeles | London | New Delhi
Singapore | Washington DC | Melbourne

SAGE Publications Ltd
1 Oliver's Yard
55 City Road
London EC1Y 1SP

SAGE Publications Inc.
2455 Teller Road
Thousand Oaks, California 91320

SAGE Publications India Pvt Ltd
B 1/I 1 Mohan Cooperative Industrial Area
Mathura Road
New Delhi 110 044

SAGE Publications Asia-Pacific Pte Ltd
3 Church Street
#10-04 Samsung Hub
Singapore 049483

Editor: James Clark
Assistant editor: Rob Patterson
Production editor: Tom Bedford
Copyeditor: Christine Bitten
Proofreader: Andy Baxter
Marketing manager: Dilhara Attygalle
Cover design: Sheila Tong
Typeset by: C&M Digitals (P) Ltd, Chennai, India
Printed in the UK

First edition published 2012
This second edition first published 2018

**Library of Congress Control Number: 2017933988**

**British Library Cataloguing in Publication data**

A catalogue record for this book is available from the British Library

ISBN 978-1-4739-7431-9
ISBN 978-1-4739-7432-6 (pbk)

At SAGE we take sustainability seriously. Most of our products are printed in the UK using FSC papers and boards. When we print overseas we ensure sustainable papers are used as measured by the PREPS grading system. We undertake an annual audit to monitor our sustainability.

For mum

# Contents

# About the Author

Dr Julia Lawrence has worked in initial teacher education for over 15 years and is currently based at The University of Hull. She has previously taught in Bedfordshire and Buckinghamshire, and worked at Brunel and Leeds Metropolitan Universities.

Julia has contributed to a number of textbooks associated with supporting those training to work in the education profession, both in physical education and the wider teaching context.

Her research focuses on pupils' experiences of physical education, in particular during the transition from primary to secondary school, as well as trainee teachers' experiences and mentoring in teacher education.

# Foreword

*Teaching Primary Physical Education* provides both theoretical and practical perspectives on teaching physical education in primary schools. The clear presentation and well-argued positions covered in the book should help teachers in the primary school to develop their understanding of the subject and hence become reflective practitioners in relation both to their work in this curriculum area and to the contribution physical education can make to the education of primary school children. This critically reflective stance should enable them to improve their practical day-to-day teaching of the subject as well as have the confidence and understanding to take on leadership roles in physical education, arguing for its unique and significant place in the curriculum.

This is a particularly valuable text as little has been written on the philosophy underpinning physical education in the primary school. Most recent research, debate and textbooks about physical education centre on secondary education. There are a number of reasons for this, including the fact that physical educationists involved in secondary school are specialists who have followed an in-depth study of the subject, whilst there are very few teachers in the primary school who have specialist knowledge of the subject area. Primary teachers are, in the main, generalists who have to cover the whole curriculum. These teachers have had minimal time to reflect on physical education on account of the multiple demands on their time in training and in school. Regrettably this lack of training has resulted in lack of knowledge of the movement and its importance in the all-round education of the child.

This leaves the impression that physical education in the primary school is of less importance than that in the secondary school. This is far from the truth. Physical education in the primary school is the critical foundation for work at secondary level and can establish attitudes to involvement in physical activity that can persist throughout life. There is an urgent need for scholarly work in the area of physical education in the primary school to enhance the teaching and standing of the subject. I therefore welcome this book in adding to the literature available on physical education in primary schools.

Susan Capel

Emerita Professor (Physical Education),
Brunel University

# Acknowledgments

SAGE would like to thank the following reviewers whose comments have helped shape this book:

Ian Todd, University of Cumbria
Dawn Daley-James, University of Bedfordshire
Sarah Williams, Sheffield Hallam University
Rachel Mackinney, University of Chichester

# Companion Website

*Teaching Primary Physical Education*, 2nd edn is supported by a wealth of online materials to aid study and support teaching, which are available at https://study.sagepub.com/lawrence2e.

Support materials for Chapter 2

- Examples of resource cards

Support materials for Chapter 3

- Lesson planning templates

Support materials for Chapter 4

- Resources for developing motor skills

Support materials for Chapter 5

- Resources for athletics
- Resources for dance
- Resources for games activities
- Resources for gymnastics
- Resources for swimming
- Resources for problem solving
- Resources for orienteering

Support materials for Chapter 6

- Behaviour management strategies
- Keywords for areas of activities
- Differentiation strategies

Support materials for Chapter 7

- Sport Education

Support materials for Chapter 8

- Activity specific websites
- Warming up and cooling down activities
- Entering and exiting pools
- Examples of risk assessments

Support materials for Chapter 10

- Promoting cross curricular themes

# Links to the *Teachers' Standards* Across All Chapters

| Standard | Description | 1 | 2 | 3 | 4 | 5 | 6 | 7 | 8 | 9 | 10 | 11 | 12 |
|---|---|---|---|---|---|---|---|---|---|---|---|---|---|
| Standard 1: Set high expectations which inspire, motivate and challenge pupils | establish a safe and stimulating environment for pupils, rooted in mutual respect | ✓ | ✓ | ✓ |  | ✓ | ✓ | ✓ | ✓ | ✓ | ✓ | ✓ |  |
|  | set goals that stretch and challenge pupils of all backgrounds, abilities and dispositions |  | ✓ | ✓ |  | ✓ | ✓ | ✓ | ✓ | ✓ | ✓ |  |  |
|  | demonstrate consistently the positive attitudes, values and behaviour which are expected of pupils | ✓ |  |  |  |  |  |  | ✓ | ✓ |  |  |  |
| Standard 2: Promote good progress and outcomes by pupils | be accountable for pupils' attainment, progress and outcomes |  |  | ✓ |  | ✓ |  |  |  |  |  |  | ✓ |
|  | be aware of pupils' capabilities and their prior knowledge, and plan teaching to build on these |  | ✓ | ✓ |  | ✓ | ✓ |  |  |  |  |  |  |
|  | guide pupils to reflect on the progress they have made and their emerging needs |  |  |  |  | ✓ |  |  |  |  | ✓ |  | ✓ |
|  | demonstrate knowledge and understanding of how pupils learn and how this impacts on teaching |  | ✓ | ✓ |  | ✓ | ✓ | ✓ |  |  | ✓ | ✓ |  |
|  | encourage pupils to take a responsible and conscientious attitude to their own work and study |  | ✓ | ✓ |  | ✓ | ✓ | ✓ |  |  | ✓ |  |  |
| Standard 3: Demonstrate good subject and curriculum knowledge | have a secure knowledge of the relevant subject(s) and curriculum areas, foster and maintain pupils' interest in the subject, and address misunderstandings | ✓ | ✓ | ✓ |  | ✓ | ✓ | ✓ | ✓ |  | ✓ |  | ✓ |
|  | demonstrate a critical understanding of developments in the subject and curriculum areas, and promote the value of scholarship | ✓ |  | ✓ |  |  | ✓ | ✓ |  |  | ✓ |  |  |
|  | demonstrate an understanding of and take responsibility for promoting high standards of literacy, articulacy and the correct use of standard English, whatever the teacher's specialist subject |  |  |  |  | ✓ |  |  |  |  | ✓ |  |  |
| Standard 4: Plan and teach well-structured lessons | impart knowledge and develop understanding through effective use of lesson time |  | ✓ |  |  |  |  | ✓ |  |  |  |  |  |
|  | promote a love of learning and children's intellectual curiosity |  | ✓ | ✓ |  | ✓ | ✓ | ✓ |  |  | ✓ |  |  |
|  | set homework and plan other out-of-class activities to consolidate and extend the knowledge and understanding pupils have acquired |  |  | ✓ |  |  |  |  |  |  | ✓ |  |  |
|  | reflect systematically on the effectiveness of lessons and approaches to teaching |  |  | ✓ |  |  |  | ✓ |  |  |  |  |  |
|  | contribute to the design and provision of an engaging curriculum within the relevant subject area(s) |  |  | ✓ |  | ✓ | ✓ | ✓ |  |  | ✓ |  | ✓ |

*(Continued)*

(Continued)

| Standard | Description | 1 | 2 | 3 | 4 | 5 | 6 | 7 | 8 | 9 | 10 | 11 | 12 |
|---|---|---|---|---|---|---|---|---|---|---|---|---|---|
| Standard 5: Adapt teaching to respond to the strengths and needs of all pupils | know when and how to differentiate appropriately, using approaches which enable pupils to be taught effectively | ✓ | ✓ | ✓ | ✓ | ✓ | ✓ | ✓ | ✓ | | | | |
| | have a secure understanding of how a range of factors can inhibit pupils' ability to learn, and how best to overcome these | | ✓ | ✓ | ✓ | ✓ | ✓ | ✓ | ✓ | ✓ | ✓ | | |
| | demonstrate an awareness of the physical, social and intellectual development of children, and know how to adapt teaching to support pupils' education at different stages of development | ✓ | ✓ | | | ✓ | | | | ✓ | ✓ | | |
| | have a clear understanding of the needs of all pupils, including those with special educational needs, those of high ability, those with English as an additional language and those with disabilities, and be able to use and evaluate distinctive teaching approaches to engage and support them | | ✓ | | | | ✓ | | | | | | |
| Standard 6: Make accurate and productive use of assessment | know and understand how to assess the relevant subject and curriculum areas, including statutory assessment requirements | | | | ✓ | | | | | | | | |
| | make use of formative and summative assessment to secure pupils' progress | | | ✓ | | | | ✓ | | | | | |
| | use relevant data to monitor progress, set targets, and plan subsequent lessons | | | | | | | | | | | | ✓ |
| | give pupils regular feedback, both orally and through accurate marking, and encourage pupils to respond to the feedback | | | ✓ | | ✓ | ✓ | | | | ✓ | | |
| Standard 7: Manage behaviour effectively to ensure a good and safe learning environment | have clear rules and routines for behaviour in classrooms, and take responsibility for promoting good and courteous behaviour both in classrooms and around the school, in accordance with the school's behaviour policy | | | ✓ | | | ✓ | | ✓ | | | | |
| | have high expectations of behaviour, and establish a framework for discipline with a range of strategies, using praise, sanctions and rewards consistently and fairly | | | | | | ✓ | ✓ | | | | | |
| | manage classes effectively, using approaches which are appropriate to pupils' needs in order to involve and motivate them | | | | | ✓ | | | | ✓ | | | |
| | maintain good relationships with pupils, exercise appropriate authority, and act decisively when necessary | | | | | | ✓ | | ✓ | | ✓ | | |
| Standard 8: Fulfil wider professional responsibilities | make a positive contribution to the wider life and ethos of the school | | | | | ✓ | ✓ | | | | ✓ | ✓ | ✓ |
| | develop effective professional relationships with colleagues, knowing how and when to draw on advice and specialist support | | | | | ✓ | ✓ | | | | ✓ | ✓ | ✓ |
| | deploy support staff effectively | | | | | | ✓ | | | | ✓ | ✓ | ✓ |
| | take responsibility for improving teaching through appropriate professional development, responding to advice and feedback from colleagues | | ✓ | | | | | | ✓ | | ✓ | ✓ | ✓ |
| | communicate effectively with parents with regard to pupils' achievements and wellbeing | | | ✓ | | | ✓ | | | | ✓ | ✓ | ✓ |

# Introduction

The teaching of physical education in primary schools has always been debated and questioned. Changes to national curricula and continuing debates around physical activity and healthy active lifestyles have seen a rise in the importance of physical education as a core subject helped by financial support through the introduction of the Primary Physical Education and School Sport Premium. This book provides an overview of key aspects associated with the development and delivery of effective physical education experiences.

Chapters 1 and 2 provide an overview of physical education and the contribution it makes to the development of pupils and allow the reader to develop a deeper understanding of the theories of learning and development associated with the subject.

Chapter 3 encourages the reader to think about the planning process, prior to Chapters 4, 5 and 6 which look at the development of specific skills through physical education building from the development of basic motor competences to the skills associated with physical education, and how all pupils can be included within the learning experience.

Chapter 7 looks at the range of pedagogical approaches that can be used to deliver physical education and is supported by Chapter 8 which looks at how safe practice can be reflected in the delivery of high quality lessons.

Chapters 9, 10 and 11 explore education in the contribution of physical education to the health and wellbeing of pupils, the wider curriculum and cross-curricular themes, as well as links to the wider community. To conclude, Chapter 12 looks at how you might develop as a subject leader within physical education.

Throughout the book practical activities, case studies and extended readings provide you with an opportunity to reflect upon your own learning and development, while materials available from the companion website provide further support. This can be found at https://study.sagepub.com/lawrence2e and by clicking on the Sample Materials tab.

Each chapter is also linked to the *Teachers' Standards* (Department for Education, 2011) to allow you to evidence attainment against each standard using a range of evidence.

The chief update to the second edition of the book is a new chapter on health and wellbeing (Chapter 8). This is in response to the growing prominence of these topics in understanding pupil's performance and behaviour in school. Chapters 1 (Why Physical Education?), 2 (How Pupils Learn and Develop) and 3 (Planning the Learning Experience) have all been updated to include new content and additional case studies.

In addition to this, each chapter has been closely mapped to the Teachers' Standards (DfE, 2011) with a detailed table in the prelims and a chapter-specific table at the start of every chapter which illustrates links to the Standards.

# Why Physical Education?

## Chapter aims

- To define physical education
- To develop an understanding of the role and benefits of physical education
- To provide opportunities for you to reflect upon your personal experiences of physical education
- To develop an understanding of changes in physical education over the last century

## Links to *Teachers' Standards*

In working through this chapter, you should develop your knowledge associated with the *Teachers' Standards* (Department for Education, 2011) detailed in Table 1.1.

## Introduction

For many of us, our experiences of physical education have shaped the way we feel towards the subject. At times during your schooling, you probably questioned why you had to do the subject at all, especially when it was too cold, raining or too hot! For some of you, it was more about the relevance of the activity. Why was physical education on the curriculum? Why did you have to run the 1500m? These are questions that were asked but possibly never really answered.

**Table 1.1**  How this chapter links to the *Teachers' Standards* (DfE, 2011)

| | |
|---|---|
| Standard 1: Set high expectations which inspire, motivate and challenge pupils | • demonstrate consistently the positive attitudes, values and behaviour which are expected of pupils |
| Standard 3: Demonstrate good subject and curriculum knowledge | • have a secure knowledge of the relevant subject(s) and curriculum areas, foster and maintain pupils' interest in the subject, and address misunderstandings<br>• demonstrate a critical understanding of developments in the subject and curriculum areas, and promote the value of scholarship |
| Standard 5: Adapt teaching to respond to the strengths and needs of all pupils | • demonstrate an awareness of the physical, social and intellectual development of children, and know how to adapt teaching to support pupils' education at different stages of development |
| Standard 8: Fulfil wider professional responsibilities | • take responsibility for improving teaching through appropriate professional development, responding to advice and feedback from colleagues |

If we as practitioners do not understand why we are teaching a subject, there is potential for our attitudes, beliefs and values to impact on the experiences of those whom we teach. It may become difficult for us to motivate not only ourselves, but also our pupils. Therefore, before we start to look at the teaching of physical education within the primary school, we must define and explore the concepts associated with the subject, and understand how physical education has evolved over time. In doing so we can start to reflect upon our own perception of the subject, and how this might influence our teaching of it.

The aim of this chapter is therefore to provide the opportunity for you to develop a clearer understanding of physical education as a curriculum subject. It will allow you to reflect upon your own and others' experiences of physical education. By the end of the chapter you should be able to provide a clear rationale for the inclusion of physical education within a school curriculum.

# Defining physical education

So, what is physical education and what does it mean to me? Research (Capel, 2015) suggests that our own values and beliefs about physical education coupled with our socialisation within the school environment (how we experienced physical education), impacts significantly on our content and modes of delivery. She stresses that teachers of physical education should be 'not only aware of and recognise their beliefs and values, but also that these are challenged' (Capel, 2015: 169).

Thus, a starting point for defining physical education should be to look at our own experiences of physical education and the extent to which this may influence our own definition of the subject. Task 1.1 will help you do this.

## Task 1.1

1   Using your own experiences to provide examples, reflect on what physical education was like for you in the following contexts:

    a   primary school
    b   secondary school
    c   outside of school.

2   From these experiences identify the following:

    a   what activities did you experience?
    b   what did you most enjoy about physical education?
    c   what did you dislike about physical education?

3   What impact did these have on your participation?
4   What physical activities do you now participate in?
5   How might you use these experiences when teaching physical education?

Your experiences of physical education will have varied across phases of education (between primary and secondary school), as well as between contexts (what you did in school compared with what you did outside of the school day). Some of these experiences may have been positive while others may have been negative. You will have experienced a range of activities; some you enjoyed, some less so. If you have had the opportunity to discuss these experiences, you may well have found that they differed between males and females. Many of your experiences will have been based on the staff who taught you and their own beliefs about physical education. Understanding how our previous experiences have shaped our attitudes, beliefs and values towards physical education, provides us with the opportunity to reflect on what we might therefore teach and how we might teach it. However, we still need to look at how the profession and those who prescribe our curriculum define physical education.

## Curriculum development in physical education

The Department for Education (2013) identifies the purpose of physical education as follows:

> A high-quality physical education curriculum inspires all pupils to succeed and excel in competitive sport and other physically-demanding activities. It should provide opportunities for pupils to become physically confident in a way which supports their health and fitness. Opportunities to compete in sport and other activities build character and help to embed values such as fairness and respect. (DfE, 2013: 247)

Detailing that:
  The national curriculum for physical education aims to ensure that all pupils

- develop competence to excel in a broad range of physical activities
- are physically active for sustained periods of time
- engage in competitive sports and activities
- lead healthy, active lives. (DfE, 2013: 247)

However, this overview provides us with some detail as to what physical education looks like in the mind of policy makers. It does not detail specifically what it is. Therefore in working to construct a definition of physical education, it is important to review current literature in the field both nationally and internationally. This will allow us to establish how different people and organisations define physical education, allowing for personal reflection as to what it means to ourselves.

Physical education has and will probably continue to be defined not only as a single subject in its own right but also in relation to other aspects of physicality and how this manifests itself. Therefore alongside physical education you may also see references made to Physical Activity (PA), Physical Literacy (PL), Physical Education and School Sport (PESS), Physical Education School Sport and Community Links (PESSCL), Physical Education and Sport Strategy for Young People (PESSYP) and Health and Wellbeing or Healthy Active Lifestyle. Such terms are used by many interchangeably in the context of the physical education environment, or in relation to national policy. Therefore definitions for these will be provided within this chapter. A starting point in understanding what physical education is, is to review how the physical education curriculum has evolved over time, to establish current thinking from those responsible for the design and delivery of the subject.

The Board of Education identified that 'the object of Physical Education and Training is to help in the production and maintenance of health in body and mind' (1933: 9), identifying the effects of engagement with the subject as physical and educational. Whilst physical effects may seem obvious, it is also the educational aspects associated with mental and moral development; specifically, they argued that 'exercises, if rightly conducted, also have the effect, not less important, of developing in the children a cheerful and joyous spirit, together with the qualities of alertness, decision, concentration, and perfect control of the brain over body' (1933: 10).

Physical education at the turn of the twentieth century focused on physical training. Curriculum content encouraged the development of motor competences through gymnastic-based and drill-style activities. Such practice was reflective of the Swedish Gymnastics movement. A lesson would typically be composed of a series of drills, for example arm rotations or trunk rotations, with activities being taught outside. A focus on gymnastic and dance-based activities coincided with the development of movement frameworks with the emphasis not only on the physical skill being developed but also on concepts such as space, effort and relationships. In many ways, there was a continuation of the ideas surrounding physical education as more than just the physical, but also the emotional and social aspects of growth and development (see Chapter 2 for domains of learning).

The 1970s and 1980s saw a movement towards a much more games-focused approach, a tradition that is still evident in many school curricula. The development and introduction of the first national curriculum in 1991 (Department of Education and Science, 1991) saw a focus on planning, evaluation and participation in physical education. Pupils within the primary school were expected to participate in the six defined areas of activity, to include athletic activities, dance, games, gymnastic activities, outdoor and adventurous activites (OAA) and swimming. A review published in 1995 (DfE, 1995) saw a reduction in the range of activities taught at Key Stage 1 to dance, games and gymnastic activities, with the expectation that pupils would experience all six at Key Stage 2. The only exception here was swimming which could be taught during either key stage. Further revisions occurred in 1999 (Department for Education and Employment and QCA, 1999) with an emphasis on the development of knowledge, skills and understanding associated with the subject, focusing specifically on the acquisition and development of skills, the selection and application of skills and the development of tactical awareness as well as the ability to compose sequences of movements. The ability to evaluate and improve performance remained, and a new focus on the development of knowledge and understanding associated with fitness and health was introduced.

The Rose review (Rose, 2009) considered the integration of physical education into a thematic curriculum within primary schools. The aim of this curriculum was to develop:

- **successful learners** who enjoy learning, make progress and achieve
- **confident individuals** who are able to live safe, healthy and fulfilled lives
- **responsible citizens** who make a positive contribution to society. (Qualifications and Curriculum Development Agency, 2010a: 4 and b: 12)

Such an approach reflected the emerging focus on the wider contributions physical education can make to the development of pupils (we look at this concept in more depth in Chapter 2). However, a change of government in 2010 led to the recommendations of the Rose review being dropped, and consequently another curriculum review.

The most recent iteration of the curriculum (DfE, 2013) whilst much briefer in its detail still emphasised the need to develop pupils' ability to perform and more importantly 'excel in competitive sport and other physically-demanding activities' (DfE, 2013: 247). Aspects such as co-operation and competition are also evident with reference made to the curriculum providing 'opportunities for pupils to become physically confident in a way which supports health and fitness. Opportunities to compete in sport and other activities build character and help to embed values such as fairness and respect' (DfE, 2013: 247).

What becomes apparent is that curriculum design and consequently how physical education is viewed by policy makers (albeit with some consultation with experts within the field of physical education) remains changeable. However, throughout the development of physical education across the curriculum a focus on the physical, mental (emotional and cognitive) and the moral (to include social) aspects is high-lighted, suggesting that physical education is more than just developing physical skills. It is more focused on the development of the individual as a whole. It allows the child to make progress across a number of areas of development and we will now look at the literature to draw out more explicitly the meaning of physical education.

## Aims and benefits of physical education

Research and personal reflections have allowed individuals to review and revise the processes involved in the subject, looking again at the potential benefits of physical education and most appropriate methods of delivery. Emerging from the previous section of this chapter is an acknowledgement that physical education is not just about the physical. What is clear is that in terms of the policy changes across time, physical education has been seen as a vehicle for addressing issues such as the physicality of individuals – which included not only their skill development, but also their knowledge of their body – and that physical education could address wider issues concerning the engagement of individuals with others and their society, par-ticularly how they worked together, development of personal skills around character and also address health issues. However, as well as looking at policy around phys-ical education, it is also important to review academic literature.

Corbin (2002) suggests 'a physically educated person must be fit, be skilled, know the benefits of physical activity, and value physical activity' (2002: 134), with Whitehead (2004) arguing that physical education is more than just the learning of specific sport-related skills. While successful participation in physical education may be an initial aim of the curriculum (indeed it was highlighted as a key focus in original National Curriculum documentation published in 1991), it is the development of pupils' abilities to assess their own and others' performance, take increasing responsibility for their own progress and finally apply their knowledge in increas-ingly challenging situations that allows them to develop what is commonly referred to as higher order thinking skills (Corbin and Lindsey, 1997).

In their review of the educational benefits of physical education, Bailey et al. (2006) argue that the strength of the subject lies in the development that pupils can experi-ence physically, socially, affectively and cognitively. They conclude that as pupils engage in a range of physically active pursuits during the school day, the overall physical education of the individual can be seen as much more than the activities they are taught or experience within the school curriculum. In fact, the knowledge, skills and understanding that they develop during curriculum time can be applied in a range of differing contexts, for example during playtime, after school and away from the school environment in respect of any extra-curricular classes they may attend during the evening or at weekends. Such a premise reinforces what we have already started to highlight, namely that physical education is much more than participating in specific activities. Further, it highlights that physical education whilst taught in schools, is applied across a range of other contexts outside of the school environment. Thus it can be argued (as with all curriculum subjects) that what we teach in school is preparation for continued engagement in the subject across the individual's life time.

In this regard, some researchers (Haydn-Davies, 2005; Whitehead, 2004, 2005) have argued that rather than physically educating pupils, which suggests 'mastery of a measurable profile of achievements, of a prescribed set of skills' (Whitehead, 2004: 5) a move should be made towards developing physical literacy. Whitehead provides the following definition for physical literacy:

> As appropriate to each individual's endowment, physical literacy can be described as the motivation, confidence, physical competence, knowledge and understanding to maintain physical activity throughout the lifecourse. (2010: 12)

Embedded within this definition, Whitehead (2010) identifies six key attributes associated with physical literacy, these being: motivation, confidence and competence, ability to interact across environments, sense of self, interaction with others, and knowledge and understanding. Central to the philosophy supporting physical literacy is the view of the individual as a whole, with the body and mind as a single entity, rather than early definitions (BoE, 1933) that can be interpreted as seeing the body and mind as separate.

More recently the Association for Physical Education (AfPE) have identified the outcomes for the child as a result of high quality physical education as associated with health, skill development and emotional development with Almond (2015) arguing that we can look to refocus physical education away from traditional viewpoints to ones that focus on:

- Health as a resource
- Promoting purposeful physical pursuits to enrich lives
- Developing personal capital
- Helping young people to learn to give their life shape and purpose. (Almond, 2015: 22)

Thus, drawing on curriculum design and academic writing around the subject we can start to unpick some of the key ways in which physical education supports the development of the child. Table 1.2 attempts to summarise these with Task 1.2 providing an opportunity for you to reflect in more depth on your own thoughts of what the aims of physical education should be.

**Table 1.2** Concepts of physical education and physical literacy

| BoE (1933) | Bailey et al. (2006) | Whitehead (2010) | Almond (2015) |
|---|---|---|---|
| Healthy body | Physical development | Motivation | Health |
| Healthy mind | Social development | Confidence and competence | Purposeful |
| Emotional | Affective development | Self | Personal capital |
| • cheerful | Cognitive development | Knowledge | Empowerment |
| • joyous | | Understanding | |
| Cognitive | | Interaction with others | |
| • alertness | | | |
| • concentration | | | |

## Task 1.2

1   Look at the different ways in which physical education supports the development of the child shown in Table 1.2.

    a   Would you agree that these are the key areas?
    b   Would you identify any other ways in which physical education can support the development of the child?

2   In reviewing your responses to Question 1, what do you feel the key aims of physical education should be?
3   How are these aims reflected either in your current teaching of the subject, or in your previous experiences of being taught physical education?
4   Discuss these with a colleague to identify any similarities and differences in how you think about physical education.

Having completed Task 1.2, you should have started to identify what you feel are the key aims of physical education and started to develop a definition of physical education. What should be coming clearer is that physical education is more than just being physical. When taught to a high quality, it has the capacity to provide learning experiences across the range of pupils' developmental domains (see Chapter 2) and that it is the ways in which physical education is delivered that will be most influential on the learning that takes place (see Chapter 7). Therefore, as a teacher of primary physical education, you should continually reflect upon and review how you yourself define physical education.

However, as was identified earlier in the chapter, when looking to define physical education, it is important to explore other terms commonly associated with the subject. The next section makes an attempt to do this.

# Physical education terminology

As identified earlier in the chapter, physical education is often referred to in association with other concepts, for example, physical activity (PA), healthy active lifestyles, health and wellbeing, school sport. It is therefore important to look at how these are defined and how they are linked to physical education.

PA is associated with any activity that means that your body is working harder than normal.

> Any force exerted by skeletal muscle that results in energy expenditure above resting level. The term physical activity therefore includes the full range of human movement, from competitive sport and exercise to active hobbies, walking, cycling, or activities of daily life. Physical activity *per se* is a complex, multi-dimensional behaviour. (Department of Health, 2004: 81)

Daily recommended levels of physical activity are published. In the United Kingdom the recommended level of physical activity for children and young people is:

> a total of at least 60 minutes of at least moderate intensity physical activity each day. At least twice a week this should include activities to improve bone health (activities that produce high physical stresses on the bones), muscle strength and flexibility. (Department for Health, 2004: 10)

Within this published report, guidance is provided on the type of activities that can be undertaken, as well as the levels of intensity for the activities. While the guidance is for an hour of physical activity per day, this can be made up of a series of smaller blocks of time, for example walking or cycling to and from school, playground activities and pre-lesson activities (such as Wake Up Shake Up). This minimum suggested time for daily physical activity continues to be reinforced (Department of Health, 2010), with more recent research suggesting that minimum expected engagement should be increased further. With increasing child obesity levels, increasing emphasis is being placed on schools to look at how, through healthy diets and exercise, they can support pupils and parents to understand the impact of such lifestyles on their overall health and wellbeing (see Chapter 9 for a more detailed analysis and overview of health and wellbeing). Key then is looking at how opportunities for pupils to be physically active can be embedded throughout the school day.

What is clear, however, is that physical education has the potential to influence PA levels. If we refer to Table 1.2, one of the key characteristics of the subject is the influence it can have on the attitudes pupils hold towards it. If the experiences of the subject are positive, it is likely that pupils will hold a positive attitude towards it, resulting in a willingness to persist with it – in essence their levels of motivation, seen by Whitehead (2010) as the first of her six key attributes of physical education. However, we also need to acknowledge that in terms of the recommended physical activity levels we are not necessarily going to be able to achieve these within our lessons.

Therefore it is important that we look to develop links with other organisations to support the development of the child away from the school environment.

PESSCL, established in 2002, had the aim of raising sporting opportunities for children and young adults. It suggested that physical education, and sport in schools, both within and beyond the curriculum, can improve the following:

- pupil concentration, commitment and self-esteem; leading to higher attendance and better behaviour and attainment;
- fitness levels; active children are less likely to be obese and more likely to pursue sporting activities as adults, thereby reducing the likelihood of coronary heart disease, diabetes and some forms of cancer; and
- success in international competition by ensuring talented young sports people have a clear pathway to elite sport and competition whatever their circumstances. (Department for Education and Skills, 2002: 1)

This strategy was superseded in 2008 by the PESSYP. The key aim of this strategy was to extend the current provision of two hours' high quality PESS to a five-hour offer comprised of two hours of curriculum and an additional three hours of extra-curricular provision. With both strategies, the emphasis on supporting the development and maintenance of high quality physical education was central. Developing strong links between primary and secondary schools was encouraged as well as links with external organisations (this will be explored in greater depth in Chapter 11).

Additional funding and support for physical education saw another change in 2013 with the introduction of the Primary PE and Sports Premium which provides funding for schools to support the growth and development of physical education and sport across the school. The Association for Physical Education and Youth Sport Trust (2016) report that the aim of the funding is to ensure that '**ALL** pupils leaving primary school are **physically literate** and with the **knowledge, skills and motivation** necessary to equip them for a **healthy, active lifestyle** and **lifelong participation** in physical activity and sport'. The objective is:

To achieve **self-sustaining** improvement in the quality of PE and sport in primary schools against 5 key indicators:

- the engagement of all pupils in regular physical activity – kick-starting healthy active lifestyles
- the profile of PE and sport being raised across the school as a tool for whole school improvement
- increased confidence, knowledge and skills of all staff in teaching PE and sport
- broader experience of a range of sports and activities offered to all pupils
- increased participation in competitive sport. (AfPE and YST, 2016: 1; bold as in original text)

Guidance on how schools can use the funding is given with the requirement that schools publish details of how they have spent their premium. Use of the funding also forms part of the school inspection process.

Most recently *Sporting Future: A New Strategy for an Active Nation* (Cabinet Office, 2015) has been published. The strategy focuses on five key outcomes:

- Physical wellbeing
- Mental wellbeing
- Individual development
- Social and community development
- Economic development

The report argues 'a person's attitude to sport is often shaped by their experience – or lack of experience – as a child, and many people drop out of sport before they even reach the age of 14' (2015: 10). Thus there continues to be an emphasis on providing opportunities for children to engage in activities outside of the school curriculum.

As can be seen, review of physical education provision continues to take place. It is important as you progress through your training and professional career that you engage in regular reading around the subject and access your professional subject association which will allow you to keep abreast of new initiatives and curriculum development.

Having looked at some of the key concepts and characteristics associated with physical education, Task 1.3 provides an opportunity for you to reflect upon your own definition of the subject. If you have not already done so you may wish to complete Task 1.2 to support your thinking.

---

## Task 1.3

1 Literature sources provide a range of definitions for physical education and its associated terms. Using the sources included within the above section and any others you may access, identify the key aspects of physical education.
2 Develop your own working definition for physical education.
3 Share this definition with others to identify similarities and differences in your interpretation of the literature.

---

It is clear from the literature and your responses to Tasks 1.2 and 1.3, if you have been able to complete them, that there are similarities and differences in how the subject is interpreted. You therefore need to be clear about how you define the aims and benefits of participating in physical education. As we have previously alluded to, how you see the subject will impact on how and what you teach. Kirk suggests that 'early learning experiences are crucial to the continuing involvement in physical activity' (2005: 2), a belief further acknowledged with the *Sporting Future* strategy (Cabinet Office, 2015). More specifically Kirk (2005) argues that it is the development of pupils' competence within physical education during their early schooling that may ultimately impact upon their overall engagement with the subject – a premise supported across the physical education fraternity. Our role as physical educators therefore becomes focused on ensuring that early experiences of physical education are positive and that they build pupils' motivational levels to ensure sustainability of engagement across their primary experiences and provide strong foundations for continued participation into their secondary education and beyond. How this can be achieved is embedded across the remaining chapters of this book.

Thus the key aspect of the teaching of physical education is the way in which the activities are presented, a premise that reflects the work of both Gallahue and Ozmun (1995) who argue that it is the way in which the task is presented that is important, and Corbin (2002) who suggests that 'learning skill builds confidence, but confidence is needed to build skill' (2002: 133). Therefore we should look to develop a teaching environment based on concepts of personal mastery where success is reflected in the completion of a given task rather than by comparison against others, or a 'person-centred participation model' (Whitehead, 2005: 7). This underlines the relationship between our aims and definition of physical education and the approaches we adopt in respect of the delivery of the subject.

We have now spent some time looking at the aims of physical education. We have also started to think about the content of our curriculum, specifically at the range of other areas where physical education can be used to support development beyond mere participation. We have looked at how curriculum changes have taken place over the last century, but also how the core aims of physical education have remained in many respects unchanged.

It is evident from the literature reviewed and the progressions seen in curriculum design that perspectives on the subject have changed over time and as a teacher of physical education, you will find it beneficial to reflect upon why physical education is taught within the school. Task 1.4 will help you to do this.

## Task 1.4

Physical education has been defined in many ways. Each of these definitions contains different core aims and related benefits for the subject. Using these aims and benefits of physical education, provide a rationale for the inclusion of physical education as a curriculum subject within the primary school.

# High quality physical education

In defining and reviewing the aims of physical education, we can start to identify what makes a high quality physical education experience. The AfPE (2016) suggests that high quality physical education is reflected through the curriculum taught, how the subject is taught, high levels of behaviour and safety, inclusion practices, and leadership and management. According to Ofsted (2013), schools demonstrating good or outstanding teaching in physical education demonstrate the following:

- Consistently high expectations of all pupils
- Teacher–pupil relationships that promote engagement and enjoyment
- Inspired pupils
- Purposeful and appropriately paced learning activities
- Modelling of techniques by teachers

As a professional we have a duty to promote high quality physical education within our classes and across the schools in which we teach. AfPE (2016) published their *Physical Education Declaration* which states:

> AfPE believes passionately in the value of high quality physical education, physical activity and participation in school sport. Each has an enormous impact on health and emotional wellbeing as well as significantly impacting on whole school improvement, so we would ask that you help us to ensure that:
>
> - **H**ealth and emotional wellbeing of all young people are improved.
> - **E**ducation is an entitlement and therefore the impact of physical education across the curriculum should be valued and recognised.
> - **L**eadership by all head teachers, governors, subject leaders and heads of departments promotes and celebrates the value of physical education, physical activity and school sport.
> - **P**hysical education is 'Powerful Education' and that you support and recognise the impact is has on whole school development, making a real difference to the lives of young people and preparing them for an ever-changing world.

Thus if we are to ensure the delivery of high quality physical education, it is how we work in partnership within and across schools and our local community that will define success.

## Chapter summary

The aim of this chapter has been to look at defining physical education and to review changes in its focus and content over time. It has required you to identify your own aims for the subject and the ways in which these might be reflected in

*(Continued)*

*(Continued)*

your personal planning and delivery. Hayes et al. (2006) suggest that in terms of education, what we believe are the key outcomes must be reflected in the way we deliver our lessons. Further that if we view pupils as central in the educational process then they must be at the centre of the planning process. Thus, in reflecting on your own understanding it is important that you review your thinking on a regular basis. It would therefore be appropriate at this point to spend some time reflecting on the following review questions.

1    Why should we teach physical education?
2    What do I see my role as a teacher of physical education to be?
3    How do I define physical education?
4    What will I prioritise when teaching physical education?
5    How do I see my personal experiences impact upon on my ability to deliver high quality physical education?

It is important to recognise and appreciate how you personally define and value physical education as this will impact on your motivation and delivery of the subject. As Hayes et al. state 'Individual teachers have more impact on student outcomes than do whole-school effects' (2006: 2).

# Further reading

Bailey, R., Armour, K., Kirk, D., Jess, M., Pickup, I. and Sandford, R. (2006) *The Educational Benefits Claimed for Physical Education and School Sport: An Academic Review.* London: British Educational Research Association (BERA).
This review provides a comprehensive research-focused overview of physical education and school sport and the associated educational benefits.

Whitehead, M. (ed.) (2010) *Physical Literacy through the Lifecourse.* London: Routledge.
Drawing on a range of experts across the field of physical literacy, this edited textbook provides an overview of the philosophical underpinnings of physical literacy and how the development of physical literacy can be achieved.

Pickup, I., Price, L., Shaughnessy, J., Spence, J. and Trace, M. (2008) *Learning to Teach Primary PE.* Exeter: Learning Matters.
This easy to read textbook includes a detailed chapter on physical education and its associated benefits. It builds on the content of this chapter to clearly identify how a rationale for physical education can be developed, as well as how the arguments for the inclusion of physical education in the curriculum can be addressed.

In developing your knowledge and understanding of physical education and physical literacy you may wish to access the Physical Literacy website at www.physical-literacy.org.uk which provides access to a range of articles and conference presentations published by active researchers working in the field of physical literacy.

# How Pupils Learn and Develop

## Chapter aims

- To develop an understanding of the domains of learning
- To develop an understanding of theories of learning
- To be able to identify a range of learning environments and their character-
  istics and how these may impact upon the learner
- To develop an ability to apply learning theories within a physical education
  context

## Links to *Teachers' Standards*

In working through this chapter, you should develop your knowledge of the
*Teachers' Standards* (DfE, 2011) detailed in Table 2.1.

## Introduction

The previous chapter explored the aims of physical education and encouraged you
to develop your own rationale for the inclusion of the subject within the primary
curriculum. What started to emerge was that physical education was more than just
developing pupil's ability to perform; it was about how physical education also

**Table 2.1**   How this chapter links to the *Teachers' Standards* (DfE, 2011)

| | |
|---|---|
| Standard 1: Set high expectations which inspire, motivate and challenge pupils | • establish a safe and stimulating environment for pupils, rooted in mutual respect<br>• set goals that stretch and challenge pupils of all backgrounds, abilities and dispositions<br>• demonstrate consistently the positive attitudes, values and behaviour which are expected of pupils. |
| Standard 2: Promote good progress and outcomes by pupils | • be aware of pupils' capabilities and their prior knowledge, and plan teaching to build on these<br>• demonstrate knowledge and understanding of how pupils learn and how this impacts on teaching<br>• encourage pupils to take a responsible and conscientious attitude to their own work and study. |
| Standard 3: Demonstrate good subject and curriculum knowledge | • have a secure knowledge of the relevant subject(s) and curriculum areas, foster and maintain pupils' interest in the subject, and address misunderstandings |
| Standard 4: Plan and teach well-structured lessons | • impart knowledge and develop understanding through effective use of lesson time<br>• promote a love of learning and children's intellectual curiosity |
| Standard 5: Adapt teaching to respond to the strengths and needs of all pupils | • know when and how to differentiate appropriately, using approaches which enable pupils to be taught effectively<br>• have a secure understanding of how a range of factors can inhibit pupils' ability to learn, and how best to overcome these<br>• demonstrate an awareness of the physical, social and intellectual development of children, and know how to adapt teaching to support pupils' education at different stages of development<br>• have a clear understanding of the needs of all pupils, including those with special educational needs, those of high ability, those with English as an additional language and those with disabilities, and be able to use and evaluate distinctive teaching approaches to engage and support them |
| Standard 6: Make accurate and productive use of assessment | • make use of formative and summative assessment to secure pupils' progress<br>• give pupils regular feedback, both orally and through accurate marking, and encourage pupils to respond to the feedback |
| Standard 7: Manage behaviour effectively to ensure a good and safe learning environment | • have high expectations of behaviour, and establish a framework for discipline with a range of strategies, using praise, sanctions and rewards consistently and fairly<br>• maintain good relationships with pupils, exercise appropriate authority, and act decisively when necessary |

supported the development of the child, socially, emotionally and mentally, as well as their knowledge and understanding. It also provided you with opportunities to reflect upon your own experiences of the subject and to consider how that might influence your teaching of the subject.

If you have taken the opportunity to discuss these experiences with others, you may well have identified similarities and differences in such experiences. These differences may have been related to the activities you had undertaken, or the ways in which the subject was presented and delivered. Implicit within your interpretations would have been your personal learning journey and how this changed over time. As with developing an understanding of the inclusion of a subject within the curriculum, it also becomes important to consider how you learnt about and developed within the subject area. Developing a deeper understanding of how pupils learn and develop allows you to reflect on all aspects of teaching, from how and why we should have high expectations, to how behaviour can be most effectively managed, and how you can scaffold learning activities to support pupils to attain to the best of their abilities.

Therefore, this chapter aims to look at the theories and processes associated with learning and how these may impact upon the delivery of curriculum subjects. We will consider the different domains in which learning occurs and the key theories associated with these. We will then look at how environmental factors may impact on learning experiences and what learning opportunities exist within the school curriculum. Throughout links will be made to the delivery of physical education.

---

## Task 2.1

Thinking about your experiences of education and more specifically physical education, reflect upon the following questions.

1  How would you define learning?
2  How do you learn?
3  In what areas does learning take place?

---

Task 2.1 invites you to start thinking about learning as a process that can occur in different domains or areas. For example, you have had to go through a learning process in order to gain qualifications thereby developing academically or cognitively; you have learnt how to work with other people thereby developing socially and emotionally; and you may also have learnt different physical skills thereby developing within the psychomotor domain. However, before we start to look at the specific domains of learning, it is important to develop an understanding of what we mean by learning in the context of this chapter.

Learning can be defined as 'the process whereby knowledge is created through the transformation of experience. Knowledge results from the combination of grasping and transforming experience' (Kolb, 1984: 41). Sugden and Connell argue that learning occurs when a child 'progresses from an absolute beginner to a performer of relative maturity' (1979: 131). Delignieres et al. view learning as 'a transitional process, from an initial response to more effective and/or efficient patterns' (1998: 222). Learning therefore relates to the acquisition of knowledge, the storage of such knowledge and the ability to use knowledge in different situations or contexts. Furthermore, learning can be seen as progressive, suggesting that it occurs in stages. In viewing learning in this way, there is an acknowledgement of the individual differences we see among those learners with whom we work, and also that the speed of progression varies among different learners. If you look at the content of the National Curriculum (DfE, 2013), you will see that such a premise is reflected in the different aspects of knowledge, skills and understanding that pupils are expected to attain through the different key stages.

Having defined learning, it becomes important to acknowledge the role the learner plays within the learning process. Katz argues that learners can adopt two roles within any learning process: they are either active and engage in 'reasoning, the process of reflection, the development and analysis of ideas' (2003: 16), which results in the development of a deeper level of understanding; or passive whereby the learner is instructed, resulting in a lack of opportunity to construct their own ideas.

In adopting a learner-centred approach to learning, we need to develop a clear understanding of what we want learners to achieve from a task, and present the task in such a way that the learning outcomes can be achieved. This concept will be developed further in Chapter 3 which looks at the planning of learning experiences.

Having developed an understanding of learning and the different roles a learner may take, the next section of this chapter focuses on the domains in which learning occurs.

## Domains of learning

Learning occurs within three domains: the cognitive (thinking) domain (Bloom et al., 1956), the affective (social) domain (Krathwohl et al., 1964) and the psychomotor (skill development) domain (Simpson, 1971). You should now be able to see how teaching high quality physical education provides opportunities for learning to take place across these domains.

Cognitive learning is reflected in the development of knowledge and understanding. Within this domain learning is evidenced through learners' ability to move from being able to recall data during the early stages of their development, to being able to use their knowledge to evaluate and assess their level of understanding during later stages.

Within the affective domain, learning occurs around the development of attitudes and social and emotional skills. Development is reflected in learners' increasing awareness of those around them resulting in the establishment of value systems identifying what is important to them. These value systems are then reflected in the behaviours exhibited by those learners towards themselves and others.

The psychomotor domain of learning focuses on the development of skills. Learners move from being able to copy simple skills, to being able to combine skills in increasingly complex situations resulting, at the later stages of development, in them becoming proficient in performing specific skills.

It is important to acknowledge at this point that while these domains of learning provide an opportunity to categorise learning, they are not mutually exclusive, with aspects of learning occurring across domains. For example, in the early stages of cognitive and psychomotor development, learning is evidenced through an individual's ability to recall and copy, which is embedded within early learning goals as well as curricular design.

Each domain is of equal importance, although the learning environment or task presentation may prioritise learning within a specific domain. Task 2.2 provides an opportunity to reflect upon your knowledge and application of domains of learning within your own teaching.

---

## Task 2.2

1   Using a typical teaching day, and the lessons you have taught or observed, reflect upon which domains of learning were included.
2   Try to identify specific examples of activities undertaken and how effective they were within the lesson.
3   Discuss your reflections with a colleague or peer and answer the following:

  •   How will developing my knowledge of domains of learning impact on my effectiveness as a teacher?

---

Having started to look at the domains in which learning occurs, the next section of this chapter focuses on the theories associated with learning.

# Learning theories

If you look at your teaching experiences to date, you will have noticed that no class or lesson is the same. When planning lessons, or learning experiences, it is important as a teacher that you have an understanding of the major theories of learning. This will allow you to plan activities based on a theoretical perspective rather than by chance. (Chapter 7 looks in more detail at the range of teaching approaches that can be adopted in physical education lessons while Chapter 3 looks at planning in more depth.) As with the concepts discussed in Chapter 1, you will need to develop a rationale for why you have chosen the adopted approach.

## Cognitive domain of learning

Learning theories associated with the development of knowledge can be categorised as behaviour (behaviourist), thinking (cognitivist), social interaction (social learning) and experiences (experiential). For the purpose of this chapter we will focus on the behaviourist and constructivist theories. It is important to acknowledge that in narrowing our focus you are encouraged to read some of the further reading texts identified at the end of this chapter to develop your understanding further.

## Behaviourist theories of learning

Behaviourist theorists argue that learning occurs as a result of changes in the behaviour exhibited by the individual. Bates suggests that it 'is based on the principle of stimulus and response' (2016: 23), arguing that 'people need to be directed and that if the stimulus is something that the individual wants (a reward) or fears (a punishment), the individual will respond accordingly' (Bates, 2016: 23). Thus, emerging from these theories is the concept of behaviour modifications highlighted by theorists such as Thorndike, Watson, Pavlov and Skinner.

Thorndike focused on the concepts of trial and error, arguing that in trying to solve a problem, there will be rewards achieved by solving the problem and failures. It is the reinforcement of these successes that reinforces these behaviours. What is important to recognise is that there may be multiple ways of solving the problem, and thus in a physical education context such an approach encourages aspects of exploration and experimentation, a concept we have already noted within physical education curricula. Watson focused on stimulus and response, whereby the individual becomes trained to respond to a specific stimulus. Within the context of physical education, this might be evident in the behaviour expectations you have of them and the consequences of them not achieving those expectations. Pavlov focused on conditioned responses and is best known for his salivating dogs. Here the emphasis is on training the individual to respond, but according to Bates (2016) it can also be used to support pupils to confront their fears by addressing how they respond to any specific situation. I know from working with trainee teachers that when I mention the word 'bleep' to them during a warm-up activity I deliver, their reaction is to think it is the 'bleep test' (or multistage fitness test) that many of you would have experienced when in secondary school. The challenge then is to make them aware that what I am expecting from them is different to what they have experienced in the past.

B.F. Skinner is well known for his theory of operant conditioning. Operants are effects or a consequence of a stimulus. Aubrey and Riley (2016) suggest that Skinner considers behaviour to be 'determined by consequence, such as positive and negative reinforcers, and that application of these will increase the possibility of a behaviour occurring again' (Aubrey and Riley, 2016: 60). Specifically, Skinner argued that where a behaviour is positively reinforced it is more likely to be repeated. Bates (2016) concurs with this arguing that 'not only does positive reinforcement have a longer-lasting effect on behaviour than negative reinforcement, but that negative reinforcement could actually be counter-productive' (Bates, 2016: 32). Application of a behaviourist approach is commonly seen in a school environment in relation to behaviour management, as well as the management of expectations. This requires us to look at the responses, be they rewards or sanctions, we provide to ensure the behaviours to which we aspire are adopted. Many schools have rewards and consequence charts where pupils are clearly shown the consequences of their behaviours. However, with any behaviour management, we must be consistent in our approach to avoid giving out mixed messages. In a physical education context, it will focus on, for example, the rules and routines you establish in terms of, for example, appropriate kit, expected behaviours when changing, or in the distribution and collecting of equipment. However, it also links to how and when we praise a pupil.

Task 2.3 provides you with an opportunity to reflect in more detail on your application of behaviourist theories in practice.

---

## Task 2.3

1   From your current experiences, identify five examples of the application of a behaviourist learning theory.
2   Think about what behaviour was modified and how, then look to identify ways in which you will apply such an approach within your own teaching.
3   How will you embed behaviourist principles within your own teaching?
4   Use this reflection to evidence progress against your teachers' standards.

---

## Cognitivist theories of learning

Cognitivist theories of learning focus on the development of the individual's ability to think and reason. Some focus on how learning is constructed and built upon, whilst others focus on how interactions with others impact on learning.

Constructivist theorists (for example, Piaget [1898–1980], Vygotsky [1896–1934] and Bruner [1915–2016]) argue that learning is constructed, and occurs as a result of progression through a series of stages. According to Piaget, learning occurs as a result of interactions between the individual and their environment. However, Vygotsky and Bruner argue that the interactions occur between the individual and others, within a social environment. In addition, Vygotsky argues that the society and culture of the individual's environment strongly influence their learning experience. This is referred to as a social constructivist approach. References to construction of learning are evident within the curricula we teach, which place an emphasis on the development and application of knowledge skills and understanding across phases of education. You may wish to take some time to look again at the National Curriculum and how these theories of learning are reflected in programmes of study.

Piaget suggests that learning occurs as a result of exploration and experimentation; he argues that over time children develop from using basic aspects of sensory and reflexive learning to being able to make links between objects and contexts. This allows them to develop the ability to adopt and adapt appropriate knowledge and understanding. Garhart Mooney develops this further suggesting that 'children learn best when they are actually doing the work themselves and creating their own understanding of what's going on, instead of being given explanations by adults' (2000: 62). Therefore, when planning, there is a need to provide such opportunities within the learning experience. For example, you can provide pupils with a range of equipment to hit a ball, thereby building differentiation into the activity and allowing opportunities for pupils to experiment to solve a basic challenge.

Within his theory of cultural–historical social activity theory, Vygotsky argued that for learning to be most effective the learner should work within their zone of proximal development (ZPD). Garhart Mooney defines this concept as 'the distance between the most difficult task a child can do alone, and the most difficult task a child can do with help' (2000: 83). If learning is to be achieved, learners must be engaged in an activity which challenges them. Setting a task that is too easy or too difficult would result in frustration and an absence of effective learning. Again, it is quite easy to think of examples when you might have experienced this. There will have been times when you have set pupils an activity which they completed very quickly, but because you have scheduled it to last a set period you did not move on to the next activity resulting in pupils becoming disruptive. In contrast, you may have set an activity which you understood, but when it came to pupils actually doing the activity their performance did not reflect your expectations. While this could have been a communication issue, it may well have been that you had overcomplicated the activity. Therefore, differentiating the tasks you provide will ensure that you provide sufficient levels of challenge for all learners, allowing them the opportunity to succeed. While tasks could be differentiated to support the learner, the second part of the definition of the ZPD identifies the opportunity for learning to be supported by others. Vygotsky also explores the concept of the expert in the learning experience, defining this individual as anyone with a greater level of knowledge than the learner. This individual may well be a learner in the same class, which offers the opportunity for peer teaching to occur. For example, in physical education the use of reciprocal activities whereby pupils work in pairs providing feedback and guidance on performance and improvements that could be made (see Chapter 7 for more information on practical teaching approaches) could be included.

## Task 2.4

Vygotsky argues that learning reflects the social and cultural influences of the learner's environment.

1   Reflecting on your own learning, what social and cultural influences impacted on you?

2 Based on your knowledge of schools, what factors might now impact on pupils' learning?

3 How will you take account of these influences in your planning and delivery of physical education?

Bruner develops the concepts of constructivism further, arguing for the need to provide structured learning opportunities that build progressively. His concept of a spiralling curriculum proposes that learners should revisit concepts and processes progressively, but at increasing levels of difficulty to allow them to develop a deeper level of understanding. He suggests the concept of scaffolding, 'a flexible and child-centred supportive strategy which supports the child in learning new things' (Smith et al., 1998: 431), which requires the teacher to provide a series of structured activities that build upon the learner's existing knowledge base. It is important here to understand what the learner's starting point is. On many occasions, especially when you first meet your class, there is a tendency to start by undertaking some baseline assessment. This can be detrimental to skill development as you run the risk of adopting a 'fresh start' approach thereby setting activities at a lower level than the learners are capable of. Effective liaison with the previous teachers to understand what they have undertaken and what they have achieved will ensure a higher level of continuity allowing for the opportunity for progress to be maintained. For example, setting of progressive practices or challenges that allow pupils to build on their level of skill without becoming too competitive, which may result in a decline in overall skill performance.

The theories discussed above place the learner at the centre of the process (a concept identified in Chapter 1 in relation to the development of physical literacy). The teacher acts as the facilitator of learning opportunities or experiences. Thus, within a physical education context we need to look closely at the tasks we set, and think about how they build upon previous experiences. We need to think about the inter-relatedness of the skills we ask pupils to perform, in order that they can make connections between these skills. If we look to apply this in the context of jumping, we might ask pupils to think about instances when we might jump, for example, to catch a ball, to head a ball, jumping on and off a piece of equipment or when we are doing athletics. By doing this, we are asking pupils to think about their previous experiences and therefore build upon them. We can then get pupils to go away and think about how they jump, thus providing them with the opportunity to think about the specific skill and practise its application. Examples such as these will be explored in much more depth in Chapters 4 and 5.

Bandura's social cognitive theory argued that 'people are more likely to exhibit modelled behaviours if it results in valued outcomes than if it has unrewarding or punishing effects' (2001: 24). Whilst seeming to link more to behaviourist theories, Bandura's work was focused more on the use of role models to shape behaviours, suggesting that 'children model their behaviour on what they see and hear around them, choosing behaviours they identify as positive in respect of desirability' (Lawrence, 2009: 71). Thus within our teaching we must provide appropriate role modelling if we are to achieve the expectations of our pupils. Within a physical education context this might be reflected in the establishment of clear routines around the kit pupils are expected to wear, or the way pupils enter and leave the changing rooms. Equally it can be related to the ways in which teachers behave towards their pupils, for example teachers who continually arrive late with an unprepared lesson are not demonstrating attributes such as punctuality and preparation that they are likely to expect from their pupils. By setting and modelling such behaviours we provide benchmarks for pupils to assess their own performance.

So, as teachers of physical education, what specific aspects do we need to take into account when looking to develop learning within the cognitive domain? Consideration must be given to how learning is structured, for example, how does each activity build upon prior learning to either reinforce or develop new knowledge? We need to consider how success is rewarded to ensure pupils remain motivated, and we need to be clear in relation to how we manage behaviour in order that we create an environment that facilitates learning.

## Affective domain of learning

When looking at development within the affective domain we are focusing on aspects of emotional development. Sheridan (1991) argues that affective development is of at least equal importance as cognitive development. This is not a new concept. Piaget and Inhelder suggest: 'The affective and social development of the child follows the same general process [of cognitive development], since the affective, social, and cognitive aspects of behaviour are in fact inseparable' (1969: 114). Central to Sheridan's view is the need for pupils to 'gain positive self-concept, greater self-esteem and a more developed sense of competency' (1991: 29) and that 'these key facets of personality development are crucial to children's attitudes concerning learning and their sense of motivation for applying their skills in learning situations throughout life' (1991: 29). Katz suggests that 'experiences of the early years of life have a powerful influence on the later ones' (2003: 15). Consequently, the learning experiences we provide have the potential to impact on children's lifelong learning experience. Such a premise is further evidenced in the work of Kirk (2005) and Corbin (2002) which we looked at in Chapter 1 and is fundamental in the concept of physical literacy (Whitehead, 2010). What emerges is a need for teachers to build confidence and the importance of effective early learning experiences if continuing participation is to be encouraged.

Within this domain we are looking at the development of the learner's emotional aspects, specifically their attitude and feelings towards themselves and those around them (Chapter 9 explores concepts around social and emotional wellbeing in more depth). One of the key theorists associated with this is Erik Erikson (1995). Erikson identified eight stages of emotional development, aligned to conflict resolution or crisis.

With reference to the primary environment, he acknowledged that changes in the affective domain were associated with learners becoming more independent, developing the ability to cope with the demands of the environment in which they learn and to interact with others, and beginning to establish their own identity (Keenan and Evans, 2009). Therefore, effective learning experiences should include opportunities for the development of more pupil-centred and interactive activities (see Chapter 7 for the range of different teaching approaches).

Sheridan (1991) acknowledges a need to consider how the expectations of learners, which are reflected in the way we present tasks, can impact upon pupils' development, specifically how we provide feedback upon and acknowledge learners' achievements. This is closely linked to behaviourist theory and requires learners to reflect on their own self-efficacy, self-esteem and motivation.

Learners' willingness to engage in learning activities depends heavily upon the values they associate with the activity. You will know from your own experiences that if you enjoy something and see it as being beneficial you are more likely to persist with it, even when it becomes challenging, than when you are asked to do something that you see as irrelevant. This is sometimes referred to as the effort–benefit ratio (Fox and Biddle, 1988).

Within his social cognitive theory, Bandura (1989) developed the premise of observational learning arguing that learning is affected by the attention applied, the retention of the information, the translation of this learning into different contexts and the motivation to continue to engage within the learning. Additionally, Erikson (1995) identified the use of social comparison between the self and others as an influential factor in the formation of identity. Note here that once again learning is seen as a social activity, and therefore links to Vygotsky can also be made.

When structuring activities around the affective domain, we need to think carefully about the activities planned and the impact that they might have. Physical education is a very visual subject. The nature of the learning experiences provided allows for a high level of social comparison, especially when we are asked to demonstrate or perform to the rest of the class. I am sure that you can remember having to perform your gymnastics sequence at school, but in our planning we need to understand how the activities we plan might impact on the affective development of the pupil. Do we really need to get each group to demonstrate their routine to the whole class, or might sharing their ideas with a partner or another group produce the same outcome? We also need to consider how we group pupils so that they work with a range of different pupils and potentially take on a range of different roles. We also need to think about how our experiences of physical education at school impacted on how we felt about ourselves and consequently look at how we can reduce any negative impacts, for example changing rooms, having to wear a certain uniform, feeling less able than others in your class can all impact on the pupils' willingness to participate and is reflected in the learning environment you create. As practitioners within physical education you therefore need to be sensitive and acknowledge this domain within your teaching.

## Psychomotor domain of learning

The final domain of learning occurs around psychomotor development. Here we are looking at how the learner develops specific skills. As with all aspects of development, learning is progressive. Gallahue and Ozmun (1995) argue that in the context of physical education such stages encompass the movement from reflexive to rudimentary actions, through to the development of fundamental skills and finally to specialised skills. Their work builds upon that of Haywood (1986) who identified a transition from basic locomotion and movement skills during early childhood (ages 1–8) to the development of strength and improved efficiency during late childhood (ages 8–18). It is important to acknowledge that learning within this domain is not just associated with physical education but is also focused on motor skills in general, for example within the early years it links to skills such as handwriting and construction. Chapters 3 and 4 will explore psychomotor development in the context of primary physical education in more depth.

It is also important to acknowledge the impact learning within this domain may have on other domains, especially the affective domain. Early research (Breckenridge and Vincent, 1965) identified that demonstrations of physical competence (in the context of physical education the ability to perform skills) positively impact on the confidence of the individual. If we refer to the previous section on affective development, we can infer that a confident individual is more likely to engage in social interactions. If we go back further to the section on cognitive development, we can argue that this increased confidence in social interactions would impact upon development in this domain as well.

## Section summary

So far, this chapter has provided a general overview of the theories of learning and the impact these may have within physical education. What emerges is that there are commonalities between theories and therefore adopting one specific theoretical perspective may not always be possible, or appropriate. Equally the domains of learning are inter-related and not mutually exclusive. It therefore becomes important during the planning of any learning opportunity that consideration is given to the impact of these on the developmental needs of the learners with whom you work. Chapter 3 explores these concepts in more depth.

## Learning preferences

We have established that learning is staged and that movement through these stages will depend upon the individual learner. Linked to this is the fact that learners have preferred learning approaches. If you think again about your preferred approach to learning it may well be different to those of others. Traditionally these have been seen as the visual (V) (reading/seeing), the auditory (A) (listening) and the kinaesthetic (K) (doing), shortened to VAK. Fleming and Mills (1992) developed the concept further arguing that the visual was better described as two, allowing reading (R) to be a discrete preference resulting in VARK.

Learning preferences allow us to think about how we present tasks to pupils. Remember, it is the way we present the task that will ultimately impact on its success or failure. If we think about pupils who learn best through the visual medium, tasks need to be presented or supported with written text, for example, in physical education resource cards may be provided to support the learning of a new skill. Pupils will be able to see how key aspects of the skill are performed as well as being given key words or explanations of the skill. In reflecting the needs of the auditory learners, verbal explanations of the skill would be given. Here we would need to consider the length of the instructions and understanding what information is needed to allow successful completion of the task rather than overloading them with information. Kinaesthetic learners would need to be able to practise the skill.

In looking at learning preferences we start to acknowledge the range of teaching approaches that need to be adopted to reflect the diversity of pupils. Gardner (1999) identified that as well as learning preferences, pupils also demonstrate learning across a range of 'intelligences'. In this regard, Gardner (1999) identified that intelligence could be reflected both in knowledge acquisition and in creation.

Gardner identified seven intelligences:

- Traditional intelligence:

  - Linguistic – learners demonstrate knowledge through the use of language, for example, they may be asked to write about a specific skill or a match report.
  - Logical mathematical – learners demonstrate knowledge through their ability to solve problems, for example, they may be asked to identify different ways of passing an opponent.

- Artistic intelligence:

  - Musical – learners demonstrate an appreciation of musical interpretation, for example, they may be asked to choreograph a short dance sequence.
  - Bodily kinaesthetic – learners demonstrate knowledge through the ability to perform physical skills, for example, they will be required to demonstrate their ability to perform specific skills.
  - Spatial – learners demonstrate knowledge through their understanding of the use of space, for example, they may be asked to develop short gymnastic sequences using a defined set of equipment and space.

- Personal:

  - Inter-personal – learning reflects understanding of working with others, for example, learners may be asked to work in groups of different sizes and with different peers.
  - Intra-personal – learning reflects an understanding of an individual's own personal development, for example, they may be asked to reflect upon their own performance and offer suggestions as to how they might make improvements.

# Barriers to learning

So far we have identified the processes and preferences associated with learning. However, it is equally important to look at the barriers some pupils have to learning. While this is covered in much more detail in Chapter 6, a general overview is now provided.

The Department for Education and Skills identifies: 'Difficulties in learning often arise from an unsuitable environment – inappropriate grouping of pupils, inflexible teaching styles, or inaccessible curriculum materials' (2004: 31). As practitioners we need to reflect on how we make learning accessible to pupils. This suggests that barriers may be associated with development within the cognitive, affective and psychomotor domains of learning. In some respects this brings us full circle. Having looked at domains of learning we can now consider how development within these may impact on the learner's ability to access learning.

# Learning environments

While we as teachers tend to focus on learning occurring within the curriculum, acknowledgement needs to be made of other learning opportunities that exist (Chapter 10 explores these in greater depth). For many learners the knowledge, skills and understanding that they develop may occur outside the confines of the classroom. On average pupils are only in the school environment for six or seven hours per day. Examples where pupils may participate in physical activity outside the classroom include attending out-of-school clubs, playing for a local team or participation in physical activity encouraged by their parents. Residential activities organised by a pupil's school may also support learning across the domains.

While traditional learning environments have focused on classroom-based opportunities, and for physical education this may also include the school hall, gym, playing fields or playground, much social learning may occur outside the confines of the classroom through informal play opportunities. Take time to look at the interactions that take place before class and during break and lunchtimes. Opportunities for learning outside the school environment can also occur through educational trips and residential activities. While the planning and organisation of these raise issues around safe practice (see Chapter 8), such environments also widen the breadth of learning opportunities and learning experiences.

## Chapter summary

Smith et al. argue that 'physical education can and should contribute to the physical, emotional, social, moral and intellectual development of pupils' (1998: 169). Further, AfPE (2016) identify that high quality physical education contributes to the development of key aspects in relation to physical, affective and cognitive aspects as detailed in Table 2.2.

**Table 2.2**  How physical education contributes to the development of the child

| Physical | Affective | Cognitive |
| --- | --- | --- |
| Stamina, suppleness and strength | Desire to improve | Understanding |
| Healthy, active lifestyle | Enjoyment | British citizenship |
| Skills | Commitment | Thinking and decision making |
| | Personal development and wellbeing | |
| | Confidence | |
| | Participation | |
| | Spiritual, moral, social and cultural | |

What is clear is that physical education can make a significant contribution to the development of the child. This chapter has explored aspects associated with learning focusing not only on the theoretical premises of learning, but also on the practical application of them within a physical education context. It has also built upon the aims of physical education to demonstrate how the subject can contribute to development across domains of learning. Key themes that emerge from the process of learning demonstrate that learning is progressive and that stages of learning and development are individual, and as such we cannot adopt a one-size-fits-all approach. Clear similarities are evident between the theories, allowing us to identify that any learning experience that focuses on one particular domain would not necessarily preclude learning within other domains. This concept is developed in much more detail in Chapter 7.

We have looked at how learning can occur across a range of environments, and that exposure to these will impact upon the lifelong learning opportunities for those with whom we work. Much of what has been covered in this chapter will be developed within subsequent chapters, so it may be useful to reread this chapter from time to time. However, to review your learning in this chapter you may wish to respond to the following questions.

1   Using practical examples to support your response, identify two key theories associated with the way pupils learn, and reflect on how you have used these when teaching to impact positively on pupils' progress.
2   Explain in your own words the different domains of learning, and how these can be reflected in the planning and delivery of effective learning experiences.

*(Continued)*

*(Continued)*

3   Review the range of learning environments you have experienced as a pupil, during your initial teacher education or when you have been teaching. Identify the key characteristics of these environments and the specific opportunities for pupil development they allowed.

4   Based on your reading of this chapter, identify what you feel are the key factors you should take into account when planning your physical education lessons. Use this to support your reading of Chapter 3.

## Further reading

Aubrey, K. and Riley, A. (2016) *Understanding and Using Educational Theories*. London: Sage.
This text provides detailed analysis of the major theories of learning and their application to the classroom.

Bates, B. (2016) *Learning Theories Simplified, and How to Apply Them to Teaching*. London: Sage.
This easy-to-read text provides brief overviews of the main learning theories and models. Its strength is its accessibility, the clear links to application within the classroom, and the breadth of theories and models reviewed.

Gallahue, D.L. and Ozmun, J.C. (1995) *Understanding Motor Development: Infants, Children, Adolescents, Adults*, 3rd edn. Iowa: Brown and Benchmark Publishers.
This text breaks down the basic concepts of motor development. It provides examples of expected progressions of development through clear pictorial representations that can be adapted and used not only for observation of pupils and their development, but also to support pupils' assessment of their own and others' performance.

Keenan, T., Evans, S. and Crowley, K. (2016) *An Introduction to Child Development*, 3rd edn. London: Sage.
This text provides details of development across the domains of learning. Its strength lies in the embedding of research examples throughout the text so providing clear supported evidence of the impact of the relevant theories on development. A balanced standpoint is taken, using analysis of the strengths and weaknesses of the theories covered, as well as the application of the theories to teaching.

# Planning the Learning Experience

## Chapter aims

- To develop an understanding of the processes involved in developing effective learning experiences
- To develop an understanding of the process of planning and its application within physical education
- To develop an understanding of assessment and its effective use within teaching and learning
- To integrate existing knowledge within the process of planning

## Links to *Teachers' Standards*

In working through this chapter, you should develop your knowledge associated with the *Teachers' Standards* (DfE, 2011) detailed in Table 3.1.

## Introduction

Ofsted, in reviewing physical education inspections between 2008 and 2012, suggest that weaker teaching is reflected by 'teachers' limited subject knowledge and use of assessment which led to superficial planning and insufficient challenge,

**Table 3.1**   How this chapter links to the *Teachers' Standards* (DfE, 2011)

| | |
|---|---|
| Standard 1: Set high expectations which inspire, motivate and challenge pupils | • establish a safe and stimulating environment for pupils, rooted in mutual respect<br>• set goals that stretch and challenge pupils of all backgrounds, abilities and dispositions |
| Standard 2: Promote good progress and outcomes by pupils | • be aware of pupils' capabilities and their prior knowledge, and plan teaching to build on these<br>• guide pupils to reflect on the progress they have made and their emerging needs<br>• demonstrate knowledge and understanding of how pupils learn and how this impacts on teaching<br>• encourage pupils to take a responsible and conscientious attitude to their own work and study. |
| Standard 3: Demonstrate good subject and curriculum knowledge | • have a secure knowledge of the relevant subject(s) and curriculum areas, foster and maintain pupils' interest in the subject, and address misunderstandings<br>• demonstrate a critical understanding of developments in the subject and curriculum areas, and promote the value of scholarship |
| Standard 4: Plan and teach well-structured lessons | • promote a love of learning and children's intellectual curiosity<br>• reflect systematically on the effectiveness of lessons and approaches to teaching |
| Standard 5: Adapt teaching to respond to the strengths and needs of all pupils | • know when and how to differentiate appropriately, using approaches which enable pupils to be taught effectively<br>• demonstrate an awareness of the physical, social and intellectual development of children, and know how to adapt teaching to support pupils' education at different stages of development |
| Standard 6: Make accurate and productive use of assessment | • give pupils regular feedback, both orally and through accurate marking, and encourage pupils to respond to the feedback. |
| Standard 7: Manage behaviour effectively to ensure a good and safe learning environment | • have clear rules and routines for behaviour in classrooms, and take responsibility for promoting good and courteous behaviour both in classrooms and around the school, in accordance with the school's behaviour policy |
| Standard 8: Fulfil wider professional responsibilities | • take responsibility for improving teaching through appropriate professional development, responding to advice and feedback from colleagues |

particularly for the more able pupils' (Ofsted, 2013: 5). Further that teachers should 'plan learning in PE that builds on what pupils of all abilities already know, understand and can do, and identifies what pupils need to do next in order to improve' (Ofsted, 2013: 8).

In Chapter 1 we looked at the aims of physical education and built on these during Chapter 2 to look at how pupils learn and develop and how such learning and development takes place across domains of learning. The final task in Chapter 2 asked you to identify key aspects that should be taken into account when planning and it may be useful to reflect again upon these prior to reading this chapter.

This chapter builds upon your learning to date to provide you with the opportunity to look at how it can be used in the planning of learning experiences, as well as how continuity and progression in the learning experiences of pupils can be achieved. As you read this chapter, links to future chapters will be made, allowing you to add more detail to your planning.

A good starting point is to think about why we need to plan, as it is important that we understand why it is necessary if we are to accept it as an essential process and thereby give it the importance that it needs.

---

## Task 3.1

Planning is a key part of ensuring pupils experience an effective learning episode. This task encourages you to reflect upon your understanding of planning and the processes you currently undertake.

1   When you are planning a lesson what part of the plan do you start with? Why?
2   When do you identify the intended learning outcomes of the lesson?
3   How does evaluation of the previous lesson inform your planning?
4   What aspect of planning a lesson do you find the easiest? Why?
5   What aspect of planning a lesson do you find the hardest? Why?

---

In completing Task 3.1 you are being encouraged to reflect upon your current approach to planning. We will now explore in a little more depth what effective planning may look like, noting that everyone will approach planning differently and therefore in reading this chapter you should try to establish what works best for you. Effective planning requires us to look at the whole picture of what we want to achieve; we need to make learning visible so that we can assess the impact we have on the progress of the pupils we teach. Planning can be short term, what we want to achieve in a lesson (a lesson plan); medium term, where we are looking at what we want to achieve over a period, for example a term (scheme of work); and long term, what we might want to achieve over a year, or a key stage (National Curriculum). What is important is to develop an approach to planning that is practical and not too onerous.

QCDA (2010a: 24–5) identifies three key questions that we should look to address when engaging in any planning process, broken down into a seven-step design and planning process. While individual schools may adopt different approaches the principles involved in the process will be similar.

Focus within the seven-step process is centred on three key themes.

* What are you trying to achieve?
    o   Identify your priorities.
    o   Record your starting point.
    o   Set clear goals.

- How will you organise learning?

  o   Design and implement a lesson.

- How will you know you are achieving your aims?

  o   Review progress.
  o   Evaluate and record the impact.
  o   Maintain, change or move on.

We will now explore these in more detail.

## What are you trying to achieve?

When working with teachers around the planning process I encourage them to think about the end of the lesson as their starting point. This may seem odd, but if you are clear about what you want the pupils to be able to do at the end of the lesson, it will provide you with a framework that you can use to structure the learning episodes that need to be completed in order to achieve the end goal. In particular I ask them to picture what it will look like, focusing specifically on what the pupils will be doing and what success will look like. I then get them to think about what they will need to include within the lesson to ensure the picture is achieved. By doing this you can start to plan the activities you wish to include within the lesson as well as think about how you will move between these activities. It also allows you to think about the extent to which you plan to develop knowledge, skills and understanding across the domains of learning (see Chapter 2) or if you are focusing on a specific domain. The initial plan may be in the form of a 'mind map' or as bullet points, which you develop further when you engage in the formal planning process. In planning you are thinking not only about the pupils with whom you are working, but also about yourself. Knowing what you are doing and when provides an element of security for you. It gives you a sense of purpose and direction as well as allowing you time to prepare and organise resources. It also means that you are better placed to react to situations during the lesson. Being well planned and prepared also shows the value you place on the lesson (see Chapter 1).

Looking at what the focus of the lesson is to be allows us to reflect on our own priorities, and clearly identify what we want our learners to achieve. It allows us to think about the order in which activities might be placed to provide continuity, ensuring that activities build upon what has already been taught. It also provides us with the opportunity to think about what information or knowledge we will need to complete subsequent tasks. When looking to promote continuity we are focusing on delivering the curriculum. However, we also need to ensure that there is some form of progression in the activities taught. Progression focuses on knowledge acquisition and application, ensuring that pupils are challenged at an appropriate level.

From such explanations you can start to see how both terms – continuity and progression – are closely aligned; in fact, they tend to be referred to together. Such terminology and principles should not be new to you as they are linked to the theories associated with learning (see Chapter 2). They also link to the ideas that will be explored in Chapter 6 where we look at inclusion and differentiation in more depth.

As we start to look at planning in greater depth, we need to consider the makeup of the class we are working with. For example, we need to understand what pupils can already do, what were they taught last year, who they might best work with. Within the primary school you might be teaching your own class so this is simple, but if you are teaching as a specialist across the school you will need to consider when you first start teaching your classes who might be able to support you with this. You will need to consider what you want to achieve by the end of the scheme as well as how many lessons you have in which to accomplish this. These basic questions will form part of any planning meetings you may be involved in. They are also some of the questions you may be expected to ask during orientation visits for school placement.

Having taken time to answer and reflect on the questions above, we can start to identify the goals or learning objectives we wish pupils to achieve. Shilvock and Pope summarise the process as follows:

> Before planning a lesson it is important to identify your exact learning objectives. Consider your students' learning as a long journey. Before setting off you need to be clear where you are, decide where you want to go and the most effective route for getting there. By outlining your objectives at the start of the lesson, students will have a clear idea of where they are heading and why and can be informed of progress along the way to make the journey more fulfilling. Students will follow your instructions in lesson and do what you ask, but won't know the purpose of separate activities unless you explain. (2008: 35)

So we have identified our journey's end and considered our starting point. It is now time to look at writing our objectives. Learning objectives provide the initial structure for the lesson – you might say that they are the skeleton of the lesson. As such they need to reflect what you want pupils to achieve by the end of the lesson. Again, there is no one-size-fits-all approach to the process. Bassett et al. (2016) suggest that 'learning objectives describe the learning intention for the lesson and are recorded in terms of what pupils are expected to know, understand and be able to do' (2016: 115). What is important is the phrase 'allows you to identify if learning has occurred'; your learning objectives not only outline what you are striving to achieve within the lesson, they also provide you with terms of reference against which you can assess the learning that has taken place, as well as a framework against which you can evaluate your overall lesson. They allow you to provide clarity of instructions to the pupils in your class by being specific about what you are expecting. A number of schools use the anagrams WALT (We Are Learning To …) and WILF (What I'm Looking For …). More recently the use of Dedicated Improvement and Reflection Time (DIRT) has been adopted within lessons to allow pupils to spend time reviewing and improving their own work. When first starting to work in a school it is important that you identify the approaches adopted.

In the context of physical education, we are looking predominantly at what we want pupils to know, perform and apply and at how they evaluate their own and other performances. It is important that you are clear about what you want them to do, in what situation and what it will look like, which draws on both WALT and WILF. Thus a learning objective for gymnastics might be: to be able to perform three balances (what you want them to do) in a sequence (in what situation) demonstrating good body tension through pointed toes and being still (what it will look like). The companion website provides further examples of learning objectives.

However, if we are to reflect on the diverse nature of the classes we teach we need to consider if we can only use one learning objective. While the example provided is generic in its writing as it does not specify the types of balance or the length of sequence, you might wish to consider writing learning objectives that link to different levels of attainment. Some schools use 'All pupils will …', 'Most pupils will …' and 'Some pupils will …'. Using such sentence beginnings allows you to identify what you want everyone to be able to do, what you are expecting most pupils to be able to do, and what you acknowledge only some of the pupils will be able to achieve. This also allows you to identify key performance indicators which can be linked to formal assessment activities. In some cases you might look to have learning objectives that cover the three domains of learning identified in Chapter 2.

## Case study (part 1)

Pete is a mature teacher with 15 years' experience. He is seen as a traditionalist with a lesson structure of warm-up, skills development and if time permits a game at the end. Pete is keen to change his practice and therefore worked with colleagues in his school to review their approaches to planning. Pete is starting to plan a lesson focusing on throwing for accuracy and distance. By the end of the lesson Pete wants the class to be able to play a game of target ball, which requires them to work as a team to move the ball from their area into their opponent's area using only overarm throws.

- What could his learning objectives be?

Regardless of the approach you adopt, it is important, as Shilvock and Pope (2008) identify, that you share these learning objectives with pupils at the start of the lesson so they have a clear understanding of the lesson 'journey'. Of equal importance is the need for pupils to refocus on these objectives in order that they can assess where they are and what they need to do next in order to achieve the objective. Consequently, the depth and complexity of the objectives you set or share with pupils will vary across age groups. What is important is that your learning objectives are not something that you keep to yourself. They should be shared with the pupils, for example, written on a board and explained at the start of the lesson, as well as referred to throughout the lesson. Pupils need to know what is expected of them and what success will look like. This will help them remain focused and motivated as well as providing opportunities for them to review their own learning during the lesson.

The quality of your objectives will directly impact on your ability to evaluate both the performance of the pupils and how the lesson was taught. It also allows you to think about how you will share these with your class. Therefore, time spent in this initial process is important. The case study below shows how the way you think about planning and setting learning objectives might influence how the pupils behave and the outcomes of the lesson.

## Case study (part 2)

Feedback from lesson observations identified that it was not clear what Pete was trying to achieve by the end of the lesson and this resulted in pupils not understanding what was expected of them. Working with his colleagues they looked at the approaches to planning and objective setting and how they made pupils aware of what was expected of them. At the start of the next lesson Pete shared the learning objectives with the class. They spent a short time thinking about what this would look like, so that all pupils had an understanding of what they were aiming to achieve. Pete provided all pupils with a Post-it note with their name on, and asked them to identify where they thought they were at the start of the lesson in relation to the learning objective. As a result, pupils appeared much more focused and motivated to participate.

- Thinking about Pete's experience how will you share your learning objectives at the start of the lesson?

The start of this chapter identified three main focal points within planning, the second of which focuses around the organisation of the learning. The next section of the chapter therefore looks at how this can be achieved in more detail.

## How will you organise learning?

When designing and implementing a lesson there are a number of aspects that need to be considered. While the objectives might be the skeleton of the lesson, the design and content form the flesh. In this section we will start to consider aspects of lesson design focusing specifically on:

- what we want pupils to do
- how we plan to organise pupils
- how we will ensure that all pupils are able to achieve
- the specific material that we will need to cover, and at which point in the lesson.

This section clearly identifies what the lesson will look like. If the objectives are a 'journey' this section is 'a recipe'.

As mentioned previously in this chapter, different organisations will plan in different ways and use different templates on which to plan. Below is a simple example of a planning template (see Figure 3.1) that you might find useful (it is likely that

| Class | | Number of pupils | Gender | |
|---|---|---|---|---|
| Lesson number | | Lesson length | | |
| | | | | |
| Previous experience | | | | |
| | | | | |
| Evaluation from previous lesson (focus should be on pupil learning) | | | | |
| | | | | |
| Lesson objectives | | | | |
| | | | | |
| Equipment needed | | | | |
| | | | | |
| Lesson content | | | | |
| Timing | Activity | Organisation | Equipment | Differentiation (space, task, equipment, people) |
| | | | | |

**Figure 3.1** Planning template

your training establishment or school will provide additional examples of planning templates). What is key is that you undertake some form of planning process for each lesson to ensure that you are confident with the objectives, content and progression of the lesson.

If we now start to think about how we will use this template, we first need to identify our learning objectives. For example,

Learning objectives:

- To be able to send and receive the ball over different distances showing accuracy (focuses on skill development – psychomotor domain).
- To develop the ability to play small-sided games (focuses on application of the skill – cognitive domain); and working with others (affective domain).
- To be able to review your own performance and identify ways of improving (focuses on application of the skill – cognitive domain); and working with others (affective domain).

If we unpick these learning objectives, we are looking at developing pupils' abilities to send and receive a ball (this could be throwing and catching, kicking and trapping, hitting and fielding) over different distances. We want them to be able to demonstrate these skills within small-sided games and demonstrate accuracy in their passing. We also want them to review their own performance. Therefore we need to ensure that within the lesson opportunities arise for pupils to practise sending and receiving, and that this occurs over varying distances. They need to develop an understanding of what a successful pass looks like, so we need to ensure that at some point we give them clear terms of reference (learning or teaching points and modelling of what a good one looks like) that give them a framework against which they can assess their own performance and that of others. Finally, we need to include opportunities for them to demonstrate their skill development within a small-game situation. This is the basis of our lesson, and would be reflected in our planning template within the lesson objectives section (see Figure 3.2).

As with any lesson we need to look at the constituent parts. We need to be clear about the order of the activities we are planning to deliver, and also how we ensure opportunities for ourselves and the pupils to review the progress they are making towards achieving the learning objectives are embedded throughout the lesson. This is crucial as the quality of a lesson is reflected in the impact you as the teacher have on the progress of the pupils. Once you have an image of the lesson you can start to look at each part of the lesson in more depth.

When planning, many people focus on the taught part of the lesson, rather than the lesson in its entirety. Traditionally in physical education the starter activity would be seen as a warm-up (see Chapter 8 for the purpose and components of a warm-up). However, your lesson starts from the time pupils begin to change and therefore this should be included in your planning. Are there any set routines you expect pupils to follow while changing? How will you supervise changing? What

| Class | | Number of pupils | Gender | |
|---|---|---|---|---|
| Lesson number | | Lesson length | | |
| | | | | |
| Previous experience | | | | |
| | | | | |
| Evaluation from previous lesson | | | | |
| | | | | |
| Lesson objectives • To be able to send and receive the ball over different distances showing accuracy • To develop the ability to play small-sided games • To be able to review your own performance and identify ways of improving | | | | |
| | | | | |
| Equipment needed | | | | |
| | | | | |
| | | | | |
| Lesson content | | | | |
| Timing | Activity | Organisation | Equipment | Differentiation (space, task, equipment, people) |
| | Starter | | | |
| | Main activities | | | |
| | Plenary | | | |

**Figure 3.2**  Planning template including lesson objectives

will pupils do when they are changed? Is there anything you can get them to do once they have changed (for example find a partner and talk about what they can remember from the last lesson, or identifying which group they are working in for the lesson)?

Consideration also needs to be given to the general organisation of the lesson. Effective organisation limits the time pupils spend off task (that is the time when learning is not taking place).

Key questions to consider here are as follows.

- How will I group my pupils?

  o Do I want pupils to be of similar ability or do I want to mix them up?
  o What group size do I need?
  o What is the optimum size for the activity – can the activity be done alone? One point to think about is that the smaller the group, the more opportunities occur for pupils to engage in the activity.
  o How can I get them into groups?

- Will I need to change the group sizes through the lesson?

  o How can I minimise group size changes?
  o What is the final group size (threes, fours)?
  o How will I get there?

For example, if you have planned for the end game to be played as 4 v 4 you might have pupils working on their own to begin with, then with a partner, and then look to combine two pairs to form a group of four. The key is to avoid splitting groups once they have been formed, for example going from pairs to threes.

- What equipment do I need and where will this be placed?

  o How will equipment be collected and returned to the store?

Are you going to have full responsibility for taking the equipment out and bringing it back? Or is this a task you can give to designated pupils? A key point to note is that it is your responsibility to ensure that all equipment is fit for purpose (see Chapter 8) and also that all equipment taken out is returned. You need to train your pupils to count the equipment out as well as counting it back in. It is also important that equipment stores are kept tidy, not only because it means that your equipment will last longer, but also because you will not waste time trying to find equipment at the start of the lesson.

  o How will pupils collect equipment for each activity?

This might seem like an odd question, but I am sure that you can all remember racing to choose the brightest ball, and everyone fighting over the new equipment – at times choosing your equipment became a survival of the fittest, or whoever got there first. If you have pupils working on their own, identify a small group at a time to go and collect their equipment or hand the equipment out as you are talking to them. If they are working in pairs or small groups, get them to identify an individual with responsibility to collect the equipment. You may set up equipment stations so that pupils go to different places to collect what they need.

It is also important to consider when the best time to collect the equipment is. You will want to avoid handing out and collecting in equipment too frequently. However, when distributing equipment you also need to be very clear what it is you want them to do once they have the equipment. Are they expected to go straight into an activity? Or will they just return to their work space and await further instructions? Giving out equipment and then giving further instructions runs the risk of pupils becoming distracted and in many situations this will result in behaviour management issues.

- What space do I have and how can I make effective use of it?
  - o  How will I designate boundaries – can I use cones or are line markings available?
  - o  Do I want to change the size of the workspace during the lesson and what is the best way of doing this?

Traditionally physical education lessons will take place in the school hall, or on the school playground or field. If you are teaching inside, you will need to be very conscious of other equipment that might be stored in that area, for example lunch tables, chairs, pianos (Chapter 8 looks at safe practice in physical education). What is important is that you establish a clear workspace. You may consider using cones to form your boundary areas, although you do need to be aware that they will move during the lesson and can become a trip hazard. However, you will also need to think about the progressions in your lessons and how you may need to change the space over time. You may also need to consider other users, for example, does your lesson take place when another class is having their break and will this impact on the outdoor area you can use? Is your lesson in the main hall prior to or immediately after lunch and how will this be affected by setting up for lunch and the clean up afterwards?

Over recent years there has been an increase in the use of the playground and development of playground markings and 'playzones'. Again, the facilities you have will vary between schools, so you should spend time familiarising yourself with what you have available prior to undertaking any detailed planning.

In terms of organisation we need to be clear about what behaviour management strategies we might employ, as well as health and safety considerations we need to take into account.

Having started to focus on our organisation, we now need to think about how we will present our lesson and what teaching approaches we intend to use. One of the most frequently used approaches for the teaching of physical education is the spectrum developed by Mosston and Ashworth (1994, 2008). Whilst this concept is explored in greater depth in Chapter 7, put simply, the approach looks at the different ways in which an activity can be presented and completed in relation to the extent to which the activities are centred around the learner. For example, is the teacher controlling the content and delivery or are pupils encouraged to take greater responsibility for their own learning?

## Task 3.2

Look at the learning objectives for our lesson.

- To be able to send and receive the ball over different distances showing accuracy
- To develop the ability to play small-sided games
- To be able to review your own performance and identify ways of improving

1   What teaching approaches do you feel are most appropriate for these activities (remember you can use different approaches for different activities)?
2   How might you group your pupils for this activity?

The learning objectives require us to provide pupils with the opportunity to practise a specific skill – sending and receiving the ball. This suggests that we are looking at using a reproductive style whereby they are reproducing a skill. The most probable approach in learning new skills is the practice style, whereby pupils are shown a skill and then asked to reproduce it through practising. However, we could also deliver this through a more discovery approach, whereby pupils are challenged to think about the different ways in which they can send and receive. Further, a reciprocal style could be adopted particularly as we are looking at accuracy and direction in our learning objectives as well. We also need to consider how opportunities for feedback will be embedded, again, a reciprocal approach might be best here allowing the pupils to observe either themselves (through reviewing videos of their performances) or feedback to each other using resources cards.

Having chosen our teaching approaches, we can start to think more about the actual content: what we are going to be doing in each part of the lesson.

We introduced the concept of starter activities earlier in this chapter. Such activities should provide a link for pupils between what they learnt in their previous lesson and what they are going to work on during the current lesson. They engage pupils from the start of the lesson and should allow pupils to gain an understanding of the learning objectives for the lesson. For example, in physical education we might engage them in a warm-up activity, but in doing so ask them to think about specific skills that they have learnt. Or we might plan an activity which requires them to demonstrate the skills they had learnt in the previous lesson to identify what they have retained.

Having started the lesson with some form of starter activity we now need to have a smooth transition into our next activity. We need to be clear how the starter activity relates to the main body of the lesson. We also need to consider how activities should be differentiated to support the whole class (see Chapter 6 for more detail regarding differentiation). As we move through the lesson we need to consider opportunities for assessment.

## Assessment

> If we are to develop truly effective schools, educators must understand how to gather dependable evidence of student achievement and use the assessment process and its results either to support or certify student achievement depending on the context. (Stiggins, 2014: 67)

Assessment is embedded within everything we do. We constantly make judgements about ourselves in relation to others, criteria, expectation. But why? Is it because we live in societies where everything is judged and therefore must by default involve a form of assessment? We all take exams and degrees, undertake appraisals, apply for jobs based on criteria. Our success is reflected in the judgements we and others make against these criteria.

'Assessment covers all those activities which are undertaken by teachers and others to measure the effectiveness of their teaching and the extent to which pupils learned what they were trying to teach' (Haydn, 2016: 447). More recently Stiggins (2014) defines assessment as 'the process of getting information to inform instructional decisions' (Stiggins, 2014: 69). Such a definition provides us with the three key points of assessment: that it is an active process, that it is undertaken by a range of individuals, and that there must be clear criteria on which judgements or observations are made.

Assessment must be meaningful. It must have a clear purpose and have clear and measurable outcomes. Ensuring the pupils themselves understand the purpose of the assessment is vital in order for them to reflect upon their own learning and identify opportunities for further development and target setting. Assessment is therefore a way in which we feedback to our pupils. As Mosston and Ashworth (2008) state 'feedback shapes perceptions, personality, and one's view of humanity. Since each form of feedback acknowledges events from a particular point of reference, expanding the use of all the forms of feedback can expand our perceptions of the teaching–learning process' (2008: 46).

Further to this, AfPE state:

> Effective assessment in physical education engages supports and motivates pupils to become competent, confident, creative and reflective movers. It can support and encourage young people to work together in order to excel in physically demanding and competitive activities. Approaches to assessment must be meaningful and embedded throughout a high quality physical education curriculum; which enables learners to make progress and improve their attainment. (2015: 2)

A range of assessment approaches including self-check, peer and teacher assessment, all are underpinned with the need for clear performance criteria to be identified and shared. Knowing what they need to be able to do to show success is important and reflects the principles associated with learning detailed in Chapter 2.

Thus, when choosing to assess, we need to be clear about its purpose. For example, are we using assessment to inform us or our pupils and support learning (formative assessment), which would require us to engage in assessment throughout the lesson; or to summarise the learning that has taken place (summative assessment), which suggests that the assessment takes place at the end of a learning process?

Three main types of assessment are commonly associated with education: norm referenced, criterion referenced and ipsative. When using norm referencing we are looking at comparing our pupils against each other. An example in physical education may be when we are engaging them in some form of timed event, where we identify the fastest and consequently the slowest pupil. While such a process allows us to rank pupils, the associated impact can be detrimental to the development of pupils' self-esteem (see Chapters 2 and 9).

A more appropriate approach may be that of criterion-referenced assessment. Here assessment is based upon achievement against specific criteria. If we think about our current lesson, we are looking at pupils being able to perform specific skills and therefore we need to provide them with the criteria (learning or teaching points) to be able to perform the skill. These then become our criteria for assessment.

A further type of assessment that we may wish to use is ipsative assessment. This is sometimes referred to as value-added assessment. Here the focus is on the individual (pupil) assessing their own progress against themselves. In such a way, they are able to identify what they were able to do at, for example, the start of the lesson, and then at the end of the lesson to gauge the progress they have made. Such an approach reflects recent governmental policy around the process of assessment for learning which encourages pupils to gain an understanding of what they have already learnt, what they need to do next and how they might achieve this.

Ofsted (2013: 19) suggest that effective assessment includes:

- Building on prior learning and using baseline assessments to monitor progress.
- Identifying core tasks as the basis for assessment.
- Tracking pupils' progress against the core tasks.
- Providing a best fit for achievement.
- Sharing progress across key stages.
- Sharing feedback with pupils.

For assessment to be successful, pupils need to understand the purpose of the assessment and how the outcomes of it will be used to support their own learning. Lopez-Pastor et al. (2012) suggest that in a physical education context, there is a tendency to focus on summative rather than formative assessment approaches. Further, in planning for assessment, consideration needs to be given to what it is we are assessing, for example attainment, progress, effort or behaviours. Stiggins argues that 'Students judge their chances of future success based on their interpretation of their past success' (2014: 70), therefore we must acknowledge the power of assessment and how it is used on the overall outcomes of pupils. Success and failure will have a huge impact on pupils' willingness to continue to engage in an activity.

As we have previously identified within this chapter, pupils should be clear about what the learning objectives are and what success will look like in achieving them. They should be encouraged to reflect on their own progress towards these objectives and identify with or without support how improvements can be made to make further progress. In essence, both the teacher and the pupil become accountable for the progress that is made towards achievement of the learning objective, encouraging a focus towards mastery of the skill. In acknowledging this, pupils have the potential to become more engaged, showing higher levels of learning and motivation (Lopez-Pastor et al., 2012).

In our planning we need to be considering how and when we can build in opportunities for pupils to assess themselves or each other, asking ourselves how we as teachers will engage in assessment. At the end of the lesson we need to consider how we provide pupils with opportunities to reflect upon their learning.

Earlier in the chapter we identified that at the start of the lesson you would have provided an overview of the learning objectives. At the end of the lesson you need to provide pupils with an opportunity to identify their level of success against these criteria as well as think about what they would need to do to improve further.

## Task 3.3

1    Spend some time thinking and researching the different methods of assessment that can be employed within the primary classroom.
2    Identify those with which you are familiar and consider how you may use such approaches within your physical education lessons.

## Case study (part 3)

If you recall in Case study (part 2), Pete shared the learning objectives with his class and asked them to identify where they thought they were in relation to these.

Throughout the lesson, Pete refers to the learning objectives and encourages pupils to think about whether they need to move their Post-it to reflect the progress they have made. At the end of the lesson Pete asks all pupils to check whether they have achieved the learning objectives, and asks some to explain in their own words how they have achieved this.

• How is Pete assessing the learning that has taken place?

# How will you know you are achieving your aims?

Having planned and implemented your lesson, you now need to reflect upon the extent to which you achieved your aims. Some of this reflection will take place during the lesson itself as you modify your lesson to reflect pupils' progress (do not think that you have to stick to every detail of your lesson plan – if something is going really well or particularly badly, work around it).

Amos and Postlethwaite argue that reflection is important as it allows the individual to:

> practise a way of thinking about teaching which will enable them to keep their knowledge updated by reference to changing circumstances, and to changing awareness of the formal theories and research as that develops. (1996: 14)

Schon (1983) identifies two types of reflection:

- reflection in action, which occurs while you are doing the activity (during the lesson)
- reflection of action, which occurs once something has been done (at the end of the lesson).

So, what do we reflect on? Ideally we want to reflect upon the learning objectives. To what extent did pupils achieve the learning objectives? What were the strengths and weaknesses of the lesson, in other words what went well and what do I need to improve next time? Avoid the temptation to always focus on the negative. Bailey (2006) suggests the focus should be around the content, organisation and presentation of the lesson. You should use the results of your evaluation to identify where you are going next. This is the time to either plan the next lesson or at least jot down a few ideas to use as a basis. By doing this you are already thinking about the next lesson in the scheme and can either plan it straight away or at least make some notes to come back to later. Lawrence et al. (2016) working with teachers of differing experiences to look at reflection post lesson delivery in physical education identified the following key areas against which review could be undertaken:

- The impact their teaching had on the progress of the students.
- Specific critical incidents that occurred during the lesson identified either by the teacher or the observer.
- Reflection against the teaching characteristics on which teaching observations were based.
- Identification of two positive aspects of the lesson.
- Identification of one area for improvement.
- Identification of key areas of focus for the next lesson.
- A summary of what they intended to teach in the next lesson.

You might find it useful to think about some of these each time you review your lessons. As well as evaluating your own teaching, during your initial teacher education programme you will also be evaluated against your teaching standards. Thus when planning your lesson, you also need to consider how you will demonstrate attainment against your specific standards. Professionally you should therefore keep abreast of any changes to the standards so that you clearly understand what you are expected to have achieved against each standard.

## Task 3.4

1    During your initial teacher education programme you will engage in a range of evaluation situations. During one placement try and have your lesson videoed (you will need to check with your school if this is possible as it has potential issues associated with safeguarding pupils). Having completed an initial evaluation of your lesson, watch the video of your lesson and complete a second evaluation based on what you have observed.

   a    What differences have you noted?
   b    How will your teaching change as a result of this?

2    Try and observe other staff (this could be a fellow student) with whom you work and with their permission complete an evaluation of their lesson.

   a    What do you notice about the way they deliver their sessions?
   b    What can you take away from your observations?

## Chapter summary

The aim of this chapter has been to develop your knowledge and understanding of the planning process in physical education. While much of what you have read will support your existing knowledge of the planning process you may wish to reflect upon the following review questions.

1    What key factors do you need to consider when planning a physical education lesson?
2    What constitutes an effective lesson?
3    How will you include assessment within your lesson planning?
4    Why, how and when should you evaluate your lesson?

# Further reading

DinanThompson, M. and Penney, D. (2015) 'Assessment literacy in primary physical education', *European Physical Education Review*, 21(4): 485–503.
This research piece looks specifically at the assessment practices of teachers within physical education. It identifies the challenges associated with effective assessment.

Green, N. (2015) 'Are assessment practices in physical education developing with PACE?' *Physical Education Matters*, 10(3): 17–20.
This research piece explores how assessment can be conducted across the physical, affective and cognitive domains, and through different educational contexts. It identifies progression in learning through six key areas, from the beginner through to the exceptional.

# Developing Motor Competences

## Chapter aims

- To develop a deeper understanding of the concept of physical literacy and its application in the early years and primary setting
- To develop an understanding of the principles of motor competences in physical education
- To develop an understanding of the fundamental motor skills relevant to physical education
- To develop an understanding of motor development in pupils

## Links to *Teachers' Standards*

In working through this chapter, you should develop your knowledge associated with the *Teachers' Standards* (DfE, 2011) detailed in Table 4.1.

## Introduction

In Chapter 1 we looked at what physical education is and how it can be defined. Embedded within the chapter was the concept of physical literacy. Chapter 2 introduced you to the principles of child development predominantly focusing on learning across

**Table 4.1**   How this chapter links to the *Teachers' Standards* (DfE, 2011)

| | |
|---|---|
| Standard 1: Set high expectations which inspire, motivate and challenge pupils | • set goals that stretch and challenge pupils of all backgrounds, abilities and dispositions |
| | • demonstrate consistently the positive attitudes, values and behaviour which are expected of pupils. |
| Standard 2: Promote good progress and outcomes by pupils | • be accountable for pupils' attainment, progress and outcomes |
| | • be aware of pupils' capabilities and their prior knowledge, and plan teaching to build on these |
| | • demonstrate knowledge and understanding of how pupils learn and how this impacts on teaching |
| Standard 3: Demonstrate good subject and curriculum knowledge | • have a secure knowledge of the relevant subject(s) and curriculum areas, foster and maintain pupils' interest in the subject, and address misunderstandings |
| | • demonstrate a critical understanding of developments in the subject and curriculum areas, and promote the value of scholarship |
| Standard 4: Plan and teach well-structured lessons | • promote a love of learning and children's intellectual curiosity |
| | • contribute to the design and provision of an engaging curriculum within the relevant subject area(s). |
| Standard 5: Adapt teaching to respond to the strengths and needs of all pupils | • know when and how to differentiate appropriately, using approaches which enable pupils to be taught effectively |
| | • have a secure understanding of how a range of factors can inhibit pupils' ability to learn, and how best to overcome these |

the developmental domains. The aim of this chapter is to look in detail at physical literacy and the development of the fundamental motor skills and movement patterns you will be expected to teach within the early years and primary classroom. Reference will also be made to how physical education can be delivered within the early years setting to promote physical development across early learning goals. The chapter will also consider a range of developmental activities that can be integrated into lesson planning in order to emphasise key teaching points associated with skill development.

# Developing the concept of physical literacy

As early as the Board of Education syllabus of 1933, reference to the delivery of specific activities within the physical education have been identified. Detailing dance, games and swimming as the key areas of foci, the syllabus also identified free play and the need to 'create a love of open air and a healthy way of living' (BoE, 1933: 9), suggesting a requirement for outdoor activities and the promotion of health-related activities. Whilst current curricula are less prescriptive, underpinning all areas of activity are the fundamental movement skills that form the foundations for development over time.

In Chapter 2 we looked at stages of development across the domains of learning. Whitehead and Murdoch (2006) identify six development periods ranging from birth through to older age. For the purpose of this text, we will focus on those most relevant, these being pre-school and the foundation and primary school period.

During the pre-school period the focus should be on developing the basic attributes associated with physical literacy, with a particular reference to encouraging children to be active (Whitehead and Murdoch, 2006). Maude (2013) suggests that the increasing prevalence of play-based learning and outdoor learning opportunities within early years' settings increases the diversity of learning experiences available to children. Thus developing physical literacy should not be seen as the role of only physical education teachers. Within the early years setting, development of motor competences through the physical development early learning goals will be seen not only in the physical education activities in which they engage, but also in activities such as writing and construction.

During the foundation and primary school period, the development and establishment of the fundamental concepts become important. Here an emphasis on motivation, confidence, competence and confidence become important.

## Physical literacy and the learning environment

In Chapter 1 we explored the concept of physical literacy and how it should be a goal of high quality physical education experiences. Whilst views regarding physical literacy as a pedagogical approach vary, ensuring opportunities for its development must be embedded in the learning environments we create. Specifically, we need to be looking at how we ensure an engaging learning environment is created that allows pupils to develop working relationships with others and take ownership of aspects of their own learning. In essence, we must create learning environments that allow the individual to feel safe and able to develop across the domains of learning.

Morgan et al. (2013) argue that a mastery climate is crucial for successful physical literacy development. Evolving from the work of Ames (1992) on achievement motivation, it is suggested that where there is a task-orientated focus (whereby success is reflected by the ability of the individual to achieve the task, rather than the comparison of the individual in relation to how others perform the task), the willingness to persist in an activity is more evident than in situations where the focus is ego-orientated. Thus clarity in the purpose of the activity, and how success will be demonstrated are paramount (a concept discussed in Chapter 3). Thus identification of individual learning goals and tracking of progress against these become important, reflecting a focus on ipsative and self-assessment (see Chapter 3 for further details on this).

## Physical literacy and fundamental movement skills

For many, physical literacy is reflected in the ability of the individual to become competent in the fundamental movement skills identified later in this chapter. Whilst the development of competence in these skills is important, becoming too prescriptive in their achievement limits the central concept of physical literacy being a journey. More important is the belief that it is the empowerment of the individual to undertake and value physical activity allowing them to take personal responsibility for their own 'physical literacy journey'. It also limits how those with some form of barrier to participating in physical activity become physically literate in their own context.

Development of movement skills occurs from birth onwards. As teachers of physical education, we develop an understanding of how those we teach develop over time in order that we can create effective learning opportunities for them to secure progress. We have previously indicated that central to the teaching of physical education is the goal to create physically literate individuals. With an increasing number of schools taking pupils in from the age of two, as teachers we have a duty to maintain our subject knowledge in order that we can fully support pupils across the phases of education. In the early years and foundation stage (EYFS) of the curriculum, this is supported through the EYFS framework (DfE, 2014). Within this framework seven 'areas for learning and development' (DfE, 2014: 7) are identified. Table 4.2 provides a breakdown of these and some of the activities that physical education can support.

**Table 4.2**   Learning and development areas within the EYFS framework (DfE, 2014) and their links to physical education

| Areas | Sub categories | Physical education activities |
| --- | --- | --- |
| Communication and language | Listening and attention | Describing activities |
| | Understanding | Talking partners |
| | Speaking | |
| Physical development | Moving and handling | Movement skills |
| | | Manipulation skills |
| | Health and self care | Effects of exercise on our body |
| Personal, social, emotional development | Self-confidence and self-awareness | |
| | Managing feelings and behaviour | Sharing of equipment |
| | Making relationships | Working with others |
| Literacy | Reading | |
| | Writing | Dough disco |
| | | Fine motor skills development: |
| | | Bead threading |
| | | Cutting out |
| | | Tracing |
| | Numbers | Counting activities |
| | Shape, space and measures | Measuring activities |
| Understanding the world | People and communities | |
| | The world | |
| | Technology | |
| Expressive arts and design | Exploring and using media and materials | |
| | Being imaginative | Dance activities |
| | | Sequences |

# Skills we would expect pupils to achieve during their early years' development

In the context of the time spent teaching physical education this results in potentially pupils mastering five skills per year. Thus in the planning of the curriculum, consideration must be given to how maximisation of learning can occur. In Chapters 3 and 7 we look in depth at how planning and a range of teaching approaches can be applied to maximise learning opportunities, but it is probably important that consideration is given to the key approaches at this point.

To maximise learning we need to consider the following:

• How much equipment do I have?

Equipment is important as ideally, and if the skill permits, you should ensure that each pupil has their own piece of equipment. In doing so you ensure that they can all be working on the skill at the same time and reduce the amount of waiting time.

• How many instructions do I need to give the pupils for them to be able to complete the task?

In observing the teaching of physical education over the last 20 years, a reoccurring issue is the amount of time teachers take to explain an activity. In doing so they reduce the amount of time available for pupils to practise the skill and also raise opportunities for off-task activities. Think carefully how much information pupils need to start the activity and then add other information as or when required.

# Assessment within the EYFS framework

Assessing pupil progress across their physical education development is an important aspect. Most assessment will take place as a result of observing the pupils performing the skills or engaging within the activity. Within the context of EYFS, it is the observation of pupils' ability to perform a skill that becomes central to your requirement to provide progress against the physical development prime area (DfE, 2014). Central to pupils' progress is the feedback they receive and how they are encouraged to make further progress. In Chapter 7 we look at the use of feedback on progress including the potentially negative consequences it can have. Therefore, in creating an effective learning environment, consideration needs to be given to how observations will be undertaken and how outcomes will be recorded and reported. Within the context of the EYFS framework, staff are required to report progress in relation to pupils' strengths and areas for development, with the formal completion of an EYFS profile for all pupils to support their transition into Year 1.

Strategies that can be used to support assessment include:

- Note taking – can you set up a system whereby any observations are noted and then used to show how pupils have progressed during the lesson, or across a series of lessons?
- Photographic evidence – can images of pupils' work be taken and then stored to allow you to share with parents the work they have been doing?

# Developing early motor skills

Developing an understanding of what fundamental movement skills look like is crucial if you are to be able to assess levels of competency and identify areas/ aspects for further development. In many ways, the process of observing reflects those skills evident within the primary classroom as a whole. 'The first of skills children usually practice and master are those of importance and interest to them and their peers' (Haynes and Miller, 2015: 406). Thus in planning for the development of skills it is important to identify what pupils know and can do before adopting a one-size-fits-all approach (theories associated with learning are covered in Chapter 2, whilst details of the different approaches for teaching physical education can be found in Chapter 7). The notion of interest is also important in respect of motivational levels (Drost and Todorovich) who argue: 'Students often lack motivation to persist in skill practice because they lack an understanding of the usefulness of a specific skill' (2013: 54).

Skill development occurs over time and, in many instances, is linked to the physical development of the individual (see Chapter 2). This must be taken into consideration when considering what skills and progression pupils will be capable of achieving (Gosset, 2016). This concept is also important when reviewing the safe teaching of physical education and is covered in greater depth in Chapter 8.

According to Gallahue and Ozmun (1995) and QCDA (2010a) three discrete stages of motor development occur: the initial or early, the elementary or middle and the mature or late. In contrast, the Physical Education Association of the United Kingdom (2003) identified two stages: the early and late motor pattern. These developmental stages, however they are constructed, include different motor skills, and the development of these skills will be reflected to some extent in the curriculum, both in England and in other countries.

Most of the pupils with whom you work will already have experienced a wealth of developmental opportunities during the early stages of their development as a result of their interactions with different individuals or environments. They will have started to develop basic motor skills associated with stability (balance), locomotion (movement) and manipulation (use of hands). These concepts will therefore underpin any physical work in the Foundation Stage and early years of primary education (and are detailed above in Table 4.2).

---

## Task 4.1

1    From your current experience, what would you regard as the fundamental motor skills pupils should learn?
2    Why do you think these are important?
3    Do you think there is any specific order in which they should be developed?

---

What emerges from the available literature and resources is a generic approach to developing fundamental skills through engaging pupils in a range of activities, underpinned by a guiding principle that children need these basic skills for lifelong participation in physical education and physical activity (as reflected in the concept of physical literacy). What we as teachers therefore need to do is to understand these specific skills and identify activities that can be used to support their development.

The range of supporting resources currently available demonstrates not only the recent investment in physical education, but also an increased awareness of the need to support those who work with pupils during the early stages of their development (www.youthsportdirect.org.uk provides examples of such resources). Such resources build upon the work of researchers looking at growth and development within the physical domain (see Chapter 2 for more detail). The progressive nature of skill development is a common theme within this literature. In the early stages of development we concentrate on basic motor skills and concepts rather than expecting pupils to engage in more complex games and activities. As a consequence, the remainder of this chapter will focus on the development of generic skills rather than on specific games or activities (examples of these can be found on the companion website). This will demonstrate the inter-relatedness of many of the skills discussed.

A common classification of fundamental skills used by physical education practitioners is ABC (Agility, Balance and Co-ordination) (Sports Coach UK, www.sportscoachuk.org). This categorisation has been used to produce a Multi-Skills Club of resources and activities designed to develop pupils' competences within these areas (Youth Sport Trust – www.youthsporttrust.org.uk). In a similar vein, national governing bodies of sport have also started to develop FUNdamental resources (British Gymnastics), which are designed to support learning activities that not only develop basic motor skills, but are also enjoyable for children.

As well as these ABC skills, we should also look at the categories of motor skills which include locomotion, core stability and those involving some form of manipulation (see Table 4.3).

## Task 4.2

1 Using Table 4.3, reflect upon the skills identified.
2 What knowledge do you have of performing these skills?
3 What do you feel are the key teaching points for each of these skills?

You may wish to develop a resource file to collate the tasks completed in this chapter so that you can use them in your teaching.

**Table 4.3**   Categories of motor skills

| Locomotion | Stability | Manipulation |
| --- | --- | --- |
| Walk | Bend | Throw |
| Run | Stretch | Catch |
| Leap | Reach | Kick |
| Hop | Twist | Trap |
| Jump | Turn | Roll |
| Slide | | Strike |
| Gallop | | Volley |
| Rotation | | Write |
| | | Construct |

Looking at the skills listed in Table 4.3, you will appreciate that fundamental motor skills are those which we take for granted in any activities we engage in, and form the basis for any physical education that we might participate in as adults. For example, we run in many games-based activities, in athletics, in dance and in gymnastics, as a means of developing our fitness. We turn when we change direction in games-based activities, in gymnastics and in dance. We throw in games activities, in aquatic activities and in athletic activities. When we view skill development in this way, we can begin to acknowledge the inter-related nature of skills in physical education.

## Fundamental motor skills

The teaching of fundamental movement skills (FMS) provides the foundations for development across the physical domain. Drost and Todorovich identify fundamental motor skills as 'locomotor, manipulative and non-manipulative' (2013: 54). Research indicates that the 'rationale behind the focus on the development of FMS is based on the notion that they have been considered the precursor for successful and satisfying participation in healthy lifelong leisure activities and sport' (Haynes and Miller, 2015: 398). Further, that there is a clear link between physical ability and emotional development.

We can divide fundamental motor skills into skills that focus on specific body parts. One of the simplest ways to do this is a top-down approach to the human body, for instance by thinking about what the head is doing, what the arms are doing, what the main body is doing, and finally what the legs and feet do (PEAUK, 2003). This allows us to observe performances in detail, affording the opportunity to give focused and specific feedback. The next section of the chapter focuses on specific skills.

## Locomotor skills

You may wish to refer to Table 4.3 for a complete overview of the different locomotor skills.

## Running

Running is the basic movement that allows us to cover ground at speed, and the speed at which we run will vary depending upon the activity. For example, if we are running to develop our fitness then we are likely to travel at a gentle pace over a longer period of time, while in many activities we undertake within physical education we will run at speed. In essence, a run is an extension of a walk, so the adage that 'you can't run before you can walk' is indeed correct.

With any skill, key teaching or learning points can be used to guide the performer as well as providing a framework through which feedback about performances can be given. When developing the skill of running the following points should be focused upon.

- **Teaching point 1:** The head must remain as still as possible with the eyes focused upon a point in the direction of travel – when learning to run it can be common for children to rotate the head from side to side, and this rotation can lead to a lack of co-ordination and balance in the upper body (torso and shoulders). A further common fault occurs as a result of the learner focusing their gaze towards the floor leading to forward rotation of the body. An easy way to think about how this would feel is to imagine yourself running very quickly down a hill and the lack of balance and co-ordination you would feel when doing this. An easy way to address this is to get children to identify a spot on the horizon or wall of the hall and focus on that when running.
- **Teaching point 2:** Arms and legs work in opposition – this may seem self-explanatory, but that is because this is a skill that we perform habitually, without really thinking about it. If a pupil is performing the skill with the same arm and leg moving at the same time, you will see a lot of body rotation (you might find it useful to have a

go at running in this way to fully understand). The key to this teaching point is to encourage the learner to relax and do what comes naturally. You could start any activity at walking pace, and as pupils' confidence and competence develop encourage them to increase the pace at which they are working.

- **Teaching point 3:** Arms pump by your side rather than across the body which results in upper body rotation – again this teaching point is better appreciated if you have a go at doing it yourself. While standing on the spot pump your arms as though you are running, but rather than your arms going forwards and backwards, move your arms across your body so that your right arm finishes across the left side of your body and your left arm finishes across your right side. What you should feel is that your torso rotates. Now try the same practice with your right and left hands finishing pointing forward. Can you feel the difference?
- **Teaching point 4:** Upper body leans forward – as the first teaching point was that we should encourage learners to look straight ahead, leaning forward while running could seem contradictory; however, a slight forward lean will enhance balance.

What activities can we use to encourage skill development? With the running-related activities discussed above it is sensible at first to encourage pupils to perform the skill on the spot. As they become more confident they can start to perform the skill at walking pace and over time increase their speed. If they are struggling to run in a straight line you can encourage them to follow a line on the ground, or provide them with two cones to run between. To develop agility you can then get them to run round cones (slalom). You can consider setting up relay activities to encourage co-operative opportunities, although you need to be aware that as competition is introduced you may find that the skill level declines as children emphasise winning over following set techniques. You will also need to consider the learning environment you are creating by introducing competition.

## Jumping

Jumping can be used across activities. As with running, the performance will be influenced by what we are trying to achieve. In jumping we might wish to jump for height, to catch a ball, or for distance in a long jump. However, when we look at jumping in gymnastics and dance-based activities, we can identify five different ways to jump:

- one foot to one foot (hop)
- one foot to the other (leap)
- two feet to one foot
- two feet to two feet
- one foot to two feet (hopscotch).

Again, we can break the skill down to reflect what the body parts are doing.

If we look at the skill from the top down, we can start by thinking about what our head is doing. As with running, we want to encourage the learner to focus their eyes forward on a spot in front of them. This ensures that they are not looking at their feet and avoids unnecessary forward rotation. We then need to focus on the arms and legs. It is important that children bend their knees to provide power for the take-off, and bend them again when landing to absorb the impact. You may already know that the knee joint is sometimes referred to as a hinge joint. If the knees are not bent on landing, then the shock-absorbing mechanisms of the joint will not function, resulting in shock waves (a jolting sensation) being experienced throughout the body. Over time this may cause an injury.

While the legs act as the power behind the skill, the arms also contribute. Depending on the purpose of the jump, the arms will act differently. If you are encouraging jumping for height, the arms will swing forward and up; when jumping for distance the arms will swing forward and back. Practising this part of the skill standing still will allow you to feel the impact of the movement of the body.

In terms of setting suitable challenges to support skill development we can ask pupils to jump up and touch an object, for example a suspended balloon. This will encourage them to jump for height. If we are looking at encouraging them to jump for distance, then we can ask them to jump forward to a cone. A fun challenge is to get them to predict how far they can jump and place a cone on the floor. Children can then try to reach this cone and either move it forward if they have passed it or backwards if they have not reached it. As they become more proficient they can be encouraged to jump over objects. As with all physical activities you will need to consider relevant aspects of health and safety, a topic discussed in greater depth in Chapter 8.

As your pupils' ability to perform basic jumps improves you can get them to think about the shapes their bodies make when in the air. For example, a straight jump requires them to jump up with their hands stretched above their heads, their fingers pointing up and their toes pointing towards the floor. A tuck jump requires them to jump up and bring their knees to their chest. Caution is suggested when introducing this skill as learners may have a tendency to bring their chest to meet their knees resulting in them forming a ball shape which will lead to a lack of stability.

## Rotation

Rotation skills can be used to travel in both gymnastics and dance activities. Perhaps the easiest roll to perform is the log roll, also known as the pencil roll. The log roll requires pupils to lie on their backs flat on the floor. Hands and arms should be stretched up above the head with fingers pointed. Toes should be pointed towards the floor. If pupils are struggling to understand this, an easy way for them to get a feel for the position is to ask them to stand upright on their toes with their arms stretched up above their heads. You can also get them to link the starting position to how they perform a straight jump.

**Figure 4.1** The log roll

Pupils start by lying on the floor on their backs. The aim of the log roll is to rotate the body to either the left or the right, moving from lying on the back to lying on the stomach and then finishing on the back (see Figure 4.1). In order to achieve this, learners will need to form a shallow dish shape and rock slightly to the side to gain enough momentum to roll over.

A consideration when teaching this skill is the muscular development of the pupil, in particular around the neck region. Ideally the head should remain in-between the arms when the skill is performed. Those performing the skill at an early developmental stage, however, may lift their head so that it destabilises the movement. This has a resulting impact on the direction of travel. One way to address this is to encourage pupils to roll between two cones, or to place a cone on the ground above their fingers and another below their toes before they begin and then place a series of cones along their direction of travel to see how much they move off course. If using mats (see Chapter 8 for information on the safe use of equipment) they can use the side of the mat as a target.

Having looked at the three basic locomotor skills you might wish to think about how you would develop these within your own lessons. Task 4.3 gives you the opportunity to do this.

---

## Task 4.3

1   Observe either a lesson or a play-based session (this could include a break time).

    a   Identify pupils performing basic locomotor skills.
    b   Using the key teaching points identified for each skill, identify at what levels pupils are performing (for example, an early or a late motor pattern).
    c   Identify how you might improve pupils' performance by including activities you might encourage pupils to participate in.

2   If you have the opportunity, provide feedback to those you have observed and revisit their skill at a later date to identify any progress that has been made.

---

## Stability skills

Stability skills encourage the development of control and co-ordination and are therefore closely aligned to the requirements of both early childhood documentation and Key Stage 1 development. As Table 4.3 identifies, the key skills are associated with bending, stretching, reaching, twisting and turning.

When looking at bending, stretching and reaching, we can see similarities in the activities we may encourage pupils to perform. When we think of bending we might consider the directions in which we might bend, for example forwards or to the side. We might consider bending as relating to stretching and therefore use bending activities during the warm-up aspect of our lesson (see Chapter 8 for developing warm-up activities and also the associated health and safety aspects of the activity). As with many locomotor skills, stability skills are core components of many types of activities.

As well as integrating such activities into the warm-up phase of the lesson, we can also develop focused activities within the main body of the lessons. Returning to bending, we can ask pupils to think about what parts of their body they can bend to form different shapes. This will encourage pupils to start thinking about what different body parts can do. For example, our body tends to bend predominantly from the middle, so we can bend to move toward our toes, and then reach up to go up on to our toes to make ourselves tall and thin. This is a good activity to encourage children to consider how they will feel when doing a straight jump, or equally what their starting point is for the log roll discussed in the previous section. We may also consider getting children to make shapes with their bodies lying on the floor, for example 'star shape'. Alternatively, we could set the challenge of making as many different letters using their bodies, for example S, L, X, T, P, O, I. Such activities can then be developed into gymnastic or dance-based activities, for example over time pupils can be encouraged to repeat these movements using different pieces of equipment, or work with a partner to form different body shapes.

We need to think about how we can develop pupils' reaching skills. Again, it is important that we think about the range of movements and activities that require some form of reaching. If we think about throwing and catching (covered in more detail later in this chapter) we reach to catch a ball. We could encourage pupils to reach up when performing a straight jump; equally we want pupils to reach up when starting the log roll.

Twisting and turning skills are not limited to gymnastic or dance-related activities; we might also turn to change direction, or twist when we try to move away from an opponent. If we think about a simple warm-up game such as 'Stuck in the mud' (if playing such games, you will need to be very specific about how players are released, for example ensuring pupils move under the arms from front to back), pupils will be regularly required to twist and turn to avoid capture by the 'tagger'. If we are playing a game that requires pupils to change direction on command (see the companion website under the section on warm-up activities for a range of appropriate activities) it is likely that they will use twisting and turning activities.

We can develop twisting and turning activities using jumps, for example asking pupils to jump and turn to face the opposite wall thereby rotating 180 degrees.

We can also consider developing twisting and turning movements to move along, on, off or over equipment. This can be developed by encouraging pupils to explore different ways of moving, or by giving them a range of movements that they can try.

## Manipulation skills

Table 4.3 also identifies the range of manipulative skills we need to encourage during the early stages of development. These skills are used in activities which require pupils to use different body parts to hold, move, receive and send objects.

## Rolling an object

Developing pupils' ability to roll a ball can be used as a precursor to developing the skills of throwing and catching. The benefit of introducing this skill early on is that it allows for the development of the basic characteristics of throwing and is performed in such a way as to encourage pupils' confidence in receiving a moving object. Many aspects associated with this skill can be performed in small areas and allow for the development of control as well as co-operative skills.

An effective way to roll an object would involve a pupil standing side-on to an intended target, although at the early stages of development pupils will tend to face the intended target, which restricts the amount of power that can be generated. The rolling hand should start extended backwards away from the body, and the opposite foot should be placed forward. The hand should end up pointing at the intended target, and this is a key teaching point for many skills used to send objects (see the section on throwing for a development of this concept).

When receiving a rolled ball, the receiver should be positioned behind the ball, with their hands low to trap the ball.

In developing this skill, the following paired activities can be used.

1  Pupils lie on their stomachs facing their partner. They roll the ball to each other with the aim of trapping the ball in front of the chest. By lying on their stomachs, power is generated from the shoulders. Variations include:

    a   using one hand, using both hands, using the non-preferred hand (the one they would not usually use to send the ball)

    b   using different sized balls

    c   placing two cones in between the pair to form a goal and challenging the participants to get the ball through the goal before it reaches their partner – this encourages the development of directional skills and can be made more challenging by decreasing the size of the goal

    d   increasing the distances the ball has to travel

    e   challenging the pairs to see how many passes can be made in a specified time.

2    Pupils sit on the floor, their legs apart forming a V shape, opposite their partner. They roll the ball to their partner who aims to trap the ball in their hands. By being seated the power for the pass must come from the upper body. Variations to the activity can include those listed under the first activity.

3    Pupils stand opposite their partner and roll the ball to each other. The emphasis here is on developing pupils' abilities to use all parts of their bodies to generate power and control using the whole of the body. If you are working in clearly defined work areas, this activity can be developed to encourage movement. Instead of sending the ball directly to their partner, they could send the ball to the side of them so their partner changes position before receiving the ball.

## Throwing

Throwing involves the sending of an object over a distance. When performed effectively this should demonstrate movement of the thrower's body from back foot to front foot using a stepping action where necessary. This is commonly known as weight transfer. A number of different throws can be performed (underarm, overarm, chest pass, bounce pass), although the principles for their effective performance are similar.

As with locomotor skills we can analyse throwing by looking at what different body parts do when performing this skill. A pupil performing a throwing action during the early stages of development will tend to stand facing the intended direction of the throw, and when releasing the ball will tend to rotate forward from the waist with a limited transference of weight. In developing this aspect of the skill, pupils should be encouraged to stand sideways on to the target with the opposite foot forward to their throwing hand, so if they are throwing with their right hand their left foot would be forward. You may wish to identify on the floor the position of their feet using cones, chalk marks or even feet shapes. The sideways stance will allow pupils to step forward, thereby transferring their weight from back to front and giving power to their throw.

Having looked at general body position we will now turn to the arms. Arms and hands contribute power and direction to throwing. If we think back to the basic biomechanical principles learnt during science lessons, we will remember that the body is made up of a series of joints. The elbow is known as a hinge joint, allowing movement in general forwards and backwards. The other major arm joint is located at the shoulder. This ball and socket joint allows much more movement, including a capacity for rotation. As the ability to throw develops there is a change from the predominant use of the elbow joint, which will result in the hand pointing towards the floor, to the use of the more powerful shoulder joint, which allows for greater power to be exerted and for the ball to travel further. The finishing position of the hand should be pointing in the intended direction of the throw. This is a key teaching point for any skill or action that involves sending any object over a distance (including kicking and hitting, which will be covered later in this chapter). Whatever the physical action performed, the finishing position of the body part being used to send that object will point in the direction the object has gone. Therefore, when throwing, if pupils want the ball to go to a specific partner, their hands should end up pointing at them. The action of the arms can be mimicked by the eyes, which should follow the direction of travel.

Four key teaching points for throwing can be identified as follows:

1   The pupil stands sideways on to the target.
2   The throw comes from the shoulder.
3   The throwing hand ends up pointing at the intended target.
4   The eyes follow the direction of the ball.

Activities that can be used to develop the skill of throwing are closely linked to those that also support the development of catching skills, which we cover next. When learning throwing and catching skills it is important that pupils are given a defined working area which can be marked out by using cones (Chapter 5 explores this in further detail).

## Catching

Catching involves controlling an object that has been thrown to us. This is commonly taught at the same time as the throw. It is important when catching to ensure that the object to be caught is of an appropriate size, shape and weight. When learning to catch, large, round, light balls are most effective as they give the catcher time to move to the ball as well as providing them with a larger target to catch.

It is important to have a stable body position to receive the ball. Ideally the stance should involve children standing with their feet shoulder-width apart, and with their body facing the direction from which the object is coming. As the actions of the hands and arms are crucial in the development of this skill it is important that we look at these in a little more detail. Hands should form a cup shape with the little fingers together, which can be one of the most challenging parts of the skill for younger children in the earlier stages of development. There are several common reactions for pupils at this level as the ball comes towards them: to move away, to clap their hands together resulting in either the ball falling to the floor or bouncing off their hands, or to grasp the ball in a reflex gripping action similar to when a baby clutches a finger.

A child may move away from a thrown ball due to a fear of being hit, therefore we need to be conscious of the speed and direction the ball is travelling. If pupils are throwing the ball to themselves by throwing it straight up in the air, encourage them to only throw the ball up a short distance. This will also ensure that you do not have lots of balls flying around the working area. As they try to put more power into the throw pupils are likely to swing their arms too much resulting in their hands pointing over their heads thereby reducing the accuracy of their throws. If a child is throwing a ball against a wall and receiving the ball back towards their body, monitor the distance between the thrower and the wall; the closer they are the more control they will have. If a child is receiving the ball from a partner, emphasise the co-operative nature of the activity and set challenges that reward success. For example, a child scores a point only if their partner catches the ball, thereby emphasising the need for consideration in the pass being sent. When working with younger children you could consider allowing the ball to bounce before it is caught, which will reduce the speed at which it is travelling into the hands. Catching activities can be varied through using balls of different sizes and weights. A larger ball is much easier to catch due to its increased surface area. A lighter ball will travel more slowly, giving children more time to position themselves and make the catch. For those tending to catch objects using a grasping reflex, bean bags or cosh balls can be used. In all catching activities the eyes should focus on the returning object.

Four key teaching points for catching can be identified as follows:

1    The body faces the direction from which the ball is coming.
2    The hands form a cup shape, with the little fingers together.
3    As the ball comes into the hands the fingers should be cupped around the ball.
4    The caught ball should be pulled in towards the body.

The following activities can be used to develop throwing and catching skills (more activities can be found on the companion website).

Children working on their own:

1    Working in their own defined space, children bounce the ball in front of themselves and attempt to catch the ball as it comes toward their waist.
2    Children throw the ball up level with their heads and catch the ball as it comes down, or alternatively allow the ball to bounce and then catch it. For added variety use different types of balls.
3    Children throw a ball against a wall and catch the ball as it rebounds (remember you can encourage them to let the ball bounce before they catch it). Once they have completed a set number of catches successfully they can be challenged to move back, increasing the distance they have to throw the ball. However, they should also be given the option of moving closer to the wall should their level of success decrease.

Children working with a partner:

1    Children can throw a ball to each other. Those who are not at a level to achieve this can start by rolling the ball to each other.
2    Over time the distance thrown can be increased. You might apply similar rules to those above whereby children move further apart if successful, but move towards each other if they are not catching the ball.
3    Children can be challenged to see how many successful throws and catches they can do in a timed period.

## Kicking

Kicking is used to send the ball over a distance using the feet. In some respects, it can be argued that the principles associated with kicking are similar to those of the throw, with the power being generated from the hip joint (ball and socket) rather than the knee. Contact with the ball should be made with the side of the foot which has a greater surface area and will therefore provide better control than with the toe, which will tend to result in the ball being lifted into the air. When making contact, the ball should be slightly in front of the body and to the side. When sending the ball, the upper body should lean slightly over the ball with the head looking at the ball. If the head is looking up, there is a tendency for the body to lean back, which can result in the ball being lifted into the air. When kicking, the arms are used to maintain stability, remaining to the side of the body with the head looking over the ball when contact is made.

The following paired activity can be used to develop the skill.

1   Standing opposite one another, pupils pass the ball to their partner who can trap the ball by:
    a   using their hands as they would when rolling the ball to each other
    b   placing a foot on the ball to stop it
    c   moving the foot they are trapping the ball with backwards as the ball arrives (similar to the movement they will perform when catching a ball).

Further activities are located on the companion website.

## Striking a ball

Striking the ball is an integral part of racquet sports such as tennis and badminton, and invasion games such as hockey. Objects are introduced to assist in the sending of a ball, puck or shuttlecock. We should regard these objects as extensions of our hands and as such the basic principles associated with these skills reflect many of those already discussed.

For tennis-based activities, we are introducing an extension to the hands in the form of a racquet, and in doing so we are starting to develop hand–eye co-ordination. Consequently, many of the initial activities introduced will focus on the development of the ability to co-ordinate the striking of a moving object.

A good starting point is to encourage children to bounce the ball using their hands, and in doing so they will be aware of the need to co-ordinate their movements in order to carry out this activity (this is also a good starting point for teaching dribbling skills – see Chapter 5). As with the other skills discussed in this chapter, differentiation can be introduced through the types of balls used. In bouncing a ball, pupils should be encouraged to use the palm of the hand, which creates the biggest surface area, and push the ball towards the floor. They can then be encouraged to bounce a ball while simultaneously walking around their working area. This activity can be developed further by introducing a racquet; these may be wooden or plastic and have varying head sizes as well as handle lengths. Having practised pushing the ball to the floor with their hands, children can repeat the activity using a racquet. You will need to emphasise that the ball should be to the front and side of the body. Pupils should be encouraged to hold the racquet as close to the racquet head as possible, especially if not using short-handled racquets, as this will allow hand–eye co-ordination to develop progressively, and pupils can slowly move their hand down the racquet shaft as they become more confident. As well as pushing the ball towards the floor, pupils can be encouraged to bounce the ball upwards, and then alternate between pushing down and bouncing upwards. This can then progress to hitting the ball towards a target; this may be a wall or a partner.

A hitting action mimics some aspects of throwing and kicking insofar as the body should be sideways on to the intended target, with the striking hand at the back and the opposite foot at the front to allow for weight transfer. The racquet should swing from back to front to meet the ball. The racquet head should finish pointing at the intended target. Again, the head should follow the flight of the ball.

Once confidence in ball control has been developed and pupils are performing the skill with some efficiency, they can move on to receiving a ball from a partner. Consideration now needs to be given to the speed and direction from which the ball is fed. Normally this will be from the front, and will be performed by their partner. It is important that the feed is controlled and effective. By the time this skill is being introduced pupils should be quite proficient in throwing and catching. Initial feeds should be bounced as this will mean that the speed at which the ball is travelling is reduced. This can be achieved in the following ways.

1   Pupils feed the ball by bouncing it into a hoop, which will increase the accuracy of the feed, and then send the ball to their partner to either catch on the full, allow to bounce and then catch, or allow to roll towards them.
2   Partners feed the ball to each other using a bounce feed. Again, a hoop can be used to encourage accuracy, with a downward throw being used as the feed. This ensures that the ball will then bounce up to meet the person striking the ball.

The previous section of this chapter focused on the development of fundamental motor skills. However, skill development by itself cannot provide a full appreciation of physical education. Children also need to develop an understanding of what are often referred to as motor concepts. These concepts require pupils to think about the skill they are performing in relation to their body, the space they are working in, the effort they are applying and the relationships involved. The next section of the chapter provides an overview of these, and they are discussed in greater depth in Chapter 5.

# Motor concepts

## The body

We have looked at the concept of the body performing movements in relation to key teaching and learning points focusing on what specific body parts do during a given skill. We have also discussed actions by the body, for example the transference of weight. We now need to consider other actions such as how the body is used to support a movement, as in performing some form of balance, and other movement concepts associated with gymnastic and dance-related activities. We can also think about the shapes the body is making, for example, wide, tall, star.

## Space

This concept focuses on the space in which a skill is being performed, and how this space is used within activities. In doing so we are trying to develop pupils' understanding of direction. This might be the direction they are travelling, for example forwards, backwards or sideways, the level at which they are working, for example on the floor, or using pieces of equipment which will increase the height at which they are working. We should also consider the pathways children make when performing an activity, for example we can encourage them to make movement patterns on the floor either in the form of shapes (squares, circles, triangles) or letters. This latter concept will be explored in Chapter 8, which looks at warming up, and also earlier in this chapter. It will be explored in further depth in Chapter 10, which looks at the promotion of cross-curricular themes.

## Effort

The concept of effort is associated with the speed at which the skill is performed, for example a quick or slow movement. Do we speed up when we are performing a specific movement or do we slow down?

## Relationships

The concept of relationships can include the people we are working with during a specific activity, for example, alone, with a partner or with a larger group. We have discussed specific examples in the developmental activities earlier in this chapter. We can explore the relationships we have with the objects we use, for example, allowing pupils to explore different ways of moving over or under equipment. We can also think about whether we are performing the movement at the same time as someone else (sometimes referred to as unison), or after someone else thereby repeating the movement (sometimes referred to as canon).

So far we have looked at the generic skills and concepts most relevant to pupils in the 3–8 age range. However, we should also think back to some of the previous chapters to establish whether we are covering the breadth of skills reflected in the aims of physical education (see Chapter 1) and also how these link to the overall principles of child development (see Chapter 2). As you have read this chapter you should have been keeping a record of some of the practice activities identified. Task 4.4 encourages you to develop this further.

---

## Task 4.4

1    For each of the fundamental motor skills, identify a series of practices you would use during your physical education lessons.

    a    Where possible try these ideas in your lessons.
    b    Evaluate the effectiveness of these practices noting any modifications you might make.
    c    Include examples of these practices in your portfolio.

---

## Chapter summary

This chapter focuses on the skills necessary to become competent in physical education activities. This is by no means an exhaustive list and further resources that may support your subject knowledge development are available on the companion website. We have looked at a range of activities that can be undertaken in support of the teaching of fundamental movement skills across early years and into Key Stage 1. To embed your learning from this chapter you may benefit from reflecting on the following review questions.

1    How would you define motor competence?
2    Identify a range of activities that you could use to develop pupils' ability to send and receive an object.
3    For each of the fundamental motor skills identify a series of practices you would use during your physical education lessons. Use the practices to compile a resource folder for each of the skill areas.

# Further reading

Gallahue, D.L. and Ozmun, J.C. (1995) *Understanding Motor Development: Infants, Children, Adolescents, Adults*, 3rd edn. Iowa: Brown and Benchmark Publishers.
This comprehensive text provides guidance on a range of fundamental movement skills and the expected stages of development.

Department for Education (2014) *Statutory Framework for the Early Years Foundation Stage: Setting the Standards for Learning, Development and Care for Children from Birth to Five*. London: DfE
This framework document provides details of the key principles and learning goals for pupils from birth to five. It provides details around assessment and also tracking of progress.

Early Education (2012) *Development Matters in the Early Years Foundation Stage (EYFS)*. London: The British Association for Early Childhood Education.
This comprehensive guidance material provides detailed breakdowns of expected behaviours associated with the areas of learning and development. It provides support in relation to the characteristics of effective learning evidenced through engagement, motivation and thinking.

Physical Education Association of the United Kingdom (2003) *Observing Children Moving*. Worcester: Tacklesport (Consultancy) Company.
This CD-ROM provides visual images of the development of fundamental movement skills allowing for comparisons between early and later motor patterns. It contains a wealth of resources that can be used to support learning including a detailed breakdown of each skill as well as a range of developmental activities that can be integrated into planning.

# Developing Knowledge, Skills and Understanding Across Areas of Activity

## Chapter aims

- To develop knowledge, skills and understanding across areas of activity in physical education
- To develop your depth of knowledge and understanding specific to areas of activity
- To develop practical understanding of the delivery of different areas of activity

## Links to *Teachers' Standards*

In reading this chapter and completing the associated tasks you will be able to collect evidence in relation to the *Teachers' Standards* (DfE, 2011) as detailed in Table 5.1.

## Introduction

Chapter 4 looked at the fundamental movement skills associated with the delivery of physical education. This chapter aims to build on this knowledge and understanding, with an increased focus on specific areas of activity. We will look at activities associated with athletics, dance, games, gymnastics, swimming and OAA. Each sub-section focuses on generic principles appropriate to each area of activity, with additional practical examples located on the companion website.

**Table 5.1**  How this chapter links to the *Teachers' Standards* (DfE, 2011)

| | |
|---|---|
| Standard 1: Set high expectations which inspire, motivate and challenge pupils | • set goals that stretch and challenge pupils of all backgrounds, abilities and dispositions<br><br>• demonstrate consistently the positive attitudes, values and behaviour which are expected of pupils |
| Standard 2: Promote good progress and outcomes by pupils | • be accountable for pupils' attainment, progress and outcomes<br><br>• be aware of pupils' capabilities and their prior knowledge, and plan teaching to build on these<br><br>• guide pupils to reflect on the progress they have made and their emerging needs<br><br>• demonstrate knowledge and understanding of how pupils learn and how this impacts on teaching |
| Standard 3: Demonstrate good subject and curriculum knowledge | • have a secure knowledge of the relevant subject(s) and curriculum areas, foster and maintain pupils' interest in the subject, and address misunderstandings<br><br>• demonstrate a critical understanding of developments in the subject and curriculum areas, and promote the value of scholarship<br><br>• demonstrate an understanding of and take responsibility for promoting high standards of literacy, articulacy and the correct use of standard English, whatever the teacher's specialist subject |
| Standard 4: Plan and teach well-structured lessons | • promote a love of learning and children's intellectual curiosity<br><br>• contribute to the design and provision of an engaging curriculum within the relevant subject area(s) |
| Standard 5: Adapt teaching to respond to the strengths and needs of all pupils | • know when and how to differentiate appropriately, using approaches which enable pupils to be taught effectively<br><br>• have a secure understanding of how a range of factors can inhibit pupils' ability to learn, and how best to overcome these<br><br>• demonstrate an awareness of the physical, social and intellectual development of children, and know how to adapt teaching to support pupils' education at different stages of development |
| Standard 6: Make accurate and productive use of assessment | • know and understand how to assess the relevant subject and curriculum areas, including statutory assessment requirements<br><br>• make use of formative and summative assessment to secure pupils' progress<br><br>• give pupils regular feedback, both orally and through accurate marking, and encourage pupils to respond to the feedback |
| Standard 7: Manage behaviour effectively to ensure a good and safe learning environment | • have clear rules and routines for behaviour in classrooms, and take responsibility for promoting good and courteous behaviour both in classrooms and around the school, in accordance with the school's behaviour policy<br><br>• manage classes effectively, using approaches which are appropriate to pupils' needs in order to involve and motivate them |

Physical education has traditionally been delivered through activity areas and there has been a tendency for such activities to be focused around traditional games activities. Recently the focus has shifted towards the development of more rounded opportunities to develop a lifelong commitment to physical activity resulting in the engagement of pupils in healthy and active lifestyles beyond schooling age, as reflected in the work of Whitehead (2010) in relation to the development of the concept of physical literacy (see Chapters 1 and 4). Thus there has been a move away from a purely skills-based curriculum, where success is reflected through performance, to a more learner-centred approach where learning is evident through pupils engaging in exploration and experimentation, building upon existing knowledge to construct new learning (see Chapter 2 to refresh your understanding of theories of learning and learning domains). This reflects an increasing emphasis being placed on developing those positive values, beliefs and attitudes that will sustain lifelong participation.

The next section looks in greater detail at a range of specific activities that can be taught within each area of activity. Practical activities are provided alongside discussion of how they could be delivered (supporting material is included on the companion website). A series of tasks are also included that you may wish to complete and add to your portfolio.

# Athletic activities

In teaching athletics, pupils should be encouraged to engage in a range of challenges designed to develop their ability to run, throw and jump in different contexts. The National Curriculum for England clearly indicates at Key Stage 1 that pupils must 'master basic movements including running, jumping, throwing and catching, as well as developing balance, agility and co-ordination, and begin to apply these in a range of activities' (DfE, 2013: 248). This is further developed during Key Stage 2 with a growing emphasis on their ability to 'compare their performances with previous ones and demonstrate improvement to achieve their personal best' (DfE, 2013: 248). You will have a basic level of understanding around what key athletic events are, for example, sprinting, middle distance, shot, javelin, high jump and long jump. In the primary school we are looking to introduce pupils to the concepts associated with these activities, rather than the full events themselves.

## Running activities

Chapter 4 looked at running technique. Through the delivery of athletic activities, we will now look at how this technique can be developed and used in different contexts. In essence, we are looking at pupils' ability to run at speed, over longer distances and over barriers.

## Running for speed

Running for speed is reflected in sprint activities where the focus needs to be on shorter distances, for example, 25, 50 and 100 metres. However, initially pupils should be encouraged to find out how far they can run in a specified time. Thus pupils are encouraged to work at increasing speeds through the execution of a range of challenges.

**Activity** Ask pupils working in pairs to predict how far they think they will be able to run in a specified time, for example, three seconds. Ask them to place a cone at the point they think they will reach in the allocated time. They are then timed by their partner and the cone is moved to the point they actually reached (this may result in the cone being moved either forwards or backwards). Pupils can then work on refining their running technique, for example working on their head position, body position, arm action and leg action, and are given the opportunity to see if they can beat their original distance. The focus is on pupils reviewing their own personal progress, rather than looking at who is the fastest.

## Running for distance

Here the emphasis is on developing endurance capacity. Again, the full range of activities will not need to be taught; what is important is that you look at building pupils' ability to run for extended periods of time. Again, the emphasis should be placed on personal development through the setting of appropriate challenges.

**Activity** As with the sprinting activity identified in the previous section, cones can be used to set appropriate challenges. For example, a grid is created with cones approximately 20 metres apart. Pupils are then challenged to predict how many cones they will pass in a set time, for example, three minutes. They are then timed and either count, or have their partner count the number they pass. The emphasis is on encouraging pupils to keep going over a period of time (the time can be increased based on your understanding of the group), and therefore running and walking can be used in the completion of the task. Over time the aim should be that the majority of pupils will be able to participate for the duration of the challenge. The number of cones passed should be recorded and compared with the prediction (an example recording sheet is included on the companion website). During the activity, pupils can be encouraged to think about what impact it is having on their bodies, in order that they start to develop an understanding about the impact longer periods of activity have on their bodies (see Chapter 10 for further ideas on how such activities can be used to develop cross-curricular learning).

## Using skills in combination – hurdling

Activities such as hurdling can be used to combine running with other skills in order to develop pupils' abilities to co-ordinate movements. Hurdling combines running at speed with clearing an object. This might be a cane or pole which over time is increased in height. Alternatively, commercially available equipment can be purchased.

**Activity** A good way to begin a hurdling activity is to start by asking pupils to run 20 metres with hurdles placed at 5-metre intervals (you may wish to change the frequency or the number of hurdles). As confidence improves, the height at which the hurdles are set can be increased, for example they could be placed on cones of increasing heights, although when doing this the distance between hurdles may need to be increased. It is possible to differentiate the activity by setting up three lanes of hurdles with each lane using hurdles of a different height thereby allowing pupils to choose which lane to run in.

## Jumping activities

Chapter 4 looked at the basic techniques associated with jumping for height and distance. We will now look at these in the context of athletic activities focusing specifically on the standing long jump, long jump with a walked take-off and the standing height jump.

## Long jump

**Activity**  The standing long jump involves taking off from a static two-footed stance and jumping forward to land two-footed. The distance achieved is measured from the front of the take-off position, normally represented by a take-off board or a line on the floor, to the back of the heel of the foot landing closest to the take-off position. As with running activities, cones can be used to set targets and make predictions as to how far pupils think they will reach with their jumps. Their partners can observe their efforts and either move their cone to the point achieved or alternatively place a new cone at the landing point so the difference between the prediction and the actual jump can be identified. In the early stages, there may be a tendency for pupils to over-predict the distance they will achieve, in which case as the teacher you may wish to provide defined distances and mark these out.

As pupils start to challenge themselves further teaching points will need to be reinforced, particularly on the need to lean forward on landing in order that they do not fall back. Reciprocal cards may be used at this point which detail the specific teaching points (examples of which are available from the companion website). To encourage height in the activity, a small barrier can be placed just in front of the take-off position, which pupils need to clear before landing.

A further variation is for pupils to take a three-step walk-up; here the emphasis is on walking rather than running, and consideration will need to be given to the landing area being used. If you are fortunate enough to have access to an indoor athletics set (your feeder secondary school may have this), this should be used; alternatively, you can use mats, and standard health and safety concerns when using equipment apply.

Taking this activity further, pupils can start to look at combining movements, and in doing so start to perform the hop, step and jump that make up the triple jump.

## Jumping for height

The standing height jump is designed to encourage pupils to think about how their bodies can be used to gain height.

**Activity**  This activity is best taught indoors, or where a wall is available. From a standing start, pupils bend their legs and swing their arms to jump up as high as they can. As they jump they use a piece of chalk to mark the wall, or some other measure. While there are commercially available measuring devices, you may wish to provide coloured lines to identify the distances jumped. Pupils can then identify the distance achieved (for example red, amber, green), record this on their activity log and then make a second attempt. As with other examples, the activity can be performed in groups with different roles being assigned, for example performer, coach, scorer (see Chapter 7 for more information).

## Throwing activities

In looking at throwing activities we are focusing on pushing (for example, shot put), pulling (for example, javelin) and slinging (for example, discus) actions. In Chapter 8 we will look at the organisation and management of athletic activities to ensure safe teaching of activities; however, you may wish to read that section prior to planning and delivering any athletic activity. The aim in throwing events is to develop pupils' competence in the activities, and in doing so it may be that you use adapted equipment. Your local secondary school or athletics club may be able to source this for you.

## Throwing – using a pushing action

The action of pushing an object in the context of athletic activities relates to shot put. It is likely that you will be limited in the specialist equipment to which you have access; however, equipment such as bean bags or larger balls can be used. At this level the most important point is for children to get a feel for the principles that underpin the activity.

When throwing with a pushing action the starting position sees pupils standing sideways on to the direction of throw. This will allow them over time to transfer weight and thereby increase the amount of power put into the throw. Initially this can be achieved by getting them to step into the throw; once this has been successfully accomplished they can try placing their weight on their back foot (you can even get them standing on only their back foot) before stepping forward as they throw, remembering that they must not step over the throw line.

The throwing arm is at the rear of the body (so if right-handed a pupil's left shoulder will point towards the direction of throw), with the object to be thrown held in the throwing hand and placed into the neck. Ideally the throwing arm elbow should be pointing out at right angles to the body. When ready to throw, pupils push the object forwards ideally at an angle of approximately 45 degrees. To aid the flight of the object, pupils can use their non-throwing arm to point, or alternatively pupils can identify a target on the horizon to aim at. In Chapter 4 we identified that a common principle for the flight of an object is that wherever the implement being used to send the object ends up pointing tends to reflect where the object finishes; a concept equally applicable to throwing activities.

Here is an example of how this activity can be managed within a lesson. It is equally applicable for the other types of throwing actions.

**Activity**  The following process can be repeated for all three types of throw. Working in groups of three, pupils assign themselves roles: a performer who completes the activity, a coach who gives feedback to the performer based on predetermined criteria (see athletics support material) and an official who has responsibility for the safety of the throw as well as the collection of the object.

The official sets up a safe throwing area, with cones used to identify throwing distances, or targeted distances, for example, 5, 10 or 15 metres (it may be that in the initial stages of teaching, you as the teacher set these up). Once safety has been confirmed, the performer has three attempts at the activity. After each attempt the coach provides feedback based on the criteria sheet provided, and the official records the approximate distance (this may be related to the colour of the cone reached) and collects the thrown object. The performer then repeats the cycle until all three throws have been completed. At this point the roles are rotated so that each pupil has the opportunity to perform each role. In adopting such an approach, you are limiting the number of pupils throwing and collecting at any one time, as well as introducing opportunities for developing communication and observation skills.

## Throwing – using a pulling action

When throwing with a pulling action the principles involved are those associated with the javelin. Financial and health and safety concerns are likely to prevent the use of actual javelins, although foam javelins are now available which reduce many of these concerns.

The initial stance should involve pupils facing the direction of throw. If pupils sit with their legs apart this isolates the legs and arms, ensuring that the arms become the main providers of power. Pupils then hold a ball (a football or netball will suffice) behind their heads. When told to do so pupils should then release the ball forward. Typical problems that may occur in this activity include pupils releasing the ball too early so that it goes straight up in the air rather than forwards or getting insufficient height in the throw resulting in the ball making contact with their head.

A more advanced version of this activity involves pupils standing sideways on to the direction of the throw which is then made using only one hand.

## Throwing – using a slinging action

In this activity the arms swing around the side of the body, and as a result this activity can potentially be the most challenging in respect of ensuring health and safety as well as the skill itself.

The key issue in this skill is the release of the object. The general principle is that the object is released from in front of the body. When thrown with the right hand, if released too early it will go to the right, if released too late it will go to the left and this has major implications for the safety of pupils to either side of the thrower. Hoops or quoits can be used for this activity. If using a hoop, the grip is with the throwing hand holding the hoop with the arm outstretched. The arm is swung back with the hoop going towards the back of the body. Remaining outstretched, the arm is then swung around the side of the body, with the hoop being released when the arm and hand are facing forward. If a quoit is being used, then it is held with the hand over the top with the fingers gripping the far side gently.

This section has looked at the introduction and development of athletic activities including running, jumping and throwing. Included in each activity are key teaching points as well as key processes and activities to support progression. These are summarised, with further supporting materials included, on the companion website. To further consolidate your knowledge of this area you may wish to complete Task 5.1.

---

## Task 5.1: Athletic resources

1   Design a set of resources (one per activity) which outline the following:

   a   an overview of how the skill is performed
   b   the key teaching points
   c   progression activities
   d   feedback opportunities.

2   Trial your resources with your class and make any modifications as you feel appropriate.
3   Add these resources to your portfolio.

---

# Dance activities

Dance can be defined as 'the rhythmic movement of the human body, usually to music. It is one of the oldest forms of human expression' (see *Encyclopaedia Britannica*, 2016). With the English National Curriculum, dance is an area of activity that is taught across the phases of the primary school. It allows pupils to develop a deeper understanding of what their bodies can do. During the early stages of primary education, it allows pupils to develop 'balance, agility and co-ordination' and 'perform dances using simple movement patterns' (DfE, 2013: 248). As pupils develop the emphasis is focused towards their ability to develop sequences and the movement vocabulary in order that they can assess their own and others performances. To support this, pupils should be taught to use a range of stimuli, for example music, poetry, pictures. In Chapter 4 basic movement, skills and concepts were introduced. However, to develop these further Table 5.2 provides an overview of key vocabulary that can be explored.

By teaching dance, pupils are provided with an opportunity to gain an understanding of the different forms of dance, from different periods of time or from different cultures. This can allow them to develop an appreciation of aspects of different cultures and provides opportunities for cross-curricular teaching, an aspect explored in more detail in Chapter 10. Dance also allows for the development of communication skills associated with observation and the giving and receiving of feedback.

So how can we go about delivering dance? As identified within Chapter 1 the values, beliefs and attitudes held by the teacher will impact on how they perceive an activity. That coupled with their experiences of the specific activity might well impact on their confidence and competence to provide effective learning opportunities for pupils to develop within that area. From my perspective, it is about keeping things simple and developing a basic structure that can be followed. For example, during the warm-up, basic movements that you will later integrate into your dance are introduced; this could include getting pupils to explore how they move using different body parts or at different levels by using either moving or stretching activities. Immediately you are using the key vocabulary that you can rely on later in the lesson as well as allowing pupils to be creative in their interpretation. Further you can include specific movements that will be used within the motif of the dance sequence. When introducing the motif you might find it useful to provide resource cards to prompt pupils to remember the actions. For example, if you are using characters (say the Mr Men©) you could provide pictures of the characters and the sequence in which you want them to appear in the dance.

However, as has been previously indicated, dance is not just specific movements. In developing the pupils' movement vocabulary, opportunities for pupils to develop their own movement patterns arise. If we think about how we encourage pupils to construct

**Table 5.2**  Key words that can be used in dance

| Direction | Levels | Size and shape | Actions | Dynamics | Relationships |
|-----------|--------|----------------|---------|----------|---------------|
| Forwards | High | Decreasing | Jumping | Weight | Mirror |
| Backwards | Low | Increasing | Travelling | Flow | Canon |
| Upwards | Medium | Large | Stillness | Speed | Shadow |
| Downwards | | Small | Gesture | | Lead |
| Sideways | | Twisted | Turn | | Follow |
| | | Stretched | | | Formation |

paragraphs, we might provide them with the basic content, and then encourage them to improve the content through changes to the words they use. Dance is no different. If you refer to Table 5.2 these words and definitions can be used as a resource for pupils to improve their performance. For example, having mastered a basic movement, pupils can be encouraged to think about and include changes of speed, or to think about the pathways they might use. In essence, the key vocabulary becomes an additional word wall, a concept that they are used to using within a classroom-based lesson.

However, in using specific vocabulary to form the dance, you are also providing them with specific criteria against which they can evaluate their own and others' performances. In doing so you are guiding and providing support for them to effectively engage in self or peer assessment. The activity below provides a simple example of how this might look in practice.

**Activity: Animal dance**  As part of the warm-up, pupils working on their own explore different ways of moving like animals (for example mini-beasts, jungle animals). They are encouraged to think about the speed at which they move and also the direction they are moving, for example, can they form a letter as they move?

Pupils are then paired and share their ideas of animal movements with each other and identify four moves that they can both do. At this point counting can be integrated into the performance, so that each move or series of moves has to be completed in a set time, for example, by the count of 8.

They can then perform their four moves to another pair who give feedback on their performance using key words identified during the lesson introduction. These words can be displayed in the working area. Pupils are then provided with the opportunity to use the feedback to practise their skills again and further refine their movements.

The above activity encourages a productive approach to teaching where pupils are encouraged to explore and experiment with their own ideas and share these with others (this concept is explored in more detail in Chapter 7). However, you may also feel that it would be beneficial for all pupils to be doing the same moves at the same time. In dance terms this is referred to as a motif. In developing a synchronised series of movements, consideration needs to be given to the pupils' level of development.

**Activity**  Using the animal dance developed in the previous activity you can design a motif lasting 32 beats (4 × 8 – which is the same length of time the pupils have designed their sequences to last). Pupils then practise and perform the motif, and when you are happy you can ask pupils to add their individual sequences at the end of the motif. Over time you can build this up further so that you have the format:

MOTIF – PUPIL SEQUENCE – MOTIF – PUPIL SEQUENCE – MOTIF

Another way to look at it is as a song with the motif representing the chorus!

Other potential themes can be taken from a range of teaching topics, for example the Egyptians where the stimuli for the dance could come from hieroglyphics in tombs and temples or a text they are reading.

## Task 5.2: Dance resources

1   Design a set of resources for dance activities which outline the following:

  a   theme/stimulus for pupils to use to develop their dance
  b   key words you want pupils to use when reviewing performances.

2   Trial your resources with your class and make any modifications as you feel appropriate.
3   Add these resources to your portfolio.

# Games activities

Like dance activities, games activities are taught across phases of primary education and can be used to develop pupils' abilities to perform basic skills associated with sending and receiving objects as well as moving with such objects, for example, through the use of a net/wall and in striking and fielding activities and invasion activities (see Chapter 1 for more information on activity groupings). The National Curriculum (DfE, 2013: 248) states that Key Stage 1 pupils should 'master basic movements including running, jumping, throwing and catching, as well as developing balance, agility and co-ordination, and begin to apply these in a range of activities' and 'participate in team games, developing simple tactics for attacking and defending'. Progression in Key Stage 2 is seen through them being able to 'use running, jumping, throwing and catching in isolation and in combination' allowing them to 'play competitive games, modified where appropriate [for example, badminton, basketball, cricket, football, hockey, netball, rounders and tennis], and apply basic principles suitable for attacking and defending' (DfE, 2013: 248).

Thus, in developing competence in games-related activities, we are encouraging children to think about the correct skills to use in different situations and the strategies and tactics for a given activity. Whilst Chapter 4 looked at the basic skills associated with games activities, this next section develops more complex skills.

## Dribbling

Dribbling occurs when we move with a ball, for example, when running with a ball in football, hockey or basketball-based activities. It allows us to move with the ball at pace. The generic teaching points associated with the skill are that the ball should be to the side and slightly in front of the body, allowing for a greater level of control. If you have sufficient equipment, you should attempt to allow all pupils to work on their own in the first instance so that they can have the maximum opportunity to practise the skill.

**Activity**   On their own pupils move around a defined area, identified either by the use of line markings or a coned area. If they are dribbling using their hands or their feet, they can practise using both sides of their body in an attempt to establish their preferred side. When dribbling with the hand the ball should be bounced at waist height with a pushing action. Pupils new to the skill may try to bounce the ball as high as they can, which limits precision and control. When dribbling with feet or a stick the ball needs to be kept as close to the foot or stick as possible. In the early stages of development there is a tendency for pupils to kick or hit the ball forward and then chase after it.

As pupils become more confident, they can start to speed up the skill and can be encouraged to change speed and direction (remember the principle that as the level of challenge or competition increases the quality of the skill may decrease). This can be played as part of the warm-up whereby pupils change speed and direction on hearing a whistle. Thus, as has previously been indicated, the warm-up is acting as a starting point for the lesson and is providing the pupils with the opportunity to practise skills they will be using throughout the lesson. A further progression is that on the teacher's instruction pupils attempt to knock each other's ball out of the playing area – this starts to encourage them to think about how they keep possession of the ball within a more competitive situation. You will have to have clear rules for this activity, for example what to do when their ball is knocked out, and I would encourage that wherever possible they collect their ball and rejoin the activity to ensure that maximum levels of participation are maintained. A scoring system can also be introduced, for example, if their ball is knocked out they lose a point, but if they knock someone else's ball out they gain a point.

Once pupils have developed a basic level of understanding and proficiency in dribbling, they can start to combine skills. They can dribble the ball over a distance and then send the ball to a partner. Initially this might be completed in small groups as follows:

1   Pupils work in groups of four:

   a   Pupils line up in pairs opposite each other.
   b   Player 1 dribbles forwards, sends the ball forward and goes to the back of the pair to whom they are running towards.
   c   Player 2 receives the ball and dribbles forward, sending the ball to Player 3.
   d   Player 3 controls the ball, dribbles forward and sends the ball to Player 4.
   e   The activity is repeated until all pupils reach their starting point.

2   Pupils work in pairs:

   a   Player 1 dribbles forward and passes the ball to Player 2.
   b   Player 1 moves into a space to receive the ball back from Player 2.
   c   The emphasis is placed on pupils looking up to see where their partner has moved to as well as thinking about the concept of space.

As with all games activities at this level the emphasis is on developing basic skills and proficiency. We are not expecting pupils to play full versions of the games but to experience small-side activities.

## Net/wall activities

Chapter 4 looked at the basic principles of striking a ball. In net and wall activities, we are initially looking to develop pupils' ability to strike the ball in such a way that they can return it to their partner. Accuracy will develop over time, so that rather than sending the object to their partner, they will be able to send it into space.

We can start developing pupils' hitting skills through the use of a single personal square. As pupils progress to working with a partner they can use both squares with the middle of the squares acting as a net (see Figure 5.1).

A simple game activity can involve partners throwing the ball underarm to each other and allowing the ball to bounce prior to catching it. The emphasis is on sending the ball to the partner. Points can therefore be awarded for each successful catch. Using the same set up, pupils can then use their hands as racquets to send the ball to their partner. Again, the ball should bounce before it is sent back. By letting the ball bounce, the receiver has more time to get into an appropriate position before having to decide upon the speed at which the ball is travelling and where they want to send it back to. In using only the hands, the power that is generated in each hit is limited and therefore provides a safer opportunity to practise the skill.

Once pupils have progressed to an acceptable level of skill (i.e. they can control their hits so that they go to their partner), racquets can be introduced. Introducing a piece of equipment with which to hit will raise some organisational issues, for example, how the racquets will be distributed (see Chapter 8 for more information on this).

Because pupils are still in the early stages of development, allocating only one racquet per pair is probably the best approach. In this way pupils can continue to use the same grid areas to carry out this activity, although hitting needs to be outwards, away from the feeder (see Figure 5.2 for a more focused explanation).

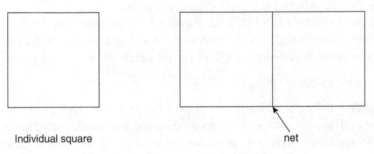

Individual square                                                    net

**Figure 5.1**  Individual square and two squares with a net in the middle

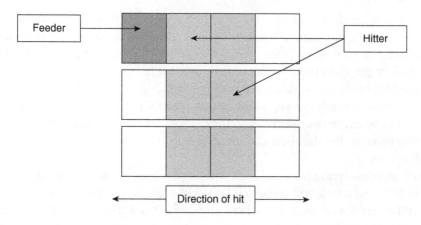

**Figure 5.2**   Grid areas for hitting or striking

By having pupils hit outwards, the opportunities for them to hit each other are limited. However, clear guidance on the collection of balls that are not returned to partners needs to be given. For example, you need to avoid pupils running into each other's working areas, so they should wait until the ball arrives at a safe place before collecting it.

## Striking and fielding activities

In striking and fielding activities we are providing opportunities for pupils to select and apply a range of existing skills (throwing, catching, striking, fielding the ball) in different contexts.

While the principles associated with striking a ball in rounders and cricket are the same as for short tennis, the quality of the feed becomes more important. In rounders, a bowl is essentially an underarm throw, while in cricket it starts from an overarm throw position but is aimed towards the ground. One of the easiest ways of ensuring striking of the ball early on is to remove the bowler entirely. This is easily achieved using cones or tees. Doing so means that pupils are hitting the ball from a static position (as in golf) and this limits the information processing needed to co-ordinate the striking of a moving object. If we are developing striking skills associated with cricket-based activities we can use small cones (like those we might use to set out our working areas) or small tees (which are commercially available and form part of Kwik Cricket sets). For rounders activities we will need to use cones at pupil waist height, for example traffic cones (again commercial products are available).

As progress is made in the striking action, pupils can begin to receive a moving ball. Feeds can be from the side or from in front of the striker. At this point consideration needs to be given to the direction of the swing that the striking pupil will make. For example, a right-handed pupil will hit with the bat travelling from right to left, with a left-handed batter hitting from left to right. Thus the positioning of the feeder is vital to avoid injury. When progressing from a static feed (off cones) to a moving feed, the next stage is for the feed to be received from the side. When doing this the ball is dropped (you might wish to place a hoop so that the bowler can see where the ball needs to be dropped) and the striker hits the ball as it bounces back up. If you have already taught short tennis, pupils may well have experienced a similar action when bounce-feeding to themselves when starting a rally. Once pupils are confident with this the feed can come from the front, reflecting a more realistic bowling action.

As well as considering how the feed will be performed, thought needs to be given to where the struck ball will travel to. You may wish to use the practice method we introduced for net/wall activities where pupils hit outwards within their grid areas. As they progress further and group sizes increase, you might wish to adopt the fan shape introduced during throwing activities (see Chapter 8 for a more detailed explanation). This will allow you to set up more small-sided games which will enable pupils to practise their skills more.

A range of additional games activities associated with developing striking and fielding skills can be found on the companion website.

## Invasion activities

Invasion activities focus on games that are associated with 'invading' an opponent's goal, such as football, rugby, netball, hockey, basketball. However, this is not an exhaustive list and more recently activities such as rock-it-ball (www.rock-it-ball. com) and pop lacrosse have started to be delivered in schools.

As with the previous activity, the use of a defined area is beneficial for management purposes. The main skills associated with such activities include throwing, catching and dribbling, although we may need to adapt the skill based on the activity being performed. As we increase the range of activities being experienced we may need to look at aspects such as trapping the ball – as in receiving a pass in football or hockey – or cradling the ball as in rock-it-ball or pop lacrosse.

Once we have established the basic movement skills such as sending (throwing, kicking), receiving (catching, trapping) and moving with the ball (dribbling) we can start to think about basic games-related skills, for example, the use of space, shooting, basic games play.

Throughout, the emphasis should be placed on playing small-sided games (for example 3 v 3) which allow for maximum participation and give pupils more opportunities to practise skills. Again, the use of defined areas allows for greater levels of management, for example, if the pupils are playing a 2 v 2 game, then they can use four squares, a 3 v 3 game would then use six grids (see Figure 5.3).

The use of coned areas allows you to control the movement of pupils in the early stages of development by confining their movements to either their own area or

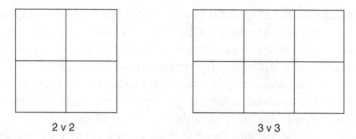

Figure 5.3   Grids for a 2 v 2 and 3 v 3 game

across two adjacent areas (a principle evident in netball). Alternatively, they can be used to create 'safe areas' where the number of pupils allowed in is restricted, which offers some protection for pupils with less confidence.

Common skills that we can develop include moving into a space to receive the ball, basic interception skills and skills associated with scoring points.

Earlier in this chapter we identified basic relay activities where pupils worked in small groups to pass and follow the ball. In more realistic games activities, pupils are more likely to pass the ball and then move into a space.

**Activity**   In pairs pupils pass the ball to each other. Once they have passed they move into a new space to receive the ball. The next progression is for the same 'game' to be played in groups of four (the easiest way to get to this number is to ask two pairs to join together). At this point, rather than sending the ball back to the person who sent it, an opportunity for decision making occurs, whereby the receiver has to think about who the best person to send the ball to is.

Once pupils have become confident and competent, you can start to introduce a defender into the activity. This is a progression for groups of both three and four, and in essence reflects the playground game of 'piggy in the middle'. Within this practice all pupils become involved in more complex decision-making opportunities. The sender has to think about who is best placed to receive the ball based on the position of their team mates and also the position of the defender. The receivers need to think about where they are best placed in relation to their team mates and the defender. The defender has to decide who to mark. If working in groups of four the attacking team (three people) have more time to make a decision so, if the learning objectives of the activity are based around attacking, this is a better group size than working in groups of three where the balance between attack and defence is more evenly distributed. To score a point the attacking team has to complete a set number of passes without the ball being touched or intercepted (this figure is flexible and should be based on the ability of the pupils). Once the point has been scored or the ball touched or intercepted, the defender becomes an attacker and vice versa. Before moving on, all pupils should have experienced both attacking and defending roles.

The activity can be developed further by bringing together two groups (3 v 3 or 4 v 4). The previous activity can then be repeated, although you may set a higher number of passes that need to be completed before a point is scored (this can be different for each team). Alternatively scoring areas can be introduced. These might be in the form of end zones (as you would find in American football), where a goal is scored if the ball is received in the end zone, or actual goals, for example, the ball must be bounced in a hoop, or passed through a set of cones.

One issue that can occur with these activities is a tendency for pupils to start following the ball. If this is occurring you may consider restricting the areas as mentioned earlier in the chapter, so, for example, a maximum of two pupils are allowed in any one area (see Figure 5.4).

Consideration should also be given to the location of the goal. If the goal is located in the middle of the end zone, typically the pattern of play will be up and down the middle of the playing area. If you want to increase the use of the playing area and also the movement of the play across it, you can consider setting up two goal areas at each side of the end zone. A further adaptation is to set scoring areas along the side of the playing zone (in this case it is best to use coloured goals so that each team is clear about which colour they need to score in). As with all the activities included in this chapter, supporting work cards and information are included on the companion website.

As pupils' competence levels develop, more easily recognisable versions of games can start to be played. For example, Kwik Cricket is a modified version of cricket but played in groups of up to 12, with teams made up of pairs for scoring purposes. High 5 Netball is played with teams of five players offering more space and time for decision making to occur. Further information on these can be found on the companion website.

It is important that, as pupils' skills, knowledge and understanding increase, opportunities are created that allow them to develop within the affective domain through working effectively in groups to create, participate in and manage games activities.

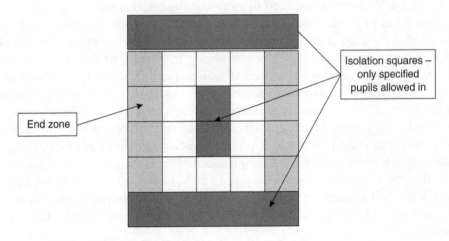

**Figure 5.4**  Grid showing restricted areas

In doing so they can begin to take responsibility for game creation (see Chapter 7 for more information on different approaches to teaching that can be used within physical education, for example Teaching Games for Understanding and Sport Education), as well as refereeing and umpiring games activities.

---

## Task 5.3: Games activities resources

1    Design a set of resources for one net/wall, one striking and fielding, and one invasion activity (one per activity) which outlines the following:

    a    range of skills per area
    b    series of games activities.

2    Trial your resources with your class and make any modifications as you feel appropriate.
3    Add these resources to your portfolio.

---

# Gymnastic activities

Gymnastic activities build upon the fundamental movement skills associated with locomotion and stability (see Chapter 4). Specifically in relation to early development, pupils should engage in activities that develop 'balance, agility and co-ordination, and begin to apply these in a range of activities' (DfE, 2013: 248) with the emphasis on quality of the movements more prominent as they make progress. Pupils should be given opportunities to develop these skills working on their own and in groups and to perform skills on different equipment. As with dance activities, gymnastic movements can be linked together to produce sequences which pupils can perform and receive feedback on, providing them with the opportunity to use the feedback to make further improvements. Further, a movement vocabulary (as previously mentioned in the context of dance) can be utilised within the gymnastic context. This allows you the opportunity to develop pupils' understanding of the inter-relatedness of many aspects of physical education – for example, encouraging them to see that much of the work they have done in dance can also be applied to gymnastics.

In breaking down the requirements for gymnastic activities further we can focus on skills associated with travelling, jumping and balance.

## Travelling

In travelling, we are looking at pupils' ability to move between two points. This might be in the form of rotation, which might include simple rolls such as a log roll (also referred to as a pencil roll), an egg roll, a side roll, or a circle roll (also referred to as a teddy bear roll), or more developmentally challenging rolls such as forward and backward rolls. Further information on the specific teaching points for each of these rolls can be found on the companion website.

However, travelling can take many other forms. For example, you can ask pupils to explore different ways of travelling using different body parts, or to copy how different animals might move (an idea we have already explored in the section on dance activities).

**Activity**  As a warm-up activity, pupils move around a designated area using different body parts, such as hands and feet, side, bottom, front (these should be identified by the class teacher to ensure appropriate health and safety regulations are enforced). Alternatively, pupils could copy different ways in which animals move, for example, if the pupils are exploring a topic in class around mini-beasts, they could imitate the movements of different creatures such as a ladybird, butterfly, caterpillar or snail.

During the warm-up, pupils can explore a range of different ways of travelling. They can practise these on the floor to improve performance. At this point key words may be introduced, which can be posted on the walls of the gym or hall in the form of a word wall. Pictorial display cards can also be used to support those who struggle with ideas.

Pupils can share the different movements they have identified with a partner, choosing three movements that they can both perform (this process can also be used for rolling activities as well as forming the basis for the introduction and development of other skills around jumping and balance). They should then practise these to improve their performances. Pupils can note their movements down using a gymnastics storyboard (see the companion website for examples) to produce a record of their developing sequence (this concept is developed further in Chapter 10).

Once pupils have become competent in performing travelling movements on the floor, they can be introduced to small apparatus, for example, benches, movement tables, and can transfer their sequence onto this equipment.

Developing this activity further, each pair can join up with another group to perform their sequence. They should start by describing their sequence to the other pair using the storyboard to support them. They can then perform their sequence to each other, receiving feedback about their performance from the observing pair. Feedback should be focused around the key words you have introduced at the start of the lesson, and again you might find it useful to use focused word walls. Pupils should then have the opportunity to go away and practise their sequence based on the feedback they have received.

## Jumping

Chapter 4 looked in some detail at different types of jump, so you may wish to refer to this now. You can adopt a similar progressive approach to the previous activity by asking pupils to explore different ways of jumping. They can then share their ideas with a partner, identifying a series of jumps that they can both perform. Individual feedback is provided using key words held on the word wall. Their jumps are then added to their original travelling storyboard. You may wish to give a set of skill pictures to each group which will not only provide them with examples of the movements they can perform, but also allow them to stick these onto their story boards to aid feedback and recall skills. (An example set is provided on the companion website.)

If appropriate, pupils can be encouraged to perform jumping activities using equipment. They will need to be taught about safe practice associated with jumping onto, over and off equipment (see Chapter 8). They can also start to think about the shapes they make when jumping, allowing for the introduction of specific jumps such as straight, tuck and straddle.

## Balancing

Balancing is usually associated with being still. As with the section looking at travelling, during the lesson warm-up, we can provide pupils with the opportunity to explore balances using different body parts. These body parts may be referred to as large (or patches) – for example, shoulders, side, bottom – or small (or points) – for example, hands, feet, elbows, knees. You can introduce the different body parts or provide pictorial resource cards to support those who struggle to come up with ideas.

The model applied in the previous activities can also be used here, with pupils exploring ideas on their own, sharing these with a partner and then adding them to their emerging sequence. By the end pupils should have a storyboard containing travel, jump and balance movements.

As the sequence evolves, pupils can start to think about how they can perform it using apparatus. Pupils will need to consider the key concepts introduced in Chapter 4 associated with direction, level and speed. They can start to build upon their prior learning focusing specifically on improving their effectiveness in executing a skill as well as looking at a wider range of apparatus that can be used.

---

## Task 5.4: Gymnastic resources

1    Design a set of resource cards for a range of rolling, jumping and balancing skills which outlines the following:

   a    key teaching points for each skill
   b    a series of progression activities for pupils to complete
   c    key words pupils need to use when giving feedback.

2    Trial your resources with your class and make any modifications as you feel appropriate.
3    Add these resources to your portfolio.

# Swimming activities and water safety

When teaching swimming activities to pupils, emphasis should be placed on the development of water confidence and safety, including entry into and exit out of the water, as well as what happens when pupils are in it. Specifically, by the time they leave primary school pupils should be able to:

- swim competently, confidently and proficiently over a distance of at least 25 metres
- use a range of strokes effectively [for example, front crawl, backstroke and breast-stroke]
- perform safe self-rescue in different water-based situations. (DfE, 2013: 249)

Chapter 4 introduced the concept of FUNdamentals (British Gymnastics). In the context of swimming activities our initial teaching needs to focus on balance, agility and co-ordination, progressing to gliding, speed, sculling and floating.

## Developing water confidence

To develop water confidence, emphasis needs to be placed on getting pupils familiar with the water, including entry and exit. In looking at how pupils should enter and exit the pool, consideration needs to be given to the depth of the pool, whether steps are available and special needs of pupils (Chapter 8 provides further information on health and safety issues associated with using swimming pools).

Once pupils are confident entering and exiting the pool, consideration can be given to developing their confidence in the water. Basic warm-up activities similar to those identified in the earlier sections looking at dance and gymnastics can be used in order to get pupils to explore different ways of travelling through water. 'Toys' can be used to introduce an element of play through games activities, for example, floating objects and sinking objects. Pupils can be encouraged to blow objects across the pool, drop objects into the water and then go underwater to retrieve them, and throw and catch objects in the water. Alternatively, you can call out different actions or shapes you want pupils to make, for example, jump up, bob down, make a star (which could be floating face up, floating face down, standing up). Simple activities such as 'washing their face' or 'ring a ring o' roses' can also be used to encourage pupils to submerge themselves.

As always, organisation of the working space is important. In the teaching of physical education lane ropes can be used to section off work areas. These might be lengthways, but can also be attached across the width of the pool.

Once pupils are confident in the water you can start to look at more specific skill development. In terms of stroke development, we can identify common principles, specifically body position, leg action, arm action, breathing and co-ordination (which relates specifically to breathing).

## Body position

Here we are focusing on pupils' ability to hold a floating position, which may be on their back or their front. The focus is on the creation of a streamlined position. In many respects this position is similar to the starting position for a log roll/straight roll or the position in flight achieved when doing a straight jump. In linking it to other skills which they may have already performed, pupils can start to think about how they can apply skills across different contexts.

Once pupils are able to perform this position they should be encouraged to push and glide. This involves pushing from the side of the pool and forming an arrow shape to see how far they can travel (see the companion website for a more detailed analysis). Common faults which may occur include the feet sinking resulting in the body bending from the middle. This can be rectified by encouraging pupils to tense their stomach muscles, or through the use of a floatation belt.

## Leg action

Once pupils become confident at pushing and gliding from the side of the pool, we can start looking at the leg action of the stroke being taught. For many the first stroke they learn will be breast stroke. This is mainly due to the fact that the stroke can be performed without the head going under water so breathing is easier.

Initial activities can encourage pupils to practise the skill from a static position. This might include holding onto the side with their hands and then performing the skill. This approach allows you to observe the kick itself. Where pupils struggle to keep their feet up, floatation belts can again be used. As progress is made pupils can be asked to push away from the side and, using a handheld float, perform the leg action to travel across the pool. If pupils have the confidence to submerge their faces, they should be encouraged to do this, coming up for air as appropriate. This will encourage the streamline position.

## Arm action

The next step is to introduce the arm action. There is a need here to isolate the arms, so any floatation aids are now used by the legs. Again, depending upon the stroke being taught, variation in arm action will be evident. When practising breast stroke the hands push forward to straighten the arms. With palms facing outwards a semi-circle is drawn by each hand with the finishing point in line with the chest, before hands push forward once again.

## Breathing

Once the arm movement has been introduced, activities aimed at combining both the leg and arm action can be developed. At this point the focus should be on breathing.

Breathing in beginner breast stroke swimmers is a slow exhalation of breath followed by a deep breath inwards. Because the head tends to be above the water level this is easier than for other strokes. As they become more proficient and the hands move forward the head will bob down and the swimmer will breathe out underwater, with the intake of breath occurring as the hands make their semi-circular movements which will naturally cause the head to rise slightly. Further analysis of the other strokes can be found on the companion website.

---

### Task 5.5: Swimming activities resources

1   Design a set of resources for each stroke which outlines the following:

   a   how the skills should be performed (pictures)
   b   the key teaching points for each aspect of the stroke
   c   differentiated activities for beginners, intermediate swimmers and advanced swimmers.

2   Trial your resources with your class and make any modifications as you feel appropriate.
3   Add these resources to your portfolio.

---

## Outdoor and adventurous activities

While not commonly taught in primary schools, outdoor and adventurous activities (OAA) offer pupils opportunities to participate in a range of challenges across different learning environments. Skills associated with problem solving and basic orienteering can be developed, as can social skills associated with working in groups and in challenging situations. In some respects, it is the contribution to the development of skills within the affective domain (see Chapter 2) – for example, working with others, and developing confidence and resilience – that marks OAA out from other aspects of the physical education curriculum. There is also a general lack of confidence among primary school teachers in the delivery of the activities, which for many are seen as dangerous, or as carrying a higher than acceptable level of risk. You will need specialist qualifications to deliver those more 'risky' activities and for many of you, your pupils will experience them during a residential experience. However, simple problem-solving and orienteering activities can be delivered by most people.

### Problem solving

Problem-solving activities provide opportunities for pupils to develop knowledge, skills and understanding of working in group situations as pupils are required to engage in a range of different roles and responsibilities. While specific motor skills may not be developed, it is the associated development both within the cognitive and affective domains of learning that encourages pupils to transfer existing knowledge, skills and understanding and apply them to different situations.

**Activity: Shepherd and sheep** In this activity the emphasis is placed on effective communication using a variety of methods. Working in pairs, one pupil is blindfolded. Their partner is then responsible for guiding them along a path (which can be set out using cones) avoiding obstacles that may have been placed along the path. The guide may choose to hold their partner's hand or describe the obstacles as they approach. As pupils become more confident they can call out instructions from a distance, for example, forwards, backwards, step over, bend down. The final progression is for two pairs to join together. One pupil becomes the shepherd, who has responsibility for communicating to the other pupils (the sheep). They can be encouraged to use other forms of communication, for example, whistles to direct the sheep into a pen.

At the end of the activity, pupils can feedback to each other about what they felt went well and how they might improve next time. In doing so they are developing skills associated with communicating with others through the giving and receiving of feedback. What is important at this point is that pupils have the opportunity to use the feedback they receive to make improvements to their approach.

**Activity: Group spell** In this activity, pupils are required to work in small groups to spell as many words as they can using their bodies to form the letters. Points can be awarded relative to the number of letters contained within the word (for example, a three-letter word would be awarded three points). Time limits can be set so pupils have to make as many words as they can in two minutes.

**Activity: Bench swap** This activity requires pupils to change positions while standing on a bench. If they fall off the bench they must return to the spot on the bench they started at. Having randomly stood on the bench, you ask pupils to change positions so that they become ranked, for example, in height order with the shortest pupil at the front and the tallest at the back. Using balancing and supporting techniques pupils swap places with each other until this is achieved. Once they have achieved their ranking you can ask them to swap again so they are ranged by, for example, month of birth, day of birth, shoe size.

These are just a few ideas that you can use. Further examples can be found on the companion website.

## Orienteering

Orienteering-focused activities can be as simple as following trails to encouraging pupils to develop those skills associated with map reading.

## Trails

Pupils can be asked to follow simple trails set out in the school grounds, for example they could follow a string that is laid out to form a course. Once they become confident with the activity they can be blindfolded with a partner giving them instructions. Map reading and drawing skills can be developed with pupils drawing simple plans and maps, or through the use of more detailed maps.

**Activity: Designing and using simple maps** The basic concepts of a map will need to be explained to pupils at the outset, for example, that it is a two-dimensional representation of an area. Working in pairs pupils draw a simple plan of the gym or outdoor space where the lesson is taking place. Using a key or legend they should include features such as windows, doors, wall bars, benches, mats (if indoors) or pitch markings, playground markings, trees, benches (if working outdoors).

The next step is for pupils to design a course for someone to follow using their map. In orienteering a course is completed by collecting a stamp from locations identified on a map. These stamps are attached to controls which are red and white in colour. While these can be bought for use in schools (orienteering equipment packs are commercially available) a simple red and white card can be made and laminated with letters or numbers written on them. Plastic cups can also be used with coloured pencils attached to identify which control has been visited. Permanent courses can be established within the school grounds by painting numbers and letters on permanent fixtures, for example, walls and fences (make sure you get permission to do this from the school). Further details on setting up orienteering courses and resources can be found on the companion website.

Using their maps pupils can be asked to design a course by putting red circles on the map where they have placed their controls. Each control should be numbered, but this does not mean that they have to be collected in that order. On a separate piece of paper they can record the control number and whatever piece of information is on the card. For example, if the course requires pupils to collect a series of letters which can be used to spell a word, then the record card would show the control number and corresponding letter. Once the course has been set up, pupils swap maps and complete each other's courses.

Developing this idea further, you can produce a map of the school grounds (this can be done commercially, or simply by acquiring a copy of the school plan). You can then identify a series of courses which can be differentiated by the distance pupils have to cover and the difficulty of finding the controls. Alternatively, you can set up timed events where pupils have a set time to find as many controls as they can. Different controls will carry different points so those that are close to the starting point and easy to find are worth fewer points than those that are further away or are harder to find. In this way pupils are engaging in planning activities prior to the task to think about strategies they might employ to get the most points.

As with any aspect of learning, activities need to be structured in such a way that pupils become confident in the process they are engaging in. Chapter 2 talked about scaffolding of learning, and it is likely that pupils will find this approach helpful when first introduced to the concept of orienteering. In practice this could be achieved by walking through a course so pupils know what they are looking for. As they become confident you may wish to let some of them continue with the course on their own while you walk the rest of the class round the course. Alternatively, pupils can engage in a 'star event' which requires them to return to the start point after visiting each control so that you can check on their progress and give feedback.

You can also be creative in what pupils have to do at each control. For example, each control could have an assigned letter and these letters could either form a word or be used to make as many words as possible. A similar approach can be used with numbers and mathematical symbols so that they solve a problem. Alternatively, pupils could complete the course in groups and at each control have a problem to solve.

## Reviewing activities

Reviewing activities can be used extensively within OAA as a means of getting pupils to reflect upon their own performance and the performances of others. In their simplest form they can be used by pupils to identify what went well (WWW) with the activity, or 'even better if' (EBI) to identify the improvements they would wish to make. Alternatively, they can be used to support pupils' reflections upon their feelings during each activity. Using chuff charts pupils can rate their 'chuffness' at specific time points during the activity. This approach is particularly useful for reflecting on longer events when you have taken pupils on a residential experience.

---

### Task 5.6: OAA resources

1   Design a set of resources for problem-solving activities (one per activity) which outlines the following:

   a   problem-solving task (to include the equipment you will need)
   b   key points that might help pupils to solve the problem
   c   review activities which encourage pupils to reflect upon how they achieved the activity.

2   Trial your resources with your class and make any modifications as you feel appropriate.
3   Add these resources to your portfolio.

## Chapter summary

This chapter has attempted to provide a general overview of a range of activities that can be taught in the primary school. However, this is not an exhaustive list and further resources are available from the companion website. As you have read the chapter you will have identified commonalities in how activities can be taught. Perhaps the three most important points are as follows.

1    Wherever possible progress pupils from working on their own, to working with a partner, to working in small groups.
2    Give pupils opportunities for exploration and experimentation rather than just telling them how to perform a skill. This will allow them to modify the skill to their individual needs.
3    Practices are transferable across activities.

The following review questions give you the opportunity to review your learning through this chapter.

1    What are the key skills that need to be developed within each area of activity?
2    How can teaching in physical education support learning across the domains of learning?
3    What approaches to teaching are applicable across the areas of activity?

# Further reading

Griggs, G. (2012) (ed.) *An Introduction to Primary Physical Education*. London: Routledge. This text provides support materials for the delivery of physical education across the curriculum.

Pickard, A. (2014) *Teaching Physical Education Creatively*, Learning to Teach in the Primary School Series. London: Routledge.
This text provides a range of support ideas for the delivery of primary physical education. It pays particular focus to the teaching of the key areas of activity.

# Inclusion in Physical Education

## Chapter aims

- To develop an understanding of inclusion as a principle in physical education
- To review the range of educational needs evident in schools
- To develop an understanding of how physical education can be modified to include all pupils
- To understand the principles of differentiation

## Links to *Teachers' Standards*

In reading this chapter and completing the associated tasks you will be able to collect evidence in relation to the *Teachers' Standards* (DfE, 2011) as detailed in Table 6.1.

## Introduction

Previously we have looked at the development of physical education over time and the theories of learning and the developing child. The next chapter will look at the range of different approaches to the teaching of physical education you can adopt. This chapter introduces you to a range of educational needs within the school environment and how physical education can be used to support such needs. By the end of the chapter you should be able to identify and reflect upon a range of educational needs within your classroom, with the aim of creating an inclusive learning environment.

**Table 6.1**  How this chapter links to the *Teachers' Standards* (DfE, 2011)

| | |
|---|---|
| Standard 1: Set high expectations which inspire, motivate and challenge pupils | • establish a safe and stimulating environment for pupils, rooted in mutual respect<br>• set goals that stretch and challenge pupils of all backgrounds, abilities and dispositions |
| Standard 2: Promote good progress and outcomes by pupils | • be aware of pupils' capabilities and their prior knowledge, and plan teaching to build on these<br>• demonstrate knowledge and understanding of how pupils learn and how this impacts on teaching |
| Standard 3: Demonstrate good subject and curriculum knowledge | • have a secure knowledge of the relevant subject(s) and curriculum areas, foster and maintain pupils' interest in the subject, and address misunderstandings |
| Standard 4: Plan and teach well-structured lessons | • promote a love of learning and children's intellectual curiosity<br>• contribute to the design and provision of an engaging curriculum within the relevant subject area(s) |
| Standard 5: Adapt teaching to respond to the strengths and needs of all pupils | • know when and how to differentiate appropriately, using approaches which enable pupils to be taught effectively<br>• have a secure understanding of how a range of factors can inhibit pupils' ability to learn, and how best to overcome these<br>• demonstrate an awareness of the physical, social and intellectual development of children, and know how to adapt teaching to support pupils' education at different stages of development<br>• have a clear understanding of the needs of all pupils, including those with special educational needs, those of high ability, those with English as an additional language and those with disabilities, and be able to use and evaluate distinctive teaching approaches to engage and support them |
| Standard 7: Manage behaviour effectively to ensure a good and safe learning environment | • have high expectations of behaviour, and establish a framework for discipline with a range of strategies, using praise, sanctions and rewards consistently and fairly<br>• maintain good relationships with pupils, exercise appropriate authority, and act decisively when necessary |
| Standard 8: Fulfil wider professional responsibilities | • make a positive contribution to the wider life and ethos of the school<br>• develop effective professional relationships with colleagues, knowing how and when to draw on advice and specialist support<br>• deploy support staff effectively<br>• communicate effectively with parents with regard to pupils' achievements and wellbeing |

## Task 6.1

Use your experiences of teaching and being in schools to answer the following:

1    What does inclusion mean to you?
2    How do you include all pupils in lessons at the moment?
3    What evidence do you have that your approaches have been successful or not?
4    What strategies have you seen other staff use to include pupils?

5   Organise a meeting with the Special Educational Needs Co-ordinator (SENCo) in school to discuss how you can work with them to develop your knowledge and understanding of SEN and disability within school, and to discuss possible strategies that can be employed to support the pupils identified as requiring additional support within the classes you teach.

6   Record your answers so that you can refer to them at the end of the chapter.

## Effective inclusion

The *Special Educational Needs and Disability Code of Practice: 0 to 25 years* published jointly by the Department for Education and Department of Health (2015) states 'All children and young people are entitled to an appropriate education, one that is appropriate to their needs, promotes high standards and the fulfilment of potential' (2015: 92). Further that they must 'ensure that children and young people with SEN engage in the activities of the school alongside pupils who do not have SEN' (2015: 92).

This document builds on the National Inclusion Framework (Ofsted, 2003: 92), which identified that effective inclusion occurs when there is:

- a climate of acceptance of all pupils
- careful preparation of placements for special educational needs (SEN) pupils
- availability of sufficient suitable teaching and personal support
- widespread awareness among staff of the particular needs of SEN pupils and an understanding of the practical ways of meeting these needs in the classroom
- sensitive allocation to teaching groups and careful curriculum modification, timetables and social arrangements
- availability of appropriate materials and teaching aids and adapted accommodation
- an active approach to personal and social development (PSD), as well as to learning
- well-defined and consistently applied approaches to managing difficult behaviour
- assessment, recording and reporting procedures which can embrace and express adequately the progress of pupils with more complex SEN who make only small gains in learning and PSD
- full involvement of parents/carers in decision making, keeping them well informed about their child's progress and giving them as much practical support as possible
- development of and participation in training opportunities, including links with special schools and other schools.

Inclusion can also be facilitated as a result of the teacher designing suitable learning objectives (see Chapter 3), making learning accessible for all pupils and responding to the diversity of need (explored in more detail within this chapter).

In a physical education context, the Inclusion Spectrum (Stevenson and Black, 2011) has evolved as a model of supporting pupils with SEN or disabilities to become more integrated into the classroom. They identify five stages of the spectrum:

- Open – everyone can play: here few modifications are needed. Pupils are encouraged to work at a level appropriate to them.
- Modified – change to include: the emphasis here is on all pupils doing the same activity but with some level of challenge or support integrated to allow progress to be made.
- Parallel – ability groups: here pupils are grouped according to their ability and are provided with an activity appropriate to their needs. The basis of the activity remains the same for all groups.
- Alternative or separate activity: here individuals are given a separate activity and practise on their own. Once they are able to complete the task they should be reintegrated into the activities planned for the rest of the class as appropriate.
- Adapted physical activity and disability sport – here adapted activities are delivered (for example, boccia, seated volleyball) to the class allowing for greater integration of disabled pupils.

Central to the spectrum is the STEP model (Youth Sport Trust, 2004; Teacher Development Agency, 2009; English Athletics, 2012) which acts as a guide in thinking and planning for differentiation within lessons which will be developed in more depth later in the chapter.

In preparation for this, in the next section we will look at the range of educational needs evident within the classroom environment and how barriers to learning associated with such needs can be overcome within physical education.

## Key groups of need within education

It is suggested that 'a child has special educational needs if he or she has a learning difficulty which calls for special provision to be made for him or her' (Departments for Children, Families and Schools, 2008: 12). The *SEN and Disability Code of Practice* identifies four 'broad areas of need' (DfE and DoH, 2015: 97) with examples of needs within education as detailed in Table 6.2.

**Table 6.2**   *SEN and Disability Code of Practice* (DfE and DoH, 2015) areas of need

| Area of need | Example |
| --- | --- |
| Communication and interaction | Autistic Spectrum Disorder (ASD) |
| Cognition and learning | Moderate Learning Difficulties (MLD) |
|  | Severe Learning Difficulties (SLD) |
|  | Profound and Multiple Difficulties (PMLD) |
|  | Specific Learning Difficulty (SpLD) |
| Social, emotional and mental health difficulties | Isolation |
|  | Attention Deficit Hyperactive Disorder (ADHD) |
|  | Eating disorders |
| Sensory and/or physical needs | Vision Impairment (VI) |
|  | Hearing Impairment (HI) |
|  | Multi-Sensory Impairment (MSI) |

The next part of the chapter discusses these groupings in more detail, provides you with the opportunity to reflect upon your current practice and supports your professional development. It will also provide practical examples of how physical education can be modified to allow access for all pupils.

# Communication and interaction

The ability to communicate is an essential life skill for all children and young people in the twenty-first century. It is at the core of all social interaction. With effective communication skills, children can engage and thrive. Without them, children will struggle to learn, achieve, make friends and interact with the world around them. (Bercow, 2008: 16)

Common difficulties can be associated with:

* listening to and understanding instructions and information
* learning and understanding concepts and words
* responding to questions and sharing ideas
* collaborative and social interactions.

The group includes for example, pupils who suffer with Autistic Spectrum Disorder (ASD) and Asperger's Syndrome.

## Autistic Spectrum Disorder and Asperger's Syndrome

ASD is generally thought to be associated with developmental problems which are exhibited during both childhood and adulthood. According to *Social Policy Report* published in the United States of America, autistic disorder can be defined as 'the presence of deficits or unusual behaviours within three domains: reciprocal social interaction, communication, and restricted, repetitive interests and behaviours' (Lord and Bishop, 2010: 4). Within these three areas common behaviours may be evidenced as follows.

* Social interactions – evident through the way the individual relates emotionally to others. This may include their limited ability to communicate non-verbally and to establish peer relationships.
* Language and communication skills – reflected in the ways in which the individual may talk to others. This may include a lack of speech in general, or the adoption of alternative methods of communication.
* Physical behaviour – reflected in patterns of behaviour and routines, that if disrupted may cause distress. Such behaviours may include repetitive movements or compulsive behaviours.

Webster identifies that other common characteristics might also include 'over- or under-sensitivity to sounds, touch, tastes, smells, light or colours' (2016: 37). Therefore pupils may struggle with changes to routines and patterns, working with others, loud noises or changes in volume and in extreme cases may self harm.

In a physical education context, Webster suggests 'autistic people are less likely to participate in sport and physical activity due to factors related to the condition including heightened fear and anxiety in social situations, difficulty in understanding body language and metaphor, and sensory challenges' (2016: 37).

## Classroom strategies

Having spent some time talking through the key characteristics of ASD we will now look at some of the classroom strategies that can be used.

***Only give one instruction at a time***    When introducing a new skill in physical education pupils need to be given the key teaching points over a period of time, rather than all at the same time. Giving only limited information reduces the chances of information overload, and as a result limits the opportunities for the pupil to become frustrated, leading to off-task activity. Furthermore, if the pupil is asked to repeat the instructions back to you, you can assess their level of understanding. In physical education this may occur when you are introducing a practice. You may ask pupils to repeat key aspects of the practice to ensure that they understand what you have said. You will need to consider how you ask such questions and how you deal with unexpected responses but such a strategy will help you gauge the level of understanding of all pupils.

***Give extra time for processing information***    We can often assume that pupils will process the information we give to them within a set time. However, the discussion of growth and development in Chapter 2 established that different pupils develop at different rates and therefore their ability to receive, process, retain and retrieve information will vary. Giving pupils time to think about their answers allows these processes to be enhanced. For example, when giving instructions, provide sufficient time for the pupil to take them on board and then respond. This is particularly important when asking questions. One practical application may be to introduce learning objectives (see Chapter 3) at the start of the lesson and include the key questions you will ask the pupils at the end. This allows pupils time to think about the answer during the course of the lesson, and if you continually refer to the question during the lesson, it will allow them time to formulate their response. You might even target specific pupils with specific questions so that they know what they are going to be asked to respond to.

***Pair pupils***    Another technique appropriate here would be to pair pupils so that they spend time during the lesson discussing their answers so that they have more confidence in being able to respond. For example, at the start of the lesson you might get pupils to warm up with a partner and as they are warming up to talk about the changes occurring to their body. At the end of the warm-up they could be asked to identify three changes that they have experienced. By working with a partner, they can gain confidence in their responses as well as being able to share their ideas.

*Use established routines* All pupils need some form of structure if they are to perform effectively. Pupils with ASD struggle with changes in routines; you should therefore endeavour to establish routines and maintain them at an early stage. Examples within physical education may include when and where the pupil changes – do they go to a separate area to change and then come to the lesson with a member of support staff? Who do they work with? Do they stay with the same partner throughout the lesson?

## Case study

Pat is a Year 8 pupil who suffers with some characteristics of autism. He is able to work within the class for some activities. Pete has worked closely with the SENCo within the school to identify and create a profile of what Pat likes and dislikes in order that these can be used to support planning of the lessons. It has been identified that Pat struggles with changes to routines and also sudden changes in noise levels.

Pat is due to participate in gymnastics this half term. Pete has therefore prepared a series of resources to support Pat's work. These include pictures of the specific skills that Pete wants Pat to practise which can be attached to a sequence storyboard so that Pat has a clear structure to their sequence. Pete has also identified who Pat will work with to complete the partner and group aspect of the work, as this will ensure that Pat has a clear structure.

Questions:

Where on the inclusion spectrum would you suggest that Pete is planning to work in relation to Pat's needs?

Do you think the strategies that Pete is planning to include are appropriate for Pat's needs?

What other suggestions of strategies would you suggest that Pete employs?

## English as an Additional Language (EAL)

When working with pupils who demonstrate language difficulties, we are also looking at pupils who may have English as an Additional Language (EAL). Appropriate strategies revolve around the clarity and speed of instruction. For example, when teaching pupils with language difficulties, you will need to think about the amount of information you can give at any one time. You need to consider the language you use and equally the words you would expect pupils to use in their responses. Consideration also needs to be given to the amount of time pupils are given to respond to questions. Many of the strategies used with ASD sufferers are therefore equally applicable here.

An example in physical education would be to use key words during the lesson which can be placed on walls within the learning environment to reflect the word walls that pupils would find within their main classrooms. Pupils can then be encouraged to use these words in the responses they give during the lesson. For example, in delivering a session looking at gymnastics, key words such as flight, balance, shape, jump may be displayed around the teaching space to focus pupils on the words they should use in their responses.

Pupils can also be encouraged to communicate through other mediums, for example through the sequences they compile in dance and gymnastics. They might be asked to produce a storyboard for their sequence where they either draw or use pre-prepared cards to show what movement they are making at each stage of their routine. This will provide not only a record of their sequence, thereby enhancing recall, but also some form of assessment opportunity.

It is important that you understand these behaviours if you are to engage pupils as fully as possible in your lessons. As you teach your class or classes, you will become aware of the range of behaviours evident within the pupils you teach. Many can be fully integrated into your class, but you should seek advice and guidance from those designated within the school to support those with SEN and disabilities. However, Task 6.2 provides you with an opportunity to start to collate evidence and strategies.

---

### Task 6.2

To support your emerging knowledge and understanding of inclusion this task encourages you to build on the information provided within this chapter to develop an overview of the key characteristics of the needs identified within the *Code of Practice* (DfE and DoH, 2015) to identify possible strategies to support pupils and then to reflect on the impact of these strategies on the progress of pupils within your class. You should complete the table after each sub-section in order that you have a complete overview to support your planning.

| Area of need | Example of specific need with associated characteristics | Strategies that can be employed to support learning | Reflection on the impact of the strategies used on pupil progress within my lessons |
|---|---|---|---|
| Communication and interaction | Autistic Spectrum Disorder (ASD) | | |
| Cognition and learning | Moderate Learning Difficulties (MLD) | | |
| | Severe Learning Difficulties (SLD) | | |
| | Profound and Multiple Difficulties (PMLD) | | |
| | Specific Learning Difficulty (SpLD) | | |
| Social, emotional and mental health difficulties | Isolation | | |
| | Attention Deficit Hyperactive Disorder (ADHD) | | |
| | Eating disorders | | |
| Sensory and/or physical needs | Vision Impairment (VI) | | |
| | Hearing Impairment (HI) | | |
| | Multi-Sensory Impairment (MSI) | | |

# Cognition and learning

Within this group of needs, there may not be any physical signs of the challenges being faced by the individual. Further psychological characteristics might not be obvious. What is evident is that individuals involved struggle to learn in the same way as their peers. The level of challenge in this group can range from moderate learning difficulties (MLD) – where attainment is lower than expected level of attainment in relation to National Curriculum expectations – through to severe learning difficulties (SLD) and in extreme situations, profound learning difficulties (PLD).

## Specific Learning Difficulty (SpLD)

Also identified within this group are the specific learning difficulties. Here pupils within this area of need demonstrate characteristics of dyslexia, characterised by difficulties with reading and writing; dyscalculia, whereby pupils struggle with mathematical sequencing and numbers; and dyspraxia, where pupils struggle with motor competence and control.

# Social, emotional and mental health difficulties

Pupils who experience social, emotional and mental health difficulties have previously been categorised as experiencing difficulties in respect of behaviour, emotion and social skills (BESD) and were defined as those who 'demonstrate features of emotional and behavioural difficulties such as: being withdrawn or isolated, disruptive and disturbing; being hyperactive and lacking concentration; having immature social skills; or presenting challenging behaviours arising from other complex special needs' (DCFS, 2008: 12). If you refer to Chapter 2, which looked at the processes associated with development within the affective domain, you can start to make connections between what you see in the classroom and the associated stage of development.

## Classroom strategies

As with autism, a range of classroom strategies can be employed to support pupils within the school environment. Such strategies include setting clear expectations around behaviour and grouping of pupils. These will now be explored in greater depth. Supporting journals and websites are included at the end of this chapter where you will be able to access further practical support.

***Set clear expectations of behaviour and reinforce these when appropriate*** Pupils need to be clear about their expected behaviours. Expectations need to be clear, reinforced and established as soon as possible in order to effectively manage behaviour (Chapter 5 looks at behaviour management strategies in more detail and support materials are available on the companion website). Where a pupil is seen to exhibit good behaviour, this should be highlighted. This will ensure that pupils receive positive feedback and reinforcement, which may enhance the likelihood of the behaviour being repeated (you may wish to look back at Chapter 2 and the behaviourist theories of learning).

***Consider pupil groupings*** You will need to give consideration to how you group your pupils. For example, do you want them to work in friendship or ability groups? Are there pupils who can, and others who cannot, work together? Can you give pupils different levels of responsibility within your groups (you might wish to look at the range of teaching approaches introduced in Chapter 7)? You will also need to consider how you get pupils into the group sizes you desire. For example, during the warm-up you may do an activity that requires pupils to get into the corresponding group size to the number you call out (grouping will be covered in more detail later in this chapter). It is important that the time taken to group pupils is kept to a minimum in order that opportunities for pupils to move off task are reduced.

# Sensory and/or physical needs

As well as specific learning difficulties, some pupils you teach may also exhibit physical disabilities, for example visual impairments, hearing impairments or a physical impairment. Here an understanding of the level of impairment and its impact on participation is vital to ensure an effective learning experience. Each of these impairments will carry different requirements. A pupil with a visual impairment may need larger equipment to perform a task. The way we give instructions will need to be different for a hearing-impaired pupil, for example you need to know their preferred communication style (which might be lip reading). Those pupils with a physical impairment may have to be provided with an adapted activity, for example the equipment may need to be adapted or the rules of the game modified to provide them with a defined space in which only they are allowed to work. Whilst somewhat dated, TDA (2009) provides a comprehensive overview of working with pupils with SEN and disabilities.

## Gifted and talented pupils

Thus far we have looked at supporting pupils with educational needs that may limit their involvement. However, we also need to acknowledge that there will be pupils who work beyond the expected level of attainment. Such pupils are commonly referred to as gifted and talented. Strategies associated with accelerated learning (Smith, 1998) should be used with these pupils, for example, problem solving, reflective activities, application of knowledge across differing contexts and the development of independent thinking skills. What is clear is that opportunities for learning are reflected in the approaches we adopt when planning and delivering lessons and these should meet the needs of the pupils with whom we work. Chapter 7 provides more detail regarding the range of teaching approaches we might adopt within physical education.

### Task 6.3

Looking at the strategies identified for working with pupils across the areas of need, what common approaches can you establish with the strategies used to support pupils across these needs?

When comparing strategies, you should begin to notice similar approaches that can be used to support any pupil within the classroom regardless of their defined special need. In fact, it could be argued that many of the strategies identified can be employed to ensure the inclusion of all pupils within the school environment. We will now explore this further by looking at differentiation in more detail.

# Differentiation

Many pupils who have some form of SEN or disability want to be involved within the lesson (Back up and Active Assistance, 2013), therefore it is important that we look at ways in which we can address this, and reflect the inclusion spectrum within our own teaching. This section of the chapter looks at a range of strategies that can be employed to identify and support pupils through the process of differentiation.

Vickerman (2010) argues that as a teacher you are:

> required to work flexibly and creatively to design environments that are conducive to learning for all. This involves identifying potential barriers to learning, teaching and assessment, whilst using strategies that offer access and entitlement to PE. (2010: 168)

Thus, when looking at differentiation we need to consider: the teaching approaches adopted (see Chapter 7); the activities we are undertaking and how these might need to be adapted to reflect the range of needs; how we evaluate the learning that has taken place. Central to the process is the premise that 'all' pupils make progress, and thus we are looking at extending the performances of those identified as gifted and talented, as well as those who may be identified as working below curriculum expectations.

While much work has been undertaken that looks at the process of differentiation Bailey (2006) gives one of the main summaries of approaches that can be adopted. Specifically, he identifies three key differentiation groupings: organisation, presentation and content.

## Organisation

A key aspect of organisation is the structuring of the learning episode in which consideration needs to be given to how you group pupils. As mentioned earlier in the chapter, this is particularly important to pupils who may have associated needs. As well as deciding how you intend to group pupils, you will also need to consider how they get into these groups. Singling out team captains and getting them to pick individuals to join their group is not the best way of either getting efficient and effective groups or enhancing pupils' self-esteem, especially if they are the last chosen. A more effective way may be to call out numbers during a warm-up activity and get pupils to make that group size. When grouping you also need to consider the activity being undertaken. For example, when practising a new skill, pupils may find it more beneficial to be working on their own in order to get the opportunity to practise the skill more frequently. If you want to put the skill into a game situation, you may wish to work with small-sided games so pupils have more opportunity to practise the skill as they will be more likely to receive the ball due to the smaller number of team mates.

A second organisational aspect is to think about the size of the area you might wish to use. When teaching physical education, never feel that everyone has to be doing exactly the same thing at the same time. For example, if you are developing a skill such as passing the ball, you might want to change the distance over which pupils pass; thus groups passing over different distances will evolve naturally. Further, if you want to put pupils under greater pressure when practising passing, you might reduce the size of the playing area so that they have less time to make decisions. Conversely, you might extend the playing area, thereby increasing the space available as well as the time in which decisions can be made.

Consideration also needs to be given to the roles that pupils undertake. For example, the Sport Education model provides opportunities for pupils to undertake a range of specific roles and responsibilities (see Chapter 7). The integration of these into the learning environment may provide pupils with increased levels of responsibility and can enhance BESD.

We can also look at the ways in which pupils interact with each other. As has previously been identified, many pupils with SEN will have associated communication needs. Consequently, you will need to consider the opportunities you provide for pupils to communicate either with each other or with you as the teacher. You may need to think about the questions you ask, the time you give pupils to respond, as well as to whom they respond. Is it necessary for them to talk to the whole class, or will sharing answers in small groups be more appropriate?

## Presentation

When looking at the way we present the lesson, we need to consider the way the lesson is structured (see Chapter 7 for the range of teaching styles that can be adopted); the responses that are expected from pupils (this may be the questions that will be asked, the answers expected, or in physical education the practice opportunities and demonstrations you might be planning); the resources you are intending to use (in physical education this may be more than just practical equipment, for example, they may include resources or reciprocal cards or ICT equipment); and any additional support that may be provided (many pupils with identified learning difficulties may have an assigned teaching assistant to support them in lessons).

Chapter 7 looks extensively at the teaching approaches and styles that can be adopted within lessons. It is important to identify the objectives of your lesson and the most appropriate approach to adopt. Looking at the domains of learning (see Chapters 2 and 7) may provide you with further guidance in these areas.

When looking at the responses that you are expecting from pupils, consideration needs to be given to how questions are introduced and the depth of response you are expecting. A range of questioning strategies can be used. You may ask closed questions where a specific answer is required, for example, 'do you understand?' which would elicit a yes or no response, or 'give me three teaching points for passing the ball'. While there may be more than three teaching points available you have been very specific in what you are looking for. Alternatively, you could ask open-ended questions which would give pupils the opportunity to give a range of responses. For example, 'how many different ways of passing a ball can you think of?'. You can get pupils to expand their answers by asking them why they have chosen to do something in a certain way.

It is important to consider the ways in which pupils are encouraged to respond. For example, how can you ensure they will all be able to give a response? We have identified throughout this chapter aspects of giving pupils time to provide answers by thinking about when questions are asked, and when a response is expected. However, other strategies can include 'no hands up'. In such a strategy you are providing an opportunity for all pupils to provide a response as you identify the person from whom the response should come. In such a way you can gauge the first question (for example, a closed question) and then ask supplementary questions (open questions) to allow other pupils to expand on the first response.

If pupils are struggling to answer a question you might modify the question being asked, or alternatively provide them with 'help' strategies. For example, you might ask pupils to identify someone in the class they want to ask for help ('phone a friend'), they might pass the question over to someone else or they might 'ask the audience'. Such strategies are common in many games shows, but provide support mechanisms for pupils thereby limiting the impact of getting the question wrong. What is important is to establish a learning environment where it is acceptable to make mistakes; after all, much of what we have learnt throughout our lives came as a result of getting something wrong in the first place!

The resources that are to be used are also important. In physical education our resources tend to be associated with the equipment we use, so we may want to think about the activity we are delivering and whether the equipment can be modified to ensure that all pupils achieve success. For example, when playing a racquet sport (tennis, badminton) can we use racquets with shorter handles to improve hand–eye co-ordination? Can we use racquets with large heads, so that there is a greater surface area with which to make contact with the ball or shuttle? Does the ball or shuttle have to be of a normal size, or can enlarged versions be used? When looking at introducing throwing or catching, can balls of different shapes and sizes be used? These are just a few examples of how equipment may be modified to support learning. More detail is included in Chapter 3, which looks at planning, and Chapters 4 and 5, which focus on the development of fundamental and activity specific skills.

However, the resources we use may not necessarily be restricted to equipment. Within physical education we may also use word walls or resource cards. It is therefore important to look at how these are developed and utilised within the context of the lesson.

The way we support learning within the physical education classroom is another important consideration. Many pupils with identified learning needs will be assigned a measure of support. This may include a designated staff member who accompanies pupils to lessons. It is important, if a pupil in your class is accompanied, that you provide adequate guidance to the staff member enabling them to provide the support that you require. This might involve meeting with them prior to the lesson to provide a brief overview of their role. You will be conscious of this process anyway as a result of your use of teaching assistants within your classroom-based lessons.

The support you provide may come from other pupils within your class. If you refer to Chapter 2 and the theories of learning, you will remember that Vygotsky highlighted the use of peers to support learning. If you look at the teaching approaches identified by both Mosston and Ashworth (1994) and Metzler (2011), they too identified the use of peers to support learning. It is therefore important that if you are using such approaches clear guidance and structures are identified to ensure pupils are clear about their expectations and roles.

## Content

The final group of strategies identified by Bailey (2006) around differentiation are associated with the content of the lesson. Specifically, we are looking at:

- the tasks set
- the pace of the lesson
- the level at which pupils are being expected to work
- the style of practice being used.

You will be familiar with setting differentiated tasks within your classroom-based lessons. For example, you may group your class by ability represented by the tables they sit at, so that when setting work different tables are assigned different tasks. This practice is equally appropriate for physical education. Thinking back once more to the discussion of child development in Chapter 2, you will remember that different pupils will progress at different rates, and therefore setting the same task for all pupils may result in it being too easy for some pupils and too difficult for others. You need to be clear about the purpose of the task, and what you want pupils to get out of it. Earlier in this chapter we looked at the different ways in which we ask questions of pupils and also the ways in which they may respond. It may be that while we may set a similar task for pupils, the outcome we are expecting from them is different. What is crucial here is that the pupils are fully aware of what outcome is expected.

The pace of a lesson refers to the speed at which the lesson progresses. It is a difficult skill to master. At times you will rush through things to ensure that you complete all the activities you have planned, while at other times you may move through the activities too slowly. The key here is to watch the class. They will send signals out as to whether they have completed the task, and therefore are starting to go off-task, or are struggling and therefore not fulfilling the requirements of the task. Both instances will require some form of intervention from you as the teacher. It may be that you need to refocus the group, move them on to the next task, or simplify the activity. Again, this needs to be considered within your planning. Whatever you choose to do, you must be confident that it reflects the needs of the pupils. Do not be afraid to have different groups working on different tasks at different times. You do it all the time in the classroom! Organisationally it may also support you. For example, if one group has already completed the initial practice to the level you expect, move them onto the next practice. After completing the new practice, they can then demonstrate to other groups what you want them to move on to. In this way, you do not have to spend as much time explaining, thereby increasing the levels of activity within the lesson.

When we refer to the level of the activity we are making reference to the levels of attainment pupils are working at or towards. While there have been many changes to the content and organisation of the National Curriculum, there has been less change to the levels of attainment (see Chapter 1). Thus, when looking at the content of the lesson, you need to also think about what level of attainment you are expecting. This may be written into the learning objectives set (see Chapter 3). Again, consideration will need to be given to the range of levels you are addressing. Equally you will need to think carefully about how you might inform pupils of the levels at which they are working. This might be through identifying specific skills they must achieve for each level, remembering of course that in terms of the National Curriculum, levels are not just associated with the skills they can perform, but also their levels of understanding and ability to communicate. It may well be that the tasks you set already reflect the different levels of attainment, or that the task set can be achieved through the demonstration of different skills reflective of different levels of attainment. This is particularly relevant if the tasks are of a very open-ended nature, as discussed earlier in the chapter.

Finally, we look at the style of practice being used. Specifically, we are looking at the ways in which the skills are practised. For example, would it be most appropriate for pupils to practise the skill on their own, with a partner or in a small group? How will they gain feedback about their performance – from each other, from you as the teacher, from watching their own performances using video?

While Bailey (2006) gives a detailed overview of differentiation across physical education, alternative models also exist. The STEP model (Youth Sport Trust, 2004; TDA, 2009; English Athletics, 2012) is now becoming more embedded within primary physical education teaching and identifies four key aspects of differentiation:

- **Space**: this relates to the space (area) in which the activity is being performed, and can include distances. Key questions might focus around:
  - What size space do pupils need to have to complete the activity?
  - Do all pupils need to be using the same size space?
  - Can I increase/decrease the size of the area to make it more/less challenging?

- **Task**: the activity you are asking the pupils to perform. For example:
  - How can I structure the activity in order that all pupils can complete the task on their own or with help?
  - How will I ensure that pupils have sufficient time to complete the task?
  - How will I ensure that all pupils have equal access to the resources to practise the skill I am developing?
- **Equipment**: what the pupils are using to complete the task. For example:
  - Do I need to provide a range of equipment for pupils to use to complete the task?
  - How will pupils select the equipment they want to use?
- **People**: who the pupils work with. For example:
  - How will pupils be grouped?
  - Who will have what role within the group?
  - What size group do I need to maximise learning opportunities?
  - How will I use any learning support staff I have?

---

## Task 6.4

1  Using the previous section of the chapter, identify a range of differentiation strategies that you wish to try within your lessons.
2  For each strategy identify:

   a  the activity you plan to deliver
   b  the differentiation activities
   c  how you will gauge the level of success.

3  Ask your school mentor colleague to observe the lessons in which you have planned to use these strategies and provide feedback to you on the outcomes of the approaches.

---

## Chapter summary

The aim of this chapter has been to look at the range of individual needs evident within education and more specifically in the context of physical education. Further examples of differentiation and support strategies can be found on the companion website.

*(Continued)*

*(Continued)*

To summarise your learning in this chapter you may benefit from reflecting on the following review questions.

1    What is the range of SEN within the school environment?
2    How do these impact on the teaching of physical education?
3    How can I ensure that I plan and differentiate appropriately within my lessons to ensure that I reflect the needs of all the pupils I teach?
4    What key areas of personal development can you identify to increase your knowledge and understanding of these concepts?

# Further reading

Youth Sport Trust (2013) *Active Kids 2013 – Inclusive Resources*. Loughborough: YST.
This resource provides a detailed overview of the inclusion spectrum and STEP model, providing advice on increasing activity levels for all pupils, communicating with pupils and examples of inclusive games that can be delivered within physical education lessons.

Bates, B. (2017) *A Quick Guide to Special Needs and Disabilities*. London: Sage.
This text provides a clear yet concise overview of over 60 special needs that might be experienced in schools. Having provided an overview of the specific needs and characteristics, Bates provides examples of strategies that can be employed to support pupils within the classroom.

Teacher Development Agency (2009) *Including Pupils with SEN and/or Disabilities in Primary Physical Education*. Manchester: TDA. Available at: http://webarchive.national archives.gov.uk/20111218081624/http://tda.gov.uk/teacher/developing-career/sen-and-disability/sen-training-resources/one-year-itt-programmes/~/media/resources/teacher/sen/primary/physicaleducationpe.pdf.
This publication provides guidance on supporting pupils with SEN within the context of physical education. Whilst its publication date might suggest that it is dated, it provides a self-audit tool that encourages you to reflect on your own and other's teaching and encourages you to reflect on your application of different strategies within your classroom. It also demonstrates how the inclusion spectrum can be applied across areas of activities with practical examples provided to support the removal of barriers to learning.

Trussler, S. and Robinson, D. (2015) *Inclusive Practice in the Primary School a Guide for Teachers*. Sage: London.
This text provides an overview of how teachers can develop inclusive teaching environments to ensure that all pupils have the opportunity to learn and develop. Its easy-to-read structure guides the reader in looking at the range of needs evident in the classroom and offers a range of activities and observations that can be undertaken to review, revise and refresh practice.

## Relevant journals

*Autism*

This international and peer-reviewed journal provides practical help in the support of pupils with autism. The journal can be accessed from http://aut.sagepub.com.

*Emotional and Behavioural Difficulties*

Published four times a year, this journal provides practical support and guidance when working with pupils who have behavioural, emotional and social difficulties. Available at www.tandf.co.uk/journals/EBD.

## Other useful websites

Active for Autism – www.autism.org.uk/active

*I CAN Talk* series – www.ican.org.uk

Teacher Expertise – www.teachingexpertise.com

## Organisations

Social Emotional and Behavioural Difficulties Association (SEBDA). Available at: www.sebda.org.

I CAN – charity set up to support children with communication needs. Their associated website – www.ican.org.uk – provides support and guidance aimed at the development and improvement of communication skills.

# Approaches to the Teaching of Physical Education

## Chapter aims

- To develop an understanding of pedagogy in physical education
- To develop an understanding of different approaches to the teaching of physical education
- To develop an understanding of how different teaching approaches impact on the learning of individuals

## Links to *Teachers' Standards*

In working through this chapter, you should develop your knowledge associated with the *Teachers' Standards* (DfE, 2011) detailed in Table 7.1.

## Introduction

Chapter 2 aimed to develop your understanding of learning and the theories associated with it. It also provided an opportunity to look at different learning environments and how these could be applied to the teaching of physical education. If you have not read that chapter for some time, you may find it useful to remind yourself of the key points raised within it by looking at the review questions at the end of the chapter.

**Table 7.1** How this chapter links to the *Teachers' Standards* (DfE, 2011)

| | |
|---|---|
| Standard 1: Set high expectations which inspire, motivate and challenge pupils | • establish a safe and stimulating environment for pupils, rooted in mutual respect<br>• set goals that stretch and challenge pupils of all backgrounds, abilities and dispositions |
| Standard 2: Promote good progress and outcomes by pupils | • demonstrate knowledge and understanding of how pupils learn and how this impacts on teaching<br>• encourage pupils to take a responsible and conscientious attitude to their own work and study |
| Standard 3: Demonstrate good subject and curriculum knowledge | • demonstrate a critical understanding of developments in the subject and curriculum areas, and promote the value of scholarship |
| Standard 4: Plan and teach well-structured lessons | • impart knowledge and develop understanding through effective use of lesson time<br>• promote a love of learning and children's intellectual curiosity<br>• reflect systematically on the effectiveness of lessons and approaches to teaching<br>• contribute to the design and provision of an engaging curriculum within the relevant subject area(s) |
| Standard 5: Adapt teaching to respond to the strengths and needs of all pupils | • know when and how to differentiate appropriately, using approaches which enable pupils to be taught effectively<br>• have a secure understanding of how a range of factors can inhibit pupils' ability to learn, and how best to overcome these |
| Standard 6: Make accurate and productive use of assessment | • make use of formative and summative assessment to secure pupils' progress |
| Standard 7: Manage behaviour effectively to ensure a good and safe learning environment | • have clear rules and routines for behaviour in classrooms, and take responsibility for promoting good and courteous behaviour both in classrooms and around the school, in accordance with the school's behaviour policy<br>• have high expectations of behaviour, and establish a framework for discipline with a range of strategies, using praise, sanctions and rewards consistently and fairly<br>• manage classes effectively, using approaches which are appropriate to pupils' needs in order to involve and motivate them |

This chapter aims to look in more detail at how domains of learning are reflected in the range of pedagogical approaches that can be adopted within the classroom and applied within the physical education context. Hayes et al. (2006) state 'Individual teachers have more impact on student outcomes than do whole-school effects' (2006: 1). In striving to become the best teachers we can be, we must reflect upon our teaching and the impact it has on the learning outcomes of our pupils. We should look to move away from an isolated approach to one that allows us to share and reflect upon our own practice. In doing so we are able to test and identify the 'what' (what works well) and 'how' further progress can be achieved (even better if).

# Pedagogical approaches to teaching

Many (Hayes et al., 2006; Kirk, 2005; Penney and Waring, 2000; Simon, 1994; Shulman, 1987) have argued for the acknowledgement of a pedagogical approach to teaching. Simon (1994) identifies pedagogy as the science of teaching, where theoretical understanding is reflected in practical application, arguing that within the UK there is a tendency to shy away from such a concept, an argument supported by Penney and Waring (2000). In developing a concept of pedagogy, Shulman (1987) argues that within specific professions common characteristics and areas of knowledge are required and developed. In education, he argues for the existence of a signature pedagogy with the emphasis placed on knowledge development and enhancement across seven key categories:

- content knowledge
- general pedagogical knowledge
- pedagogical content knowledge
- knowledge of learners and their characteristics
- curriculum knowledge
- knowledge of educational contexts
- knowledge of educational ends, purposes and values.

More recently Metzler (2011) has applied such categories specifically to the context of physical education:

- content knowledge – subject matter
- general pedagogical knowledge – generic teaching methods
- pedagogical content knowledge – subject specific teaching methods
- knowledge of learners and their characteristics – learning as a process
- curriculum knowledge – how content develops
- knowledge of educational contexts – how context impacts
- knowledge of educational ends, purposes and values – educational goals. (2011: 46)

When looking to develop an understanding of the approaches to teaching, and specifically to the teaching of physical education, we need to acknowledge the breadth of knowledge we must acquire in order to provide effective learning experiences. We need to question ourselves about what we want to teach and decide what might be the best way to approach this. More specifically we need to be very clear what we want our pupils to learn, and how we will know this has been achieved. Whilst this chapter focuses on approaches to teaching, references are made throughout to other chapters. In this way, it requires you to think about the connections between teaching approaches and the aims of physical education (Chapter 1) as well as how pupils learn and develop (Chapter 2). Further, how the approaches adopted might impact on how you plan and assess pupil learning are looked at in detail in Chapter 3.

Primary education has traditionally been seen as more pupil focused than secondary education, which is seen as more subject focused. This suggests that when planning for primary lessons, the child is at the centre of the process rather than the subject. If you look at how the curriculum is structured across these phases of education, it is clear that differences do exist.

Chapter 2 looked at learning as a process and identified that most individuals will move through different stages of learning. This suggests that there must be some form of structure to the learning that takes place. Such a premise is supported by much of the work of the social constructivists Vygotsky and Bruner as well as the behaviourist theorist Skinner, and requires us as practitioners to reflect closely on what we are striving to achieve when planning our learning experiences (see Chapter 3 for more details).

Chapters 1 and 2 looked at how early learning experiences can influence lifelong opportunities. Kirk specifically argues that 'early learning experiences are crucial to the continuing involvement in physical activity' (2005: 2). The work of Morgan and Hansen (2008) identifies confidence among practitioners as key for quality learning experiences. This suggests that when looking at approaches to teaching physical education we can run the risk of adopting approaches in which we feel confident rather than approaches that provide the best learning opportunities for pupils.

Educators should act as facilitators, providing structured help and guidance to support learning. Within this we need to understand the concept of readiness to learn. Readiness to learn is the extent to which the pupil is in a state to move forward, and is influenced by many factors (see Chapter 9 which focuses on pupils' health and wellbeing). As teachers, we need to understand the stage the pupil is at and then challenge them according. Specifically, when looking at the approaches we adopt, we need to look at the different needs of the individuals with whom we are working (a concept we looked at in Chapter 6). This does not mean that we should be aiming to provide an individualised approach for all children, and nor are we suggesting a 'one-size-fits-all' approach. What is most important is that individual differences are acknowledged, and that we ensure that the tasks planned are such that all pupils can achieve success.

Penney and Waring (2000) argue that much of the research around physical education and its curriculum is focused on the *content* of the curriculum rather than on the ways in which it is taught. Furthermore, they define pedagogy as 'a concept that simultaneously embraces and informs rationale, curriculum design, teaching and learning … pedagogy is not only about the "how" of teaching, but also the "what" and "why"' (2000: 6). You will have already started considering your own personal pedagogy through the development of your understanding around the rationale for physical education (see Chapter 1). Task 7.1 provides you with the opportunity to develop this further.

## Task 7.1

As teachers of physical education in the primary school, the way we view and have experienced the subject impacts on the way we deliver it. Using your personal definition of physical education, your understanding of the aims of physical education and your personal experiences:

- Consider your current approach to teaching and think about how this pedagogical approach has been developed.
- What teaching approaches worked best for you and how do you reflect this in your own teaching?
- How would you define your teaching approach?

Teaching pedagogies are not a new concept. Much is made of the different ways in which teachers teach and the impact this has on pupil learning and progress. Whilst much focus is placed on the teaching of the core subjects (English, Mathematics and Science) with international practices highlighted (for example, China, Singapore, Finland), research into the way physical education is delivered also continues to evolve. Penney (2003) argues for the existence of two key categories of pedagogical approach in physical education. Firstly, expanded learning where the learner works in a context associated with criticism (questioning), discovery and practical application. In physical education this might involve pupils applying existing knowledge and understanding to practise skills or feedback on individual performances. Secondly, situated learning where pupils use their knowledge within different situations to further develop their understanding. For example, in physical education, pupils might be asked to apply their knowledge of one activity when being introduced to a new activity.

Penney's categories of pedagogical approach are similar to the work of Mosston and Ashworth (1994) who identified two distinct clusters of teaching styles: i) reproductive styles where there is a reproduction of knowledge and skills through the use of decision making, skill practice and feedback, and ii) productive styles, where new knowledge and skills are developed through the use of problem-solving and cognitive thought.

More recently the work of Hayes et al. (2006) focusing on pedagogy in general, has raised a focus towards the term 'productive pedagogies'. Their work identifies key dimensions such as *intellectual quality*, suggesting 'pupils need to be in intellectually challenging classrooms' (2006: 22); and *connectedness*, making connections to the real world and the world around us may impact positively on pupils' motivation to learn, understanding why we are doing something or seeing the bigger picture is important.

The next section of this chapter will develop these concepts further. We start by looking at the work of Mosston and Ashworth, before looking at instructional models, Teaching Games for Understanding and Sport Education.

## Mosston and Ashworth's teaching styles

Seen by many as the basis for subsequent approaches for the teaching of physical education, Mosston and Ashworth (1994) continue to provide structure to the teaching of physical education. Their proposed approaches are based upon a spectrum characterised by the involvement of the teacher and the learner within the decision-making processes during the delivery of learning experiences. Their premise was built around the belief that 'teaching behaviour is a chain of decision making' (Mosston and Ashworth, 1994: 3). Further that 'all teaching styles are beneficial for what they can accomplish; none is more important, or more valuable, than another' (Mosston and Ashworth, 2008: 5). Emerging from this was a formalised structure of teaching styles. Each contained their own specific anatomy (which refers to the group of decisions that are made), including who the decision makers are, the style, and the developmental effects. It is appropriate at this point to explore these structures in greater depth in order to fully appreciate the integrity of the styles, and to provide examples of how these approaches can be reflected in the teaching of physical education.

When looking at the anatomy of the style, we are looking specifically at the decision making that occurs. Mosston and Ashworth (1994, 2008) suggest that such decisions are made prior to the lesson (pre-impact), and this is reflected in the planning of the lesson (see Chapter 3 for further detail on planning), during the lesson (impact) in terms of the progression and pace of the lesson, and after the lesson (post-impact) in the evaluative process assessing a lesson. Each learning style also considers the interactions between the teacher and learner which contribute to the decision-making process, and during which development is expected to occur. This is closely aligned to the concept of learning domains (as discussed in Chapter 2) which Mosston and Ashworth (1994, 2008) define as developmental channels, focusing on development across cognitive, social, physical, emotional and ethical areas of development, arguing that 'physical education inherently embraces more opportunities to emphasise and develop a wide range of human attributes along all the Development Channels than any other content area in the curriculum' (2008: 12).

In selecting any teaching style for use in physical education Mosston and Ashworth (1994) felt the following questions should be addressed:

•   What are my learning objectives? What do I want my pupils to achieve?

For example, are we looking at skills, knowledge, understanding and/or application? This becomes a crucial question, because if we want to develop skills we might wish to use a direct teaching style, whereas if we want to develop pupils' ability to apply a skill, the approach will need to be more interactive.

- What is the best method to use to achieve these objectives?
- How should I structure my teaching?
- How should I organise the learning?

For example: How might I present my tasks?

- How do I motivate my pupils?

For example: How will I make the activity relevant to the pupils? How do I make sure that the activity is at the right level for their competence?

- How do I encourage social interactions and thinking?

For example: How will I get them to apply their knowledge? What will thinking look like? How will I structure the groups?

- How will I know that I have achieved my objectives?

For example: How will I assess learning? What will learning look like? What questions might I ask?

If we are to fully understand a range of teaching approaches and thereby reflect these in our planning, it is important to look at a general outline of each one in turn. This will allow you to reflect upon the basic principles and applications. The spectrum consists of 11 styles, five of which are categorised as reproductive (styles A–E) and six of which are associated with the productive categories (F–K).

## Reproductive styles

Reproductive styles 'reproduce known knowledge, replicate models and practice skills' (Mosston and Ashworth, 2008: 11). The emphasis here is on recall and replication using known knowledge to draw upon.

## Style A – command

Style A, referred to as the command style, is the most direct style. Here we see the decisions being made by the teacher with an emphasis on the development of specific skills within a clear time frame. It is commonly used when there is a lot of information to be transferred over a short period of time, or when the skills being developed have health and safety issues associated with them, for example when teaching throwing skills in athletics, or a specific skill in gymnastics. In utilising such a style, self-exploration and creativity can be limited. This style is also seen as a way of managing pupil behaviour. This means that at times it is used to support less confident practitioners.

## Style B – practice

Style B, or the practice style, relinquishes some of the decision making to learners as they take increasing responsibility for their own learning. As implied by its name, the style enables learners to practise a skill which allows the teacher to circulate and provide feedback to the pupils. A good example of this in physical education would be when pupils are developing their competences in throwing and catching. Once the task has been set, pupils practise the skill in pairs, while the teacher provides individualised feedback to each pair or generic feedback to the group where appropriate. While the teacher still maintains responsibility for the planning of the activity and as such the practices being undertaken, the learner has greater responsibility for the application of the skill within the practice situation. This style is used extensively within physical education teaching, and you are probably very familiar from your own experiences of this approach; however, Task 7.2 (below) allows you to think about this in more depth.

## Style C – reciprocal

Style C, or the reciprocal style, encourages learners to work together to develop their own knowledge and understanding. As with the previous style the decision-making processes are becoming more learner focused as pupils become actively involved in the giving and receiving of feedback from their peers. As much of the feedback learners receive is from their peers, this frees up teaching time that can be used to interact with and support learners. It is important that the teacher provides formalised feedback mechanisms for learners, more specifically in the form of a skill checklist (see the companion website for further details). This requires the teacher to provide a clear breakdown of the skill and its associated faults so that learners can provide detailed and specific feedback when observing. Such an approach not only engages pupils actively within their own learning, but also provides clear and sustained opportunities for them to develop their literacy skills, specifically related to speaking and listening. For example, with pupils working in pairs, one acts as the doer and performs the skill of striking a ball against a target (hitting a ball against a wall) while the other acts as an observer giving feedback based on the skill checklist provided, which might include reference to body position, arm action and leg action (see Chapters 4 and 5 for more details on specific skills). The doer then uses this feedback to make modifications to their performance, before the two swap roles.

## Style D – self-check

Style D, or self-check, gives further responsibility to learners. Here, instead of receiving from their peers, they take responsibility for checking their own work.

Again, the teacher must make structures to support the feedback process available, but learners now have responsibility for identifying their own strengths and weaknesses and start to make decisions about progressing to the next skill. With the development of handheld video cameras within the school environment this approach allows pupils to record their own performance and then provide their own specific feedback. With this approach the emphasis is on the learner giving feedback. If we use the same example of striking a ball against a wall, the doer would now observe their performance as recorded by the observer, and using the same checklist, identify what they feel they need to do to improve their performance.

## Style E – inclusion

The final reproductive style is the inclusion style, style E. Here learners are given the opportunity to select their own task and then provide personal feedback based on their completion of the task. For example, in playing a game, pupils might identify a skill which they feel they need to improve. Using checklists or other resources available to them, they can go away and practise the skill, provide themselves with feedback and then demonstrate the improvements they have made. Thus learning experiences become individualised.

## Productive styles

Productive styles focus on the production of 'a range of ideas … venture into the new … tap the yet unknown' (Mosston and Ashworth, 2008: 11–12). In essence, the approaches encourage creativity amongst the learners.

## Style F – guided discovery

Moving on to the productive styles, we start with the guided discovery style, or style F. The aim of this style is to provide learners with a series of questions which they answer to achieve completion of the overall task. In essence, the style allows learners to move through a series of progressive steps to achieve a final goal. If you think back to the theories and concepts of learning, this approach links to Bruner's thoughts on learning and the use of scaffolding to elicit learning. In simplistic terms, it allows pupils to discover their preferred way of performing a skill. An example here would be to ask pupils to think about the best way to hold a hockey stick. You can then provide them with a series of decisions or questions, for example, 'try with both hands at the top', 'what about both hands towards the bottom?', 'is it easier to have your hands together or apart?'. In responding to these questions learners will discover their preferred way of holding the stick.

## Style G – convergent

Style G, the convergent style, requires learners to engage in a process of reasoning, in effect attempting to solve a problem through trial and error. Thus the style encourages the development of reasoning, critical thinking and logical thought processing. For example, pupils may be asked to think of the different ways of crossing a hazard as a means of developing problem-solving skills during OAA. Through trial and error they can identify an appropriate solution before demonstrating this to the teacher.

## Style H – divergent

The divergent style, style H, engages learners in identifying multiple responses to single questions. Again, the focus is on the processes of reasoning, critical thinking and logical thought, but the emphasis is on learners directing the decisions rather than being supported by the teacher. For example, pupils might be set the challenge of finding different ways of beating an opponent in a 3 v 1 situation, in which they have to work as a group to practise the different approaches before demonstrating and applying this in a more formalised game structure.

## Style I – individual programme

Style I, the individual programme, engages the learner in the development of a personal programme. Examples in physical education would be the development of individual training programmes, or warm-up activities.

## Style J – learner-initiated and Style K – self-teach

Finally, the learner-initiated style (Style J) develops Style I further, but with a greater emphasis on learners evaluating their programme while Style K is exhibited by learners teaching themselves.

The work of Mosston and Ashworth (1994, 2008) encourages us as teachers to reflect upon the approaches we adopt. Whilst, as has previously been indicated, many of us will adopt an approach that we feel comfortable or that works for us, in doing so we run the risk of teaching in such a way that we may actually become a barrier ourselves for the learning of others. We are duty bound as professionals to continually review our practices. As Mosston and Ashworth (2008: 5) argue:

> How the teacher plans, selects, and sequences the content; feels about students, or envisions successful classroom learning experiences is not accidental; it primarily reflects the teacher's knowledge. The teacher's professional and personal knowledge and beliefs are sources from which the teacher makes decisions (deliberate or by default) to create classroom events.

## Task 7.2

You have now been provided with a general overview of Mosston and Ashworth's (1994, 2008) spectrum of teaching.

1    Using the information contained in this chapter reflect upon your understanding of each approach.
2    Identify a series of activities that could be used to support each style.
3    Within your future planning try to make specific reference to styles.

# Instructional models

More recently Metzler (2011) has developed the concept of instructional models. He defines these as models that 'are based on alignment of learning theory, long-term learning goals, context, content, classroom management, related teaching strategies, verification of process, and the assessment of student learning' (2011: 8). Within his approach he argues that learning within a model can occur across the three domains of learning – cognitive, affective and psychomotor (see Chapter 2) – and that learning within these domains is prioritised dependent upon the model being used. For example, if a model encourages the use of problem solving then the cognitive domain will take priority; likewise, where the emphasis is placed on group work, the affective domain will be prioritised. In many ways therefore, his work builds on and reflects the work undertaken by Mosston and Ashworth (1994, 2008).

Metzler (2011) suggests that this traditional or direct approach is based on the behaviourist theories. Skills are developed as a result of practice, with progression reflected in the mastery of specific skills. The teacher will model expected behaviours (skills) and feedback will be based on children's ability to perform and will focus on specific teaching and learning points associated with the given skill, correcting where necessary. An example would be the teaching of a skill such as an overarm throw. As the teacher you will provide a demonstration of the skill. You will identify the key teaching and learning points:

*   stand sideways
*   ball held in finger tips
*   opposite hand points at target
*   throwing arm extends back
*   rotation is from the shoulder not the elbow
*   throwing arm follows through towards the intended target.

A series of practices will then be set up, for example, after a defined number of successful throws you could increase the distance between paired pupils. As the teacher you will patrol the practice giving specific feedback based on the teaching and learning points above. Such an approach is built upon the teacher as holder of knowledge and provider of opportunities for this knowledge to be developed in the learner. Learning occurs when changes in behaviours are seen. This approach clearly demonstrates aspects of Mosston and Ashworth's reproductive styles (A – E).

In his book *Instructional Models for Physical Education*, Michael W. Metzler (2011) argues that when looking at the planning and delivery of learning episodes, in this case lessons, consideration needs to be given to where the learning is taking place (context), the learners themselves, knowledge and application of theories, the domains in which learning is being encouraged, and the overall climate or environment required for learning to be achieved.

The traditional pedagogical approach to learning prioritises skill acquisition (psychomotor) and application of this skill in different situations (cognitive). What is less evident is how such an approach develops learning within the affective domain. If we think back to our own experiences of physical education lessons, time would be spent demonstrating skills and/or performing in front of other people. As a result, social comparisons occurred whereby we would compare our performances against those of others. The common practice of using the best performer to demonstrate practices is an example. When using such an approach, it therefore becomes important to think carefully about who demonstrates skills, how feedback is given, for example, by whom and using what criteria, and how success is demonstrated. This will significantly affect the learning climate created within the lesson, a concept explored in more depth in Chapter 3.

# Teaching Games for Understanding

Another approach is that of Teaching Games for Understanding (TGFU), which is sometimes referred to as tactical games or 'games sense'. The concept of TGFU emerged from the work of Bunker and Thorpe (1982). The approach looks at the development of decision-making processes by requiring participants to solve a series of tactical problems through the playing of games. It is based on the premise that if the pupils are active in the learning process then they are more likely to achieve. Brunton (2003) argues that we need to provide appropriate learning opportunities that allow pupils to take responsibility for their own learning. As the teacher you therefore act as the facilitator creating the problems that need to be solved. For example, you might set the problem of exploring how many different ways there are of beating a defender in a 3 v 1 situation. Pupils can then go away and practise this to identify the most effective ways and to come up with reasons to explain their choices. They might consider the type of passes used or the position of the players. They could then apply these strategies within a game situation to gauge their level of success.

Such an approach offers pupils opportunities to demonstrate a deeper level of understanding. They can develop a greater appreciation of how they play rather than necessarily focusing on specific skill development. Thus the approach encourages self-reflection and the analysis of problems. Stolz and Pill (2014) suggest that similarities exist between TGFU and guided discovery approaches, with the emphasis placed on the engagement of pupils on small-sided games that maximise participation rather than more skills-based approaches. Hence there is a focus on the what, when and why before necessarily emphasising the how.

The TGFU model is comprised of six key steps (Griffin and Butler, 2005; Metzler, 2011):

- Step 1: Game – pupils need to be able to play games. These may be modified to reflect pupils' stages of development (see Chapter 4 for examples of how activities can be differentiated), but they need to have an understanding of what the game is and how it is played.
- Step 2: Game appreciation – contextually pupils are required to understand the components of the game. They learn to understand rules and regulations associated with the activity and adhere to these while playing.
- Step 3: Tactical awareness – pupils start to be presented with the tactical problems of the game. Pupils are required to think practically about how they would solve game specific problems. For example, they could explore different ways of passing the ball over different distances and be encouraged to think about where the best place to send the ball may be.
- Step 4: Decision making – pupils demonstrate practically how they would solve the problem. For example, they could perform a range of different passes dependent upon the distance they need to send the ball. The focus is therefore on demonstrating what they need to do and how they will do it.
- Step 5: Skill execution – at this point pupils start to develop skills appropriate to the activity they are undertaking. Thus pupils are now able to link tactical awareness and decision making ('what' and 'how') to being able to perform the specific skills required to execute the decision.
- Step 6: Performance – pupils demonstrate their overall performance in small and large games situations.

Stolz and Pill (2014), in reviewing the now evolving iterations of TGFU, argue that the approach has the potential to allow pupils to develop higher order thinking skills as well as encouraging them to demonstrate their application of knowledge and understanding in different contexts. However, they reinforce that this is just one way of approaching the delivery of physical education.

# Sport Education

Sport Education, as an approach to teaching physical education, has been developed through the work of the American academic Daryl Siedentop. It aims 'to educate students to be players in the fullest sense, and to help them develop as competent, literate and enthusiastic sportspeople' (1994: 4).

Sport Education is based on the premise that individuals should experience a range of roles and responsibilities within sport. It can therefore be seen as reflecting a situational learning focus, where learning occurs as a result of interacting with different situations. The approach provides pupils with the opportunity to develop competences across a range of roles and responsibilities. The benefits of using a Sport Education approach are seen as increased investment from pupils, increased skill development and increased opportunities for marginalised pupils to become more actively involved. Interactions between staff and pupils increase with a movement away from the teacher managing tasks, allowing the teacher to increase the level of pupil–teacher interactions. Thus the teacher becomes more active in the provision of feedback. Again, strong links can be made to the styles discussed earlier. However, more recently, research has raised questions about the impact of the approach in respect of skill acquisition.

Practically the model involves allocating specific roles and responsibilities to pupils within a team structure. Such roles may include coach, trainer, equipment officer and team manager. Associated with each role would be a job description, for example, the coach would be responsible for the development of a training programme to teach specific skills, while the equipment officer would be responsible for the organisation and collection of equipment. The lesson may be structured around practice opportunities, before the teams engage in some form of competitive situation. This competition is cumulative, resulting in the development of a league-type structure. The model is run over an extended period of time, defined as a 'season', with a culminating event occurring at the end of the season. If the model is being used across class groups, the opportunity for a festival event occurs when all teams compete together. Throughout the process the pupils actively engage in record keeping, either by developing match reports or training programmes, which encourages the development of literacy skills. Further details using an example of this model in practice can be found on the companion website.

# Personalised system of instruction

A further model identified by Metzler (2011) is that of the personalised system of instruction. Such an approach allows pupils to guide their own learning and is therefore more appropriate for pupils with a developing level of cognitive ability, for example, those in the older primary age range. The basis of the model is that pupils are provided with a detailed work booklet assigning them specific tasks. Throughout the process pupils are required to check their progress either through the completion of individual tasks, or tasks which require feedback from their peers or from you as the facilitator.

An example of this would be the development of a progression workbook which provides structured steps for pupils to follow as well as the use of self-check lists. This reflects similar approaches used in teaching reading whereby pupils track their own progress.

## Case study

Pete is an experienced teacher of physical education. Whilst Pete had been teaching for some time and was receiving acceptable feedback on his lessons, his style was very command in its approach. His lesson planning was very skills focused with pupils taught through a series of drill-based activities. Because of the school Pete worked in, pupils were well behaved and consequently class management was not a problem.

Recently Pete has engaged in the weekly review of one of his lessons allowing him to receive feedback on his teaching. He was also required to review the video of his teaching and provide a self-evaluation.

It was clear from the start that Pete's command/didactive approach to teaching was limiting the progress of the pupils. His tendency to spend long periods of time on one activity was leading to a number of pupils becoming disengaged resulting in some evidence of low level disruption. Pupils were given limited feedback on their performance, although praise was often heard. Analysis of the lesson also showed a high level of teacher talk with limited levels of pupil activity.

Having read this chapter – what specific pedagogical approaches might you suggest Pete use to:

1    Make the lessons more pupil centred?
2    Increase activity levels?

## Task 7.3

The articles below identify issues that may be faced when learning to implement an instructional model. Read these articles and then reflect upon your experiences of implementing a chosen model during a school experience. Some of you may be interested in exploring this as a research project at either undergraduate or postgraduate level.

McCaughtry, N., Sofo, S., Rovegno, I. and Curtner-Smith, M. (2004) 'Learning to teach sport education: Misunderstandings, pedagogical difficulties, and resistance', *European Physical Education Review*, 10(2): 135–55.

McMahon, E. and MacPhail, A. (2007) 'Learning to teach sport education: The experiences of a pre-service teacher', *European Physical Education Review*, 13(2): 229–46.

## Task 7.4

1. Having explored a number of approaches to the teaching of physical education, provide a rationale for where and when you might use the different approaches within your own teaching.
2. Focusing on one specific approach, produce a medium-term plan showing how you might implement this approach within your own teaching (refer to Chapter 3 if you need further guidance on planning).

What is clearly evident from all the approaches introduced is that as a teacher of physical education you need to have a clear understanding of the following.

* 'What do I want my pupils to learn?'
* 'Why is this important?'
* 'How and where is learning taking place?'
* 'How will I know that learning has occurred?'

In essence, we are looking at the what, why, how and where of teaching. However, this chapter has only been able to scrape the surface of each model. Further readings are therefore provided below.

## Chapter summary

This chapter has reviewed a range of teaching strategies and models currently used in the delivery of physical education. The range of approaches is possibly more extensive than those you will have experienced as part of your own education. It is important that any teaching approach you adopt reflects the aims and objectives you have set for your class. Thus, in selecting a teaching approach you need to reflect upon your individual aims and objectives, and in doing so you may find that you adopt a range of approaches within a lesson. Tasks 7.3 and 7.4 provide you with an opportunity to reflect upon teaching approaches.

Hayes et al. (2006) state 'teachers need to create classroom environments that take into account ways in which students' learning can be supported, by providing an environment where students are not criticised for their efforts and where students are provided with the structures to help them achieve' (2006: 38).

To summarise your learning in this chapter you may benefit from reflecting on the following review questions.

*(Continued)*

*(Continued)*

1   What are the major models of instruction used in physical education?
2   What approaches to physical education have you adopted, or observed being used on a school-based placement?
    a   What was the rationale for using this approach?
    b   What did you see as the advantages and disadvantages of the approach?
    c   How would you modify the approach in the future?
3   How would you define pedagogy?

# Further reading

Griffin, L.L. and Butler, J.I. (eds) (2005) *Teaching Games for Understanding: Theory, Research and Practice*. Champaign, IL: Human Kinetics.
This text provides an overview of current thinking on TGFU. Drawing on individual experiences, it provides practical examples of how the approach can be delivered.

Metzler, M.W. (2011) *Instructional Models for Physical Education*, 3rd edn. Arizona: Holcomb Hathaway Publishers.
This text provides an overview of a range of instructional models that can be used within the physical education classroom. Providing a clear rationale for the concept of models-based instruction, it provides guidance for the implementation of the models in practice.

Mitchell, S.A., Oslin, J.L. and Griffin, L.L. (2006) *Teaching Sport Concepts and Skills. A Tactical Games Approach*, 2nd edn. Leeds: Human Kinetics.
This text provides an overview of the model as well as lesson plans for both games activities and levels of development.

Mosston, M. and Ashworth, S. (1994) *Teaching Physical Education*, 4th edn. New York: Macmillan College Publishing Company.
This text provides a clear overview of the 11 styles contained within their spectrum of teaching. It provides a range of practical application examples.

Siedentop, D., Hastie, P.A. and van der Mars, H. (2004) *Complete Guide to Sport Education*. Leeds: Human Kinetics.
This text provides details of how to successfully implement Sport Education into the curriculum. As well as providing practical applications, it also covers planning and organisation.

# Safe Practice in Physical Education

## Links to *Teachers' Standards*

In working through this chapter, you should develop your knowledge associated with the *Teachers' Standards* (DfE, 2011) detailed in Table 8.1.

## Introduction

Central to the learning experiences in physical education is the need to create a safe environment, where pupils feel able to contribute effectively across a range of activities.

**Table 8.1**  How this chapter links to the *Teachers' Standards* (DfE, 2011)

| | |
|---|---|
| Standard 1: Set high expectations which inspire, motivate and challenge pupils | • establish a safe and stimulating environment for pupils, rooted in mutual respect<br>• demonstrate consistently the positive attitudes, values and behaviour which are expected of pupils |
| Standard 3: Demonstrate good subject and curriculum knowledge | • have a secure knowledge of the relevant subject(s) and curriculum areas, foster and maintain pupils' interest in the subject, and address misunderstandings |
| Standard 5: Adapt teaching to respond to the strengths and needs of all pupils | • know when and how to differentiate appropriately, using approaches which enable pupils to be taught effectively |
| Standard 7: Manage behaviour effectively to ensure a good and safe learning environment | • have clear rules and routines for behaviour in classrooms, and take responsibility for promoting good and courteous behaviour both in classrooms and around the school, in accordance with the school's behaviour policy<br>• maintain good relationships with pupils, exercise appropriate authority, and act decisively when necessary |
| Standard 8: Fulfil wider professional responsibilities | • take responsibility for improving teaching through appropriate professional development, responding to advice and feedback from colleagues |

Consideration needs to be given to the organisation and management of the learning environment in respect of safety issues associated not only with specific activities, for example, athletic activities and OAA, but also with the organisation of equipment and learning spaces. We also need to look at health and safety associated with warming up and cooling down, so that pupils can engage fully with the learning activities.

In order to assess your own current level of understanding associated with safe practice in physical education, read and complete Task 8.1.

---

### Task 8.1

1  Using the six areas of activity identified in Chapter 1 (athletics, dance, games, gymnastics, swimming, and outdoor and adventurous activities) and your existing knowledge, produce a table identifying what you feel are the key safety issues that need to be planned for within physical education.
2  Produce a checklist that you can use during the planning process to take account of the issues you have identified.

---

## What pupils need to know about health and safety in a physical education context

It is important that everyone is involved in the management of safe practice, including the pupils you teach. Within general teaching requirements there is an expectation that pupils will be taught about health and safety in education. In any teaching environment, pupils need to have a clear understanding of how their behaviours and actions may impact on their own, and others', health and safety. This might include how they collect, return and move equipment as well as aspects of behaviour related to playing specific games. They need to understand the specific risks associated with individual activities in order to think about how these can be reduced. In essence, pupils need to develop an understanding of risks and how they can be involved in the control and management of these. Task 8.2 requires you to think about some of the strategies you might employ to develop pupils' understanding of these within your lessons.

---

### Task 8.2

1   Identify a set of key behaviours you expect pupils to demonstrate within your lessons, for example:

   a   how they enter and leave your lesson
   b   how they collect and return equipment
   c   what they should wear
   d   how they behave when getting changed.

2   For each activity provide a simple rationale for why they should behave in these ways.
3   Produce a set of resource cards which can be displayed in your classroom so that pupils know and understand what these behaviours are (you could ask pupils to produce these themselves to allow them to develop a deeper understanding).

---

# Health and safety across areas of activity

## Common principles

In many respects health and safety procedures reflect common sense. Common principles can be applied to all activities focusing on the facilities and equipment being used, what pupils are expected to wear (including footwear), the organisation of the activities being taught and staff competence to teach the specific skills. Table 8.2 provides an overview of the key principles that can be applied across areas of activity, although see James and Elbourn (2016) for further information.

Each activity will have contextual safety issues which we will explore in more detail as we move through this chapter, but generic principles are also evident, and we will look at these in more detail now.

**Table 8.2**    Common principles in healthy and safe practice

| | |
|---|---|
| Facilities | Are they fit for purpose? |
| | Are they well maintained? For example, are the facilities used by the general public as well as the school? |
| | Are playing/working surfaces safe? For example, are courts frequently swept, are leaves collected? |
| | Is access to and from the facility safe? For example, do pupils have to walk across roads or through car parks to access the facilities? |
| Equipment | Is it fit for purpose? |
| | Is it well maintained? Are faulty pieces of equipment removed? |
| | How will it be distributed and collected? Will all pupils collect equipment or will it be distributed by a small number or in small groups? |
| | Does it need to be moved in a specific manner? Does work need to be done on training pupils to move equipment? |
| Clothing/ footwear | Is it appropriate for the activity? For example, if outdoors, will they be warm enough? |
| | Is there a risk of it snagging on any equipment? For example, is it too baggy? |
| | Are trainers tied appropriately? |
| | Is the footwear appropriate for the activity being taught? For example, if on grass, do pupils need studs? |
| Pupils | Is long hair tied back? |
| | Is jewellery removed? (You will need to consider cultural and religious issues here) |
| | Are there any medical conditions affecting pupils? For example, do you know who is asthmatic, has allergies? |
| | Are they fully aware of expected behaviours? |
| Teachers and adults other than teachers | Do they have appropriate qualifications? |
| | Have they undertaken appropriate training with regard to safeguarding, the Prevent agenda and school policies and procedures? |
| Planning and organisation | Are lessons appropriately planned taking into account the age and ability of pupils? |
| | Are pupils appropriately challenged? |
| | Are pupils taught skills in the correct progression to ensure that they have the appropriate level of competence? |
| | Are clear behaviour management strategies employed? |
| | Are the learning environments appropriately managed? |
| | How are pupils grouped? |

## Knowledge of the activity being taught

As the teacher, you should have a sound level of knowledge and understanding of the activities that you are teaching. This should include appropriate warm-up and cool-down activities, the skills that need to be taught and the rules that apply to the activity. You should have a knowledge of and understand the needs of the pupils with whom you are working as well as the policies and procedures to which you must adhere.

During your initial teacher education you will receive or have received a general introduction to aspects of teaching physical education. You may feel that the amount of time spent learning about physical education does not always provide adequate depth of knowledge or sufficient opportunity to practise these skills during teaching placements. It is therefore important during your initial and early professional development that, when you are teaching a new activity or an activity that you have not taught for some time, you read up on the activity and its associated risks (a list of activity specific websites can be found on the companion website to support you with this). If you have any doubts about your ability to teach the activity then you could talk to and observe a more experienced teacher, or engage in professional development opportunities such as attending coaching courses run within your local area.

## Knowledge of developmental processes

You should have an understanding of the developmental processes in physical education and the activities pupils can be expected to perform at the different stages of development. These are often referred to as 'developmentally appropriate activities' (Chapters 4 and 5 look at these in more detail). As well as thinking about the progression of the activities to be taught, you also need to have an understanding of the pupils in your group, for example, do any of them have SEN and how will you manage these? You might wish to refer to Chapters 2 and 6 at this point. How this is then reflected in the planning of the learning episode was covered in Chapter 3. It is important that pupils are not expected to do activities that are too developmentally challenging and which require skills they have not had the opportunity to develop. We also need to give consideration to the perceived risk – that is the risk that pupils may perceive to exist in an activity they may regard as too challenging – and the actual risk involved. This tends to be lower than that which is perceived. This is very common in OAA and we will follow this up later in the chapter.

## Knowledge of first aid

Knowledge of basic first aid is advantageous, and this should be supported with a clear understanding of the medical procedures and policies in place where you are employed or at the facilities that you might use to deliver physical education, for example, local sport centres or local swimming pools. You should ensure that you know if any of your pupils have a medical condition (asthma is the most common) and that they have their medication with them (this should be labelled, especially if they are giving them to you for safe keeping). If you are taking pupils off site for extra-curricular activities, running practices out of school hours or taking them on residential trips, consent forms should be completed which clearly identify any potential medical conditions. You may wish to take additional qualifications in first aid through your school to ensure that you feel confident and competent to deal with situations as they arise.

## Knowledge of behaviour and classroom management strategies

You should have a sound knowledge of behaviour and classroom management strategies. These will be similar to those procedures already in place within your lessons, allowing pupils to understand that expected behaviours are common across subject areas. Pupils should be clear about what constitutes acceptable and unacceptable behaviour (you may well have developed this during the completion of Task 8.2). Rewards and sanctions should be applied consistently in line with school policy. In some cases you might develop sanctions which reflect practice within sporting activities, for example, issuing a green card as a warning about behaviour (commonly used in hockey), a yellow card which reflects sin-binning resulting in time out of the activity (used in rugby) or a red card when pupils are removed from the activity (used in football).

Most behaviour issues within a lesson stem from times when pupils are off task and no longer engaged in a focused learning activity. Task 8.3 requires you to start looking at this in more detail.

---

### Task 8.3: Behaviour management

1   From your experiences identify a range of opportunities for off-task behaviour to occur.
2   For each opportunity identify a series of strategies you might use to reduce the impact of these opportunities.

---

Having completed Task 8.3 you will have identified some major 'problem points' where off-task behaviour may occur. Table 8.3 identifies a number of off-task opportunities and potential strategies that can be used to reduce their impact. However, in managing pupils' behaviour in a physical education context you also need to consider concepts such as fair play to ensure that pupils do not become violent towards each other.

## Safeguarding pupils

'Safeguarding is action that is taken to promote the welfare of children, and protect them from harm' (James and Elbourn, 2016: 91). Whilst as the teacher it is your responsibility to create a safe and effective learning environment, you must also consider other risks to pupils' safety that might exist. You are also required to pass on any concerns you might have regarding the health and wellbeing of pupils you teach.

As a teacher, you should have an understanding of the concepts of 'intentional' and 'unintentional' harm. Intentional harm can be seen as 'including physical, emotional or sexual abuse, neglect, bullying (including online or cyberbullying), racist abuse,

**Table 8.3**   Strategies for managing behaviour

| Opportunity | Strategy |
|---|---|
| Arriving and departing from the lesson | Require pupils to line up prior to entering the lesson |
| | Have a controlled entry into the changing areas |
| Changing – before and after the lesson | Provide a designated changing area for each pupil, for example, boys change in one area, girls in another |
| | Be clear what pupils do once they have changed, for example, spare clothing is folded and left on their chair if changing in a classroom and pupils sit on the carpet area when they are changed |
| | Play a piece of music by the end of which all pupils should be ready to start the lesson |
| Moving between the changing and teaching space | Pupils walk in silence between the areas |
| Collecting, moving with, distributing and returning equipment | Designate specific pupils to collect equipment (this can be done when they are sitting on the carpet area at the start of the lesson) |
| | Limit the number of pupils collecting equipment for specific activities |
| | Number pupils and have only one pupil per group collecting equipment. This can be repeated to return equipment |
| | Be very specific about how equipment should be moved |
| | How gymnastic equipment should be carried |
| | Number of pupils |
| | Lifting techniques |
| Changing of activities | Limit the number of changes to activities |
| | Be clear about how much information pupils need to be given for each task |
| | Change the activity one group at a time so that you are not calling them all in at the same time |
| | Ask pupils to leave equipment in their working space so they are not 'playing' with it as you try to explain the next task |

harassment, discrimination and the potential for abuse of trust by adults working with children and young people' (James and Elbourn, 2016: 92).

You will be aware of the safety checks which are undertaken when you embark on initial teacher education programmes and when you take up your first post or engage in working with young people. You should also have undertaken some safeguarding training and been made aware of the procedures in place within your schools with regarding to the reporting of concerns. As teachers of physical education, we may be one of the few groups of people who spot intentional harm because of the need for pupils to change to participate in our subject. We should therefore know and be aware of the common signs of intentional harm, for example, bruising, mood changes or personality changes.

However, schools are also responsible for ensuring that any other adults working with pupils are subject to the same regulations as teachers. Therefore all coaches and individuals working with pupils should also be subject to vetting procedures in relation to disclosure and barring services.

Safeguarding pupils means much more than vetting who is teaching a pupil. It means ensuring that pupils feel safe in the environment they are working in. This includes their physical, emotional, social and personal wellbeing. Chapter 9 looks at this aspect in more depth, focusing on the use of external providers. It also means making sure that pupils are aware how they can discuss concerns with people they trust and the likely consequences of making such disclosures. Staff also need to be aware of their responsibilities in these situations specifically in relation to how to deal with concerns raised and therefore training and development activities should be an integral part of staff development throughout the academic year.

Consideration should also be given to the recording and use of images of pupils. Chapter 10 looks at how ICT skills can be developed through the use of videoing performances which are then reviewed to provide feedback. However, in the context of schools, detailed policies and procedures should be published in relation to, for example, use of photographic images and video recordings. There should be clear information for parents regarding school policies and reflecting the intentions of the Data Protection Act. Guidelines must include details regarding how these images are then stored or deleted. Your school will be able to provide further details about their specific policies and practices. However, with significant changes in the use of digital technology within the classroom and the increased use of tablets and apps within teaching, greater consideration must be given to the use and appropriateness of these in relation to the enhancement of learning within the curriculum.

This first section has looked at the generic principles and issues associated with creating and maintaining a safe environment for learning. The next section looks in more detail at the principles associated with warming up and cooling down in physical education.

## Warming up and cooling down in physical education

Warming up and cooling down is an integral component within safe practice in physical education. Pupils need to develop an understanding of the principles associated with preparing for and recovering from physical activity. Some of the pupils you teach will participate in physical activity away from the school environment and may experience different approaches. This may be beneficial for you as the teacher as you can encourage them to support you when warming up the rest of the class, but you yourself should be clear as to what activities should be included.

James and Elbourn (2016: 170–1) provide a detailed overview of the components, purpose and content of warm-ups so you are encouraged to purchase or gain access to their book. Specifically, they identify the components of the warm-up as:

- mobility exercises or controlled movements of the joints
- pulse raisers or whole-body activities

- stretches
- sport/activity-related movements.

When warming up or cooling down, consideration must also be given to what James and Elbourn (2016: 160–4) describe as the principles of safe practice exercise, namely control ('activities performed with control are easily stoppable and usually involve a smooth continuous action'), impact ('have any risks associated with high impact been minimised?'), alignment ('can the activity/exercise be performed with correct joint alignment?') and development appropriateness ('is the activity/exercise appropriate for the physical maturation of the student?').

In essence, a warm-up provides the opportunity for pupils to prepare their bodies for the activities they are expected to perform during the lesson. Therefore, the activities included within the warm-up should be closely aligned to those planned for during the lesson. During the warm-up pupils can start to think about what is happening to their body as they are warming up (this is covered in more detail in Chapter 10). Sport-specific warm-up activities can then be introduced, for example, activities that encourage a change in speed or direction as you would encounter in games activities; this may or may not use equipment relevant to the activity, but if introduced consideration must be given to its distribution. Once the muscles have warmed up, stretching activities can be introduced. These should be performed in a static position where the stretch is held for 6–8 seconds (James and Elbourn, 2016). What is important after the warm-up is that pupils remain active, which will require you to think about how you make the transition from the warm-up to the first activity.

When cooling down the emphasis is on returning the body to a resting level. You should move from energetic to more sedate activities requiring the body to work at ever decreasing speeds. The format is similar to the warm-up culminating in static stretching; however, this time stretches should be held for longer (15–30 seconds).

A range of warming up and cooling down activities can be found on the companion website including games and stretching. The section on further reading also identifies additional literature you may wish to access.

# Activity specific safety considerations

## Athletic activities

Chapter 5 looks at specific areas of activity relating to athletics. Consideration needs to be given to the organisation and management of the working area and equipment being used as well as the pupils being taught.

Within the school environment, the teaching of athletic activities takes place either on the school field or the school playground. Consideration needs to be given to the surface being used, for example, whether the grass is dry enough. Even in the height of the summer early morning lessons may be affected by dew on the grass causing it to be slippery and limiting activities such as throwing and jumping. Playground surfaces

**Table 8.4** Checklist for health and safety considerations in athletic activities

| Jumping | Throwing | Running |
|---|---|---|
| Is the area free from foreign objects? | Has a designated throwing area been identified? | Are the facilities and equipment being used fit for purpose? |
| Is the jumping surface dry? | Do pupils fully understand the rules regarding the activity including: | |
| Are the facilities and equipment being used fit for purpose? | • When to throw<br>• When to collect? | |
| | Is the throwing area dry and free from foreign objects? | |
| | Are the pupils appropriately spaced? | |

can also be affected by dampness as well as the build-up of grit, which presents a skid hazard. Below are key considerations you should plan for in throwing lessons. Table 8.4 provides a basic checklist for you to consider when planning lessons.

## The spacing of pupils during throwing activities

Pupils need to be placed a sufficient distance apart to ensure that during the release of the object they are not going to hit anyone else. This does not mean that all pupils have to throw from the same point one after the other, but it does require you to consider whether pupils throw at the same time, or in sequence. It is important that pupils move backwards once they have thrown. Not only is this one of the rules associated with throwing events (in that they must not step out of the front of the throwing area), but it also prevents pupils throwing and then walking out to collect at the same time as others may still be throwing. The easiest way to do this is to use cones to identify throwing areas, waiting areas and observation areas.

In order to increase levels of activity, a specified throwing area can be designated in the shape of a circle or fan (see Figure 8.1). Using such an approach, which can also be used in the teaching of striking skills in games activities allows a higher level of interaction.

## The hand from which the object is thrown

It would seem logical that if a pupil is throwing right-handed the flight path of the object will be different to that of objects thrown from the left hand. Consideration therefore needs to be given to where pupils stand in relation to others, with specific attention paid to the trajectory of the equipment being thrown.

## How the thrown object is collected

In many respects the teaching of throwing activities is best controlled in the first instance through the use of direct teaching approaches, overseen by you as the

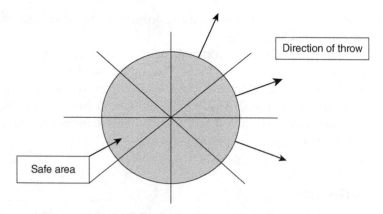

**Figure 8.1**   Throwing area in the shape of a circle or fan (adapted from Youth Sport Trust, 2004: 18)

teacher (see Chapter 7). Pupils are directed when to throw the object, normally being told when to do so. There is a tendency post-throw for pupils to walk out to collect their object. This is very dangerous particularly if others have yet to throw. Once pupils have thrown, they should return to the safe area which allows them to receive feedback from their partner about their performance, after which their partner or they should go and collect the object under the control of the teacher.

## Dance activities

When delivering dance activities, generic principles of health and safety should be addressed. These include ensuring that effective warm-up opportunities are planned for and delivered and that when specific techniques are required these are taught effectively and reflect the developmental maturity of pupils. Consideration also needs to be given to the facilities and spaces being used. In a primary school dance is likely to be taught in the school hall. If you draw a picture of your hall it probably includes a piano, seating, gymnastics equipment and dining tables. While this does not prevent the effective teaching of dance, consideration needs to be given to isolating these objects so that pupils do not climb or jump onto them, and so that they do not fall. You also need to ensure that the floor is clean and dry, especially after lunch. This will impact on the footwear you will require pupils to wear.

## Games activities

Consideration needs to be given to the playing surface, specifically to whether it is free from foreign objects, for example litter. This is particularly important if your field is open to public access. Playgrounds should be free from grit. Equipment should be developmentally appropriate, for example in hockey the sticks should be the right size for the pupils. You may need to consider using softer balls when introducing throwing and catching skills.

When establishing playing areas you will need to consider the size, as well as location in relation to other playing areas. You might want to provide grid areas either designated with line markings or the use of cones (further examples of this are included in Chapters 4 and 5). This limits pupils from running into each other's games. You will also need to think about where equipment is located and stored during activities, particularly if it is not in use.

## Gymnastic activities

Health and safety issues when teaching gymnastic activities focus on the facilities and the equipment being used. The nature of the activities taught in gymnastics requires the use of different pieces of equipment, for example, mats, benches, movement tables, wall bars. Mats need to be stored correctly so mat trolleys should be used which require mats to be stored flat or held in a vertical position. When placed on the floor the mats should be flat to avoid a trip hazard. They should be free of holes and, as with all gymnastic equipment, they should be checked and serviced regularly. Gymnastic equipment is not cheap, and therefore pupils should be taught how to look after it in regard to its storage, carriage and use.

Benches should sit flat on the floor and you should avoid placing them on mats which can cause them to rock. If using wooden benches, these need to be free of splinters and varnished regularly. Foam-topped benches need to be checked for holes which may cause a reduction in the padding. When using benches, consideration also needs to be given to the location of mats around them. A mat will tend to indicate an exit point off the equipment and this can be used to control movement around the equipment. However, a mat can also be interpreted as a landing point, and therefore you will need to be very clear about whether pupils can jump off the equipment. This links to aspects of impact already discussed.

Movement tables raise similar issues to benches. They offer the potential to increase the height at which skills are performed and therefore you will need to specify how you expect pupils to exit the piece of equipment. This is particularly important when jumping off.

As with all equipment, wall bars need regular servicing. Activities taught using wall bars encourage the use of height so depending on the age of pupils you may consider limiting the height which they are allowed to climb to.

## Outdoor and adventurous activities

If teaching OAA, such as orienteering and basic problem solving in schools, the same generic principles associated with health and safety apply. Consideration needs to be given to the location of the teacher in relation to the pupils doing the activity. You need to be confident that you can be seen by the pupils in your class as much as possible, but also need to have some form of signal should you need them to return to the lesson base at any point. When completing problem-solving activities, consideration needs to be given to the equipment being used, as well as the surfaces on which the activities are being completed.

If you are involved in residential-based activities you will need to have a detailed knowledge and understanding of the potential risks associated with each activity. While the instructors delivering the sessions will have responsibility for the specific activities, you will still be expected to reinforce expectations around behaviour management. You may find that you take responsibility for activities during the evenings and you should make sure that you fully understand any safety procedures that need to be adhered to.

## Swimming-based activities

In swimming-based activities you need to ensure pupils understand how to behave appropriately in and around the pool. For example, pupils will need to learn appropriate behaviours associated with changing, moving around the area, for example, by not running, and entering and exiting the pool (see the companion website for further details). You will need to understand the roles and responsibilities of different individuals involved in the delivery of swimming, as well as how pupils travel to and from the pool and how they are monitored in the changing rooms. There is also a need to reflect upon the organisation of the learning environment in which pupils will be working.

# Assessing risk

When embarking on any activity for the first time, you should undertake a risk assessment. This process requires you to look at the activity and assess potential problems (risks) and how you intend to reduce the potential for them to occur, and consider any actions you might need to take. Each school will have a policy and staff member with overall responsibility for the co-ordination of these assessments. However, it is everyone's responsibility to undertake risk assessments and understand the actions that must be undertaken in relation to their implementation and review. It is important that you also apply these to any external facilities that you might use. Many schools require site visits to be undertaken prior to using external facilities, so factors such as transport, changing and access to medical support might all become important requirements. Examples of risk assessments can be found on the companion website, although a detailed template for on-site and off-site activities can be found in James and Elbourn (2016).

## Chapter summary

This chapter provides a brief overview of the key principles associated with safe practice in physical education. To consolidate your learning, you should now spend some time completing the review questions below.

1    What are the key principles associated with the safe delivery of effective physical education lessons?
2    For each of the six activity areas, identify a set of rules you would expect your pupils to adhere to.
3    Produce risk assessments for a range of the activities you teach – add these to your portfolio.

## Further reading

James, A. and Elbourn, J. (2016) *Safe Practice: In Physical Education, School Sport and Physical Activity*. Leeds: Coachwise Ltd.
Written specifically for physical education practitioners this comprehensive text provides specific guidance across activity areas and sports. It also provides general guidance on areas such as competence, curriculum management, use of facilities, off-site activities and safeguarding pupils.

# 9

# Health and Wellbeing

## Chapter aims

- To develop an understanding of the underlying models and theories relating to children's health and wellbeing
- To identify and explore factors which influence children's health and wellbeing
- To discuss key policies associated with children's health and wellbeing
- To apply models, theories and policies to the primary context

## Links to *Teachers' Standards*

In working through this chapter, you should develop your knowledge associated with the *Teachers' Standards* (DfE, 2011) detailed in Table 9.1.

## Introduction

The health and wellbeing of the individual is rightly gaining prominence in understanding pupils' behaviour and performance in school. Factors such as

**Table 9.1**  How this chapter links to the *Teachers' Standards* (DfE, 2011)

| | |
|---|---|
| Standard 1: Set high expectations which inspire, motivate and challenge pupils | • establish a safe and stimulating environment for pupils, rooted in mutual respect<br>• demonstrate consistently the positive attitudes, values and behaviour which are expected of pupils |
| Standard 5: Adapt teaching to respond to the strengths and needs of all pupils | • have a secure understanding of how a range of factors can inhibit pupils' ability to learn, and how best to overcome these<br>• demonstrate an awareness of the physical, social and intellectual development of children, and know how to adapt teaching to support pupils' education at different stages of development |
| Standard 8: Fulfil wider professional responsibilities | • communicate effectively with parents with regard to pupils' achievements and wellbeing |

eating, exercise, social interactions, social media and the digital era all influence how children grow and develop. Research (Kohl et al., 2012; Standage et al., 2012) shows that current levels of activity amongst children are insufficient to maintain health and wellbeing, and that this is a global rather than a national issue.

Eime et al. (2013) argue that when looking at physical activity and physical health there is a tendency to focus around issues associated with obesity and that the corresponding impact on social emotional aspects are less focused on. They show that there is a strong argument that 'children who are active through sport are more likely to be physically active in adulthood than those who do not participate' (2013: 2). However, how the individual feels about themselves within a physical context is key for sustained participation. In Chapter 2 we looked at how the affective domain of development can be developed and how within this we can focus on the development of the individual's self-esteem and motivation to encourage greater levels of involvement. Therefore, when working in the context of physical education it becomes clear that the social and emotional aspects of the context become crucial in understanding how and why pupils may behave and react.

There is clear evidence over the past decade that a more multi-faceted approach to understanding and reacting to issues around health and wellbeing has been undertaken, most notably across health and education professionals. This is to some extent reflected in current guidelines suggesting that levels of physical activity as detailed by the Department of Health (2011a) vary across age ranges as detailed in Table 9.2.

As teachers of physical education, we have the capacity to influence the experiences pupils have of physical activity. The school environment offers a number of opportunities for pupils to engage in physical activity, be it on the way to or from school, during breaks within the school day, through timetabled physical education lessons, and through classroom-based activity. However, as discussed in Chapter 1, our attitudes, beliefs and values around the subject impact either positively or negatively on the experiences of the pupils we teach. In addition, as role models, we have

**Table 9.2** Recommended physical activity (Department of Health, 2011b)

| Early years (under 5s) | Children and young people (5–18 years) |
|---|---|
| Physical activity should be encouraged from birth, particularly through outdoor-based play and water-based activities in safe environments. | All children and young people should engage in moderate to vigorous intensity physical activity for at least 60 minutes and up to several hours every day. |
| Children of pre-school age who are capable of walking unaided should be physically active daily for at least 180 minutes (3 hours), spread throughout the day. | Vigorous intensity activities, including those that strengthen muscle and bone, should be incorporated at least three days a week. |
| All under 5s should minimise the amount of time spent being sedentary (being restrained or sitting) for extended periods (except time spent sleeping). | All children and young people should minimise the amount of time spent being sedentary (sitting) for extended periods. |

the capacity to demonstrate expected behaviours around healthy eating and exercise. Therefore, we may have to look at our own levels of activity or inactivity and reflect on how we might look to not only increase the activity levels of our pupils but potentially the activity of ourselves.

In looking at how we can improve the health and wellbeing of our pupils through physical education we must first develop an understanding of why it is important to do so, and the impact it might have on the overall development and performance of the pupil. In Chapter 2 we reviewed theories of learning and development. In this section we will make reference to some of those already identified, but also explore others that allow us to develop a deeper understanding of how children's health and wellbeing evolves.

Whilst not an exhaustive list, Figure 9.1 provides a timeline of the key theories associated with health and wellbeing. However, for the purpose of this chapter we will focus on those of Erikson (1963) and Havighurst (1972).

Central to the theories identified is the acknowledgement of developmental viewpoints. These are common beliefs around development and progress amongst individuals. Specifically, these development viewpoints are believed to be:

- Phase stage – that is changes in behaviours reflect age periods, suggesting that at or during certain age ranges common behaviours exist.
- Developmental tasks – that is specific tasks must be achieved to show developmental progress.

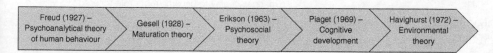

**Figure 9.1** Key theories associated with health and wellbeing

- Developmental milestones – that is key milestones must be achieved that gauge the level of development.
- Dynamic system – that suggests change may not be smooth.

In identifying development in such a way, it allows us as teachers to think about how our classes will be developing and the specific tasks we might expect them to achieve. However, it also allows us to identify when progress may not be what is expected and focus us on the fact that not all pupils will progress in the same way and that their experiences of this progression will be different.

Erikson argued that psychosocial development occurs across the life course of the individual. His eight stages of man (Erikson, 1995) identifies that the individual undergoes a series of crises during their development and is required to resolve these crises prior to movement to the next level of development. Table 9.3 identifies the key stages that occur in a primary context.

Whilst Erikson focused on emotional and relational aspects of development, Robert Havighurst focused more on how the *environment* in which the individual develops impacts on their development, and in doing so identifies key characteristics or expected behaviours that the individual should develop across distinct phases (see Table 9.4).

**Table 9.3** Erikson's (1963) psychosocial theory in relation to the primary context

| Stage | Approximate age | Characteristics |
|---|---|---|
| Trust vs mistrust | Infancy | A bond develops between the mother and child resulting in a reciprocal relationship forming |
| Autonomy vs doubt and shame | Toddler | Opportunities for autonomy become more evident |
| | | Development of self-control |
| | | Exploration evident |
| | | Development of the need for active play |
| Initiative vs guilt | Pre-school | Development of conscience |
| | | Aim for accomplishment |
| Industry vs interiority | School age | Interaction with peers |
| | | Status starts to develop |
| | | Mastery encouraged with reinforcement of success required |
| | | Dependency moves away from home to peers/school |
| | | Gender groups form |
| | | Changes in play to become more role-focused |
| Identify vs role confusion | Early adolescence | Masculinity vs femininity |
| | | Acceptance vs rejection |
| | | Conflict between what peers and society say |
| | | Role model play an increasing impact |
| | | Seeking place in society |

**Table 9.4**    Havighurst's key characteristics (1972)

| Age | Characteristics |
| --- | --- |
| Infancy and childhood (birth to 5) | Walks, eats solids, talks |
| | Becomes able to control bodily functions |
| | Starts to develop an understanding of differences between genders |
| | Starts to acquire language |
| | Begins to understand reality |
| Middle childhood (6 to 12 years) | Physical development |
| | Positive attitudes develop |
| | Starts relation building and getting on with others |
| | Enhancement of reading, writing and calculating |
| | Exhibits behaviour associated with integration |
| | Development of values and independence |

Emerging from these theories is the evolving social development of pupils during the primary phases of education. It is clear that the way the individual interacts with others in a social context is evolving and therefore it becomes important to recognise that the creation of opportunities for such interactions to occur becomes important. Embedding opportunities for pupils to interact with each other through play-based activities, resulting in them developing a better understanding of themselves in relation to others becomes an important component of their learning within the school context. We will be aware from our own school days and probably subsequent to them, how relationships develop and change so understanding that this is taking place and building in opportunities for pupils to develop such skills can become an integral part of the lessons we teach (as referred to in Chapter 3).

Having identified that these changes are taking place, it is also important to understand what might influence development. Task 9.1 provides you with an opportunity to reflect on these.

## Task 9.1

Drawing on your own experience and re-reading Chapter 2, produce a mind map to show factors that might influence the health and wellbeing of children.

1    How are these factors addressed in the schools you have worked in?
2    What are the implications in the teaching of physical education?

Having completed Task 9.1 you might have produced something similar to Figure 9.2 below.

Figure 9.2 clearly identifies a range of areas and influences that we must consider if we are to effectively support the health and wellbeing of the individuals with whom we work. We already know that the age of the individual will impact on their emotional state, particularly if their rates of development are different to that of the majority of others in their class. We appreciate that different pupils have different states of readiness to learn and for some this is influenced by the environmental influence upon them, for example the social interactions they experience away from the school environment both in relation to those with whom they socialise as well as the level of stimulation within that environment. Further, their diet may impact on their ability to access learning. If you think about your class, how many are classed as over- or underweight? How many struggle to engage in physical activity? How many withdraw from physical activity? However, the extent to which we can influence certain aspects is limited and therefore we should look to focus on those areas in which we can have the most impact.

Thus it starts to become clear that supporting children's health and wellbeing is a key requirement to support learning. The next section identifies some of the key publications coming out of England that look to support the promotion of the health and wellbeing of pupils published over the last 15 years. However, the further reading section does provide some additional resources for those who wish to look at health and wellbeing within other contexts and countries.

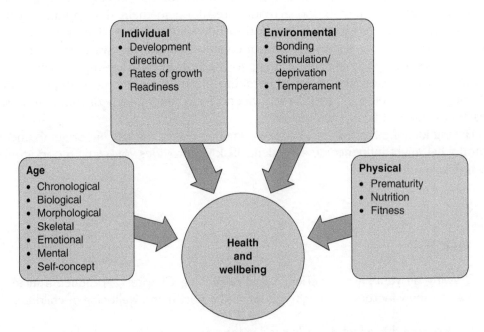

**Figure 9.2**  Potential factors influencing the health and wellbeing of pupils

Many of us will have experienced the *Every Child Matters* (ECM) initiative (Cabinet Office, 2003). It aimed to achieve the following (2003: 5–6):

- Being healthy: enjoying good physical and mental health and living a healthy lifestyle.
- Staying safe: being protected from harm and neglect.
- Enjoying and achieving: getting the most out of life and developing the skills for adulthood.
- Making a positive contribution: being involved with the community and society and not engaging in anti-social or offending behaviour.
- Economic wellbeing: not being prevented by economic disadvantage from achieving their full potential in life.

Undertaken as a result of failures in agencies associated with working with children and young adults, this publication became embedded in the ethos and practices of schools.

The development of the *Social, Emotional Aspects of Learning* (SEAL) initiative by the Department for Education and Skills in 2005, provided resources in the form of guidance materials and associated activities for teachers to support pupils. Whilst no longer commercially available, resources can still be found on the internet and links to relevant sites are included at the end of this chapter.

The *Healthy Child Programme* (Department of Health, 2009) reinforced the fact that 'Lifestyles and habits established during childhood, adolescence and young adulthood influence a person's health throughout their life' (2009: 11). Here the responsibility placed on schools focused on not only the emotional aspects for the individual, but placed a greater emphasis on how schools might influence the health of their pupils. Table 9.5 provides more details regarding the specific foci of this and the initiatives that were put in place to support it, many of which are still evident in the schools in which we work. You may find it useful to identify within your school the initiatives that are embedded within your practice resulting from this publication.

**Table 9.5**  Focused initiatives within schools relating to the health and wellbeing of the pupil as a result of the publication of the *Healthy Child Programme* (Department of Health, 2009)

| | | |
|---|---|---|
| Emotional health, psychological wellbeing and mental health | Promoting healthy weight (healthy schools) | Long standing illness or disability |
| Social aspects of learning | Physical activity (change for life) | |
| Bullying | PE Premium | |
| | Nutrition (breakfast clubs) | |

As with many centrally controlled initiatives a change in government tends to result in a change in philosophy. Thus, moving forward ECM became embedded within a new policy and practice in 2011. The introduction of the Pupil Premium (2011) focused on providing additional resources for eligible pupils. Eligibility for the grant includes those on free school meals, looked after children (those in care or who have been in care) and children whose parents are in the armed services. Grants are calculated and paid to schools based on the number of pupils within each group (each group attracts different levels of funding), but schools are responsible for providing details of how the funding is spent to support learning and the impact it has. This accountability is also monitored through routine inspections.

More recently, Public Health England (2014) in their publication *The Link Between Pupil Health and Wellbeing and Attainment* identified the following:

- Pupils with better health and wellbeing are likely to achieve better academically.
- Effective social and emotional competencies are associated with greater health and wellbeing, and better achievement.
- The culture, ethos and environment of a school influences the health and wellbeing of pupils and their readiness to learn.
- A positive association exists between academic attainment and physical activity levels of pupils. (PHE, 2014: 4)

Again the emphasis was to provide clear evidence of how supporting pupils in relation to their health and wellbeing impacts positively on their overall attainment. This focus continues with the publication of *Promoting Children and Young People's Emotional Health and Wellbeing* (PHE, 2015). This publication reinforced the argument that emotional health and wellbeing is known to impact on the cognitive development of the individual and consequently their ability to access learning opportunities. The publication suggested that supporting health and wellbeing was multi-faceted, focusing on the following seven principles (PHE, 2015: 6).

- Leadership and management: governance, improvement planning, policies, compliance.
- School ethos and environment: working practice, relationships and belonging, respect, values.
- Curriculum and teaching: PSHE curriculum, assessment of learning, resilience, mindset.
- Student voice: part of decision making, social networking.
- Staff development, health and wellbeing; training and development, support for staff, work–life balance.
- Working with parents and carers: interventions, communications, support activities.
- Targeted support: understanding home circumstances.

Emerging from this publication was that in focusing on the health and wellbeing of pupils, the health and wellbeing of colleagues should also be considered. In previous chapters (see Chapter 3 on planning and Chapter 7 on approaches to teaching) we have acknowledged the influence the teacher has on the creation of effective learning environments. This publication highlighted a growing recognition that the health and wellbeing of teachers and those working in the school environment was equally important.

Building on this, *Mental Health and Behaviour in Schools* (DfE, 2015) argues that schools have a role in supporting the development of resilience and understanding of mental health. The document details the characteristics of the mentally healthy, the factors influencing mental health and possible interventions that can be put into place. Further details are included in Table 9.6.

So, what contribution can physical education make to support pupils in this area? Eime et al. (2013), in reviewing recent research, detail clear evidence which shows that sport and physical activity participation reduces suicide rates, anxiety levels, depression and feelings of isolation. Further, it supports social development in relation to relationship formation, teamwork and social skills. In relation to emotional development engagement has been shown to support confidence, self-esteem, wellbeing, self-efficacy, perceived competence and resilience. Thus, it is easy to see why the more recent governmental initiatives promote many of these as areas that need to be addressed in schools.

In unpicking health and wellbeing, a central aspect is the emotional impact on the individual. Here we need to address the concept of motivation. We must understand why pupils decide to participate in an activity and then continue to persist. In Chapter 2 we briefly looked at the development of the pupil through the affective domain. Pupils need to develop an understanding of the benefits of exercise and its positive impact on them. The key is to hook the pupil into an activity that they enjoy and

**Table 9.6** Characteristics of the mentally healthy, factors that impact on mental health and interventions that can be put into place to support mental health (DfE, 2015)

| Characteristics of the mentally healthy | Factors affecting mental health | Interventions to support mental health |
| --- | --- | --- |
| Development | Physical | PSHE |
| Relationships | Emotional | Classroom management |
| Happy to be on their own | Communication | Social skills |
| Awareness of others | Temperament | Working with parents |
| Play and learning | Success | Peer mentoring |
| Morals and values | Esteem | |
| Resilience | Family relationships | |

conversely wish to continue. Ryan and Deci (2008) identify three key aspects of an activity maintaining motivation. The activity should have a level of *autonomy* – that is the pupil has a degree of choice in engaging in it. The pupil should have the level of *competence* required to be successful in the activity – success breeds success; how this is managed can be one of the most influential impacts on motivation. We can probably all remember when a teacher told us we were not good at something and how that made us feel as well as the impact on our continued engagement in the activity. Finally, the activity has some form of *relatedness* – that is the pupils see how engaging in the activity links to a bigger picture. In their article which investigated motivation and its use to predict physical activity, Standage et al. (2012) show that incorporating the three concepts (autonomy, competence, relatedness) into our teaching has a positive impact on the individual's physical self-concept – that is how an individual feels about themselves physically – as well as their health-related quality of life.

In this section we have reviewed a number of recent governmental and research publications that focus on the health and wellbeing agenda. Task 9.2 provides you with an opportunity to reflect on these and what initiatives have emerged from them and how these are becoming embedded within your own school.

## Task 9.2

Research (for example Standage et al., 2012) suggests that when an individual chooses to participate in an activity they are more likely to persist in it. Recent governmental initiatives and publications have highlighted the role of health and wellbeing on the development of the individual and the impact it has on learning.

Using the school you work in, look at the activities currently undertaken within the school to support pupils' health and wellbeing. Produce an overview and identify what aspect of health and wellbeing this might impact upon. For example:

| Activity | Who can access | Aspect of health and wellbeing addressed |
| --- | --- | --- |
| Breakfast club | Those on Pupil Premium receive this free; others who attend pay a small fee | Nutrition Social interactions |
| Fruit | All | Nutrition |
| Wake Up Shake Up | All | Physical fitness |

Review your list:

- Do the activities cover all aspects of health and wellbeing?
- What areas would benefit from more focus?

Plan a half term programme to address this shortfall.

# Implications for you as a teacher of physical education

Review of literature and initiatives indicates that in general primary pupils should be engaging in physical activity for no less than 60 minutes per day. Evidence suggests that even activities that last as little as 10 minutes will have an impact, and for many it is likely that exercise of this duration would be more sustainable. We must therefore look to create ways in which this can be achieved. The next sections look at a range of activities that can become embedded within the school context.

## Primary PE Premium

Introduced in 2013 the Primary Physical Education and Sports Premium provides funding for schools to support the growth and development of physical education and sport across the school. Specifically, the Department for Education argued that the vision for the funding was to ensure 'All pupils leaving primary school physically literate and with the knowledge, skills and motivation necessary to equip them for a healthy, active lifestyle and lifelong participation in physical activity and sport' (available at: www.sportscoachuk.org/node/326994 [accessed 4 December 2016]).

The objective is 'To achieve self-sustaining improvement in the quality of PE and sport in primary schools' and is measured against five key indicators:

- the engagement of all pupils in regular physical activity – kick-starting healthy active lifestyles
- the profile of PE and sport being raised across the school as a tool for whole school improvement
- increased confidence, knowledge and skills of all staff in teaching PE and sport
- broader experience of a range of sports and activities offered to all pupils
- increased participation in competitive sport. (www.sportscoachuk.org/node/326994)

Schools are offered the following advice regarding how to use the funding:

* hire qualified sports coaches to work with teachers
* provide existing staff with training or resources to help them teach PE and sport more effectively
* introduce new sports or activities and encourage more pupils to take up sport
* support and involve the least active children by running or extending school sports clubs, holiday clubs and Change4Life clubs
* run sport competitions
* increase pupils' participation in the School Games
* run sports activities with other schools.

Schools are required to publish details of how they have spent their premium with Ofsted also inspecting its use as part of their routine inspections. Guidance regarding publication of usage is provided by the Association for Physical Education and Youth Sport Trust.

# Initiatives in school

## Activity challenges

Many primary school pupils like to be challenged. Activity challenges are a good way of encouraging pupils to engage in an activity and encouraging them to record their progress. I am sure many of you will set yourselves a health and fitness goal from time to time and then actively pursue it and record your progress.

One activity challenge might be to record how they come to school (thereby linking to active transport, see below). Another might be to record the number of steps they take during the day. Older pupils could be encouraged to keep an exercise diary in which they record their out of school activities. All of these methods generate data which can be used within, for example, mathematics or science lessons for simple calculations or graphs.

## Active transport

Active transport is defined by Sport Otago (2016) as 'physical activity undertaken as a means of transport. It can include walking, cycling, using a scooter, skateboard, rollerskates or rollerblades'. The argument is that such methods increase activity levels and reduce congestion and associated issues around pollution. Linked to this approach is the use of walking buses which are commonly seen in our primary catchment areas. Here an adult is designated as the driver and walks a predetermined route picking up pupils (passengers) from designated 'bus stops'.

## Alternative activities

Schools are now encouraging pupils to participate in a range of alternative activities, for example, alternative dance activities including street dance and Zumba are now commonly seen in schools. More health-related activities such as Yoga are now embedded in the curriculum. For the more energetic, activities such as parkour and kin ball are becoming more popular (although you do need to be clear about the health and safety implications of these activities).

## Apps and tracking

Apps for electronic devices can also be used to support physical activity. A simple 'google' will highlight some of the key ones. These can then be linked to a television screen to support mass participation. The use of pedometers is also becoming more prevalent in schools, to record pupils' activity levels and distance covered, although again the implication of using such devises in relation to health and safety needs to be assessed and monitored.

## Bikeability

Bikeability is a United Kingdom initiative supported by the Department for Transport to provide basic training to pupils around safe cycling practice. Delivered on the school site and surrounding roads the programme is split into three levels; the programme moves pupils from basic balance and control to the skills they require to negotiate busier roads and situations. Again, this initiative supports the promotion of active transport in providing pupils with the skills necessary to travel to and from school safely.

## Exergaming

Go on, admit it, we've all enjoyed a dance mat challenge or playing sport/exercising using the Wii or X-Box. The British Heart Foundation (BHF) define exergaming as 'A screen-based activity which combines video game play with exercise and requires participants to use bodily movements to control and play games' (BHF, 2012: 1). Their report concluded that although there were no significant fitness benefits from participating in exergaming, it did reduce sedentary behaviours associated with poor health. However, more recent research (Ma and Qu, 2016) indicates that exergaming may have a positive impact on the development of eye–hand co-ordination in primary school pupils, as well as improving motivation and engagement in physical activity.

## Healthy eating initiatives

Encouraging pupils to eat healthy foods is a key aspect of promoting healthy and active lifestyles. There is a growing concern amongst many teachers about the number of pupils arriving at school without having eaten breakfast, an issue that is known to impact on their ability to concentrate during the school day. This has seen a rise in the number of schools offering breakfast clubs. A number of schools now also run sessions for pupils to bring their parents around to healthy eating. A popular one looks at the making of fruit kebabs.

Many schools now have gardening clubs where pupils are encouraged to grow, harvest, cook and eat their own produce. Research (Nelson et al., 2011) suggests that there are significant benefits from engaging pupils in growing their own food, including reengagement of disaffected pupils, development of scientific knowledge as well as the development of more positive attitudes towards healthy eating. Support materials for engaging in, establishing and maintaining gardening activities are widely available. You might wish to access the Royal Horticultural Society website at https://schoolgardening.rhs.org.uk/resources and download some of their resources.

## Fitness clubs

Run predominantly before or after schools these clubs provide basic fitness activities. Circuit training activities such as step ups, ladders, press ups, sit ups and speed bounce are common activities requiring limited equipment. Again, pupils can be encouraged to set individual targets for development and track their progress.

## Morning exercise

Seen in many Asian countries (in particular China and Singapore) morning exercise is a mass participation activity with all pupils (and sometimes staff) taking part in a formal series of exercise routines. The focus is on stretching, whole body movements and cardiovascular activity to include hopping and running. In the United Kingdom, a similar activity 'Wake Up Shake Up' is seen in many schools. Routines are easily accessible via YouTube, with routines lasting between 5 to 10 minutes.

## Outdoor gyms

You may have seen the introduction of outdoor gyms springing up in local parks. The concept is now becoming more evident in primary playgrounds as we look for creative ways to increase activity levels.

# Initiatives available outside of school

## Junior Parkrun

A hybrid of the increasingly popular Parkrun, junior Parkrun is designed for children aged 4 to 14 to run 2km. Events tend to run alongside those for older runners, and it is seen as an innovative way of increasing engagement of young people in basic fitness activities.

## Change4Life

A national initiative, this programme provides a range of advice, guidance and resources to encourage increased levels of activity and healthy eating. For primary school pupils, high intensity activities (over a 10-minute period) linked to recent Disney films provide fun and motivational resources.

### Chapter summary

In reading this chapter you should have started to develop a more detailed understanding of the theories and policies currently focusing on children's health and wellbeing. It is clear that there are many factors that can influence this, and as teachers and, more specifically, teachers of physical education it becomes important that we understand how we can facilitate knowledge and have a positive impact.

Take some time to consider how you could enhance the range of activities you undertake in school to support and nurture pupils' health and wellbeing.

## Further reading

Department for Education (2016) *Keeping Children Safe in Education: Statutory Guidance for Schools and Colleges*. London: DfE.
This document focuses on safeguarding, abuse and neglect and other factors which might impact on children.

International Conference on Educational Monitoring and Evaluation (2012) *Wellbeing at School*. CIEP documentary Resource Center, October 2012.
This bibliography provides abstracts from a range of published literature focusing on the wellbeing of pupils in schools. It also provides links to specific case studies as well as national organisations that support initiatives within schools.

## Useful websites/weblinks

Bikeability – http://bikeability.org.uk

Department of Education for Western Australia – http://det.wa.edu.au/curriculumsupport/physicalactivity/detcms/navigation/teaching-and-learning-support/take-the-challenge/

Exercise Move Dance Academy – www.emdacademy.org/home

Food Growing – www.foodgrowingschools.org

Royal Horticultural Society – https://schoolgardening.rhs.org.uk/resources

Social and Emotional Aspects of Learning – http://webarchive.nationalarchives.gov.uk/20110809101133/nsonline.org.uk/node/87009; http://webarchive.nationalarchives.gov.uk/20130401151715/https:/www.education.gov.uk/publications/eOrderingDownload/SEAL%20Guidance%202005.pdf

Evidencing impact of the Primary PE and Sport Premium – www.afpe.org.uk/images/stories/Evidencing_the_Impact_-_Guidance__Impact_Resource_Web_Version.pdf

School Games – www.yourschoolgames.com

Change4Life – www.nhs.uk/10-minute-shake-up/shake-ups?filter=dory#vO4k6gkLRR LK2oPV.97

School Wellbeing – www.schoolwellbeing.co.uk

Fact sheets – www.gov.uk/government/uploads/system/uploads/attachment_data/file/213739/dh_128144.pdf

Wake Up Shake Up – www.wakeupshakeup.com

Yoga at School – www.yogaatschool.org.uk

# 10

# Promoting Physical Education Across the Curriculum

## Chapter aims

- To develop a greater understanding of how physical education can be used to enhance learning across the curriculum
- To develop an understanding of cross-curricular themes evident within the school environment
- To provide a range of practical activities designed to support cross-subject and cross-curricular learning

## Links to *Teachers' Standards*

In working through this chapter, you should develop your knowledge associated with the *Teachers' Standards* (DfE, 2011) detailed in Table 10.1.

## Introduction

Previous chapters have looked at the role of physical education in developing pupils' competences across a range of physical activities. However, in defining physical education in Chapter 1, we acknowledged that physical education was more than just being physically active. Chapter 2 looked at the processes associated

**Table 10.1** How this chapter links to the *Teachers' Standards* (DfE, 2011)

| | |
|---|---|
| Standard 1: Set high expectations which inspire, motivate and challenge pupils | • establish a safe and stimulating environment for pupils, rooted in mutual respect |
| Standard 2: Promote good progress and outcomes by pupils | • guide pupils to reflect on the progress they have made and their emerging needs |
| | • demonstrate knowledge and understanding of how pupils learn and how this impacts on teaching |
| | • encourage pupils to take a responsible and conscientious attitude to their own work and study |
| Standard 3: Demonstrate good subject and curriculum knowledge | • have a secure knowledge of the relevant subject(s) and curriculum areas, foster and maintain pupils' interest in the subject, and address misunderstandings |
| | • demonstrate a critical understanding of developments in the subject and curriculum areas, and promote the value of scholarship |
| | • demonstrate an understanding of and take responsibility for promoting high standards of literacy, articulacy and the correct use of standard English, whatever the teacher's specialist subject |
| Standard 4: Plan and teach well-structured lessons | • promote a love of learning and children's intellectual curiosity |
| | • contribute to the design and provision of an engaging curriculum within the relevant subject area(s) |
| Standard 5: Adapt teaching to respond to the strengths and needs of all pupils | • have a secure understanding of how a range of factors can inhibit pupils' ability to learn, and how best to overcome these |
| | • demonstrate an awareness of the physical, social and intellectual development of children, and know how to adapt teaching to support pupils' education at different stages of development |
| Standard 6: Make accurate and productive use of assessment | • give pupils regular feedback, both orally and through accurate marking, and encourage pupils to respond to the feedback |
| Standard 7: Manage behaviour effectively to ensure a good and safe learning environment | • manage classes effectively, using approaches which are appropriate to pupils' needs in order to involve and motivate them |
| Standard 8: Fulfil wider professional responsibilities | • make a positive contribution to the wider life and ethos of the school |
| | • develop effective professional relationships with colleagues, knowing how and when to draw on advice and specialist support |
| | • take responsibility for improving teaching through appropriate professional development, responding to advice and feedback from colleagues |

with learning and how physical education may contribute to an individual's development across the different learning domains. The purpose of this chapter is to draw on these two chapters further to acknowledge the breadth of learning opportunities physical education has the potential to offer for the development and application of knowledge, skills and understanding across curriculum subjects, and of key themes or skills evident in curriculum design.

From its inception, the National Curriculum has encouraged the development of learning across the curriculum, including the promotion of: pupils' spiritual, moral, social and cultural development; citizenship; key communication, numeracy and ICT skills; working with others; improving one's own learning and problem-solving; and thinking skills. In its most recent iteration the National Curriculum (DfE, 2013: 5) states that it 'promotes the spiritual, moral, cultural, mental and physical development of pupils at the school and of society' and 'prepares pupils at the school for the opportunities, responsibilities and experiences of later life'. Whilst many of the changes have focused upon the cross-curricular aspect of provision of general teaching requirements such as inclusion (see Chapter 6), the use of ICT, the use of language, health and safety aspects (see Chapter 8) and the promotion of spiritual, moral, social and cultural aspects (see Chapter 9), a more recent focus on how physical education can support whole school improvement has made it even more important for us as teachers of physical education to understand the impact of our subject on the learning experiences of pupils across the curriculum. By completing Task 10.1, you can begin to think about these in more depth.

---

## Task 10.1

1    Using your teaching placements or current teaching timetable as a point of reference, identify subjects where physical education might be able to make a contribution.
2    For each subject try to identify examples of activities that could be undertaken in physical education which would allow pupils to consolidate and apply existing knowledge. You may wish to think about creating a portfolio in which to store these.
3    Discuss with colleagues how you feel physical education is currently used to support whole school improvement.

---

# Physical education and the core curriculum subjects

If you have completed Task 10.1, you will have already started to think about curriculum subjects that can be integrated with physical education. For example, if we look at science, one activity that you might have considered looking at is the heart and the impact of exercise on the heart (we will look at this activity in much more depth later in the chapter). For mathematics, you could consider activities such as data collection through athletic events, or the use of measuring skills. For English or literacy-based activities, we can identify activities such as writing, for example writing a match report. These are just a few simple examples of how curriculum requirements within physical education can be used to support other aspects of the curriculum. Task 10.2 provides you with an opportunity to look at this in much more depth.

## Task 10.2

1   Using the current programmes of study for Foundation Stage, Key Stage 1 and Key Stage 2 (those of you who are working with different curricula should access your own guidance materials), identify any examples of core curriculum content that could be taught in that subject and in physical education.
2   Compile a table demonstrating where similarities occur.
3   Think about how you might integrate these into your current teaching.

By completing Task 10.2, you should have identified a number of examples where curriculum content is taught through physical education and at least one other subject area. For example, knowledge and understanding associated with healthy and active lifestyles can be taught in physical education and science. However, we will start by looking at the example of the heart and the impact of exercise on it, which we mentioned earlier in this chapter.

## Physical education and science

During early stages of development pupils should be encouraged to develop their knowledge and understanding of health and growth (a premise that links closely to the concept of physical literacy we discussed in Chapters 1 and 4). The growing obesity problem and the impact this has on pupils' health and wellbeing (see Chapter 9) places a greater emphasis on schools to support the raising of awareness through an increased focus on why exercise is necessary to maintain a healthy lifestyle. If we reflect on how physical education can be used to develop pupils' knowledge and understanding of fitness and health we can clearly identify an opportunity for integration within the curriculum. However, we need to be clear about how this would look in practice.

When we get pupils to warm up we can encourage them to think about what is happening to their body as their level of activity increases. The key issue is for pupils to understand that there will be changes to their body, but that this is normal. As they move, they can be encouraged to think about what is happening to their:

• heart – it starts to beat faster; 'I feel a thumping in my chest'
• breathing – 'I breathe more'
• muscles – 'I get tired'
• colour – 'I go red'
• temperature – 'I get hotter'.

They can be asked to share their ideas with each other, thereby encouraging the development of communication skills (again we will look at this in more detail as we move through the chapter). This is only one example; further practical activities can be found throughout the chapter as well as on the companion website.

General aspects of health and wellbeing that pupils should be encouraged to learn include:

- that to stay healthy we need an adequate and varied diet
- how to present information about diet and health
- that we need exercise to stay healthy and maintain our muscles
- that when we exercise, our muscles work harder
- how to measure pulse rate and relate it to heart beat
- how to identify factors which could affect pulse rate and make predictions about changes
- that when humans exercise, muscles move parts of the skeleton and this activity requires an increased blood supply, so the heart beat increases and the pulse rate is faster. (QCDA, 2010b)

Within a physical education context, we can start to look at muscles and different exercises that can be used to stretch and strengthen them (see the companion website for a range of examples). Pupils can be encouraged to start to use appropriate terminology for the main muscle groups as they warm up (this again links to the development of literacy and language skills which we will look at in more detail later in the chapter). As they warm up we can also get them to think about muscles and bones and their roles in supporting the body. In looking at developing their understanding of pulse and heartbeat, they can be set short challenges that require them to record their pulse after different activities, for example jogging on the spot for a set period, completing a specified distance, or completing a series of specific skills such as step-ups. Later in the chapter we will explore how such activities can also be used to support knowledge development across the use of ICT as well as knowledge and understanding of the use and interpretation of data.

However, the links to science can be developed further as shown in Table 10.2.

**Table 10.2** Cross-curricular links between science and physical education

| Science theme | Link to physical education |
| --- | --- |
| Animals, including humans | Body parts |
| | Diet |
| | Impact of exercise |
| | Hygiene |
| | Growth and development |
| Everyday materials | Sports clothing |
| | Playing surfaces |
| Working scientifically | How do different types of exercise affect our heart rate? |
| | Testing |
| | Reporting results |
| Forces and magnets | How different playing surfaces affect games |
| | Forces in physical education |

## Task 10.3

1    Identify a set of key scientific terms that you wish pupils to learn and use during your lessons. For each one produce some form of resource that will allow pupils to develop an understanding of:

   a    the term itself (a definition)
   b    some form of practical application of the term (for example a picture)
   c    examples of when the term might be used (a model of the word within a sentence).

2    Plan an opportunity within your own teaching when you can use these resources and evaluate their success. Where necessary modify these resources for future use. These resources can then be added to your portfolio.

## Physical education and mathematics (numeracy)

The National Curriculum states 'Teachers should use every relevant subject to develop pupils' mathematical fluency. Confidence in numeracy and other mathematical skills is a precondition of success across the national curriculum' (DfE, 2013: 8). Thus, as teachers of physical education, we should be looking at opportunities to integrate such activities into our planning and teaching of the subject. Clear parallels can be drawn between what pupils are taught in their mathematics lessons and how these might be applied within a physical education context.

Whilst specific terminology changes with each iteration of a national curriculum, the knowledge, skills and understanding pupils are expected to develop remain generic, for example the use and application of number, as well as shapes, spaces and measurements. For instance, warm-up activities can be used to engage pupils in counting by challenging them to get into defined group sizes; simple activities such as counting the number of throws they complete in a set time or identifying when they have completed a set number can also be encouraged. Further activities can be set up so that they have to solve a problem at the end, for example pupils complete a simple orienteering course and at each control have to solve a simple mathematical problem (see the companion website support material for Chapter 5).

Pupils can be encouraged to apply their understanding of numbers to collect and use data, for example their times for running or their pulse after different activities. They can then use this data to produce graphs and charts allowing them to share their ideas with others. We will look at this in more depth in the section on developing ICT skills.

When looking at the knowledge, skills and understanding associated with concepts such as shape, space and measures, pupils can be engaged in using equipment to measure the distance they have jumped, or the time it took them to complete a set distance.

Again, this data can be used to develop statistical skills. Key terminology can be used to support learning, for example the use of geometry terminology in gymnastics and dance to describe movement direction and patterns. They can explore the different shapes they might make with their bodies when performing gymnastic movements (you may wish to refer to Chapter 5 for further examples) and can also be encouraged to think about the different shapes they make on the floor during their routines.

---

## Task 10.4

1   Look at the examples introduced of developing mathematical principles and physical education. Identify a range of activities that you could integrate into your physical education lessons that would allow pupils to develop their knowledge, skills and understanding of numbers and shape, space and measure.
2   When you plan your next week of lessons, identify specifically how physical education lessons will build on the knowledge, skills and understanding developed in mathematics/numeracy lessons.
3   Share these ideas with colleagues and integrate them into your portfolio as appropriate.

---

## Physical education and English (literacy and communication skills)

Teachers should develop pupils' spoken language, reading, writing and vocabulary as integral aspects of the teaching of every subject. English is both a subject in its own right and the medium for teaching; for pupils, understanding the language provides access to the whole curriculum. Fluency in the English language is an essential foundation for success in all subjects. (DfE, 2013: 11)

During early childhood, the development of skills associated with reading, writing and speaking is to be encouraged. As pupils become competent in reading they can start to be encouraged to explain what different physical education terms mean and be encouraged to expand the range of texts they read to include sport specific ones. Through writing, physical education allows for the development of fundamental movement skills including the fine motor skills associated with handwriting (see Chapter 4 where we discuss this further) as well as being encouraged to use physical education activities as content for their writing, for example a match report (see Chapter 7 regarding the use of Sport Education), or biography of a game or persuasive argument for new playground equipment.

Through dance and gymnastic activities pupils can be encouraged to tell a story through the sequences they perform. Storyboards can be used to allow pupils to organise their thoughts and produce a focused sequence. They can then be used as a prompt to support their explanation of the sequence, as well as a basis for feedback from other pupils. Spelling can be encouraged through the use of key physical education terminology and word walls, encouraging them to use appropriate language in describing their performances as well as during planned opportunities for them to give and receive feedback. In doing so listening skills are developed as well as their ability to use feedback to improve performances.

# Physical education and other curriculum subjects

So far we have focused on what are commonly referred to as the core subjects within the National Curriculum and identified a range of activities that can be integrated into planning to develop skills linking physical education to other curriculum areas. This section looks at how we can use physical education as a vehicle to deliver or enhance other aspects of curriculum subject areas using specific examples from geography, music and computing.

## Physical education and geography

While the teaching of OAA is not statutory within curriculum documentation, opportunities for the development of children's geographical skills are evident, such as route planning, to include reference to compass directions, as well as map-making to include use of geographical symbols. This can be achieved in a practical manner by pupils drawing simple maps of the gym and then designing a simple orienteering course. As pupils progress, simple problem-solving activities can be introduced which encourage the development of more complex skills associated with the use of maps and decision-making skills (a range of examples can be found in the companion website material for Chapter 5).

## Physical education and music

> Music is a universal language that embodies one of the highest forms of creativity. A high-quality music education should engage and inspire pupils to develop a love of music and their talent as musicians, and so increase their self-confidence, creativity and sense of achievement. As pupils progress, they should develop a critical engagement with music, allowing them to compose, and to listen with discrimination to the best in the musical canon. (DfE, 2013: 244)

Physical education and music are well aligned to support opportunities for creativity and self-confidence. Chapter 5 looked at the development of concepts, skills and processes and the teaching of dance-based activities and these can be used as a conduit for the development of such music and dance-related skills. For example, pupils might be given a theme or story and use dance movements to tell their tale. They might be given simple rhythms to move to, or different styles of music which require them to express their interpretations of that music. They may even have the opportunity to create their own music to use in their performances. Both music and physical education are performance-based subjects and therefore allowing them the opportunity to express themselves physically and emotionally increases the potential for the rehearsal and application of their skills which can deepen their overall learning experiences.

## Computing

The national curriculum for computing aims to ensure that all pupils:

- can understand and apply the fundamental principles and concepts of computer science, including abstraction, logic, algorithms and data representation
- can analyse problems in computational terms, and have repeated practical experience of writing computer programs in order to solve such problems
- can evaluate and apply information technology, including new or unfamiliar technologies, analytically to solve problems
- are responsible, competent, confident and creative users of information and communication technology. (DfE, 2013: 217)

Thus within this curriculum area, the focus is placed on pupils' ability to develop their existing knowledge of ICT and apply it to different contexts, acknowledging as they do the impact this may have. Specific skills pupils are expected to develop include the following:

- The ability to search for and select relevant information – in a physical education context, pupils can be encouraged to find information relating to the performance of a specific skill, activity or sporting event (World Cup, Olympic Games). This could then be used to support an individual or class project.
- The ability to create, manipulate and process information – this second point emphasises data generation and information processing. The focus here should be on the collection of individual data rather than group data which, if not handled sensitively, may raise potential issues around comparisons between pupils. If we think back to earlier in the chapter when we looked at the integration of science with physical education via a focus on healthy living, we considered collecting information regarding changes in pulse rate from different types of activities. By requiring pupils to record such data, they can start to analyse their own information to make predictions as well as use the data to form graphical representations of changes that may have occurred. Similar data can be collected through athletic activities, and in this way pupils are not only developing ICT skills but also working to develop skills associated with mathematics.

- The ability to review their own work and offer suggestions as to how improvements can be made – the emphasis is on the use of feedback to make improvements. In general, feedback within a physical education context has a tendency to be generated from the information given by others, for example on pupils' ability to perform a specific skill or the quality of a piece of work. Advances in technology, however, now provide opportunities for individuals to generate their own feedback. Many schools now have hand-held video cameras which allow immediate playback. In physical education, these can be used in activities such as gymnastics and athletics to video individual performance. The performance can then be reviewed by the performer, allowing them to analyse their own performance against specific criteria (for example teaching points) and suggest ways in which performance can be improved. As with any use of captured data, for example photographs and video, consideration needs to be given to how the data is then stored or destroyed (again you will need to make reference to any safeguarding pupils policy).

---

### Task 10.5

1   Spend some time collating the information provided on developing ICT capability in physical education.
2   Identify a range of activities you intend to integrate into your own teaching.
3   When possible deliver these ideas and evaluate their effectiveness.
4   Identify any changes you might make subsequent to your initial delivery, and add your completed examples to your portfolio.

---

## Physical education and other aspects of primary education

This chapter has thus far focused on developing your knowledge and understanding of how physical education can be used to deliver aspects of other curriculum areas. What we have not yet focused upon are those skills associated with personal, social and health education. These will be looked at in more detail as we move through this section of the chapter.

If we think back to Chapter 1, which looked at defining education and physical education, and Chapter 2, which looked at learning and the domains of learning, we identified that education is more than just focusing on the development of subject knowledge. We will now start to focus on some important aspects of primary education aside from subject-specific teaching. These include the inclusion of all learners (see Chapter 6), aspects of health and safety (see Chapter 8), and pupils' moral and spiritual development which can include learning and thinking skills, personal and emotional skills, and social skills (more detail regarding these aspects can be found in Chapter 9).

## Learning and thinking skills

Learning and thinking skills place an emphasis on pupils developing their ability to learn (you may wish to reread Chapter 2 to refresh your memory) and to think creatively. They are also concerned with generating ideas and problem solving. This area can be divided into the following categories.

### Investigating

Developing pupils' investigative skills can start with basic problem-solving activities. Chapter 4 looked at the development of fundamental motor skills including encouraging pupils to explore different ways of performing skills, for example getting them to think about what different body parts might do to contribute to the performance of the skills. This can also contribute to developing their understanding of the impact of exercise on their bodies. Chapter 5 looked at concepts associated with the development of strategic and tactical awareness. A vital part of this process is encouraging pupils to investigate a range of methods before deciding upon a preferred approach.

### Creativity and development

In fostering creativity, we are encouraging pupils to look at different ways to use the skills they have across different contexts. Using dance and gymnastic activities as an example, we can consider using warm-up exercises to encourage pupils to think about different body parts they might use to move in different ways or different types of balancing they might perform. They can then be encouraged to choose some of these to integrate into longer gymnastic sequences.

### Communication

We looked in detail at the development of communication skills when we explored integrating English and literacy with physical education earlier in this chapter. When exploring communication in physical education we need to consider how children deliver feedback to each other and the impact this feedback may have, as well as the visual, written and verbal ways in which they communicate.

### Evaluation

Encouraging pupils to develop evaluative skills can be done by integrating a range of approaches. It is important that pupils have a clear understanding of what they are evaluating and against what criteria; consequently, we need to consider in some depth how we introduce and support skill development in this area. For example, we need to provide clear criteria against which pupils will evaluate performance. This could be in the use of specific resources cards generated through the use of reciprocal teaching approaches. We also need to get pupils to consider how they use the feedback to make changes and improve performance. Consideration therefore may need to be given to encouraging pupils to set specific goals. Figure 10.1 provides an example of how this might be achieved.

A similar checklist can be generated for all skills allowing pupils to manage their own learning and we look at this in more depth below. This technique allows pupils to review the progress they are making, encouraging them to set specific goals, an approach that is becoming more apparent in schools to monitor and track progress over time.

## Personal and emotional skills

It is important to encourage children to take an increasing level of responsibility for their own learning. In doing so they can develop confidence and resilience ensuring they develop positive approaches and attitudes to health and wellbeing. In many ways the skills they are developing within this area mirror many of those we have already explored and specifically relate to aspects of learning evident within the affective domain (see Chapter 2 and also Chapter 9). Specifically, pupils can be encouraged to identify their strengths, manage their feelings, take part in reflection, goal setting and independent working, and develop control over their own physical skills and movements (QCDA, 2010a). More recently work looking at the mindset within the classroom

| Skill: Throw |
| --- |
| Key points |
| What I did well (what went well – WWW) |
| What I need to do better (even better if – EBI) |
| What I need to do next |
| What improvements I made |

**Figure 10.1** Skill evaluation proforma

(Dweck, 2012; Ricci, 2013; Philpott, 2016) demonstrates how encouraging pupils to develop aspirations and accept that failure is an option from which you can develop further, allows them to challenge themselves further. However, what must be acknowledged is that it is the environment created in the school or classroom that impacts most significantly on the mindset of the pupil and as such you must consider how your classroom environment may impact positively and negatively on the individual.

## Identifying strengths

Some of the practical examples of activities discussed earlier in this chapter can be used to allow pupils to identify their own strengths. If we refer to Figure 10.1 we can clearly see that the aim of the proforma is to provide pupils with the opportunity to evaluate their performance allowing them to identify not only their strengths, but also areas requiring further development as well as activities that would allow them to make improvements (goal setting).

## Developing and managing feelings

As we have previously identified, the visual nature of physical education means that it has the capacity to impact on the social development of individuals as they make comparisons between themselves and others. The complexity of the skills that pupils are expected to develop can cause frustration, in particular if they are struggling to complete the activity or not making as much progress as their peers.

---

### Task 10.6

1   Identify a recent time when you have become frustrated with yourself.
2   What was your reaction to this frustration?
3   What were the consequences of your reaction?
4   If the situation were to be repeated would you react differently?

---

As Task 10.6 demonstrates, at times we all become frustrated and will react to situations in different ways. This may be a result of prior experience, so our reaction is based on a previous outcome, or it may be a result of how we were feeling at the time; if it had happened at another time our reaction could have been different. Despite being adults, there will be times when childlike instincts surface; as such we need to appreciate that pupils in the early stages of development may not have the level of maturity necessary to make correct judgments about their own reactions. Consideration therefore needs to be given to the emotional support structures that can be integrated into lessons. For example, if a pupil is becoming frustrated at not being able to perform a specific skill, there may be a way in which the activity can be modified to allow them to experience success. This could include a change in equipment or a change in the task being completed (see Chapter 3 on planning and Chapter 6 on inclusion). It is important to create a learning environment in which pupils feel confident enough to seek help and support. Conversely pupils may become frustrated with each other because they are not all working at the same level and as a result start to blame each other for poor performances. Sadly, on too many occasions we see frustrations being played out on the sports field and then replicated in the school playground!

In completing Task 10.6, you would have identified some reaction mechanisms that occur when you vent your own frustrations. As we as adults have a level of maturity not evident in pupils we need to provide children with opportunities to develop their own understanding of reactions and the consequences of their actions and to develop an ability to manage their own behaviour. Chapter 6 looked at engaging with inclusion in physical education teaching. Some schools work closely with pupils to identify exit strategies from situations, for example pupils are able to identify when they are becoming frustrated and then remove themselves from the situation until they have calmed down. You should consult the school's policy regarding such practice. It is important that within any school the approach is applied consistently.

## Developing reflection

Throughout this book we have made reference to the provision of and processes associated with developing pupils' ability to reflect upon their own and others' performances. A key part of this is children's ability to evaluate their own performance and use such evaluations to inform subsequent performance. Earlier in this chapter we identified how reflection can be supported using ICT. Pupils may also engage in individual action planning, for example identifying what they need to do to improve and how this might be achieved. The process of reflection can also be used to support pupils identified as gifted and talented (see Chapter 6) and thereby allow for accelerated learning opportunities to be integrated into lesson planning (see Chapter 3). It is important that pupils are clear about the criteria on which they are basing any assessment, and feedback using appropriate terminology.

---

### Task 10.7

1   Review your physical education lesson plans for the last term.
2   Identify within them when opportunities arose that required pupils to reflect upon their own performance.
3   Identify a list of potential activities that can now be integrated into your planning to engage pupils in regular review opportunities.

---

## Goal setting

In setting goals, we are encouraging pupils to develop more responsibility for their own learning. The proforma in Figure 10.1 requires pupils to identify activities that they need to undertake to make further progress. We need to consider the timescale of goals, for example at the start of a lesson pupils may be encouraged to identify what it is they want to achieve by the end of the lesson or even during an activity. Taking a practical example from athletics: in developing pupils' ability to run at speed, pupils can be encouraged to identify a target distance they think they could achieve in a specified period of time. For example, they could place a cone at the distance they think they will reach in five seconds. They can then be timed by a partner to test whether they can achieve the predicted distance.

Another form of goal setting is based around levels of attainment. This engages pupils in developing an understanding of the level at which they are currently working, and from here identifying what they would need to achieve to move up to the next level and how this might be achieved.

## Social skills

Developing social skills places an emphasis on how individuals work together and again physical education offers a range of opportunities for this to occur. Much of the practical work associated with the subject requires pupils to work collaboratively towards an end goal. In many of the activities undertaken, success is a reflection of the team work in which the individuals engage. Individual skills that contribute to this development include being able to listen and respond appropriately, adapt behaviour for different situations, work collaboratively towards common goals, take turns, share, negotiate, and give constructive support and feedback.

## Listening and responding

Listening and responding are directly linked with literacy skills and focus on how pupils communicate with each other as well as with you the teacher. In physical education there is a range of opportunities across different contexts for pupils to engage in activities that cultivate these skills. In all lessons pupils will be expected to listen to instructions. These could be delivered by the class teacher or, dependent upon the teaching approaches being adopted, by the pupils themselves. Pupils should therefore spend time learning how to listen. For many they will hear the instruction being given, but being able to make sense of such instructions may be more problematic. No doubt we can all recall instances when we have given instructions and thought that all the pupils understood what they had been asked to do, only to realise as they move off to do the activity that actually they did not understand at all! While we can put this down to experience, we need to realise that at times we may need to engage some form of checking mechanism, for example 'Does everyone understand?' 'Has anyone got any questions?' 'Can you repeat back to me the instructions that I've just given you?'.

Listening to instructions is just one part of a wide range of listening opportunities in physical education as pupils will need to listen to a range of individuals including their peers. We have talked a lot about the use of feedback and how pupils use the feedback they receive to improve their own performance. Pupils need to be aware not only of how they give feedback, but also of how they interpret the feedback they are being given. It is therefore important to get pupils to draw out the key points from the information they are being given. If we refer to Figure 10.1 we can see that it provides an opportunity for pupils to note key points, again developing their ability to listen and draw out key information.

Pupils might also undertake leadership roles which require them to listen to a range of ideas offered by their peers before deciding upon a strategy. In this scenario not only are they developing listening skills, but they also have to think about how they respond to such ideas.

In the context of physical education, the development of pupils' ability to respond will be determined by how they interpret instructions, for example in OAA they might be given a series of simple instructions and equipment and then have to develop a strategy for completing the task (see Chapter 5 for an overview of delivering OAA in physical education). However, they will also need to develop the ability to respond to different ideas from different people, particularly if they are presented with a leadership role. In trying to develop one specific skill, advances in others may also occur. For example, in attempting to develop pupils' listening and responding skills, we are likely to also be working on their learning and thinking skills as well as their personal and emotional skills.

## Adapting behaviour and working collaboratively

As part of developing social skills pupils need to develop an understanding of how their behaviour may impact on others as well as the ability to take increasing responsibility for their own actions. Putting this into a physical education context we can start to think about the different roles pupils may undertake and how this may impact on the behaviour they exhibit. A good example of this is to consider the Sport Education model that was introduced in Chapter 7.

The focus of learning in the Sport Education model is on the use of a productive pedagogical approach which engages pupils in a range of roles and responsibilities, for example team captain, coach, referee. At the heart of this approach (see Metzler, 2011) lies the development not only of physical skills relating to physical education, but also of the affective domain of learning, including pupils' abilities to undertake a range of sport-related roles and to work collaboratively within these roles. In this context, pupils will start to exhibit behaviours relevant to the different roles they adopt. For example, you may expect a pupil who is taking on a leadership role to exhibit different behaviours from those who are taking on a more participatory role. If you want to see this in context, at the next training day you attend watch how different people with different levels of responsibility behave.

In the section on developing ICT capability we gave examples of how we could analyse performance in a range of activities. This can also be applied to analysing behaviour, for example pupils could be encouraged to be videoed working with others to identify their strengths and weaknesses. In doing so they could begin to understand how their behaviour impacts upon others and this process could be used to suggest improvements that could be made. This is particularly important if pupils are undertaking some form of leadership role and working with young pupils, for example as playground supervisors.

In providing learning opportunities for pupils to work together collaboratively consideration needs to be given to the appropriateness of the activities as well as the state of readiness to learn. Activities should be developed progressively, allowing pupils to take increasing responsibility for the outcomes. You may wish at this point to refresh your understanding of the theories and processes of learning in Chapter 2, as well as the approaches to the teaching of physical education in Chapter 7.

This chapter has focused on some of the more generic educational skills covered in the wider curriculum and how physical education can be used to develop cross-curricular learning. It is clear that different types of skills are connected and development in one area will lead to development in another, for example evaluative skills (which include evaluation and reflection) can be developed through literacy, numeracy, ICT capability, learning and thinking skills, and personal and social skills. You should now attempt Task 10.8 to further embed your knowledge.

## Task 10.8

Using all that you have read in this chapter, identify a range of activities that could be integrated into your physical education teaching to provide pupils with the opportunity to develop skills across the curriculum.

## Chapter summary

This chapter has investigated a range of activities that can be used to promote physical education across other curriculum subject areas. It is clear that common knowledge, skills and understanding exist between subjects

*(Continued)*

*(Continued)*

and that if we are to engage pupils and enhance their learning experiences, we should be exploring ways of providing opportunities for them to apply their skills across different contexts. To review your learning, you should complete the review questions below.

1    What is your personal rationale for promoting physical education across the curriculum?
2    What would you identify as the key skills pupils should be required to develop across all curriculum subjects?
3    What changes are you going to make to your own teaching to integrate a higher level of cross-curricular and cross-subject teaching?

## Further reading

Barnes, J. (2015) *Cross-curricular Learning 3–14*, 3rd edn. London: Sage.
This textbook provides an overview of a range of strategies that can be applied when looking to promote cross-curricular links.

Dweck, C. (2010) *Mindset: How You Can Fulfil Your Potential*. London: Hachette.
This textbook provides an overview on mindset theory and explores how it can impact on the individual across a range of areas including schools.

Philpott, H. (2016) 'Developing a growth mind set in physical education', *Physical Education Matters*, 11(1): 50–3.
A research-focused piece exploring the use of mindset theory in the teaching of physical education with a focus on gymnastic activities.

# 11

# Physical Education and the Wider Community

## Chapter aims

- To review how physical education in primary schools can be supported by the wider community
- To identify potential external providers and how they can contribute to physical education within the primary school

## Links to *Teachers' Standards*

In working through this chapter, you should develop your knowledge associated with the *Teachers' Standards* (DfE, 2011) detailed in Table 11.1.

## Introduction

Physical education has always been supported by the wider community. All primary schools will have associated secondary schools where pupils transfer at the end of their primary education. Local authorities provide facilities to support physical activity, for example, local sports centres. Some organisations have sports development officers. These might be employed by the local education authorities or an equivalent organisation and may be linked to specific governing bodies. You are also likely to find that local clubs and organisations offer links into junior provision within their own structures.

**Table 11.1**  How this chapter links to the *Teachers' Standards* (DfE, 2011)

| | |
|---|---|
| Standard 1: Set high expectations which inspire, motivate and challenge pupils | • establish a safe and stimulating environment for pupils, rooted in mutual respect |
| Standard 8: Fulfil wider professional responsibilities | • make a positive contribution to the wider life and ethos of the school |
| | • develop effective professional relationships with colleagues, knowing how and when to draw on advice and specialist support |
| | • deploy support staff effectively |
| | • take responsibility for improving teaching through appropriate professional development, responding to advice and feedback from colleagues |
| | • communicate effectively with parents with regard to pupils' achievements and wellbeing |

With the advent of extended schools and other policy changes, there has been an increase in the number and range of external providers of physical education. It is therefore important to look at how physical education contributes to the wider community as well as identifying parameters for engaging with external providers. Completing Task 11.1 should allow you to start thinking about the opportunities that exist within your community.

---

## Task 11.1

1   Produce an audit of the local sports clubs and facilities located close to your school.
2   For each one, identify a key point of contact and the opportunities they can provide.
3   Produce a display for pupils outlining the opportunities that exist within their locality for participating in sport and physical activity outside of the school curriculum.

---

Completing Task 11.1 should help you to identify the wealth of opportunities that lie outside of the school classroom for pupils to participate in. Most sports clubs and associations will have teams and activities appropriate for primary school children and many will be keen to engage with schools to promote themselves and provide opportunities for your pupils. If you are fortunate enough to live in a city with professional sports clubs, then it is likely that they will have dedicated employees with specified roles focusing on engagement with schools and the provision of training opportunities. Your local authority may have a designated sports development team, with a remit to organise sports tournaments for pupils. Additionally, you may be linked to a school sports college where opportunities for inter-school competitions exist. However, it is important that if you are encouraging young people to engage in sport outside of the school environment and sending them to targeted providers of this, that you have undertaken checks with them around aspects such as safeguarding.

The range of opportunities available can be very broad, and deciding on who and what to be involved with can become problematic. Chapter 12 looks at the role of the subject leader in identifying and working with external organisations. It is important that engagement with external organisations offers an extension to the opportunities provided within the curriculum and does not become a substitute.

We will now look in a little more detail at the range of opportunities you might engage in, focusing on working with your secondary school, using your local facilities and working with external providers.

## Working with your secondary school

Chapter 1 looked at some of the recent initiatives implemented in schools. Whilst the School Sports programmes established as part of national policy in England in the 2000s have been replaced with the Primary Physical Education and School Sports programmes, opportunities to work with secondary school partnerships continue to evolve through the establishment of Multi Academy Trusts (MATs) and Teaching School Alliances (TSAs). These provide staff opportunities, in some cases, to teach across schools and across phases of education. Such activities build upon the previously established School Sports programmes, and continue to ensure that some interaction between schools and opportunities for pupils in primary schools to experience some teaching from secondary-trained staff and to access secondary school facilities and equipment continue.

However, the development of close links between primary and secondary schools is also important to facilitate the transition across phases of education which occurs when pupils leave the primary phase of education at the age of 11. Research (Capel et al., 2003, 2004, 2007) identifies that the transition from primary to secondary school can be problematic for some pupils. Changes in approaches to teaching, characterised by a move from pupil-centred teaching in primary schools to a more subject-focused approach in secondary schools, as well as structural and organisational changes such as the change from staying in the same class for most subjects to moving classes for each subject, can impact on a child's attainment, motivation and self-esteem.

Within physical education the transition to secondary education can lead to a decline in levels of attainment, characterised by a tendency of staff to adopt a 'fresh start approach' (Lawrence, 2006). This occurs when staff choose to ignore the prior learning of pupils as they lack confidence in what has taken place in the primary school, for example, they may choose to re-teach the fundamental movement skills at the start of pupils' secondary education. Developing closer links with secondary schools through regular meetings and sharing curriculum content, planning and teaching opportunities will foster a greater level of understanding of pupils' prior learning and promote continuity and progression in learning across age phases. However, changes to curriculum assessment in relation to the removal of 'levels' of attainment, and also changes to curriculum content will continue to pose challenges for staff.

Within your school, there will be a designated staff member with responsibility for liaising with secondary schools, and it will be beneficial for you to spend some time discussing the transfer arrangements and links that exist between you and secondary schools. This is outlined in Task 11.2.

---

### Task 11.2

Working with your school transfer co-ordinator discuss the following:

1    What links currently exist between your primary and secondary school in relation to physical education?
2    Is there any shared practice in respect of the planning and teaching of physical education?
3    Is any information shared between your primary and secondary school in relation to attainment and curriculum content in physical education?
4    What improvements (if any) could be made to the links that exist?

---

## Working with local facilities

Many primary schools are limited in the range of facilities available for delivering high quality physical education and school sport. For example, few schools still have a swimming pool and those that do tend to have an outdoor facility that will not be available throughout the whole school year. As you know from Chapter 5, swimming is an integral aspect of the physical education curriculum and it is highly likely that you will need to attend a local pool as part of your teaching. Health and safety aspects related to aquatic activities will need to be considered (see Chapter 8) and it is also likely that you will need to use specialist staff to support you in delivering these sessions (we look at the use of external providers later in this chapter).

However, we should not restrict ourselves to using leisure facilities for only aquatic-based activities. It may be that you can access a sports hall either at a leisure centre or at your local secondary school. In doing so you can start to increase the range of activities pupils experience. Using facilities at a secondary school to which pupils from your primary school transfer provides further opportunities for developing links and as a result offers pupils the chance to familiarise themselves with these surroundings lessening the impact of when they transfer out of primary education.

In Chapter 5 we explored aspects of OAA. Local playing fields provide extended opportunities for engagement in orienteering-based activities and increased space for games or athletic activities. When using such spaces, you will need to take into account that the general public might also access the provision at the same time. You will therefore need to consider the safeguarding of pupils as well as health and safety issues associated with using communal environments. What therefore becomes essential is that regular risk assessments are undertaken in relation to the spaces being used, and parents are kept informed as to where activities are being undertaken.

# Working with external providers

You may also consider working with local external providers to enhance educational provision. Such providers might include local sports clubs and their coaches, local initial teacher educators or external physical education providers. The introduction of the Primary Physical Education and Sports Premium has resulted in a number of schools employing external providers to support the delivery of their physical education programme. Whilst this might provide a simple solution to a staff or competence issue, it is important to ensure that this collaboration enhances pupils' experiences as well as offering development opportunities for staff, with a view to them taking greater ownership of the teaching over time.

Chapter 1 looked at the role and values of physical education and identified what underpins high quality physical education and school sport, as well as exploring the difference between sport and physical education. Regardless of our position within a school we have a responsibility for the quality of provision. Recent changes in educational policy concerning protected preparation time and the development of school sports colleges has given rise to an increased range of external providers going into schools and in some cases delivering physical education lessons. It is essential that any individual delivering the curriculum is competent and confident in curriculum planning, assessment and evaluation processes. In essence, they must have a clear understanding of the curriculum in its entirety.

Overall responsibility for the delivery of the curriculum lies with the school and subject leader and therefore both have a responsibility to quality assure provision. Organisations such as the Association for Physical Education (AfPE) have worked hard to establish kitemarks which identify those providers who have achieved a recognised level of quality. Guidance is available from local authorities as well as publications. James and Elbourn (2016: 3) identify four key areas for consideration when engaging with anyone in delivering physical education, to include:

1   Fundamental principles of safe practice.
2   Teaching safely – principles of organisation and management.
3   Teaching safety – promoting effective learning.
4   Teaching safely – activity-specific information.

## Task 11.3

1    Identify any external individuals (including support staff) who have supported or might support you in the delivery of physical education lessons.
2    What information do you think your school should have regarding their suitability to deliver the activity?
3    How would you go about accessing such information?

# Safeguarding pupils

'Safeguarding is action that is taken to promote the welfare of children, and protect them from harm' (James and Elbourn, 2016: 91). When using external organisations and facilities the safeguarding of pupils must be at the forefront of any planning. As with any staff member, stringent checks need to be conducted on any individual who may come into contact with pupils. Accordingly, any external individual should be checked in line with school and governmental policy. Checks need to be undertaken, and clear evidence provided of appropriateness to work with pupils as outlined previously. Where possible references should be taken from organisations that have worked with these providers in the past. Some local authorities also have recommended lists of providers which you might be able to access, whilst subject associations, for example the AfPE in the United Kingdom, maintain a list of quality assured national trainers as well as accredited training around safeguarding.

External staff need to fully understand what they are expected to deliver and clear guidance on school policies, for example health and safety, and behaviour management, should be given during any induction process. You may wish to observe the individual prior to fully recruiting their services. Many individuals may have a coaching background, but may not necessarily have in-depth knowledge of varying approaches to learning and teaching. You should ensure that appropriate references are obtained. James and Elbourn (2016: 97–104) provide a comprehensive overview of criteria that need to be addressed when considering issues associated with safeguarding pupils to include consideration of the following:

- students themselves
- staff being used
- protecting children from deliberate harm
- medical conditions
- first aid provision
- digital technology
- school/department security
- drug and substance misuse
- transporting students
- health and safety

- use of appropriate physical intervention and support
- overplaying and overtraining
- intimate care issues
- responding to weather conditions.

Ensuring that the above are addressed in relation to any off-site activities or activities that are delivered by any individual outside of the school is essential if the health and wellbeing of the individual is to be protected.

## Chapter summary

The aim of this chapter has been to look at how those involved in the teaching of physical education and the wider community can work together to provide effective learning experiences for primary school pupils. We have explored a range of issues associated with working with your secondary school, local facilities and external providers. Consideration must always be given to the safeguarding of pupils when using external providers or facilities. To consolidate your learning, you should complete the following review questions.

1   What opportunities can you identify within your local area for interacting with the wider community?
2   What quality assurance criteria would you employ when working with community-based organisations?

## Further resources

Association for Physical Education – the employment and deployment of coaches. Available at: www.afpe.org.uk/physical-education/wp-content/uploads/Maximising_the_Primary_Sport_Premium_-_Coaches.pdf

Association for Physical Education – effective professional learning. Available at: www.afpe.org.uk/physical-education/wp-content/uploads/Maximising_the_Primary_Sport_Premium_Poster_One_Third_Proof.pdf

## Further reading

Whitehead, M. and Pack, K. (2010) 'Working with others to achieve the aims of PE', in S. Capel and M. Whitehead (eds), *Learning to Teach Physical Education in the Secondary School*, 3rd edn. London: Routledge. pp. 52–64.
This chapter, included in a secondary focused textbook, does provide further information concerning working with others in your own classroom as well as looking at engaging with the wider community.

# 12

# Subject Leadership in Physical Education

## Chapter aims

- To develop an understanding of the role of the subject leader in physical education
- To identify the key skills and attributes associated with subject leadership
- To identify the key areas on which subject leaders should focus

## Links to *Teachers' Standards*

In working through this chapter, you should develop your knowledge associated with the *Teachers' Standards* (DfE, 2011) detailed in Table 12.1.

## The role of subject leader

Throughout this book we have looked at the concept of physical education and its practical delivery within the primary school. While it is expected that each class teacher will have responsibility for the lessons they plan and deliver, as the subject leader you will have the responsibility of co-ordinating the day-to-day aspects around the subject. For example, this may include in some cases how the PE Premium is used (see Chapter 9 for further details on this) and where additional funding may be found,

**Table 12.1**   How this chapter links to the *Teachers' Standards* (DfE, 2011)

| | |
|---|---|
| Standard 2: Promote good progress and outcomes by pupils | • be accountable for pupils' attainment, progress and outcomes <br><br> • demonstrate knowledge and understanding of how pupils learn and how this impacts on teaching |
| Standard 3: Demonstrate good subject and curriculum knowledge | • have a secure knowledge of the relevant subject(s) and curriculum areas, foster and maintain pupils' interest in the subject, and address misunderstandings |
| Standard 4: Plan and teach well-structured lessons | • contribute to the design and provision of an engaging curriculum within the relevant subject area(s) |
| Standard 6: Make accurate and productive use of assessment | • use relevant data to monitor progress, set targets and plan subsequent lessons |
| Standard 8: Fulfil wider professional responsibilities | • make a positive contribution to the wider life and ethos of the school <br><br> • develop effective professional relationships with colleagues, knowing how and when to draw on advice and specialist support <br><br> • deploy support staff effectively <br><br> • take responsibility for improving teaching through appropriate professional development, responding to advice and feedback from colleagues <br><br> • communicate effectively with parents with regard to pupils' achievements and wellbeing |

or how all staff are supported in developing their ability to teach physical education. Subject leaders 'provide professional leadership and management for a subject to secure high quality teaching, effective use of resources and improved standards of learning and achievement for all pupils' (TDA, 1998: 5). Resources to support auditing of the subject are much more readily available and allow the subject leader to establish clear development plans that show how they intend to move provision from emerging through aspirational to embedded (Youth Sport Trust, n.d.; Randall, 2013).

While the role of subject leader has been embedded in the structure of a school for many years, recent changes in the structure and organisation of physical education, which build on the establishment of school sports partnerships, have resulted in some schools employing subject specialists for the delivery of physical education. Training programmes have been established for those wishing to become specialists, either during their initial teacher training phase, or once qualified, and include recognised qualifications. For example, a level 6 programme run by Sports Leaders in association with the Association for Physical Education, is designed to develop participants 'understanding the roles and responsibilities of a physical education subject lead, being able to determine the quality of provision, and being able to design, lead the implementation of, review and revise a targeted strategy to develop primary school physical education and its sustainability' (Sports Leaders, 2013: 2).

The role of the subject specialist in physical education is therefore focused on the management and co-ordination of all aspects of the teaching of physical education to include planning and development of schemes of work, pupil assessment, ordering and maintenance of equipment, and adherence to health and safety policy including risk assessment. You are likely to be asked to support staff development as well as co-ordinate staff who may come into the school to deliver aspects of physical education (for example, outside coaches and adults other than teachers [AOTTs]). Involvement may extend beyond the core curriculum through the co-ordination of extra-curricular provision as well as informing parents regarding what other activities might be taking place, for example, sports day. Chapter 11 looked at how physical education can contribute to and be supported by the wider community, paying particular reference to issues regarding safeguarding. You may find it useful to combine the information in Chapters 10 and 11 as your roles and responsibilities increase, to ensure that you are able to support the integration of physical education across the curriculum as well as understanding how funding can be most effectively used to enhance the competence of the staff with whom you work.

It is clear that the responsibilities associated with leading a subject area are extensive. Integral to the success of the role is the leadership of the provision. However, support of staff through mentoring and training are also key to a successful physical education experience for all. Task 12.1 provides an opportunity for you to start thinking about what qualities are associated with good leaders.

---

### Task 12.1

1    From your own experiences, what do you think makes a good leader?
2    Looking at the characteristics you have identified, explain what these skills are and what they look like practically (for example, you might identify that a characteristic is associated with being organised, and this is reflected in always knowing what you are doing).
3    Finally look at the list in front of you and identify what skills you currently possess and what skills you would like to improve.
4    Produce an action plan to identify how you will go about developing these skills, and when you will review your progress towards achieving these.

---

The next section looks at specific skills and attributes associated with leading a subject.

## Skills and attributes associated with subject leadership

In Task 12.1 you will have started to identify a range of skills and attributes you would expect in a leader. However, as a subject leader, you are also becoming a teacher educator. That is someone who takes responsibility for the education of other teachers to enhance the quality of their teaching. Research (Boyd and Harris, 2010) suggests that the appointment of an individual into a teacher educator role tends to reflect a desire and proficiency in their abilities. Thus, the appointment of a subject leader for physical education should be based on an interest and level of competence in the subject. The appointee should demonstrate expertise in the delivery and organisation of the subject and be provided with support and training to achieve the highest level. Such support may include subject-specific training as well as more generic training opportunities, for example, nationally recognised leadership programmes. What is essential is that the subject leader continues to develop their own professional competences. Specifically, Metzler (2011) suggests that they should look to focus their development around the areas detailed in Table 12.2.

**Table 12.2** Characteristics of knowledge with reference to specific examples from physical education (adapted from Lawrence, in press)

| Physical education specific links (Metzler, 2011: 46) | Physical education context |
|---|---|
| Subject matter | • Knowledge of fundamental movement skills<br>• Knowledge of athletics, dance, games, gymnastics, outdoor and adventurous activities, swimming |
| Generic teaching methods | • Generic teaching approaches<br>• Approaches to assessment<br>• Behaviour management |
| Subject specific teaching methods | • Specific teaching approaches in physical education<br>   o Teaching Games for Understanding<br>   o Sport Education |
| Learning as a process | • Theories of learning<br>   o Behaviourist, Cognitivist, Motivational<br>• Domains of learning<br>   o Affective, Cognitive, Psychomotor<br>• Continuity and progression in learning<br>• Individual needs |
| How content develops | • National Curriculum<br>• Assessment expectations<br>• Planning |
| How context impacts | • External influences<br>• Extra-curricular activities |
| Educational goals | • Aims of education<br>• Curriculum design and content<br>• Education and the wider community<br>• Health and active lifestyles/lifelong participation<br>• Safeguarding |

## Leadership and professional competence

It would seem to go without saying that a subject leader should already possess skills associated with leadership and professional competence. However, it is likely that many of you have been appointed to the role, and have learnt to develop similar skills on the job.

It is important that you have a clear focus, a common goal which you strive to achieve. The provision you lead should link not only to the fundamental aims and ethos of the school, but also link to the guidance provided by subject organisations and those working across physical education in relation to the achievement of positive outcomes for physical education. When looking to become a subject leader, you need to have a clear personal understanding of the aims of that subject and what you want to achieve (see Chapter 1). If you have confidence and a clear focus you are more likely to be able to lead staff in the direction you wish to take the subject. In many respects, you need to be convincing so that people want to follow you. For many, teaching physical education is a challenge. You as the subject leader need to be able to support other members of staff, providing opportunities where necessary for them to grow in confidence in the delivery of the subject which will result in positive experiences not only for the teacher, but also for the pupils they teach.

Leading and managing staff can be one of the most difficult roles you undertake. For some of you who undertake this role, you may find that you experience changes in the way other teachers view you as you are seen as having more authority. While you might have a clear aim and focus in mind, not everyone will share it. At times you may have to reframe your expectations, for example, if you want to introduce a different way of delivering lessons then you will need to plan how you are going to support staff in attaining the skills necessary to achieve this. You will need to work as part of a team, and it may be that part of your role is to delegate some responsibilities to others (although this will be very much dependent on the size of the school you work in). What is important is that you provide a clear rationale for the changes you are intending to make, and most importantly, show how these changes will impact positively on the progress of the pupils being taught.

You may well have to undertake a mentoring role. Here the emphasis is on providing support, guidance and feedback regarding the mentees' teaching. This can be very challenging as you may feel that you are being placed in situations whereby you are reporting on teachers' performance, whilst some teachers may feel you are making judgements on their ability to teach. If you are acting in a mentoring role, it is important that you are open and honest with colleagues as to what you feel your role is, and how you intend to go about it. You should look to identify what you see the role of the mentor as, and the variety of approaches you might adopt. It is highly likely that you will need to watch others teach or review their planning, but working with a collegiate approach is much more beneficial than a more authoritarian manner. For example, if you are observing, meet with the teacher prior to the lesson to discuss what they are intending to teach and what they are aiming to achieve. Identify aspects of the lesson you both want to focus on. Provide detailed feedback and ensure that you organise a post lesson conversation. During this meeting focus the conversation on the teacher and what they feel they have achieved, what they are most proud of and what to improve upon. Avoid becoming too judgemental; your role is to facilitate reflection. At the end encourage the teacher to identify some clear targets for development and when you will next review them.

Having identified your aims and focus for the subject, you will start to recognise priorities within physical education which may differ for different groups of pupils and staff and will require you to consider how the curriculum is structured and organised. As the 'leader' you will become a role model for both staff and pupils. While you have expectations of your team, they will also have expectations of you; don't be surprised if these differ! Some leaders find it useful to share their expectations with their team and produce some form of shared agreement of where you are going and how. This might be in the form of a rolling action plan which is updated at the end of each term, or a scheme of work based on feedback from class teachers and pupils.

However, leadership can be a lonely place and at times you may become despondent. What is important is that you share your successes, failures and frustrations with others. Throughout this book we have focused on developing your ability to reflect upon experiences and use them as learning opportunities. You might find it useful when first taking up a leadership role to identify someone who you can talk to, or keep some form of reflective journal and refer to it. You might buddy up with another subject leader either within the school or across your alliances of schools, to share good practice and experiences, or work with colleagues from other schools who have a similar role to share experiences. Support networks are important, and offer opportunities to discuss ideas, but with the growing emphasis within some schools and organisations around evidence-based practice, they also provide opportunities for you to work collaboratively with colleagues to support researching your own practice.

## Problem solving and action planning

It is very easy to think that our main job in a leadership role is to solve problems. In fact, I can remember one of my head teachers telling me that he didn't do problems, he wanted solutions. A statement such as this is somewhat cryptic but focusing on finding solutions to problems can be a more positivist approach to take. Having said that you will still have moments when you just don't see a solution.

The logical starting point when problem solving is to identify the problem or the issue that needs to be addressed. You need to be clear about the evidence you have available and how this can be interpreted. In the context of teaching the key focus must always be on the enhancement of pupil learning. A clear analysis of the issues should allow you to start to form an action plan to address them. At this point you may find that you need to refer some decisions to a more senior staff member or discuss your findings with the staff members involved. The case study at the end of the chapter provides you with an opportunity to follow through problem solving and action planning in a working example.

## Communication skills

The ways in which we communicate have expanded over time. How we talk to people depends on the context in which this communication takes place, for example, the way you talk in the staffroom may be very different to the way you talk in the classroom and the way you talk to parents. This also applies to the written word. We communicate to different groups of people, for example, colleagues, governors, external organisations, parents, pupils via email, formal correspondence and pupil reports. As a leader, you have to think about who you are communicating with. It is important that you are clear about what you want to get across and the most appropriate way to do so, for example, via email or a face-to-face conversation. Sometimes talking to the person, while potentially more difficult, will bring about a better resolution.

## Self-management

As well as managing other people, you will also need to manage yourself. The pressures placed on us in our working life have increased over time. Time is an important commodity, and occasionally you might feel that we have none left for ourselves. Personal time management becomes important if we are to achieve what needs to be done in an efficient and effective manner, while preserving time for ourselves.

As the subject leader, you will need to identify your priorities and therefore action planning becomes an important aspect of your work. You will need to set long-term, medium-term and short-term goals. By having an understanding of what needs to be done and by when, you can more effectively manage your working day. By setting attainable targets for each day you can start to develop the capacity to detach yourself from work when at home. Many of you will have heard the term 'work–life balance'. What is important is that you are able to provide much needed down time for yourself or you may suffer 'burnout'.

So how can we self-manage? The key is to identify how we work best. For example, I know I work best first thing in the morning, and that depending on what I am doing I like to listen to music. However, I also know that I am easily distracted, therefore it might be better for me to complete certain tasks at home. Take some time to think about your own preferences for working and integrate these into your working day. You might find it useful to compile a diary of the tasks you complete during a week.

One frustration we all share is that we 'never seem to get anything done'. A solution is to identify the tasks that need to be completed (best done at the end of the previous day) including one key task that you want to achieve in that day, for example, some marking, report writing, lesson planning. You should then aim to complete that task before anything else; by not checking emails and not answering phone calls for a set period of time you can become immersed in the job in hand. Once you have achieved that task you can go on to your next task. This gives us a sense of achievement even when the task is very small. If you are adopting such an approach you will need to build 'task time' into your daily programme. This is a simple premise, but if you reflect on your week so far and compare what you wanted to achieve at the start of the week with what you have actually achieved you will see that building in task time is not always as easy as it sounds.

We all have our own individual approaches to time management and self-management. What works for one will not work for another. It is therefore important that you identify a personal way of working which includes down time.

Time management is only one aspect of self-management. If you have achieved the position of subject leader, or are aspiring to become one, you should already have a focused approach to your personal career development. In order to have come into teaching you will have had to focus on the subjects you studied at school as well as the degree you achieved. Once you have qualified as a teacher, you do need to consider your continuing professional development. Most of you will be familiar with, for example, some form of career entry development profile or transition plan which you completed at the end of your initial teacher education and will have used to set development targets throughout the first year of your teaching.

Throughout this book you have been encouraged to complete a portfolio identifying your own personal strengths and areas for further development. Taking responsibility for your own personal development is an important aspect of teaching. As subject leader, you will also need to consider the developmental needs of those staff delivering the subject and provide structured opportunities for development to take place. It may be that you provide aspects of professional development yourself through training sessions, or that you engage external organisations to support this or utilise the funding provided through the Primary Physical Education and School Sport Premium.

Similar to action planning, you should review your targets on a regular basis and this will form part of the dialogue you have with your line manager within your school as you assess your progress as part of any performance review process.

## Task 12.2

Reflecting on the list of development needs you identified in Task 12.1 and your emerging knowledge based on the previous section of this chapter, review your own action plan and identify three key areas of development you wish to explore over the coming year.

# Strategic direction and development of the subject

As a subject leader, you will have aspirations around the development of your subject, however, you will need to work within the parameters set by the school. Each school will have a clear action plan or strategic plan around improving pupil learning and attainment. This will be shared regularly with you by the school management team, and your role as subject leader is to ensure that the plan is reflected in any planning you do. In essence, you have to clearly define how you will achieve the school plan through your own subject plan. As mentioned, previous programmes run through national organisations may well provide the support you need to raise the quality of the physical education taught in your school.

# Teaching and learning

We have identified that one of the key responsibilities of a subject leader is the management of effective teaching and learning of the subject area. You might find it useful to observe other staff teaching the subject as part of their own personal development. In doing so you will need to be clear about what the focus of your observations will be as well as how you will use your observations to support both the teacher observed and the development of the subject. You will also need to be clear about how you will deliver feedback drawn from your observations so that the process is seen as productive and not a threat.

It is likely that as a result of your observations you will be able to identify specific developmental opportunities. These should then be integrated into your rolling action plan.

# Efficient and effective deployment of staff and resources

As well as managing your class, yourself and the curriculum, you are also likely to be managing a budget. While the amounts will not be large you will need to carefully consider your priorities and these should be included in any action planning you undertake. Maintenance is an important aspect of resource management. You should have clear guidelines about the use of equipment with a specific focus on its storage.

You will have some form of equipment store. This should be kept tidy, with clearly defined storage areas. This will make the start of your lessons more efficient as you will find it easier to locate the equipment you need. Clear guidance on who is allowed into the equipment store should be provided including whether pupils are allowed in, and who has responsibility for any keys. You might also include a log book where staff can record any damaged equipment or equipment losses (tennis balls in summer are the main ones here).

As the subject leader, you will also have responsibility for aspects of health and safety within the physical education curriculum, and regular health and safety checks on equipment should be undertaken (see Chapter 8 for further details). James and Elbourn (2016) identify the following responsibilities that as a head of subject you should take responsibility for:

- take reasonable care of the health and safety of themselves and others
- co-operate with the employer on health and safety issues
- know and apply the employer's policy for health and safety, and incorporate this into PESSPA policy
- carry out their work as directed by the school leadership team
- report any concerns about health and safety
- do what is within their power to prevent further injury from reported concerns
- not place themselves or others at risk
- ensure they do not interfere with or misuse items for health and safety such as fire extinguishers or safety signs
- participate in safety inspections. (2016: 11)

## Case study: Action planning

In your role as subject leader, it has been brought to your attention by the head teacher that attainment in physical education is lower than that in other curriculum subjects. The head teacher has requested that you look into ways this might be addressed.

The following key questions about current levels of attainment should be asked.

1    What are the current levels of attainment and how do these differ from other subject areas?

    a    When was the data collected?

        i    How old is the data being used?

        ii   Was it collected during or at the end of a term?

        iii  Was anything else happening when the data was collected?

    b    What data was collected?

        i    Was it related to performance of specific activities?

        ii   Was it related to overall attainment across the term/year?

    c    Is the data accurately reflecting attainment?

*(Continued)*

*(Continued)*

Having collected information regarding the situation you should be able to identify developments you might undertake.

The following key questions about staff development and available resources should be asked.

1    Are staff confident in the assessment of performance in physical education?

   a    Do I need to provide any staff development opportunities?

      i    Should I involve outside agencies?
      ii    Should I look at cross-moderation of teachers' assessment?
      iii    Can I produce any support materials?

2    Are staff confident in the delivery of physical education lessons?

   a    Do I need to look at staff development opportunities?

      i    Are teachers using a range of teaching strategies within their lessons?
      ii    Are teachers differentiating to reflect the needs of all pupils?
      iii    Are teachers taking account of learning across the domains of learning?

3    Do we have enough equipment to support effective teaching?

   a    Do I need to look at requesting additional funding?
   b    Is funding being used effectively?
   c    Do I need to look again at how resources are being managed?

By drilling down to the problem and starting to look at potential solutions we can begin to add to our action plan.

In this case study your head teacher gave you a general observation of a problem. By asking questions you are starting to identify the source of the problem and in doing so beginning to identify possible solutions. For example, if you need to have more equipment so that pupils can practise their skills more frequently, do you need to negotiate an increase to your budget or undertake some fundraising activity? Do you need to provide some staff development on assessing pupils' performance and teaching strategies?

In completing this case study, you should have started to think about the integration of aspects of subject leadership into the development of action plans (see Table 12.3) as well as looking at the range of factors which might impact on pupils' learning experiences.

**Table 12.3**   Action planning: raising attainment

| Action | Success criteria |
| --- | --- |
| Develop resources and support materials for assessing performance in physical education | A range of assessment approaches demonstrated within lessons |
| | Pupils engaged in self and peer assessment against National Curriculum levels |
| Provide staff development opportunities around the delivery of physical education | Through lesson observations, staff demonstrate a range of teaching approaches |
| | Pupils report increased engagement in physical education lessons |
| Audit equipment management and storage | Improve standards of care and storage of equipment |

## Chapter summary

The aim of this chapter has been to look at how you might develop in your role of subject leader for physical education in the primary school. The chapter has focused on the knowledge, skills and understanding associated with subject leadership, as well as looking at a range of strategies you could employ to move your subject further. What is important in the organisation of the physical education curriculum is that you continue to review and refresh your own knowledge, skills and understanding in order to ensure positive learning opportunities for your pupils and to support staff within the school. Regular engagement in professional development opportunities is of course to be encouraged. To review your learning, you should reflect upon the following review questions.

1   What would you identify as the key characteristics of a subject leader?
2   What strategies would you employ to develop your competence as a subject leader in physical education?

## Further reading

Dean, J. (2004) *Subject Leadership in the Primary School: A Practical Guide for Curriculum Coordinators*. London: David Fulton Publishers.
This provides a comprehensive overview of the knowledge, skills and understanding necessary to lead subjects within the primary school.

Raymond, C. (1998) *Coordinating Physical Education across the Primary School (Subject Leaders' Handbook)*. London: Routledge.
Focusing specifically on the co-ordination of physical education, this subject-specific textbook, while potentially dated, does provide additional support and guidance for the subject leader.

# References

Almond, L. (2015) 'A change in focus for physical education', *Physical Education Matters*, 10(1): 22–6.

Ames, C. (1992) 'Achievement goals, motivational climate and motivational processes', in G. Roberts (ed.), *Motivation in Sport and Exercise*. Champaign, IL: Human Kinetics. pp. 161–76.

Amos, S. and Postlethwaite, K. (1996) 'Reflective practice in initial teacher education: Some successes and points for growth', *Journal of Teacher Development*, 5(3): 11–22.

Association for Physical Education (AfPE) (2015) *Physical Education Assessment Booklet*. AfPE: Worcester. Available at: www.afpe.org.uk/physical-education/wp-content/uploads/Physical_Education_Assessment_booklet_revised_June_2015.pdf.

Association for Physical Education (2016) *High Quality Physical Education and School Sport: The outcomes and contributions to the development of the whole child*. Poster, available at: www.afpe.org.uk.

Association for Physical Education (AfPE) and Youth Sport Trust (YST) (2016) *Evidencing the Impact of Primary PE and Sport Premium – Guidance and Template*. AfPE: Worcester. Available at: www.afpe.org.uk/physical-education/wp-content/uploads/Evidencing-the-Impact-Guidance-Impact-Resource-Web-Version.pdf.

Aubrey, K. and Riley, A. (2016) *Understanding and Using Educational Theories*. London: Sage.

Back Up and Active Assistance (2013) *Back Up Inclusive Education Toolkit*, Section 3.5, Back Up Trust. Available at: www.backuptrust.org.uk/inclusiveeducationtoolkit.

Bailey, R. (2006) *Teaching Physical Education: A Handbook for Primary and Secondary School Teachers*. London: Routledge.

Bailey, R., Armour, K., Kirk, D., Jess, M., Pickup, I. and Sandford, R. (2006) *The Educational Benefits Claimed for Physical Education and School Sport: An Academic Review*. London: British Educational Research Association (BERA).

Bandura, A. (1989) 'Social cognitive theory', in R. Vasta (ed.), *Annals of Child Development, Vol 6: Six Theories of Child Development*. Greenwich, CT: JAI Press. pp. 1–60.

Bandura, A. (2001) 'Social cognitive theory: An agentic perspective', *Annual Review of Psychology*, 52: 1–26.

Bassett, S., Bowler, M. and Newton, A. (2016) 'Schemes of work, units of work and lesson planning', in S. Capel, M. Leask and T. Turner (eds), *Learning to Teach in the Secondary School: A Companion to School Experience*, 7th edn. London: Routledge. pp. 108–21.

Bates, B. (2016) *Learning Theories Simplified, and How to Apply Them to Teaching*. London: Sage.

Bercow, J. (2008) *A Review of Services for Children and Young People (0–19) with Speech, Language and Communication Needs*. Nottingham: DCSF Publications. Available at: www.education.gov.uk/publications/eOrderingDownload/Bercow_Interim_Report.pdf (accessed September 2011).

Bloom, B.S., Engelhart, M.D., Furst, E.J., Hill, W.H. and Krathwohl, D.R. (1956) *Taxonomy of Educational Objectives Handbook 1: The Cognitive Domain*. New York: David McKay Co. Inc.

Board of Education (BoE) (1933) *Syllabus of Physical Education Training for Schools*. London: HMSO.

Boyd, P. and Harris, K. (2010) 'Becoming a university lecturer in teacher education: Expert school teachers reconstructing their pedagogy and identity', *Professional Development in Education*, 36(1–2): 9–24.

Breckenridge, M.E. and Vincent, E.L. (1965) *Child Development: Physical and Psychological Growth through Adolescence*. Philadelphia, London: W.B. Saunders Company.

British Heart Foundation (2012) *Exergaming: An Evidence Briefing on Active Video Games*. Loughborough: British Heart Foundation National Centre.

Brunton, J.A. (2003) 'Changing hierarchies of power in physical education using sport education', *European Physical Education Review*, 9(3): 267–84.

Bunker, D.J. and Thorpe, R.D. (1982) 'A model of the teaching of games in secondary schools', *Bulletin of Physical Education*, 18(1): 5–8.

Cabinet Office (2003) *Every Child Matters*, presented to Parliament by the Chief Secretary to the Treasury by Command of Her Majesty, September 2003. Norwich: HMSO.

Cabinet Office (2015) *Sporting Future: A New Strategy for an Active Nation*. London: Cabinet Office.

Capel, S. (2015) 'Value orientation of student physical education teachers learning to teach on school-based initial teacher education courses in England', *European Physical Education Review*, 22(2): 167–84.

Capel, S., Zwozdiak-Myers, P. and Lawrence, J. (2003) 'A study of current practice in liaison between primary and secondary schools in physical education', *European Physical Education Review*, 9(2): 115–34.

Capel, S., Zwozdiak-Myers, P. and Lawrence, J. (2004) 'Information exchanged between primary and secondary schools about physical education to support the transition from Key Stage 2 to Key Stage 3', *Educational Research*, 46(3): 283–300.

Capel, S., Zwozdiak-Myers, P. and Lawrence, J. (2007) 'The transfer of pupils from primary to secondary school: A case study of a foundation subject – physical education', *Research in Education*, 77: 14–30.

Corbin, C.B. (2002) 'Physical activity for everyone: What every physical educator should know about promoting lifelong physical activity', *Journal of Teaching in Physical Education*, 21: 128–44.

Corbin, C.B. and Lindsey, R. (1997) *Concepts of Physical Fitness*. Madison, WS: Brown and Benchmark.

Delignieres, D., Nourrit, D., Sioud, R., Lerpyer, P., Zattara, M. and Micaleff, J-P. (1998) 'Preferred coordination modes in the steps of learning complex gymnastics skill', *Human Movement Science*, 17: 221–41.

Department for Children, Families and Schools (DCSF) (2008) *The Education of Children and Young People with Behavioural, Emotional and Social Difficulties as a Special Educational Need*. London: DCFS.

Department for Education (DfE) (1995) *Physical Education in the National Curriculum*. London: HMSO.

Department for Education (DfE) (2011) *Teachers' Standards: Guidance for School Leaders, School Staff and Governing Bodies*. London: DfE.

Department for Education (DfE) (2013) *The National Curriculum in England: Framework Document*. London: DfE.

Department for Education (DfE) (2014) *Statutory Framework for the Early Years Foundation Stage: Setting the Standards for Learning, Development and Care for Children from Birth to Five*. London: DfE.

Department for Education (DfE) (2015) *Mental Health and Behaviour in Schools*. London: DfE.

Department for Education and Employment, and Qualifications and Curriculum Authority (QCA) (1999) *The National Curriculum for England*. London: HMSO.

Department for Education (DfE) and Department of Health (DoH) (2015) *Special Educational Needs and Disability Code of Practice: 0 to 25 Years. Statutory Guidance for Organisations Which Work with and Support Children and Young People Who Have Special Educational Needs or Disabilities*. London: DfE.

Department for Education and Skills (DfES) (2001) *Special Educational Needs: Code of Practice*. London: HMSO.

Department for Education and Skills (DfES) (2002) *Learning through PE and Sport*. London: HMSO.

Department for Education and Skills (DfES) (2004) *Removing Barriers to Achievement: The Government's Strategy for SEN*. Nottingham: DfES Publications.

Department for Education and Skills (DfES) (2005) *Excellence and Enjoyment: Social and Emotional Aspects of Learning: Guidance*. Norwich: HMSO.

Department of Education and Science (1991) *Physical Education for Ages 5–16*. London: HMSO.

Department of Health (2004) *At Least Five a Week – Evidence on the Impact of Physical Activity and Its Relationship to Health*. London: HMSO.

Department of Health (2009) *Healthy Child Programme*. London: DoH.

Department of Health (2010) *Physical Activity Guidelines in the UK: Review and Recommendations*. London: DoH. Available at: www.gov.uk/government/uploads/system/uploads/attachment_data/file/213743/dh_128255.pdf.

Department of Health (2011a) *Start Active, Stay Active: A Report on Physical Activity for Health from the Four Home Countries Chief Medical Officers*. London: DoH.

Department of Health (2011b) *UK Physical Activity Guidelines: Factsheets 1, 2 and 3*. London: DoH.

Drost, D.K. and Todorovich, J.R. (2013) 'Enhancing cognitive understanding to improve fundamental movement skills', *Journal of Physical Education, Recreation and Dance*, 84(4): 54–9.

Dweck, C.S (2012) *Mindset: How You Can Fulfil Your Potential*. London: Robinson.

Eime, R.M., Young, J.A., Harvey, J.T., Charity, M.J. and Payne, W.R. (2013) 'A systematic review of the psychological and social benefits of participation in sport for children and adolescents: Informing development of a conceptual model of health through sport', *International Journal of Behavioural Nutrition and Physical Activity*, 10: 1–21.

*Encyclopaedia Britannica* (2016) Available at: www.britannica.com/art/dance (accessed 27 October 2016).

English Athletics (2012) *Information and Advice: The Inclusion Spectrum Incorporating STEP (Black/Stevenson 2012), Inclusion Spectrum Guidance – 4*. Available at: www.englandathletics.org/shared/get-file.ashx?itemtype=document&id=13231 (accessed 4 December 2016).

Erikson, E.H. (ed.) (1963) *Youth: Change and Challenge*. New York: Basic Books.

Erikson, E.H. (1995) *Childhood and Society*, 2nd edn. London: Vintage.

Fleming, N.D. and Mills, C. (1992) 'Not another inventory, rather a catalyst for reflection', *To Improve the Academy*, 11: 137–55.

Fox, K. and Biddle, S. (1988) 'The child's perspective in physical education part 2: Children's participation motives', *The British Journal of Physical Education*, 19(2): 79–82.

Freud, S. (1927) *The Ego and the Id*. London: Hogarth Press.

Gallahue, D.L. and Ozmun, J.C. (1995) *Understanding Motor Development: Infants, Children, Adolescents, Adults*, 3rd edn. Iowa: Brown and Benchmark.

Gardner, H. (1999) *Intelligence Reframed: Multiple Intelligences for the 21st Century*. New York: Basic Books.

Garhart Mooney, C. (2000) *Theories of Childhood: An Introduction to Dewey, Montessori, Erikson, Piaget and Vygotsky*. St Paul, MN: Redleaf Press.

Gesell, A. (1928) *Infancy and Human Growth*. New York: Macmillan.

Gosset, M. (2016) 'Should we be teaching sport skills to 5–7 year olds in physical education? Not so fast', *Physical Education Matters*, 11(1): 22–3.

Griffin, L.L. and Butler, J.I. (eds) (2005) *Teaching Games for Understanding: Theory, Research and Practice*. Champaign, IL: Human Kinetics.

Havighurst, R.J. (1972) *Developmental Tasks and Education*. New York: David McKay Company.

Haydn, T. (2016) 'Assessing pupil progress', in S. Capel, M. Leask and T. Turner (eds), *Learning to Teach in the Secondary School: A Companion to School Experience*, 7th edn. London: Routledge.

Haydn-Davies, D. (2005) *How Does the Concept of Physical Literacy Affect What Is and Might Be the Practice of Physical Education?* Available at: www.physical-literacy.org.uk (accessed November 2016).

Hayes, D., Mills, M., Christie, P. and Lingard, B. (2006) *Teachers and Schooling Making a Difference: Productive Pedagogies, Assessment and Performance*. Crows Nest: Allen and Unwin.

Haynes, J. and Miller, J. (2015) 'Preparing pre-service primary school teachers to assess fundamental motor skills: Two skills and two approaches', *Physical Education and Sport Pedagogy*, 20(4): 397–408.

Haywood, K.M. (1986) *Life Span Motor Development*. Champaign, IL: Human Kinetics.

James, A. and Elbourn, J. (2016) *Safe Practice: In Physical Education, School Sport and Physical Activity*. Leeds: Coachwise Ltd.

Katz, L. (2003) 'The right of the child to develop and learn in quality environments', *International Journal of Early Childhood*, 3(1 and 2): 12–22.

Keenan, T. and Evans, S. (2009) *An Introduction to Child Development*, 2nd edn. Thousand Oaks: Sage.

Kirk, D. (2005) 'Physical education, youth sport and lifelong participation: The importance of early learning experiences', *European Physical Education Review*, 11(3): 1–16.

Kohl, H.W., Craig, C.L., Lambert, E.V., Inoue, S., Alkandari, J.R., Leetongin, G. and Kahlmeir, S. (2012) 'The pandemic of physical inactivity: Global action for public health', *The Lancet*, 380: 294–305.

Kolb, D.A. (1984) *Experiential Learning: Experience as the Source of Learning and Development*. New Jersey: Prentice-Hall.

Krathwohl, D.R., Bloom, B.S. and Masia, B.B. (1964) *Taxonomy of Educational Objectives; The Classification of Educational Goals Handbook II: The Affective Domain*. New York: Longman, Green.

Lawrence, D. (2009) *Enhancing Self-esteem in the Classroom*, 3rd edn. London: Sage.

Lawrence, J. (2006) *Negotiating Change: The Impact of School Transfer on Attainment, Self-esteem, Self-motivation and Attitudes in Physical Education*, unpublished PhD thesis. Brunel University.

Lawrence, J. (in press) 'Teacher educators in physical education', in G. Griggs and K. Petrie (eds), *Handbook of Primary Physical Education*. London: Routledge.

Lawrence, J., Low, K. and Phan, J. (2016) 'The impact of a high intensity observation programme in Singapore', paper presented at 6th Annual International Conference on Education and e-Learning, 26–27 September, Singapore.

Lopez-Pastor, V.M., Kirk, D., Lorente-Catalan, E., MacPhail, A. and Macdonald, D. (2012) 'Alternative assessment in physical education: A review of international literature', *Sport, Education and Society*, 18(1): 57–76.

Lord, C. and Bishop, S.L. (2010) 'Autism spectrum disorders – diagnosis, prevalence, and services for children and families', *Social Policy Report*, 24(2). Available at http://www.srcd.org/sites/default/files/documents/24-2.pdf (accessed 24 February 2017).

Ma, A.W.W. and Qu, L. (2016) 'The effect of exergaming on eye–hand coordination among primary school children: A pilot study', *Advances in Physical Education*, 6: 99–102. Available at: http://dx.doi.org/10.4236/ape.2016.62011.

Maude, P. (2013) 'Creativity and physical literacy', *ICSSPE Bulletin – Journal of Sport Science and Physical Education*, Bulletin 65.

Metzler, M.W. (2011) *Instructional Models for Physical Education*, 3rd edn. Scottsdale, AZ: Holcomb Hathaway Publishers.

Morgan, K., Bryant, A.N. and Diffey, F.R. (2013) 'The effects of a collaborative mastery intervention programme on physical literacy in primary PE', *Journal of Sport Science and Physical Education*, 65: 141–54.

Morgan, P.J. and Hansen, V. (2008) 'The relationship between PE biographies and PE teaching practices of classroom teachers', *Sport, Education and Society*, 13(4): 373–91.

Mosston, M. and Ashworth, S. (1994) *Teaching Physical Education*, 4th edn. New York: Macmillan College Publishing Company.

Mosston, M. and Ashworth, S. (2008) *Teaching Physical Education*, First Online Edition. Pearson Education.

Nelson, J., Martin, K., Nicholas, J., Easton, C. and Featherstone, G. (2011) *Food Growing Activity in Schools*. Slough: National Foundation for Educational Research.

Office for Standards in Education (Ofsted) (2003) *Special Educational Needs in the Mainstream, LEA policy and support services* (HMI 556). London: Office for Standards in Education.

Office for Standards in Education, Children's Services and Skills (Ofsted) (2013) *Beyond 2012 – Outstanding Physical Education for All: Physical Education in Schools 2008–12*. London: Ofsted.

Penney, D. (2003) 'Sport education and situated learning: Problematizing the potential', *European Physical Education Review*, 9(3): 301–8.

Penney, D. and Waring, M. (2000) 'The absent agenda: Pedagogy and physical education', *Journal of Sport Pedagogy*, 6(1): 4–37.

Philpott, H. (2016) 'Developing a growth mind set in physical education', *Physical Education Matters*, 11(1): 50–3.

Physical Education Association of the United Kingdom (PEAUK) (2003) *Observing Children Moving* [CD-ROM]. Worcester: Tacklesport (Consultancy) Company.

Piaget, J. and Inhelder, B. (1969) *The Psychology of the Child*. London: Routledge & Kegan Paul.

Public Health England (PHE) (2014) *The Link between Pupil Health and Wellbeing and Attainment, a Briefing for Head Teachers, Governors and Staff in Education Settings*. London: PHE Publications.

Public Health England (PHE) (2015) *Promoting Children and Young People's Health and Wellbeing*. London: PHE Publications.

Qualifications and Curriculum Development Agency (QCDA) (2010a) *The National Curriculum: Primary Handbook*. Coventry: QCDA.

Qualifications and Curriculum Development Agency (QCDA) (2010b) *Introducing the New Primary Curriculum: Guidance for Primary Schools*. Coventry: QCDA.

Randall, V.K. (2013) *Professional Learning Audit for Primary Physical Education*. AfPE: Worcester.

Ricci, M.C. (2013) *Mindsets in the Classroom: Building a Culture of Success and Student Achievement in Schools*. Waco: Prufrock Press Inc.

Rose, J. (2009) *Independent Review of the Primary Curriculum: Final Report*. Nottingham: DCSF.

Ryan, R.M. and Deci, E.L. (2008) 'Self-determination theory and the role of basic psychological needs in personality and the organization of behavior', in O.P. John, R.W. Robbins and L.A. Pervin (eds), *Handbook of Personality: Theory and Research*. New York: The Guilford Press. pp. 654–78.

Schon, D.A. (1983) *The Reflective Practitioner: How Professionals Think in Action*. London: Temple Smith.

Sheridan, M.K. (1991) 'Increasing self-esteem and competency in children', *International Journal of Early Childhood*, 23(1): 28–35.

Shilvock, K. and Pope, M. (2008) *Successful Teaching Placements in Secondary Schools*. Exeter: Learning Matters.

Shulman, L. (1987) 'Knowledge and teaching: Foundations of the new reform', *Harvard Educational Review*, 15(2): 4–14.

Siedentop, D. (1994) *Sport Education: Quality PE through Positive Sport Experiences*. Champaign, IL: Human Kinetics.

Simon, B. (1994) 'Why no pedagogy in England?', in B. Moon and A. Shelton Mayes (eds), *Teaching and Learning in Secondary Schools*. Milton Keynes: Open University Press. pp. 10–22.

Simpson, E. (1971) 'Educational objectives in the psychomotor domain', in M.B. Kapfer (ed.), *Behavioural Objectives in Curriculum Development*. Englewood Cliffs, NJ: Educational Technology Publications, Inc. pp. 60–7.

Smith, A. (1998) *Accelerated Learning in Practice: Brain-based Methods of Accelerated Motivation and Achievement*. London: Network Continuum Education.

Smith, P.K., Cowie, H. and Blades, M. (1998) *Understanding Children's Development*, 3rd edn. Oxford, London: Blackwell Publishers.

Sports Leaders (2013) *Promotional Leaflet for Level 5 Certificate in Primary School Physical Education Specialism and Level 6 Award in Primary School Physical Education Subject Leadership*. Available at: www.sportsleaders.org/media/359596/sl0623_l5-6cpd_promoleaflet_jan13.pdf (accessed 4 December 2016).

Sport Otago (2016) *Sport Otago – Getting People Active*. Available at: www.sport otago.co.nz/active-transport (accessed 3 August 2016).

Standage, M., Gillison, F.B., Ntoumanis, N. and Treasure, D.C (2012) 'Predicting students' physical activity and health related well-being: A prospective cross domain investigation of motivation across school physical education and exercise settings', *Journal of Sport and Exercise Psychology*, 34: 37–60.

Stevenson, P. and Black, K. (2011) *The Inclusion Spectrum Framework*. Available at: www.icsspe.org/documente/Ken_Black_-_Inclusion_Spectrum_summary.pdf.

Stiggins, R. (2014) 'Improve assessment literacy outside of school too', *Kappanmagazine*, 92(2): 67–72.

Stolz, S. and Pill, S. (2014) 'Teaching games and sport for understanding: Exploring and reconsidering relevance in physical education', *European Physical Education Review*, 20(1): 36–71.

Sugden, D.A. and Connell, R.A. (1979) 'Information processing in children's motor skills', *Physical Education Review*, 2(2): 123–40.

Teacher Development Agency (TDA) (1998) *National Standards for Subject Leaders*. London: TDA.

Teacher Development Agency (TDA) (2009) *Including Pupils with SEN and/or Disabilities in Primary Physical Education*. Manchester: TDA.

Vickerman, P. (2010) 'Planning for an inclusive approach to learning and teaching', in S. Capel and M. Whitehead (eds), *Learning to Teach Physical Education in the Secondary School*, 3rd edn. London: Routledge. pp. 168–182.

Webster, A (2016) 'Alternative pathways into physical activity for autistic people', *Physical Education Matters*, 11(2): 37.

Whitehead, M. (2004) 'Physical literacy: A debate', paper presented at Pre-Olympic Congress, Thessaloniki, Greece.

Whitehead, M. (2005) 'Developing physical literacy', paper presented at Primary Physical Education Conference, Roehampton.

Whitehead, M. (ed.) (2010) *Physical Literacy through the Lifecourse*. London: Routledge.

Whitehead, M.E. and Murdoch, E. (2006) 'Physical literacy and physical education: Conceptual mapping', *Physical Education Matters*, 1(1): 6–9.

Youth Sport Trust (2004) *TOP Play and TOP Sport Student Handbook: Using TOP Play and TOP Sport in Higher Education Institutions*. Loughborough: YST.

Youth Sport Trust (n.d.) *Becoming Outstanding*. Available at: www.youthsport trust.org/sites/yst/files/Sporting_Start_FinalProof_Wallplanner%20FINAL.pdf (accessed 4 December 2016).

# Index

# SECTIONAL MAPS OF THE BRITISH RAILWAYS

This atlas was originally published in 1948 as a permanent record of the British railway system as it was at the end of private ownership in December 1947. The book has been out of print for many years and the publishers are pleased to be able to make it available again in paperback form.

It will be seen that each map is divided into 10 mile squares identified by longitudinal letters and lateral numerals, so that from the Index all stations and principal junctions can be located by map number, letter and numerical reference. Stations in the index are shown in Roman type, whilst junctions and other points where there is no station are shown in italics.

Stations are normally indexed under their town name, but where there are characteristic additional names, the index will show them both under the town and such names as Thorpe (Norwich), Paragon (Hull) etc. Non-characteristic sub-titles such as Central, City, Exchange are not directly entered and one entry, eg Leeds will cover both Leeds Central and Leeds City stations. However, where a sub-title is compounded in the title of a locality the entry is direct, eg South Canterbury under S in contrast to Canterbury East under C.

Dual titles are cross-indexed, eg Claxby & Usselby is indexed both under C and U, but the map reference appears only under the first named station.

Plurality of stations and railway companies at a single place are exemplified thus:

(a) Bicester, GWR & LMS. Symbol (&) between owning companies to indicate two separate stations, separately owned.
(b) Birkenhead, BJ, *CLC, *GWR, etc. Comma (,) between owning companies to indicate separate stations, each individually owned. The CLC & GWR stations here are non-passenger, see Note*.
(c) Saunderton, GWR/LNER. Oblique (/) to indicate one station, jointly owned and used.
(d) Brecon, **GWR**/LMS. One station, owned by the company listed in bold type, but also used by the other.
(e) Aylesbury, GWR/LNER/LPTB & LMS. Two stations, of which one is "triple-joint" and the other is exclusively owned and used by LMS.

The above categories do not necessarily apply to goods stations at the places concerned.

Track Junctions — Those readily traceable by reference to an adjoining station, eg, Aynho Jc, GWR are not specifically indexed.

## WHERE IS IT ON THE MAP?

Example from Index; Framlingham, LNER, code 12, C3. Answer: on Map 12, in the square found by following Section C across until it meets the vertical column No 3.

## NOTES AND ABBREVIATIONS

| | | | | | | | | |
|---|---|---|---|---|---|---|---|---|
| **•** | ... No passenger service | **Jc(s)** | ... Junction(s) | **NSLR** | ... N. Sunderland Light Ry | **SMR** | ... Snowdon Mountain Ry (rack railway, n.g.) |
| **§** | ... Closed to all traffic | **KESR** | ... Kent & East Sussex Ry | **OAGB** | ... Oldham, Ashton & Guide Bridge Joint Ry (LMS/LNER) | **SR** | ... Southern Ry |
| **AJ** | ... Axholme Joint Ry (LNER/LMS) | **LMS** | ... London, Midland & Scottish Ry | | | **SSMW** | ... South Shields, Marsden & Whitburn (Coll.) Ry |
| **BJ** | ... Birkenhead Joint Ry (GWR/LMS) | **LNER** | ... London & North Eastern Ry | **OI** | ... Otley & Ilkley Joint Ry (LMS/LNER) | **SVY** | ... Severn & Wye Joint Ry (GWR/LMS) |
| **CLC** | ... Cheshire Lines Committee (LMS/LNER) | **LOR** | ... Liverpool Overhead Ry | **Plat** | ... Platform, = "Halt" | **SW** | ... Shrewsbury & Welshpool Joint Ry (GWR/LMS) |
| **Coll(s)** | ... Colliery (-ies) | **LPTB** | ... London Passenger Transport Board | **RCT** | ... Rye & Camber Tramy (n.g.) | | |
| **Corris** | ... Corris (n.g.) section, GWR | **ME** | ... Manx Electric Ry (n.g.) | **RHDR** | ... Romney, Hythe & Dymchurch Light Ry (n.g.) | **SY** | ... South Yorkshire Joint Ry (LNER/LMS) |
| **DA** | ... Dundee & Arbroath Joint Ry (LMS/LNER) | **Mer** | ... Mersey Ry | **RER** | ... Ravenglass & Eskdale Ry (n.g.) | **Tal.** | ... Tal-y-Llyn Ry (n.g.) |
| **DVL** | ... Derwent Valley Light Ry | **MGN** | ... Midland & Gt Northern Jt Ry (LNER/LMS) | **SBH** | ... Snailbeach Dist. Rys (n.g.) | **VR** | ... Vale of Rheidol (n.g.) section, GWR |
| **ECH** | ... Easton & Church Hope Ry (Portland) | **MJ** | ... Methley Joint Railway (LMS/LNER) | **SD** | ... Somerset & Dorset Joint Ry (LMS/SR) | **VT** | ... Vale of Towy Joint Ry (GWR/LMS) |
| **EKR** | ... East Kent Ry | **MN** | ... Mid-Notts Jt Ry (LMS/LNER) | **Sdg(s)** | ... Siding(s) | **WL** | ... Welshpool & Llanfair n.g. section, GWR |
| **ER** | ... Easingwold Ry | **MSJA** | ... Manchester, South Jc, & Altrincham Ry (LMS/LNER) | **SH** | ... Shrewsbury & Hereford Joint Ry (GWR/LMS) | **WM** | ... Wrexham & Minera Joint Ry (GWR/LMS) |
| **GWR** | ... Great Western Ry | | | **SK** | ... Swinton & Knottingley Joint Ry (LMS/LNER) | | |
| **HJ** | ... Halesowen Joint Ry (GWR/LMS) | **Mum. R** | ... Mumbles Electric Ry | | | **WUT** | ... Wisbech & Upwell Tramy. |
| **IMR** | ... Isle of Man Ry (n.g.) | **n.g.** | ... Narrow gauge | **SM** | ... Shropshire & Montgomeryshire Ry | | |
| | | **NSJ** | ... Norfolk & Suffolk Joint Ry (LNER/MGN) | | | | |

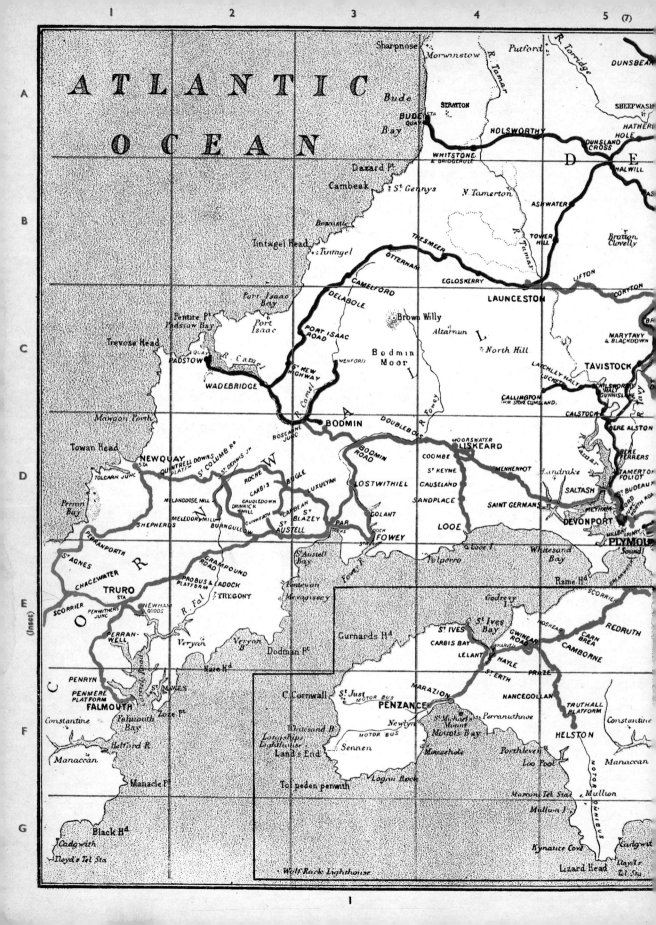

# SECTIONAL MAPS
## OF THE
## BRITISH RAILWAYS

as at 31st December 1947

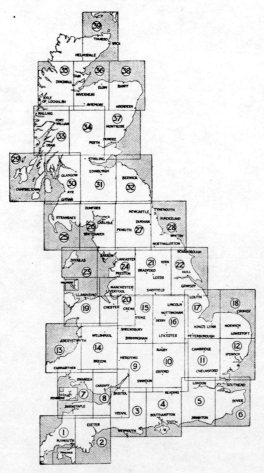

LONDON:

Ian Allan Ltd

# Explanation

| | |
|---|---|
| Great Western Railway ... ... ... | *Yellow* |
| London, Midland & Scottish Railway ... | *Red* |
| London & North Eastern Railway ... | *Blue* |
| Southern Railway ... ... ... ... | *Green* |
| Other Lines ... ... ... | *Indicated by name* |

A number bracketed in the margin indicates the continuation map.

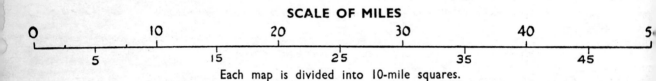

**SCALE OF MILES**

Each map is divided into 10-mile squares.

385.0941

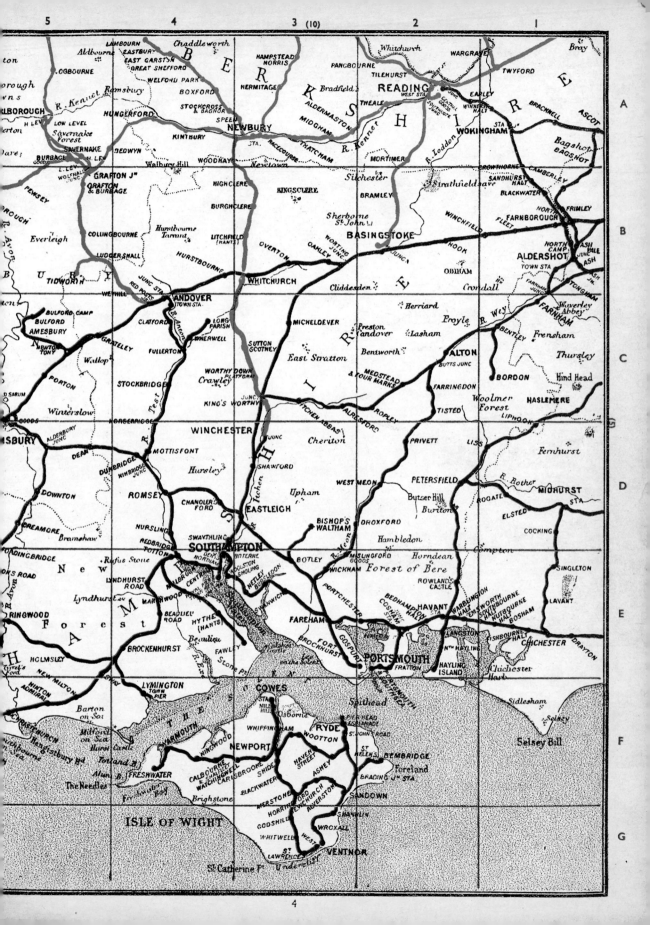

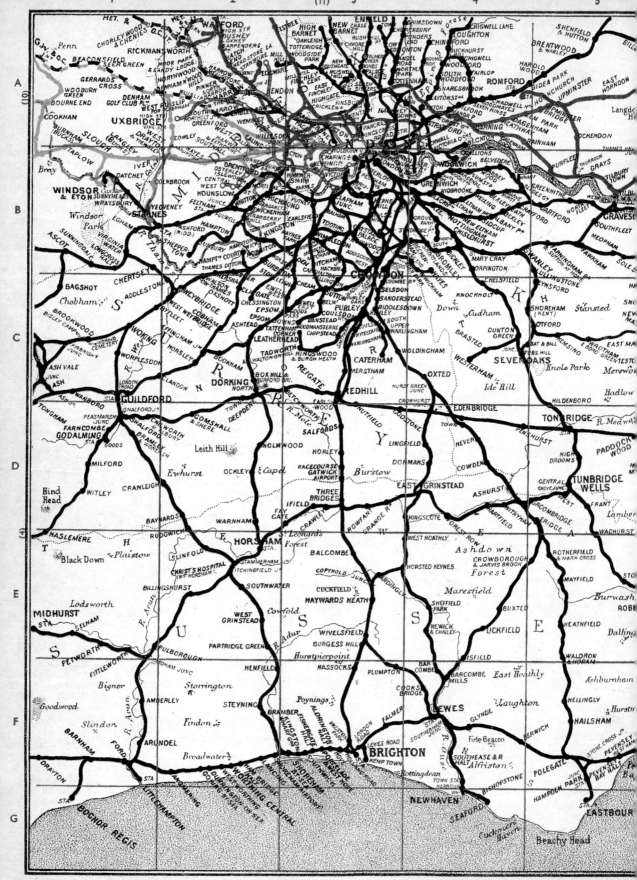

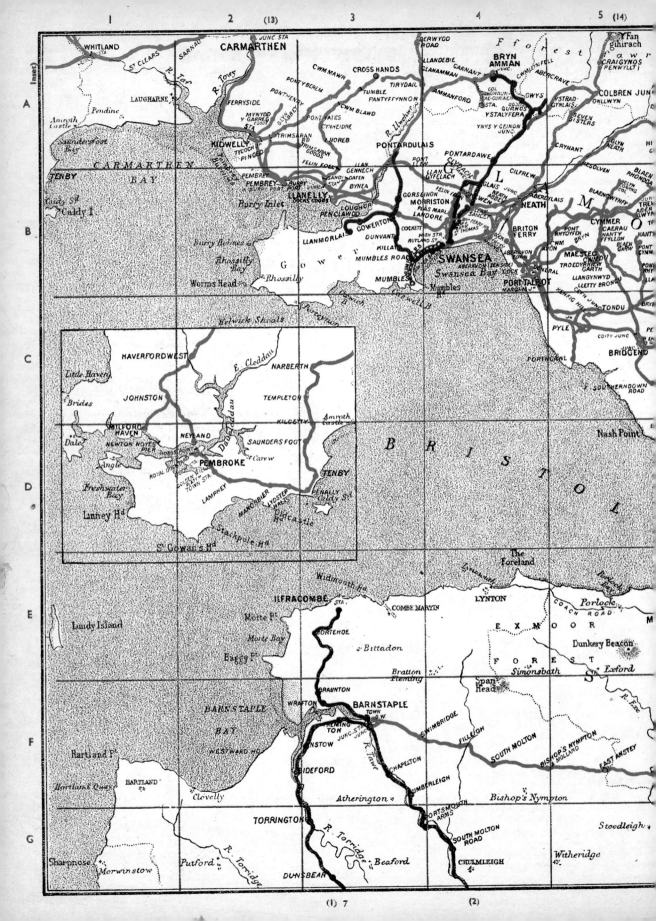

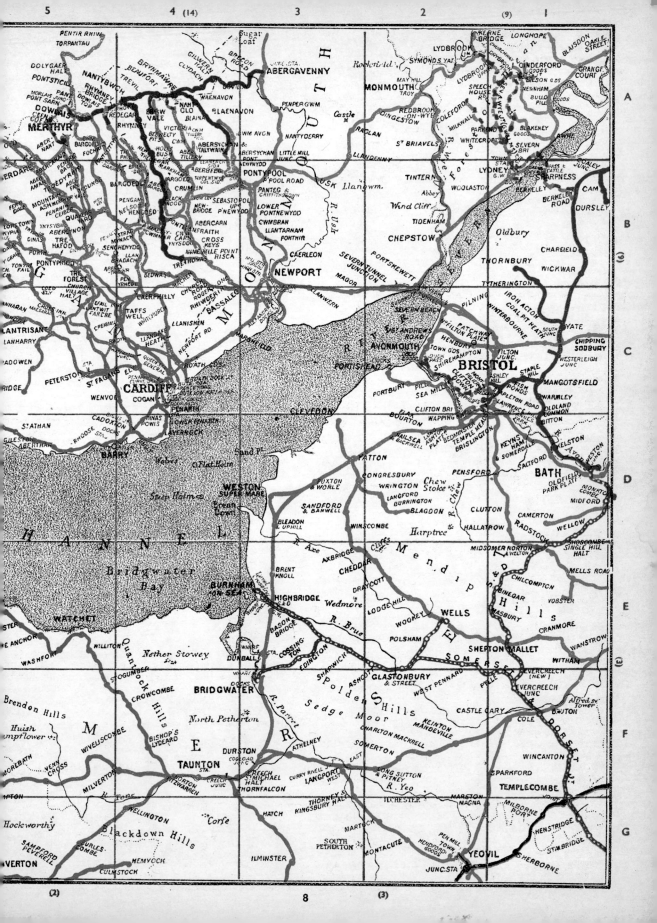

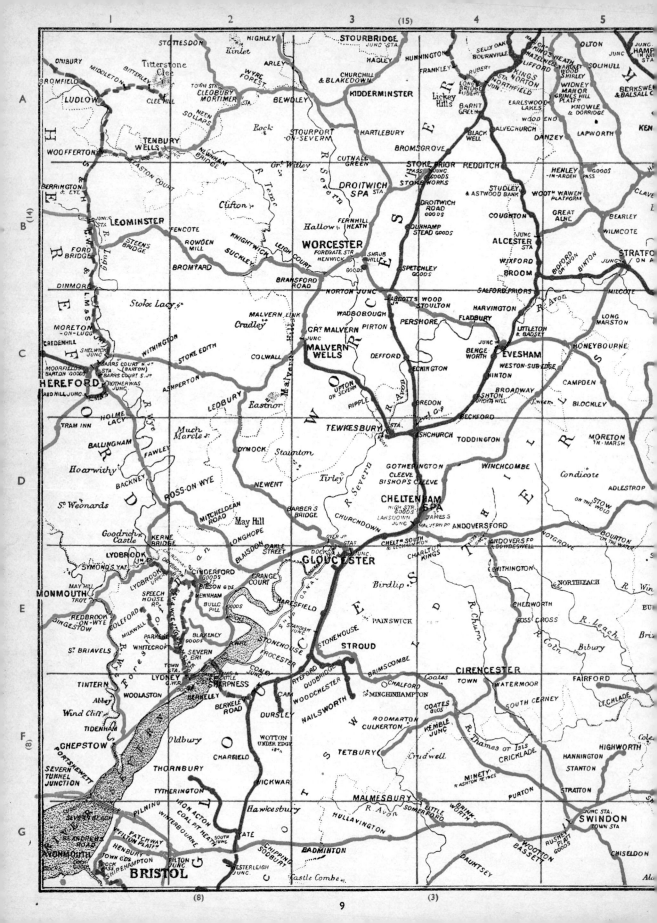

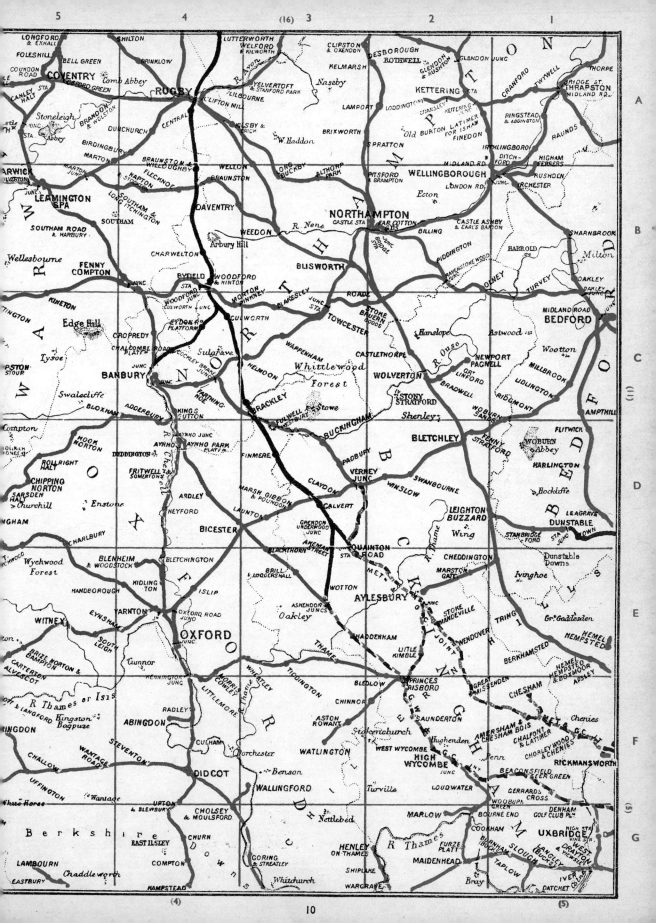

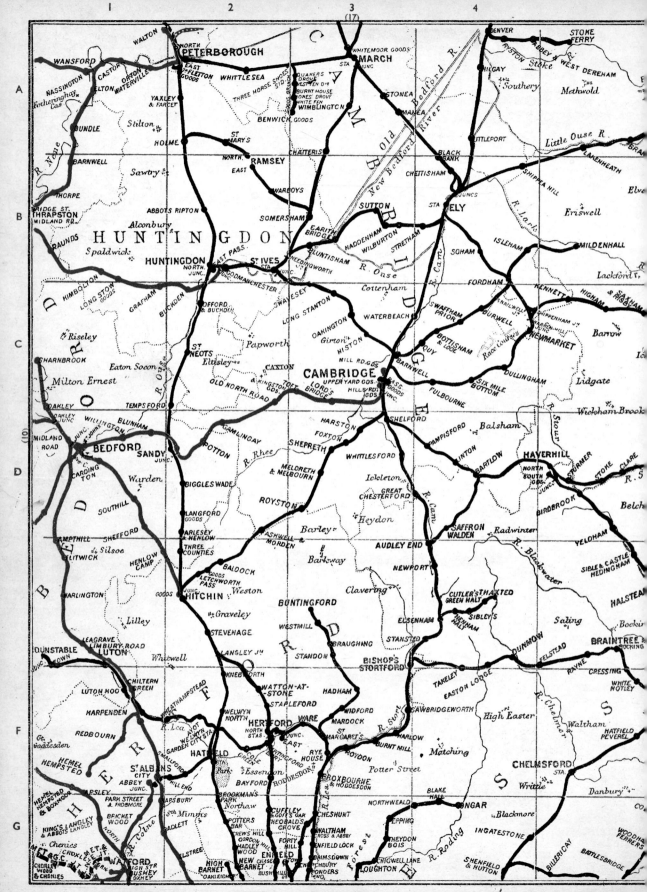

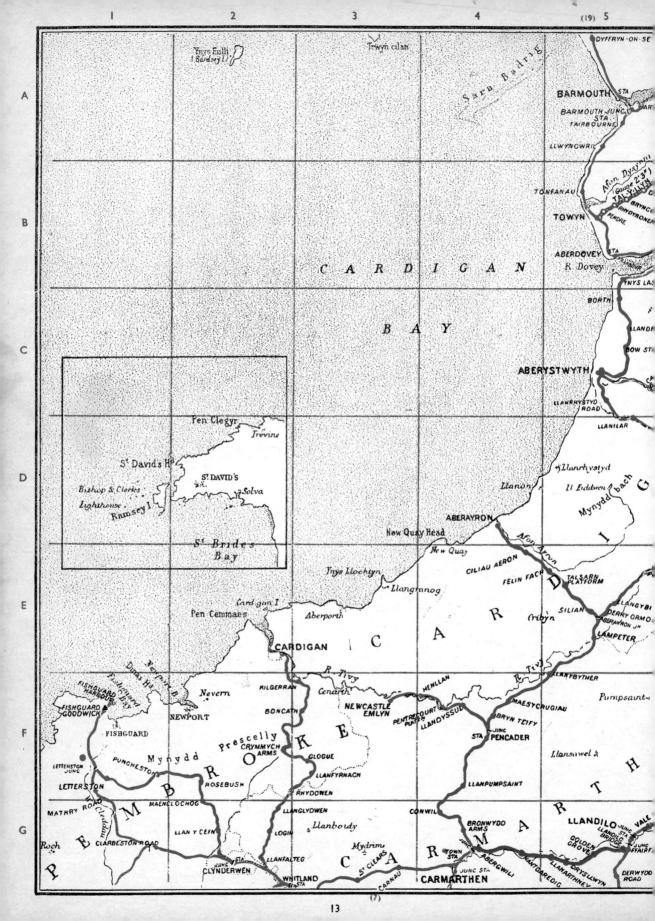

1   2   3   4

A

DYFFRYN-ON-SE

Trwyn cilan

Ynys Enlli
i Bardsey I.

Sarn Badrig

BARMOUTH   STA
BARMOUTH JUNC.
STA.
FAIRBOURNE

LLWYNGWRIL

B

C A R D I G A N

TONFANAU

Afon Dysynni
(Gauge 2'3")
TAL-Y-LLYN
BRYNG
RHYDYRONEN
PENDRE

TOWYN

ABERDOVEY
R Dovey

STA.
HARBOUR

YNYS LAS

BAY

BORTH

LLANDF

C

BOW ST

ABERYSTWYTH

LLANRHYSTYD
ROAD

LLANILAR

D

Pen Clegyr
Trevine

St Davids Hd
St DAVID'S
Solva

Bishop & Clerks
Lighthouse
Ramsey I.

Llanrhystyd

Llanon

Ll Eiddwen bach

Mynydd bach

I G

ABERAYRON

Afon Ayron

St Brides
Bay

New Quay Head

New Quay

CILIAU AERON

FELIN FACH

TALSARN
PLATFORM

D

Ynys Llochtyn

Llangranog

SILIAN

LLANGYBI
DERRY ORMO
ABERAYRON JN

E

Cardigan I.

Pen Cemmaes

Aberporth

C   A   R

Cribyn

LAMPETER

CARDIGAN

C

R. Tivy

R. Tivy

LLANYBYTHER

Pumpsaint

F

Dinas Hd

Newport B.

Fishguard B.

FISHGUARD
HARBOUR

FISHGUARD
GOODWICK

FISHGUARD

Nevern

Cenarth

KILGERRAN

BONCATH

NEWCASTLE
EMLYN

HENLLAN

PENTRECOURT
PLATF
LLANDYSSUL

MAESYCRUGIAU

BRYN TEIFY

STA   JUNC
PENCADER

Llansawel

Mynydd   Prescelly
CRYMMYCH
ARMS

E

LETTERSTON
JUNC

LETTERSTON

PUNCHESTON

GLOGUE

LLANFYRNACH

RHYDOWEN

LLANPUMPSAINT

MATHRY
ROAD

P   E   M   B   R   O   K   E

MAENCLOCHOG

ROSEBUSH

LLAN Y CEFN

LOGIN

LLANGLYDWEN

CONWIL

BRONWYDD
ARMS

LLANDILO   JUNC
LLANDILO
BRIDGE   JUNC

VALE

G

Roch

CLARBESTON ROAD

Afon Cleddau

Llanboidy

Mydrim

JUNC   STA
CLYNDERWEN

LLANFALTEG

St CLEARS

TOWN
STA

JUNC STA
ABERGWILI

CARNAU

CARMARTHEN

NANTGAREDIG

GOLDEN
GROVE

LLANDILO
JUNC
FFAIRF

DRYSLLWYN
LLANARTHNEY

DERWYDD
ROAD

WHITLAND

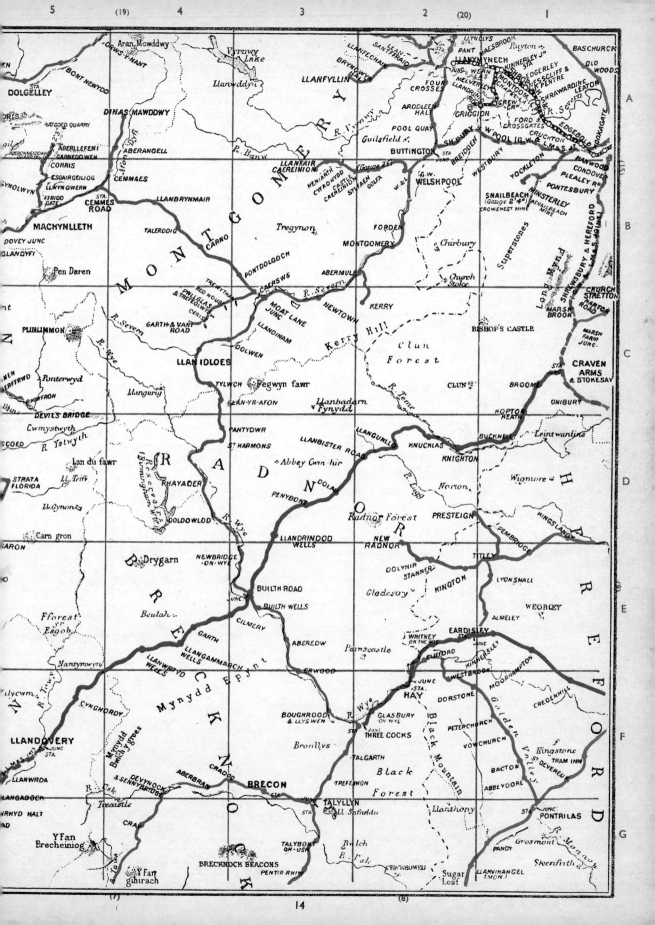

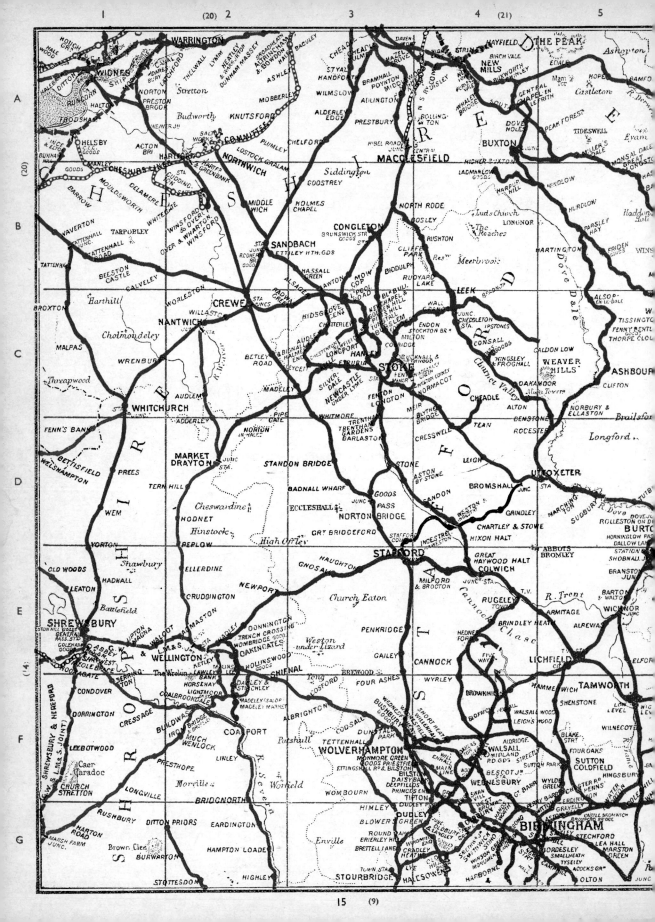

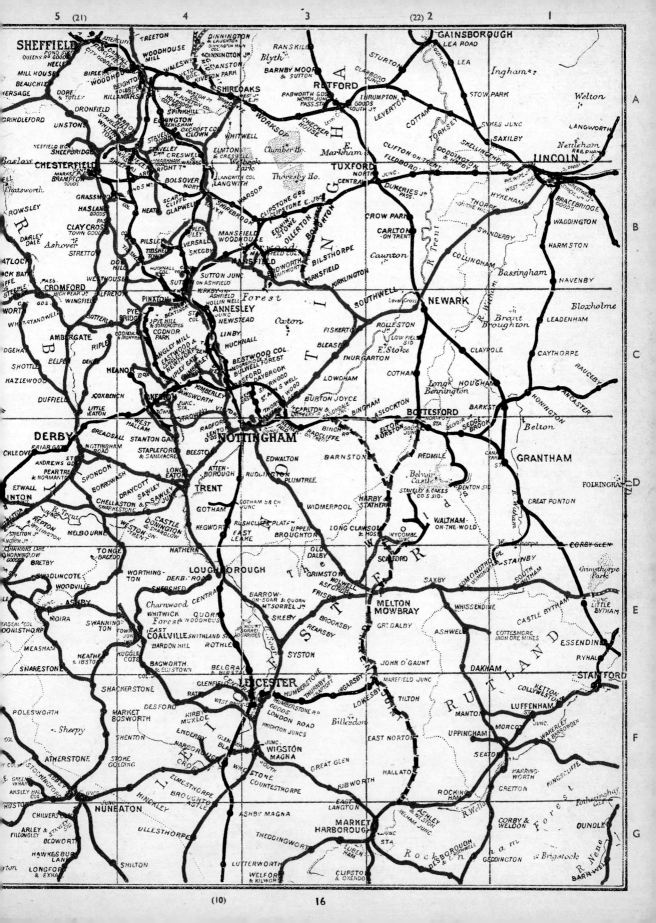

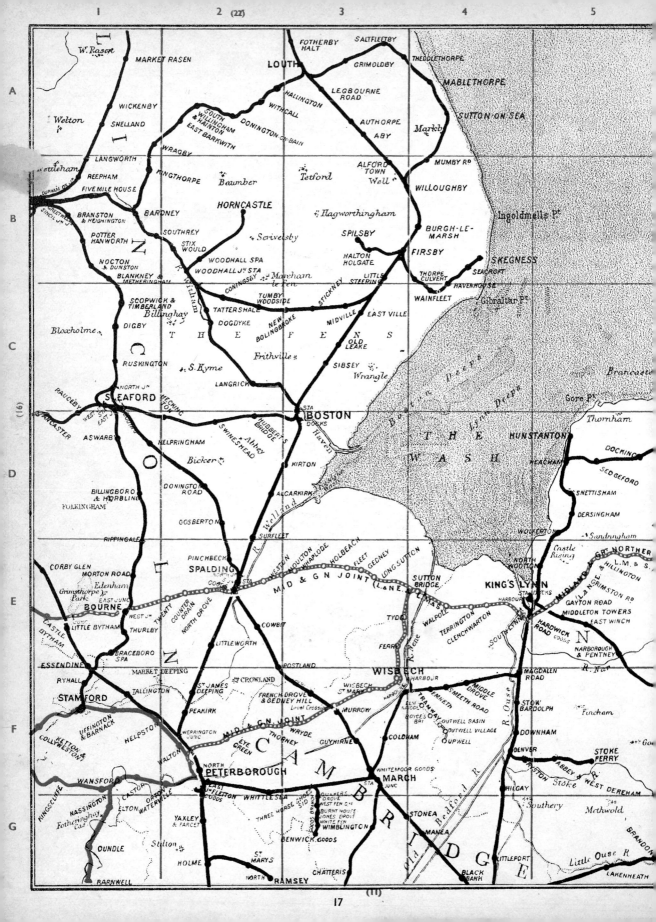

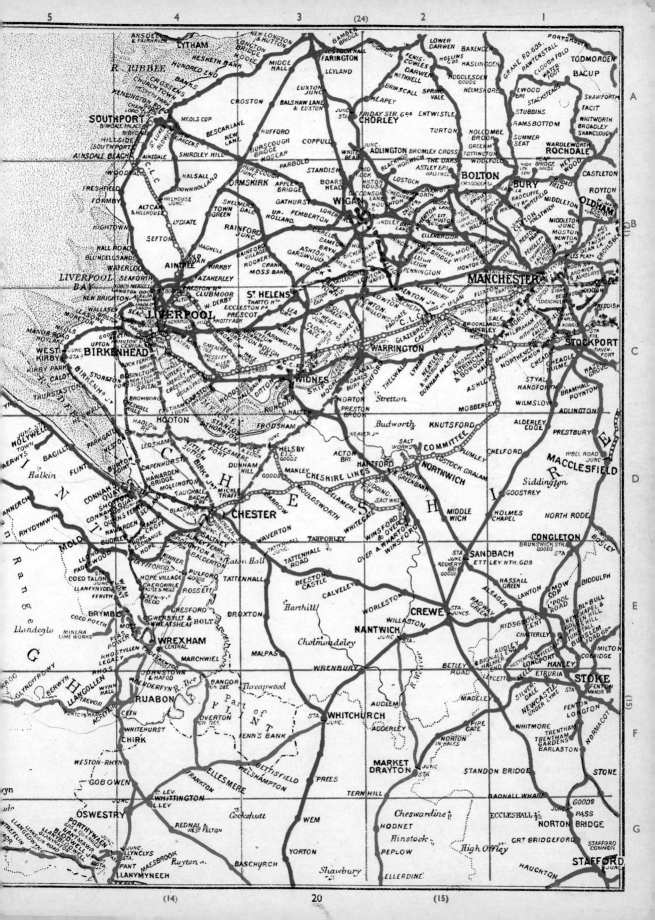

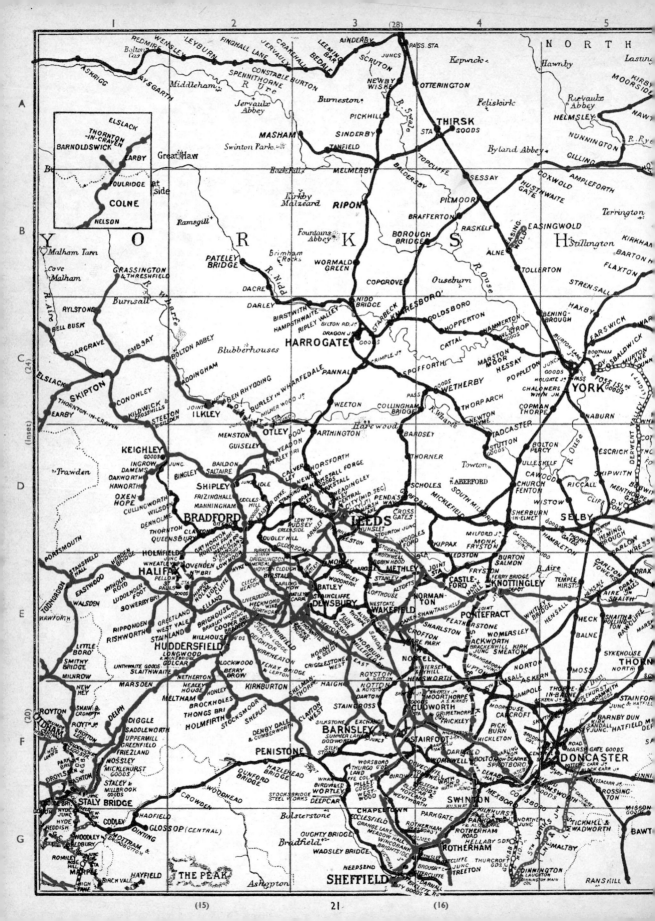

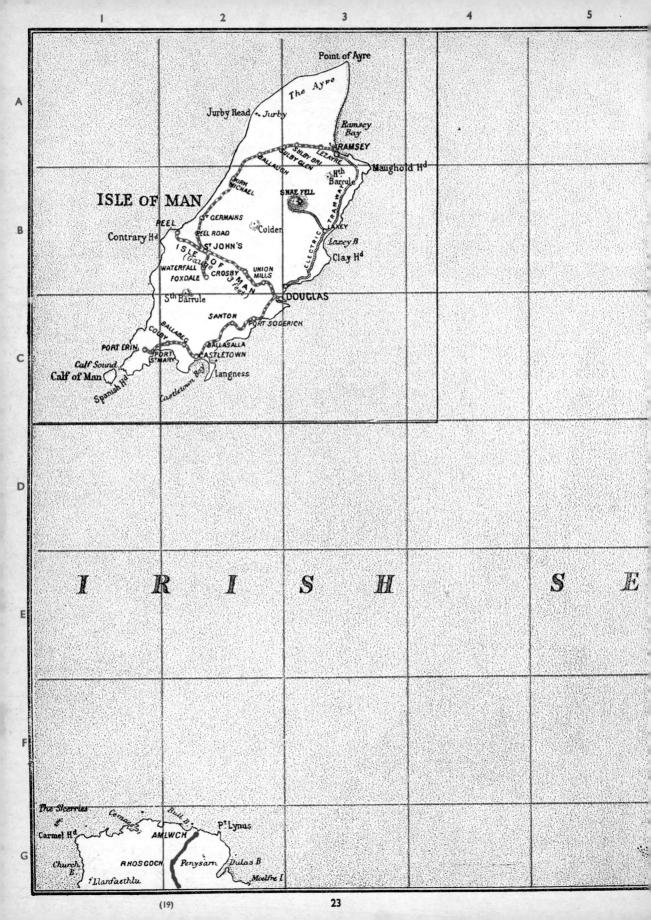

ISLE OF MAN

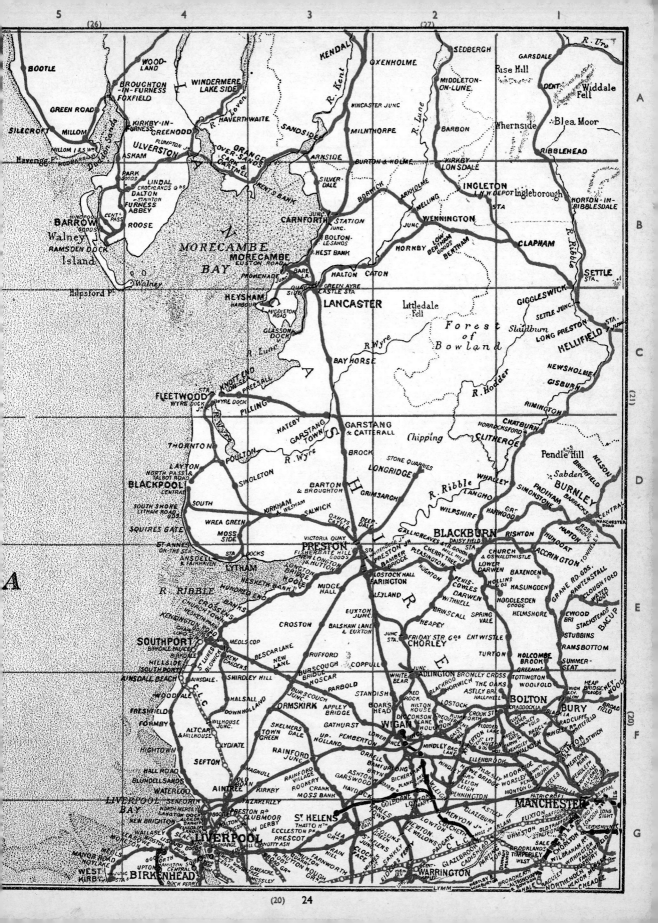

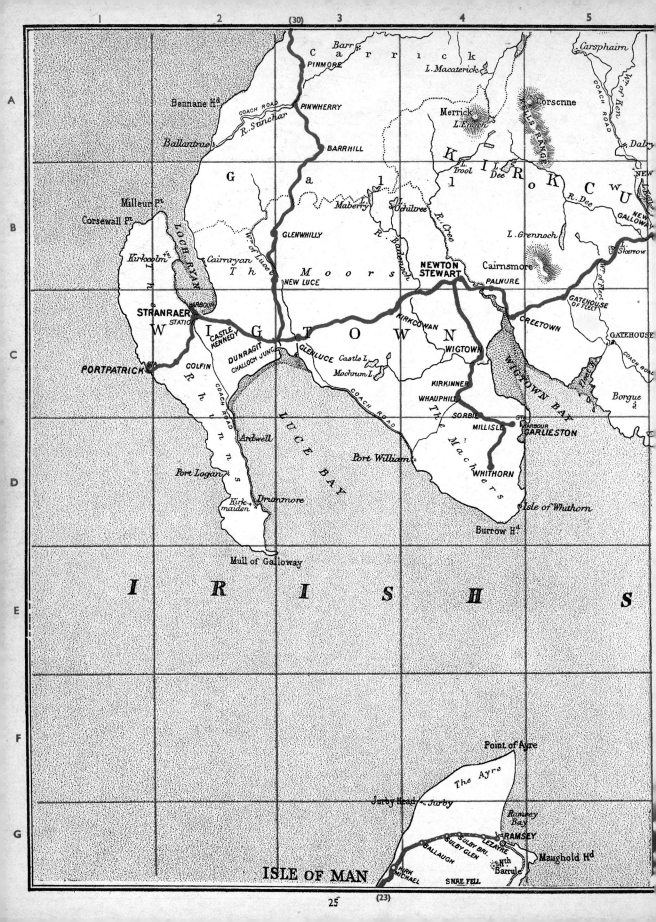

**ISLE OF MAN**

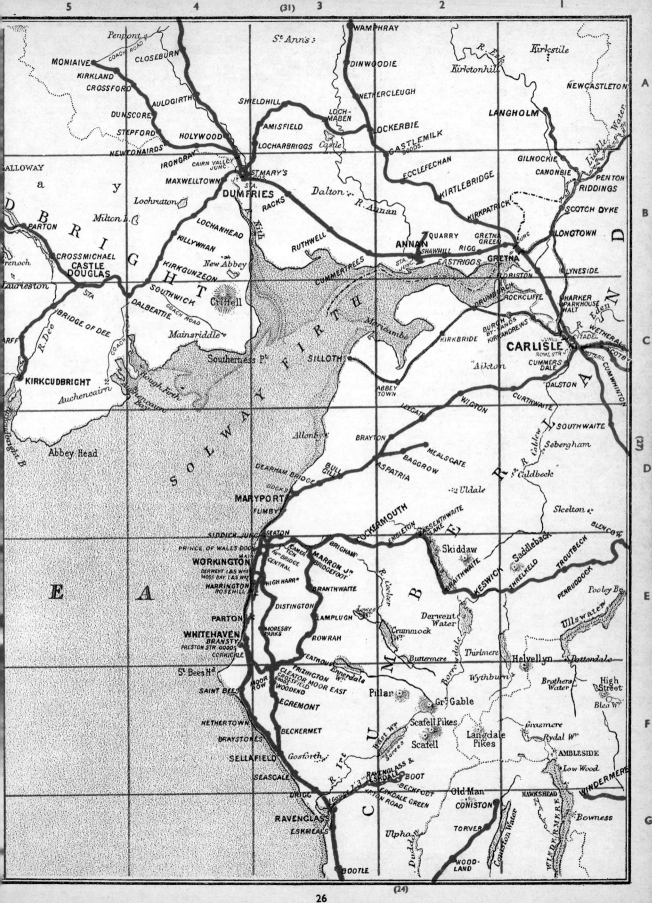

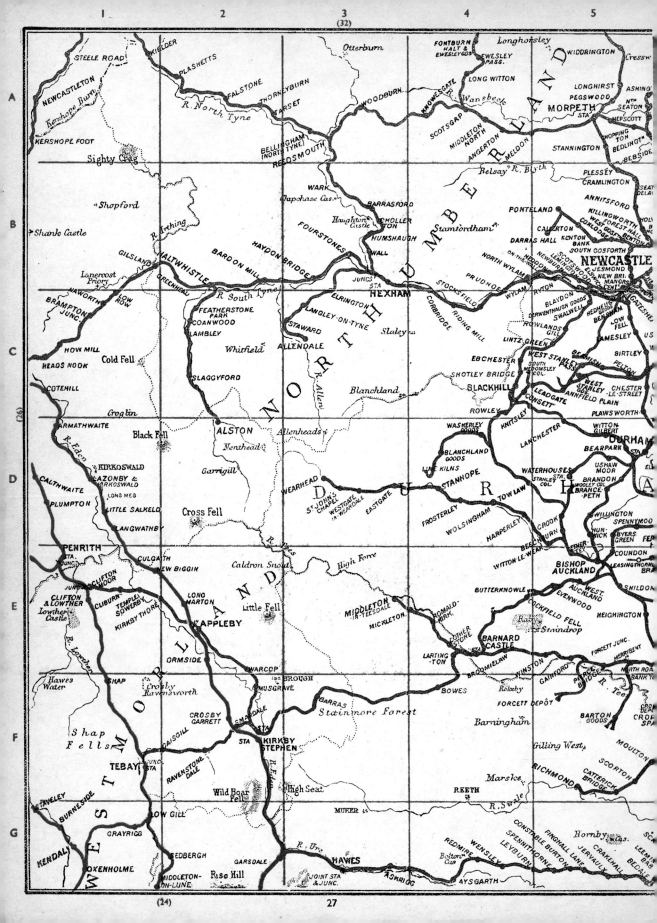

A

B

C

D

E

F

G

Snab Pt.

NEWBIGGIN-BY-THE-SEA

Camboise B.

BLYTH

NEWSHAM

HARTLEY

SEGHILL

MONK SEATON
WHITLEY BAY
CULLERCOATS
TYNEMOUTH
STA.
R. TYNE
SOUTH SHIELDS
WESTOE LANE
MARSDEN COTTAGE HALT
TYNE DOCK
MARSDEN
JARROW
BOLDON COL. STA.
EAST BOLDON

SOUTHWICK
SEABURN
NORTH DOCK
MONKWEARMOUTH
SOUTH DOCK
MILLFIELD
PALLION
HYLTON
COX GREEN
PENSHAW
SUNDERLAND
RYHOPE
RYHOPE EAST

FENCE HOUSES
SEATON
SEAHAM

LEAM SIDE
HETTON
MURTON
PITTINGTN.
Sth. HETTON
HASWELL
EASINGTON
SHERBn. COL.
HERBURN HO
HORDEN
THORNLEY COL.
SHOTTON BRIDGE
BLACKHALL COL HALT
BLACKHALL ROCKS
SHINCLIFFE
THORNLEY
M WELL FIELD
KELLOE
CASTLE EDEN
HART
COXHOE GOODS
TRIM DON
WINGATE
COXHOE BRI.
HURWORTH BURN
HARTLEPOOL
STA.
W. CORNFORTH
CHILTON JUNC.
WEST STA
Hartlepool Bay
SEATON CAREW
SEDGE FIELD
WYNYARD
GREATHAM
Tees Bay
THORPE THEWLES
HAVERTON HILL
BILLINGHAM ON TEES
NORTON ON TEES
PORT CLARENCE
SEATON ON TEES
STILLINGTON
NORTH GOODS
REDCAR
TOD POINT
AYCLIFFE
REDMARSHALL
PASS
Sth. GOODS
REDCAR EAST
MARSKE
SALTBURN
GRANGETOWN
SOUTH BANK
CARGO FLEET
BROTTON
DARLINGTON
STOCKTON
PASS
THORNABY
MIDDLESBROUGH
ESTON
NORTH SKELTON
SKINNINGROVE
LOFTUS
GRINKLE
STAITHES
Level Cross
ORMESBY
GUISBOROUGH
BOOSBECK
HINDERWELL
FIGHTING COCKS
GOODS
EAGLESCLIFFE
KETTLENESS
DINSDALE
YARM
NUNTHORPE
PINCHIN THORPE
HUTTON GATE
KILDALE MINES
Boulwick
Lythe
WHITBY
WEST CLIFF
STA.
C L E V E L A N D
GRt. AYTON
COMMON DALE
SANDSEND
ESK
CATTLE
STOKESLEY
INGLEBY
KILDALE
CASTLETON
DANBY
RUSWARP
SLEIGHTS
HAWSKER
PICTON
Gathorne
BATTERSBY
LEALHOLM
GLAISDALE
EGTON
GROSMONT
ROBIN HOOD'S BAY
ERYHOLME GOODS
WEST ROUNTON GATE
SEXHOW
POTTO
H I L L S
GOATHLAND
FYLING HALL
COWTON
TRENHOLME BAR
WELBURY
RAVENSCAR
DANBY WISKE
Osmotherley
C L E V E L A N D
STAINTONDALE
HAYBURN WYKE
BROMPTON
TOWN. GOODS
NORTHALLERTON
PASS. STA.
N O R T H   Y O R K   M O O R S
CLOUGHTON
AINDERBY
JUNCn.
Kepwick
Hawnby
Lastingham
LEVISHAM
Hackness
SCALBY
SCARBOROUGH
NEWBY
GOODS
CENTRAL
PASS

R. Wear

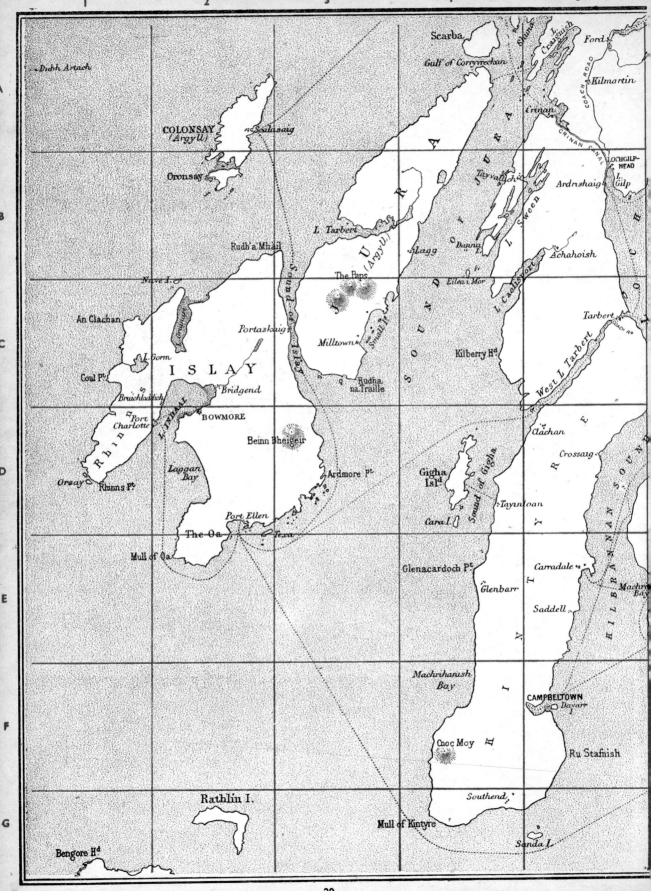

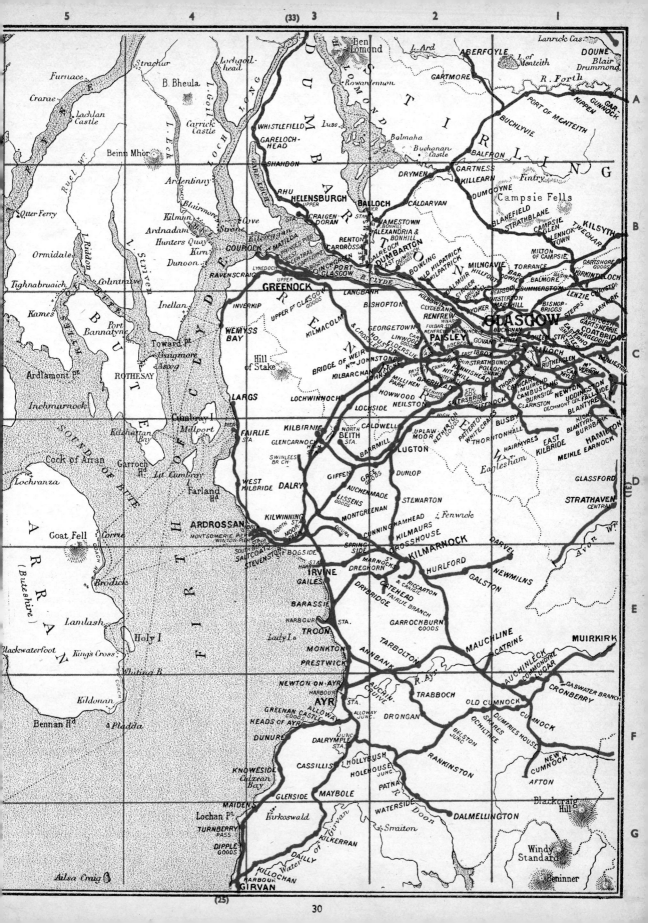

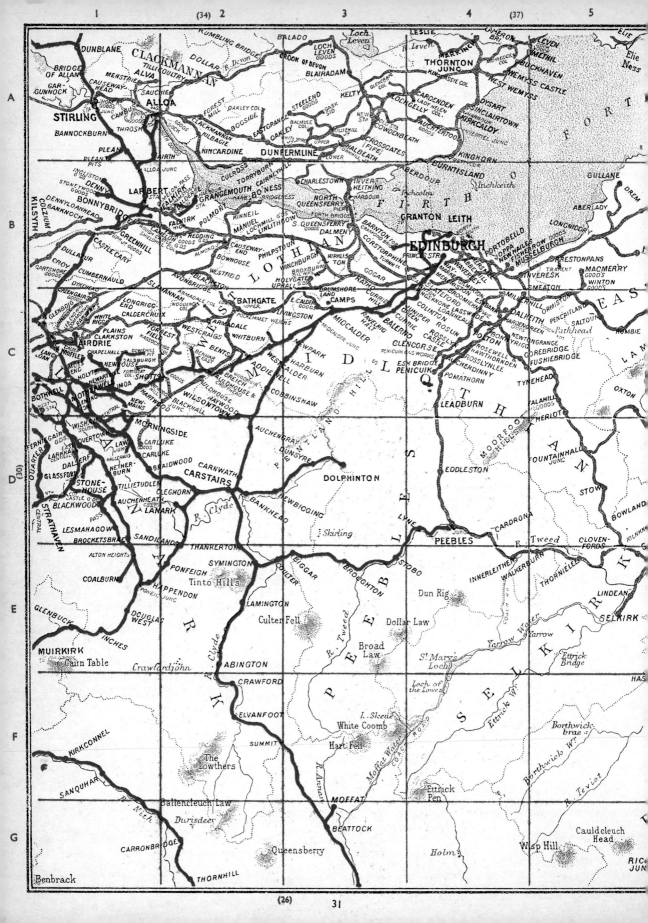

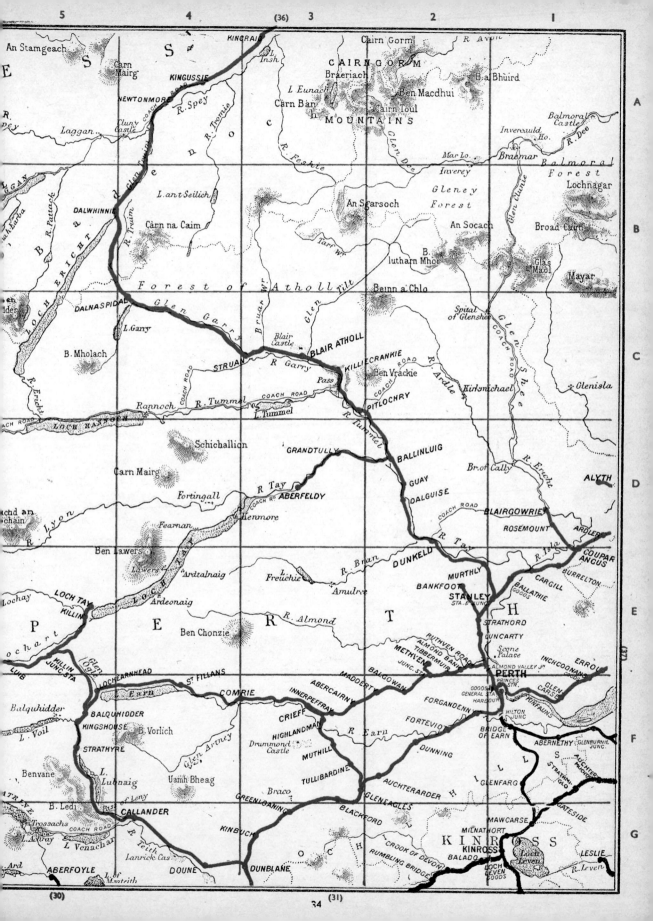

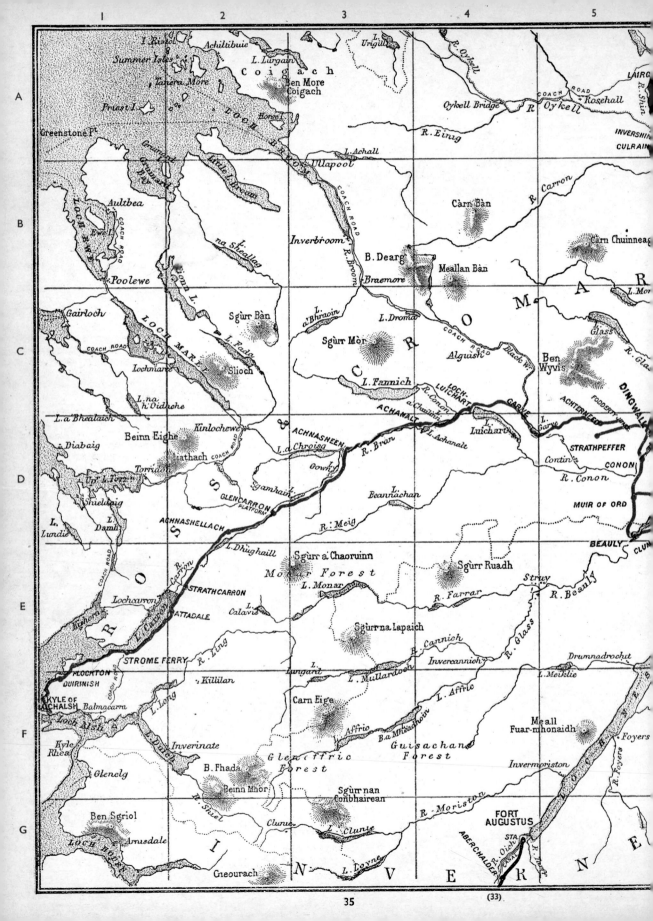

(33)

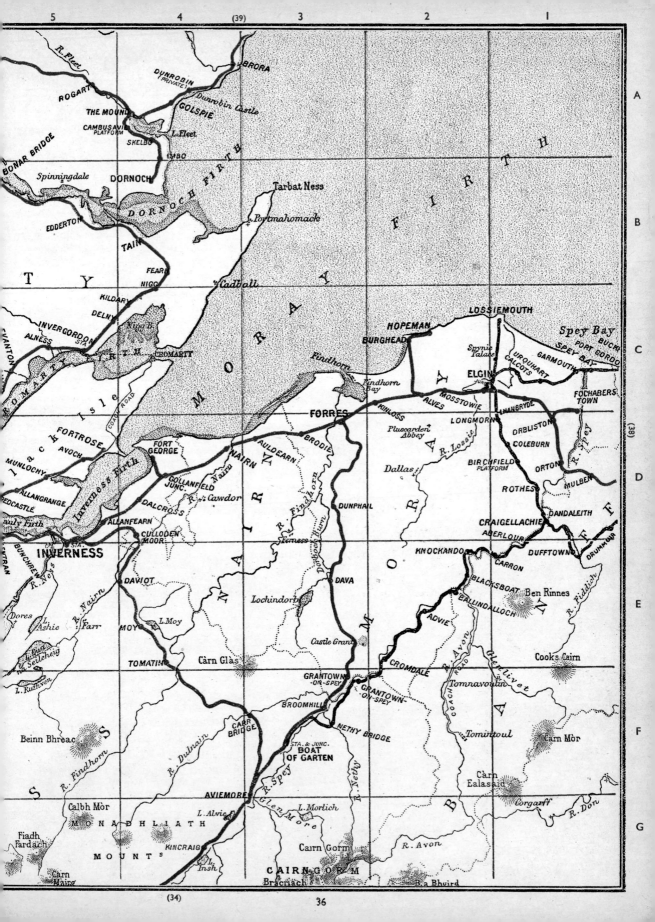

# INDEX

TO

STATIONS

SHOWN ON THESE MAPS

*(Explanation Page III)*

ABBEY—BELMONT

## A


Abbey (St. Albans), L.M.S., 11, F1.
• Abbey (Shrewsbury), S.M., 15, E1.
•Abbey & W. Dereham, L.N.E.R., 17, F5.
•Abbeydore, G.W.R., 14, F1.
Abbeyhill, L.N.E.R., 31, B4.
Abbey St.(Nuneaton),L.M.S., 16, F5.
Abbey Town, L.N.E.R., 26, C2.
Abbey Wood, S.R., 5, B4.
Abbotsbury, G.W.R., 3, F2.
Abbot's Langley, *see* King's Langley.
Abbots Ripton, L.N.E.R.,11, B2.
*Abbots Wood Jc.*, L.M.S./G.W.R., 9, C3.
Aber, L.M.S., 19, D3.
Aberaman, G.W.R., 8, B5.
•Aberangell, G.W.R., 14, A4.
Aberavon, G.W.R., 7, B4.
Aberayron, G.W.R., 13, D4.
*Aberayron Jc.*, G.W.R., 13, E5.
Aberbargoed (Mon.), G.W.R., 8, B4.
Aberbeeg, G.W.R., 8, B4.
Aberbran Halt, G.W.R., 14, F4.
Abercairny, L.M.S., 34, F3.
Abercanaid, G.W.R., 8, B5.
Abercarn, G.W.R., 8, B4.
§Aberchalder, L.N.E.R., 33, A5.
Abercorn (Paisley), L.M.S., 30, C2.
•Abercrave, G.W.R., 7, A5.
*Abercwmeiddaw Quarry*, Corris, 14, A5.
Abercynon, G.W.R., 8, B5.
Aberdare, G.W.R., 8, B5.
Aberdeen, L.N.E.R./L.M.S., 38, G2.
•Aberderfyn, G.W.R., 20, F4.
Aberdour, L.N.E.R., 31, B4.
Aberdovey, G.W.R., 13, B5.
Aberdylais, G.W.R., 7, B4.
Aberedw, G.W.R., 14, E3.
Abererch, G.W.R., 19, F1.
Aberfan, G.W.R., 8, B5.
Aberfeldy, L.M.S., 34, D3.
•Aberffrwd, V.R., 14, C5.
Aberfoyle, L.N.E.R., 30, A2.
Abergavenny, G.W.R. & L.M.S., 8, A3.
Abergavenny Jc., **G.W.R.**/L.M.S., 8, A3.
Abergele, L.M.S., 19, D4.
Abergwili, L.M.S., 13, G4.
Abergwynfi, G.W.R., 7, B5.
•Abergynolwyn, Tal., 13, B5.
•Aberlady, L.N.E.R., 31, B5.
•Aberllefeni, Corris, 14, A5.
Aberlour, L.N.E.R., 36, D1.
Abermule, G.W.R., 14, B3.
Abernant, G.W.R., 8, A5.
Abersychan, G.W.R., 8, A3.
•Abersychan & Talywain, L.M.S./G.W.R., 8, A4.
Aberthaw, G.W.R., 8, D5.
Abertillery, G.W.R., 8, B4.
Abertridwr, G.W.R., 8, B4.
Aberystwyth, G.W.R. & •V.R., 13, C5.
Abingdon, G.W.R., 10, F4.
Abington, L.M.S., 31, E2.
Aboyne, L.N.E.R., 37, A2.
Aby, L.N.E.R., 17, A3.
Accrington, L.M.S., 24, E1.
Achanalt, L.M.S., 35, D4.
Ach-na-cloich, L.M.S., 33, E3.
Achnasheen, L.M.S., 35, D3.
Achnashellach, L.M.S., 35, D2.
Achterneed, L.M.S., 35, D5.
Acklington, L.N.E.R., 32, B1.
Ackworth, S.K., 21, E4.
Acle, L.N.E.R., 18, F2.
Acocks Green, G.W.R., 15, G5.
Acrefair, G.W.R., 20, F5.
Acton, G.W.R. & L.M.S., 5, B3.
Acton Bridge, L.M.S., 20, D3.
Adderbury, G.W.R., 10, D4.
Adderley (Salop),G.W.R., 15 D2.
Addiewell, L.M.S. & •L.N.E.R., 31, C2.
Addingham, L.M.S., 21, C2.
Addington (Northants), *see* Ringstead.
Addiscombe, S.R., 5, B3.
Addlestone, S.R., 5, C2.
Adisham, S.R., 6, C2.
Adlestrop, G.W.R., 9, D5.
Adlington (Cheshire), L.M.S., 15, A3.
Adlington (Lancs), L.M.S., 20, A3.
Admaston, G.W.R./L.M.S., 15, E2.
Advie, L.N.E.R., 36, E2.
Afon Wen, **G.W.R.**/L.M.S., 19, F1.
*Afton*, L.M.S., 30, F1.
Ainderby, L.N.E.R., 28, G5.
Ainsdale, L.M.S., 20, A4.
Ainsdale Beach, C.L.C., 20, A4.
Aintree, L.M.S. & C.L.C., 20, B4.
Airdrie, L.N.E.R. & •L.M.S., 31, C1.
*Aire Jc.*, L.N.E.R., 21, E5.
Airmyn & Rawcliffe, L.N.E.R., 21, E5.
Airth, L.M.S., 31, A2.
•Akeld, L.N.E.R., 32, E3.
•Akeman St., L.N.E.R., 10, E3.
Albany Park, S.R., 5, B4.
•Albert Dock (Hull),L.N.E.R., 22, E3.
Albion, L.M.S., 15, F4.
*Albion Coll.*, G.W.R., 8, B5.
Albrighton, G.W.R., 15, F3.
Albury, *see* Chilworth.
Alcester, **L.M.S.**/•G.W.R., 9, B4.
Aldeburgh, L.N.E.R., 12, C1.
Aldeby, L.N.E.R., 18, F1.
*Alderbury Jc.*, S.R., 4, D5.
Alderley Edge, L.M.S., 15, A3.
Aldermaston, G.W.R., 4, A3.
Aldershot, S.R., 4, B1.
Aldridge, L.M.S., 15, F4.
Aldrington Halt, S.R., 5, F3.
Aldwarke, *see* Parkgate, L.N.E.R.
•Alexandra Dock (Hull), L.N.E.R., 22, E3.
Alexandra Dock (Liverpool), L.M.S., 20, C4.
*Alexandra Docks* (Newport), G.W.R., 8, C3.
Alexandria & Bonhill, L.M.S. /L.N.E.R., 30, B3.
Alford (Aberdeen), L.N.E.R., 38, F4.
Alford Town (Lincs.), L.N.E.R., 17, B3.
Alfreton, L.M.S., 16, C4.
Algarkirk, L.N.E.R., 17, D2.
Allanfearn, L.M.S., 36, D5.
Allangrange, L.M.S., 36, D5.
•Allendale, L.N.E.R., 27, C3.
Allerton, L.M.S. & C.L.C., 20, C4.
Allhallows-on-Sea, S.R., 6, B5.
Alloa, **L.N.E.R.**/L.M.S., 31, A2.
Alloa (Goods), L.M.S., 31, A2.
*Alloa Jc.*, L.M.S., 31, B1.
•Alloway, L.M.S., 30, F3.
§Almeley, G.W.R., 14, E1.
Almondbank, L.M.S., 34, E2.
*Almond Jc.*, L.N.E.R., 31, B2.
*Almond Valley Jc.*, L.M.S., 34, E2.
Alne, L.N.E.R., 21, B4.
Alness, L.M.S., 36, C5.
Alnmouth, L.N.E.R., 32, F1.
Alnwick, L.N.E.R. 32, F1.
Alresford (Essex), L.N.E.R., 12, E4.
Alresford (Hants.) S.R., 4, C3.
Alrewas, L.M.S., 15, E5.
Alsager, L.M.S., 15, C3.
Alsop-en-le-Dale, L.M.S., 15, C5.
Alston, L.N.E.R., 27, D2.
Altcar & Hillhouse, C.L.C., 20, B4.
Althorne, L.N.E.R., 12, G5.
Althorpe, L.N.E.R., 22, F5.
Althorp Park, L.M.S., 10, B3.
Altnabreac, L.M.S., 39, D2.
Altofts, L.M.S., 21, E4.
Alton (Hants.), S.R., 4, C2.
Alton (Staffs.), L.M.S., 15, C4.
•Alton Heights (Lanark), L.M.S., 31, E1.
Altrincham & Bowdon, **M.S.J.A.**/C.L.C., 20, C2.
Alva, L.N.E.R., 31, A1.
Alvechurch, L.M.S., 9, A4.
Alverstone (I.W.), S.R., 4, F3.
Alverthorpe, L.N.E.R., 21, E3.
Alves, L.M.S., 36, C2.
Alvescot, G.W.R., 10, E5.
Alyth (Perth), L.M.S., 37, D1.
Alyth Jc., (Angus), L.M.S., 37, D1.
Ambergate, L.M.S., 16, C5.
Amberley, S.R., 5, F1.
•Amble, L.N.E.R., 32, F1.
*Amble Branch Jc.*, L.N.E.R., 32, G1.
Amersham & Chesham Bois, L.N.E.R./L.P.T.B., 10, F1.
Amesbury, S.R., 4, C5.
•Amesley, L.N.E.R., 27, C5.
Amisfield, L.M.S., 26, A3.
Amlwch, L.M.S., 19, C1.
Ammanford, G.W.R., 7, A4.
•Amotherby, L.N.E.R., 22, B5.
Ampleforth, L.N.E.R., 21 B5.
Ampthill, L.M.S., 10, C1.
Ancaster, L.N.E.R., 16, C1.
Andover Jc., S.R., 4, C4.
,, Town, S.R., 4, C4.
Andoversford, G.W.R., 9, D4.
Andoversford & Dowdeswell, G.W.R., 9, D4.
Anfield, *see* Walton (Lancs.).
Angel Road, L.N.E.R., 5, A3.
Angerton, L.N.E.R., 27, A4.
Angmering, S.R., 5, F2.
Annan, L.M.S., 26, B2.
*Annan Quarry*, L.M.S., 26, B2.
Annbank, L.M.S., 26, E2.
Annesley, L.M.S. & •L.N.E.R., 16, C4.
Annfield Plain, L.N.E.R., 27, C5.
Annitsford, L.N.E.R., 27, B5.
Ansdell & Fairhaven, L.M.S., 24, E4.
*Ansley Hall Coll.*, L.M.S., 16, F5.
•Anston, L.M.S./L.N.E.R., 16, A4.
Anstruther, L.N.E.R., 37, G3.
Apperley Bridge, L.M.S., 21, D2.
Appin, L.M.S., 33, D2.
Appleby (Lincs.), L.N.E.R., 22, F4.
Appleby (Westmorland), L.M.S. & L.N.E.R., 27, E2.
Appledore (Kent), S.R., 6, E4.
*Applehurst Jc.*, L.N.E.R., 21, F5.
Appleton, L.M.S. 20, C3.
Appley Bridge, L.M.S., 20, B3.
Apsley, L.M.S., 10, E1.
•Arbirlot, D.A., 37, D3.
Arbroath, D.A., 37, D3.
Arddleen Halt, G.W.R., 14, A2.
Ardingly, S.R., 5, E3.
Ardleigh, L.N.E.R., 12, E4.
Ardler, L.M.S., 37, D1.
Ardley, G.W.R., 10, D4.
Ardlui, L.N.E.R., 33, F5.
Ardrossan, L.M.S., 30, D3.
Ardsley, L.N.E.R., 21, E3.
Ardwick, L.N.E.R., 20, B1.
Arenig, G.W.R., 19, F4.
Argoed, L.M.S., 8, B4.
Arisaig, L.N.E.R., 33, B1.
Arkholme, L.M.S., 24, B2.
Arksey, L.N.E.R., 21, F5.
Arkwright Town, L.N.E.R., 16, B4.
Arlesey & Henlow, L.N.E.R., 11, D2.
Arley (Worcs.), G.W.R., 9, A2.
Arley & Fillongley, L.M.S., 16, G5.
Armadale, L.N.E.R., 31, C2.
*Armadale Colliery*, L.N.E.R., 31, C2.
Armathwaite, L.M.S., 27, D1.
Armitage, L.M.S., 15, E5.
Armley, **L.N.E.R.**/L.M.S. & L.M.S., 21, D3.
Arnage, L.N.E.R., 38, E2.
Arnside, L.M.S., 24, A3.
Arpley (Warrington), L.M.S., 20, C2.
Arram, L.N.E.R., 22, D3.
Arrochar&Tarbet, L.N.E.R., 33, G5.
Arthington, L.N.E.R., 21 D3.
Arthog, G.W.R., 13, A5.
Arundel, S.R., 5, F1.
Ascot, S.R., 5, B1.
Ascott -under - Wychwood, G.W.R., 10, E5.
Asfordby, L.M.S., 16, E3.
Ash, S.R., 5, C1.
Ashbourne, L.M.S., 15, C5.
Ashburton, G.W.R., 2, C4.
Ashbury, S.R., 1, B5.
Ashburys, L.N.E.R., 20, B1.
Ashby (de-la-Zouch), L.M.S., 16, E5.
Ashby Magna, L.N.E.R., 16, G4.
Ashchurch, L.M.S., 9, D3.
Ashcott, S.D., 3, C1.
*Ashendon Jc.*, G.W.R./L.N.E.R., 10, E3.
Ashey (I.W.), S.R., 4, F3.
Ashford (Kent), S.R., 6, D4.
Ashford (Middx.), S.R., 5, B2.
Ashington, L.N.E.R., 27 A5.
*Ash Jc.*, S.R., 5, C1.
Ashley (Ches.), C.L.C., 20, C2.
Ashley & Weston (Northants), L.M.S., 16, G2.
Ashley Heath, S.R., 3, E5.
Ashley Hill, G.W.R., 8, C1.
Ashperton, G.W.R., 9, C2.
Ashtead, S.R., 5, C2.
Ashton (Devon), G.W.R., 2, C3.
Ashton (Lancs.), L.M.S., L.N.E.R., O.A.G.B., 21, F1.
Ashton-in-Makerfield, L.N.E.R., 20, B3.
Ashton Keynes, *see* Minety.
Ashton-under-Hill, L.M.S., 9, C4.
Ash Town, E.K.R., 6, C2.
Ashurst, S.R., 5, D4.
Ash Vale, S.R., 5, C1.
Ashwater, S.R., 1, B5.
Ashwell (Rutland), L.M.S., 16, E2.
Ashwell & Morden (Cambs.), L.N.E.R., 11, D2.
•Ashwellthorpe, L.N.E.R.,12, A3.
Askam, L.M.S., 24, A4.
Askern, L.M.S., 21, E5.
*Askern Jc.*, L.M.S./L.N.E.R., 21, F5.
Askrigg, L.N.E.R., 27, G3.
Aslockton, L.N.E.R., 16, C2.
Aspall&Thorndon, L.N.E.R., 12, C3.
Aspatria, L.M.S., 26, D3.
Astley, L.M.S., 20, B2.
Astley Bridge (Goods), L.M.S., 20, B2.
Aston (Warwicks.), L.M.S., 15, G5.
•Aston-by-Stone, L.M.S., 15, D4.
Aston Rowant, G.W.R., 10, F3.
Astwood Bank, *see* Studley.
•Aswarby, L.N.E.R., 17, D1.
Athelney, G.W.R., 8, F3.
Atherstone, L.M.S., 16, F5.
Atherton, L.M.S., 20, B2.
Attadale, L.M.S., 35, E2.
Attenborough, L.M.S., 16, D4.
•Attercliffe, L.N.E.R., 16, A5.
Attercliffe Rd., L.M.S., 16 A5.
Attleborough, L.N.E.R., 18, F4.
Attlebridge, M.G.N., 18, E3.
Auchendinny, L.N.E.R., 31, C4.
Auchengray, L.M.S., 31, D2.
Auchenheath, L.M.S., 31, D1.
•Auchenmade, L.M.S., 30,D3.
Auchincruive, L.M.S., 30, F2.
Auchindachy, L.N.E.R., 38, D5.
Auchinleck, L.M.S., 30, F1.
§Auchmacoy, L.N.E.R., 38, E2.
*Auchmuty Mills*, L.N.E.R., 37, G1.
Auchnagatt, L.N.E.R., 38, D2.
Auchterarder, L.M.S., 34, F2.
Auchterhouse, L.M.S., 37, E1.
Auchterless, L.N.E.R., 38, D3.
Auchtermuchty, L.N.E.R., 37, F1.
Auchtertool (Goods), L.N.E.R., 31, A4.
Audlem, G.W.R., 15, C2.
•Audley & Bignall End, L.M.S., 15, C3.
Audley End, L.N.E.R., 11, E4.
Auldbar Rd., L.M.S., 37, D2.
Auldearn, L.M.S., 36, D3.
Auldgirth, L.M.S., 26, A4.
•Aultmore, L.M.S., 38, D5.
Authorpe, L.N.E.R., 17, A3.
Aviemore, L.M.S., 36, D5.
•Avonbridge, L.N.E.R., 31, B2.
Avonmouth Dock, G.W.R./L.M.S., 8, C2.
Avonwick, G.W.R., 2, D4.
Awre, G.W.R., 9, E2.
Awsworth, L.N.E.R., 16, C4.
Axbridge, G.W.R., 8, E3.
Axminster, S.R., 2, B1.
Aycliffe, L.N.E.R., 28, E5.
Aylesbury, G.W.R./L.N.E.R /L.P.T.B. & L.M.S., 10, E2.
Aylesford, S.R., 6, C5.
Aylesham Halt, S.R., 6, C2.
Aylsham, L.N.E.R., 18, E3.
Aylsham, M.G.N., 18, D3.
Aynho, G.W.R., 10, D4.
Aynho Park Plat., G.W.R., 10, D4.
Ayot, L.N.E.R., 11, F2.
Ayr, L.M.S., 30, F3.
Aysgarth, L.N.E.R., 27, G4.
Ayton, L.N.E.R., 32, C3.


## B


Babworth(Goods), L.N.E.R., 16, A3.
Backney, G.W.R., 9, D1.
Backwell, *see* Nailsea.
Backworth, L.N.E.R., 28, B5.
•Bacton, G.W.R., 14, F1.
Bacup, L.M.S., 20, A1.
*Baddesley Coll.*, L.M.S., 16, F5.
Badminton, G.W.R., 9, G3.
•Badnall Wharf, L.M.S., 15, D3.
Badsey, *see* Littleton.
•Baggrow, L.M.S., 26, D2.
Bagillt, L.M.S., 20, D5.
Bag Lane (Atherton), L.M.S., 20, B2.
Bagnor, *see* Stockcross.
Bagshot, S.R., 5, C1.
Baguley, C.L.C., 20, C1.
Bagworth & Ellistown, L.M.S. 16, E4.
Baildon, **L.M.S.**/L.N.E.R., 21, D2.
Bailey Gate, S.D., 3, E4.
Baillieston, L.M.S., 30, C1.
Bainton, L.N.E.R., 22, C4.
Bakewell, L.M.S., 15, B5.
Bala, G.W.R., 19, F4.
Bala Jc., G.W.R., 19, F4.
Balado, L.N.E.R., 34, G2.
*Balby Jc.*, L.N.E.R., 21, F5.
Balcombe, S.R., 5, E3.
Baldersby, L.N.E.R., 21, B3.
Balderton, G.W.R., 20, E4.
Baldock, L.N.E.R., 11, E2.
Baldovan, L.M.S., 37, E2.
Baldragon, L.M.S., 37, E2.
•Balerno, L.M.S., 31, C3.
Balfron, L.N.E.R., 30, A2.
Balgowan, L.M.S., 34, F2.
Balham, S.R., 5, B3.
Ballabeg, I.M.R., 23, C2.
Ballachulish (Glencoe), L.M.S., 33, D3.
Ballachulish Ferry, L.M.S., 33, D3.
Ballasalla, I.M.R., 23, C2.
Ballater, L.N.E.R., 37, A1.
Ballathie (Goods), L.M.S., 34, E1.
Ballaugh, I.M.R., 23, A2.
Ballindalloch, L.N.E.R., 36, E2.
Ballingham, G.W.R., 9, D1.
Ballinluig, L.M.S., 34, D2.
Balloch, L.M.S./L.N.E.R., 30, B3.
Balmore, L.N.E.R., 30, B1.
*Balmule Colliery*, L.N.E.R., 31, A3.
Balne, L.N.E.R., 21, E5.
Balquhidder, L.M.S., 34, F5.
Balsall Common, *see* Berkswell.
Balshaw Lane & Euxton, L.M.S., 24, E3.
Bamber Bridge, L.M.S., 24, E2.
Bamford, L.M.S., 15, A5.
Bamfurlong, L.M.S., 20, B3.
Bampton (Devon), G.W.R., 8, G5.
Bampton (Oxon.), *see* Brize Norton.
Banavie, L.N.E.R., 33, C3.
Banbury, **G.W.R.**/L.N.E.R., & L.M.S., 10, C4.
Banchory, L.N.E.R., 37, A4.
Banff, L.N.E.R., 38, C4.
Banff Bridge, L.N.E.R., 38, C4.
Bangor, L.M.S., 19, D2.
Bangor-on-Dee, G.W.R., 20, F4.
Bankfield (L'pool), Goods, L.M.S., 20, C4.
•Bankfoot, L.M.S., 34, E2.
•Bankhead, L.M.S., 31, D2.
•Banknock, L.N.E.R., 31, B1.
Banks, L.M.S., 20, A4.
Bank Top (Darlington), L.N.E.R., 28, F5.
Bannockburn, L.M.S., 31, A1.
Banstead, S.R., 5, C 3.
Banwell, *see* Sandford.
Barassie, L.M.S., 30, E3.
Barber's Bridge, G.W.R., 9, D2.
Barbon, L.M.S., 24, A2.
Barcombe, S.R., 5, F4.
Barcombe Mills, S.R., 5, F4.
Bardney, L.N.E.R., 17, B1.
Bardon Hill, L.M.S., 16, E4.
Bardon Mill, L.N.E.R., 27, B2.
•Bardowie, L.N.E.R., 30, B1.
Bardsey, L.N.E.R., 21, D3.
Bare Lane, L.M.S., 24, B3.
•Bargeddie, L.N.E.R., 30, C1.
Bargoed, G.W.R., 8, B4.
§Barham, S.R., 6, C2.
Barking, **L.M.S.**/L.P.T.B., 5, A4.
Barkston, L.N.E.R., 16, C1.
Barlaston, L.M.S., 15, D3.
Barlow, L.N.E.R., 21, E5.
•Barmby, L.N.E.R., 21, E5.
Barming, S.R., 6, C5.
Barmouth, G.W.R., 13, A5.
Barmouth Jc., G.W.R., 13 A5.
Barnack, *see* Uffington.
Barnard Castle, L.N.E.R., 27, E4.
Barnby Dun, L.N.E.R., 21, F5.
Barnby Moor & Sutton, L.N.E.R., 16, A3.
Barnehurst, S.R., 5, B4.
Barnes, S.R., 5, B3.
Barnetby, L.N.E.R., 22, F3.
Barnham (Suffolk),L.N.E.R., 12, B5.
Barnham (Sussex), S.R., 5, F1.
Barnhill, L.M.S., 37, E2.
Barnoldswick, L.M.S., 21, inset.
Barnsley, **L.M.S.**/L.N.E.R., 21, F3.
Barnstaple, S.R. & G.W.R., 7, F3.
Barnstaple Jc., **S.R.**/G.W.R., 7, F3.
Barnstone, L.M.S./L.N.E.R. 16, D3.
Barnt Green, L.M.S., 9, A4.
Barnton, L.M.S., 31, B3.
Barnwell (Cambs.),L.N.E.R., 11, C3.
Barnwell (Northants.), L.M.S., 11, B1.
Barracks (Burnley), L.M.S., 24, D1.
Barras, L.N.E.R., 27, F3.
Barrasford L.N.E.R., 27, B3.
Barrhead, L.M.S., 30, C2.
Barrhead, South (Goods) L.M.S., 30, C2.
Barrhill, L.M.S., 25, A3.
Barrmill, L.M.S., 30, D3.
Barrow (Ches.), C.L.C., 20, D3.
Barrowden, *see* Wakerley.
Barrow Haven, L.N.E.R., 22, E3.
Barrow Hill & Staveley Works, L.M.S., 16, A4.
*See also* Staveley Works.
Barrow-in-Furness, L.M.S., 24, B5.
Barrow-on-Soar & Quorn, L.M.S., 16, E3.
*See also* Quorn, L.N.E.R.
*Barr's Court Jcs.*, G.W.R. L.M.S., 9, C1.
Barry, G.W.R., 8, D5.
Barry Docks, G.W.R., 8, D4.
Barry Island, G.W.R., 8, D4.
Barry Links, D.A., 37, E3.
*Barry Pier*, G.W.R., 8, D4.
Bartlow, L.N.E.R., 11 D4.
Barton (Goods), L.N.E.R. 27, F5.
•Barton & Broughton, L.M.S., 24, D3.
Barton & Walton, L.M.S., 15, E5.
•Barton Hill, L.N.E.R., 21, B5.
•Barton-le-street, L.N.E.R., 22, B5.
Barton-on-Humber, L.N.E.R., 22, E4.
Baschurch, G.W.R., 20, G4.
Basford (Notts.), L.M.S. & L.N.E.R., 16, C4.
Basingstoke, S.R. & G.W.R., 4, B2.
Bason Bridge, S.D., 8, E3.
Bassaleg, **G.W.R.**/L.M.S., 8, C3.
Bassenthwaite Lake, L.M.S., 26, D2.
Bat & Ball (Sevenoaks), S.R., 5, C5.
Bath, G.W.R. & **L.M.S.**/S.D., 3, A3, 3, Is. D., A3.
Bathampton, G.W.R., 3, A4.
Bathgate, L.N.E.R., 31, C2.
Batley, L.M.S. & L.N.E.R., 21, E3.
Batley Carr, L.N.E.R., 21, E3.
Battersby, L.N.E.R., 28, F4.
Battle, S.R., 6, F5.
Battlesbridge, L.N.E.R., 6, A5.
Bawtry, L.N.E.R., 21, G5.
Baxenden, L.M.S., 24, E1.
Bayford, L.N.E.R., 11, F2.
Bay Horse, L.M.S. 24, C3.
Baynards, S.R., 5, D2.
Beaconsfield, G.W.R. L.N.E.R., 10, F1.
Beal, L.N.E.R., 32, D2.
Bealings, L.N.E.R., 12, D3.
Beamish ,L.N.E.R., 27, C5.
Bearley, G.W.R., 9, B5.
•Bearpark L.N.E.R., 27, D5
Bearsden, L.N.E.R., 30, B2.
Bearsted & Thurnham, S.R., 6, C5.
§Beasdale, L.N.E.R., 33, B1
Beattock, L.M.S., 31, G3.
Beauchief, L.M.S., 16, A5.
Beaufort, L.M.S., 8, A4.
Beaulieu Road, S.R., 4, E4.
Beauly, L.M.S., 35, E5.
Bebington & New Ferry B.J., 20, C4.
Bebside, L.N.E.R., 28, A5.
Beccles, L.N.E.R., 12, A2.
Beckenham (Jc.), S.R., 5, B4.
•Beckermet, L.M.S., 26, F3.
§Beckfoot, R.E.R., 26, F2.
Beckford, L.M.S., 9, C4.
Beckingham, L.N.E.R., 22, G5.
•Beckton, L.N.E.R., 5, A4.
Bedale, L.N.E.R., 27, G5.
Bedford, L.M.S., 10, C1.
Bedhampton Halt, S.R., 4 E2.
Bedlington, L.N.E.R., 27,A5.
Bedlinog, G.W.R., 8, B5.
Bedminster, G.W.R., 8, D2.
Bedwas, G.W.R., 8 B4.
Bedwellty Pits, L.M.S., 8,A4.
Bedworth, L.M.S., 16, G5.
Bedwyn, G.W.R., 4, A4.
Beechburn, L.N.E.R., 27, D5.
Beeston (Notts.), L.M.S., 16 D4.
Beeston (Yorks.), L.N.E.R., 21, D3.
Beeston Castle, L.M.S., 20 E3.
Beighton, L.N.E.R., 16, A4.
Beith, L.M.S., 30, D3.
Bekesbourne, S.R., 6, C2.
Belford, L.N.E.R., 32, E2.
Belgrave & Birstall, L.N.E.R., 16, E4.
Bell Busk, L.M.S., 21, C1.
Belle Vue, L.M.S./L.N.E.R., 20, B1.
•Bell Green, L.M.S., 10, A5.
Bellingham (N. Tyne), L.N.E.R., 27, A3.
Belmont (Middx.), L.M.S., 5, A2.
Belmont (Surrey), S.R., 5, C3.

BELPER—BUTE ROAD


Belper, L.M.S. 16, C5.
Belses, L.N.E.R., 32, E5.
*Belston Jc.*, L.M.S., 30, F2.
Belton, A.J., 22, F5.
Belton & Burgh, L.N.E.R., 18, F1.
Beltonford (Goods), L.N.E.R., 32, B5.
Belvedere, S.R., 5, B4.
*Belvoir Jc.*, L.N.E.R., 16, D2.
Bembridge, (I.W.) S.R., 4, F2.
Bempton, L.N.E.R., 22, B3.
Benderloch, L.M.S., 33, E2.
Benfleet, L.M.S., 6, A5.
Bengeworth, L.M.S., 9, C4.
*Benhar East*, L.N.E.R., 31, C2.
*Benhar West*, L.M.S., 31, C2.
Beningborough, L.N.E.R., 21, C5.
Benllech, *see* Red Wharf Bay.
Ben Rhydding, O.I., 21, C2.
Bensham, L.N.E.R., 27, C5.
Bentham, L.M.S., 24, B2.
Bentley (Hants.), S.R., 4. C1.
Bentley (Suffolk), L.N.E.R., 12, E4.
Benton, L.N.E.R., 27, B5*l*
Bents, L.N.E.R., 31, C2.
•Benwick Goods Branch, L.N.E.R., 11, A3.
Bere Alston, S.R., 1, D
Bere Ferrers, S.R., 1, D
Berkeley, S.V.Y., 9, F2.
Berkeley Road, L.M.S./S.V.Y., 9, F2.
Berkhamsted, L.M.S., 10, E1.
Berkswell & Balsall Common, L.M.S., 9, A5.
erney Arms, L.N.E.R., 18, F1.
Berrington, G.W.R., 15, F1.
Berrington & Eye, S.H., 9, B1.
Berry Brow, L.M.S., 21. E2.
Berwick (Sussex), S.R., 5, F4.
Berwick-on-Tweed, L.N.E.R., 32, C3.
Berwyn, G.W.R., 20, F5.
Bescar Lane, L.M.S., 20, A4.
Bescot, L.M.S., 15, F4.
*Bessacar Jc.*, L.N.E.R./L.M.S., 21, F5.
*Bestwood Coll.*, L.N.E.R., 16, C4.
Betchworth, S.R., 5, C3.
Bethesda, L.M.S., 19, D2.
§Betley Road, L.M.S., 15, C2.
Bettisfield, G.W.R., 20, F3.
Bettws-y-Coed, L.M.S., 19, E4.
Beverley, L.N.E.R., 22, D3.
Bewdley, G.W.R., 9, A3.
Bexhill, S.R., 6, F5.
Bexley, S.R., 5, B4.
Bexleyheath, S.R., 5, B4.
Bicester, G.W.R. & L.M.S., 10, D4.
Bickershaw, L.N.E.R., 20, B2.
Bickleigh, G.W.R., 2, D5.
Bickley, S.R., 5, B4.
Biddenden, K.E.S.R., 6, D4.
•Biddulph, L.M.S., 15, B3.
Bideford, S.R., 7, F3.
•Bidford-on-Avon, L.M.S., 9, B5.
Bidston, L.M.S./L.N.E.R., 20, C4.
Biggar, L.M.S., 31, E3.
Biggleswade, L.N.E.R., 11, D2.
*Biglis Jc.*, G.W.R., 8, D4.
Bignall End, *see* Audley.
Bilbster, L.M.S., 39, D4.
•Billacombe, G.W.R., 2, D5.
Billericay, L.N.E.R., 5, A5.
Billing, L.M.S., 10, B2.
•Billingboro' & Horbling, L.N.E.R., 17, D1.
Billingham-on-Tees, L.N.E.R., 28, E4.
Billingshurst, S.R., 5, E2.
Bilson (Goods), G.W.R., 9, E2.
Bilston, G.W.R., 15, F4.
*See also* Ettingshall Road.
•Bilsthorpe, M.N., 16, B3.
*Bilton Road Jc.*, L.N.E.R., 21, C3.
Binegar, S. D., 3, B2.
Bingham, L.N.E.R., 16, C3.
Bingham Road (Notts.), L.N.E.R./L.M.S., 16, D3.
Bingley, L.M.S., 21, D2.
•Binton, L.M.S., 9, B5.
Birchfield Platform, L.N.E.R., 36, D1.
Birchington-on-Sea, S.R., 6, B2.
Birch Vale, L.M.S./L.N.E.R., 15, A4.
Birdbrook, L.N.E.R., 11, D5.
Birdingbury, L.M.S., 10, A4.
Birdwell, L.N.E.R., 21, F3.
Birdwell & Pilley (Goods), L.M.S., 21, F3.
Birkdale, L.M.S. 20, A4.
Birkdale Palace, C.L.C., 20, A4.
Birkenhead, B.J., •C.L.C., •G.W.R., •L.M.S., Mer., •L.N.E.R., 20, C4.
Birkenshaw, L.N.E.R., 21, E2.
*Birley Coll.*, L.N.E.R., 16, A5.
Birmingham, G.W.R. & L.M.S., 15, —
Birnam, *see* Dunkeld.
Birnie Rd., L.N.E.R., 37, C4.
Birstall (Leics.), *see* Belgrave.
Birstall (Yorks.), L.M.S., 21, E2.
Birstwith, L.N.E.R., 21, C3.
Birtley, L.N.E.R., 27, C5.
Bishop Auckland, L.N.E.R., 27, E5.
Bishopbriggs, L.N.E.R., 30, C1.
§Bishopsbourne, S.R., 6, C3.
Bishop's Cleeve, G.W.R., 9, D4.
Bishop's Lydeard, G.W.R., 8, F4.
Bishop's Nympton & Molland, G.W.R., 7, F5.
Bishop's Stortford, L.N.E.R. 11, E3.
•Bishop's Waltham, S.R., 4, D3.
Bishopstone, S.R., 5, G4.
Bishopton, L.M.S., 30, C2.
•Bisley Camp, S.R., 5, C1.
Bittaford Platform, G.W.R., 2, D5.
*Bitterley*, S.H., 9, A1.
Bitterne, S.R., 4, E3.
Bitton, L.M.S., 8, D1.
Blaby, L.M.S., 16, F4.
Black Bank, L.N.E.R., 11, B4.
•Black Bull, L.M.S., 15, C3.
Blackburn, L.M.S., 24, D2.
*Black Carr Jc.*, L.N.E.R., 21, F5.
Blackdown, *see* Mary Tavy.
Blackford, L.M.S., 34, F3.
*Blackhall Jc.*, L.N.E.R., 31, C2.
Blackhall Colliery Halt, L.N.E.R., 28, D4.
Blackhall Rocks, L.N.E.R., 28, D4.
Blackheath (London), S.R., 5, B4.
Blackhill, L.N.E.R., 27, C4.
Black Lane (Radcliffe), L.M.S., 20, B1.
Black Mill, G.W.R., 7, C5.
Blackpool, L.M.S., 24, D4.
Blackrod, L.M.S., 20, B2.
•Blackston, L.N.E.R., 31, B2.
Blackthorn, G.W.R., 10, E3.
Blackwater (Hants.), S.R., 4, B1.
Blackwater (I.W.), S.R., 4, F3.
•Blackwall, L.N.E.R., 5. B4.
Blackwell (Worcs.), L.M.S., 9, A4.
Blackwood (Lanark), L.M.S., 31, D1.
Blackwood (Mon.), L.M.S. & •G.W.R., 8, B4.
Blacksboat, L.N.E.R., 36, E2
Blacon, L.N.E.R., 20, D4.
Blaenau Festiniog, G.W.R. & L.M.S., 19, F3.
Blaenavon, G.W.R. & •L.M.S., 8, A4.
•Blaenclydach, G.W.R., 8, B5.
Blaengarw, G.W.R., 7. B5.
Blaengwynfi, G.W.R., 7, B5.
Blaenrhondda, G.W.R., 7, B5
•Blagdon, G.W.R., 8, D2.
Blaina, G.W.R., 8, A4.
•Blairadam, L.N.E.R., 31, A3.
Blair Atholl, L.M.S., 34, C3.
Blairgowrie, L.M.S., 34, D1.
Blaisdon, G.W.R., 9, E2.
Blakedown, *see* Churchill.
Blake Hall, L.N.E.R., 11 G4.
Blakeney (Goods) G.W.R., 9, E2.
Blakesley, L.M.S., 10, C3.
Blake Street, L.M.S., 15, F5.
Blanchland (Goods), L.N.E.R., 27, D4.
Blandford, S.D., 3, E4.
Blanefield, L.N.E.R., 30, B2.
Blankney & Metheringham L.N.E.R., 17, B1.
Blantyre, L.M.S., 30, C1.
Blaydon, L.N.E.R., 27, C5.
Bleadon & Uphill, G.W.R. 8, D3.
Bleasby, L.M.S., 16, C3.
Bledlow, G.W.R., 10, F2.
Blencow, L.M.S., 26, E1.
Blenheim & Woodstock, G.W.R., 10, E4.
Bletchington, G.W.R., 10, E4.
Bletchley, L.M.S., 10, D2.
Blewbury, *see* Upton, G.W.R.
•Blidworth & Rainworth, L.M.S., 16, B3.
Blisworth, L.M.S., 10, B3.
Blockley, G.W.R., 9, C5.
Blodwell Jc., G.W.R., 20, G5.
Blowers Green, G.W.R., 15, G4.
•Blowick, L.M.S., 20, A4.
Bloxham, G.W.R., 10, C4.
Bloxwich, L.M.S., 15, F4.
Blue Anchor, G.W.R., 8, E5.
Blundellsands, L.M.S., 20, B4.
Blunham, L.M.S., 11, D1.
•Bluntisham, L.N.E.R., 11 B3.
Blyth, L.N.E.R., 28, A5.
Blythe Bridge, L.M.S., 15, C4.
Blyton, L.N.E.R., 22, G5.
•Boarhills, L.N.E.R., 37, F3.
Boars Head, L.M.S., 20, B3.
Boat of Garten, L.M.S./L.N.E.R., 36, F3.
Bocking, *see* Braintree.
§Boddam, L.N.E.R., 38, D1.
Bodfari, L.M.S., 19, D5.
Bodiam, K.E.S.R., 6, E5.
Bodmin, G.W.R. & S.R., 1, D3.
Bodmin Road, G.W.R., 1, D3.
Bodorgan, L.M.S., 19, D1.
Bognor Regis, S.R., 5, G1.
Bogside (Fife), L.N.E.R., 31, A2.
Bogside (Renfrew), L.M.S., 30, E3.
Bogston, L.M.S., 30, B3.
Boldon Coll., L.N.E.R., 28, B5.
Bollington, L.M.S./L.N.E.R., 15, A4.
Bolsover, L.N.E.R. & •L.M.S., 16, B4.
Bolton, L.M.S., 20, B2.
Bolton Abbey, L.M.S., 21, C2.
Bolton-le-Sands, L.M.S., 24, B3.
Bolton-on-Dearne, S.K., 21, F4.
Bolton Percy, L.N.E.R., 21, D4.
Bonar Bridge, L.M.S., 36, B5
Boncath, G.W.R., 13, F3.
*Bonds Main Coll.*, L.M.S. & L.N.E.R., 16, B4.
Bo'ness, L.N.E.R., 31, B2.
Bonhill, *see* Alexandria.
Bonnybridge, •L.M.S. & L.N.E.R., 31, B1.
Bonnyrigg, L.N.E.R., 31, C4.
Bontnewydd, G.W.R., 14, A5.
Bookham, S.R., 5, C2.
Boosbeck, L.N.E.R., 28, E3.
•Boot, R.E.R., 26, F2.
*Bootham Jc.*, L.N.E.R., 21, C5.
Bootle (Cumb.), L.M.S., 26, G3.
Bootle (Lancs.), L.M.S., 20, C4.
Bordesley, G.W.R., 15, G5.
Bordon, S.R., 4, C1.
Boroughbridge, L.N.E.R., 21, B4.
Borough Green, *see* Wrotham.
Borrobol Platform, L.M.S., 39, F1.
Borrowash, L.M.S., 16, D5.
Borth, G.W.R., 13, C5.
Borwick, L.M.S., 24, B3.
*Boscarne Jc.*, S.R./G.W.R., 1, D3.
Boscombe, S.R., 3, F5.
Bosham, S.R., 4, E1.
Bosley, L.M.S., 15, B4.
Boston, L.N.E.R., 17, C3.
Botanic Gardens, L.N.E.R., 22, D3.
Bothwell, L.M.S., 31, C1.
Botley, S.R., 4, E3.
Bottesford, L.N.E.R., 16, C2.
Bottisham & Lode, L.N.E.R. 11, C4.
Boughrood & Llyswen, G.W.R., 14, F3.
Boughton, L.N.E.R., 16, B3.
Bourne, L.N.E.R./L.M.S./M.G.N., 17, E1.
Bourne End, G.W.R., 10, G2.
Bournemouth, S.R. & S.R./S.D., 3, F5.
Bournville, L.M.S., 9, A4.
Bourton-on-the-Water, G.W.R., 9, D5.
Bovey, G.W.R., 2, C4.
Bow (Devon), S.R., 2, B4.
Bowdon, *see* Altrincham.
Bower, L.M.S., 39, C3.
Bowes. L.N.E.R., 27, F4.
Bowes Park, L.N.E.R., 5, A3.
•Bowhouse, L.N.E.R., 31, B2.
Bowland, L.N.E.R., 31, D5.
Bowling, L.M.S. & L.N.E.R., 30, B2.
Bowling Jc., L.M.S., 21, D2.
Bow Street, G.W.R., 13, C5.
Box, G.W.R., 3, A4.
Boxford, G.W.R., 4, A4.
Boxhill & Burford Bridge, S.R., 5, C2.
Boxmoor, *see* Hemel Hempsted.
•Boyce's Bridge, W.U.T., 17, F4.
Braceborough Spa Halt, L.N.E.R., 17, E1.
Bracebridge (Goods), L.N.E.R., 16, B2.
*Brackenhill Jc.*, S.K., 21, E4.
Brackley, L.M.S., 10, C4.
,, L.N.E.R., 10, C3.
Bracknell, S.R., 4, A1.
Bradbury, L.N.E.R., 28, E5.
Bradfield, L.N.E.R., 12, E4.
Bradford, L.M.S./L.N.E.R., •L.M.S., •L.N.E.R. 21, D, 2.
*Bradford Jc.*, G.W.R., 3, B4.
Bradford-on-Avon, G.W.R., 3, B4.
Brading Jc., (I.W.), S.R., 4, F2.
Bradley, L.M.S., 21, E2.
Bradley Fold, L.M.S., 20, B2.
*Bradley Wood Jc.*, L.M.S., 21, E2.
Bradninch, *see* Hele.
•Bradnop, L.M.S., 15, C4.
Bradwell, L.M.S., 10, C2.
Brafferton, L.N.E.R., 21, B4.
Braidwood, L.M.S., 31, D1.
Braintree & Bocking, L.N.E.R., 11, E5.
Braithwaite, L.M.S., 26, E2.
Bramber, S.R., 5, F2.
Bramford, L.N.E.R., 12, D4.
Bramhall, L.M.S., 15, A3.
Bramley (Hants.), G.W.R., 4, B2.
Bramley (Yorks.), L.N.E.R., 21, D3.
Bramley & Wonersh, S.R., 5 D1.
Brampford' Speke Halt, G.W.R., 2, B3.
Brampton (Derby) Goods, L.M.S., 16, B5.
Brampton (Northants.), *see* Pitsford.
Brampton (Suffk.), L.N.E.R., 12, B2.
Brampton Jc. (Cumb.), L.N.E.R., 27, C1.
Bramwith (Goods), L.N.E.R., 21, F5.
Brancepeth, L.N.E.R., 27, D5.
*Brancliffe Jc.*, L.N.E.R./L.M.S., 16, A4.
Brandon (Durham), L.N.E.R. 27, D5.
Brandon (Norfk.), L.N.E.R., 11, A5.
Brandon & Wolston, L.M.S., 10, A5.
Branksome, S.R./S.D., 3, F5.
Bransford Road, G.W.R., 9 B3.
*Branston Jc.*, L.M.S.. 15. E5.
Branston & Heighington, L.N.E.R., 17, B1.
Bransty (Whitehaven), L.M.S., 26, E4.
•Branthwaite, L.M.S., 26, E3.
Brasted, S.R., 5, C4.
Bratton, *see* Edington.
Braughing, L.N.E.R., 11, E3
Braunston, L.M.S., 10, B4.
Braunston & Willoughby, L.N.E.R., 10, B4.
Braunton, S.R., 7, F3.
Braystones, L.M.S., 26, F3.
Brayton, L.M.S., 26, D2.
*Brayton Jc.*, L.N.E.R., 21, D5.
Breadsall, L.N.E.R., 16, D5.
Breamore, S.R., 4, D5.
Brechin, L.M.S., 37, C3.
Brecon, G.W.R./L.M.S., 14, F3.
Brecon Rd., L.M.S., 8, A3.
Bredbury, L.M.S./L.N.E.R., 21, G1.
Bredon (Leics.), *see* Tonge.
Bredon (Worcs.), L.M.S., 9, C3.
Breich, L.M.S., 31, C2.
Breidden, S.W., 14, A2.
Brent (Devon), G.W.R. 2, D4.
Brentford, S.R. & •G.W.R., 5, B2.
Brent Knoll, G.W.R., 8, E3.
Brentor, S.R., 1, C5.
Brentwood & Warley, L.N.E.R., 5, A5.
*Bretby Wharf*, L.M.S., 16, E5.
Brettell Lane, G.W.R., 15, G3.
Bretton, *see* Broughton.
Bricket Wood, L.M.S., 11, G1.
Bridestowe, S.R., 2, B5.
§Bridge, S.R., 6, C3.
Bridgend, G.W.R., 7, C5.
Bridgend & Coity (Goods), G.W.R., 7, C5.
•Bridgefoot, L.M.S., 26, E3.
Bridge of Allan, L.M.S., 31, A1.
Bridge of Dee, L.M.S., 26, C5.
Bridge of Dun, L.M.S., 37, C3
Bridge of Earn, L.N.E.R., 34, F1.
Bridge of Orchy, L.N.E.R. 33, E5.
Bridge of Weir, L.M.S., 30, C3.
Bridgerule, *see* Whitstone.
*Bridgeness*, L.N.E.R., 31, B2.
Bridge St. (Northampton), L.M.S., 10, B2.
Bridge Street (Thrapston), L.M.S., 10, A1.
Bridgnorth, G.W.R., 15, F2.
Bridgwater, G.W.R. & S.D., 8, F3.
Bridlington, L.N.E.R., 22, B3.
Bridport, G.W.R., 3, F2.
Brierfield, L.M.S., 24, D1.
Brierley Hill, G.W.R., 15, G3.
*Brierley Jc.*, L.M.S./L.N.E.R., 21, F4.
Brigg, L.N.E.R., 22, F4.
Brigham, L.M.S., 26, E3.
Brighouse, L.M.S., 21, E2.
Brightlingsea, L.N.E.R., 12, F4.
Brighton, S.R., 5, F3.
Brightside, L.M.S., 21, G3.
Brill & Ludgershall, G.W.R., 10, E3.
Brimscombe, G.W.R., 9, E3.
Brimsdown, L.N.E.R., 11, G3.
Brindley Heath, L.M.S., 15, E4.
Brinkburn, L.N.E.R., 32, G2.
Brinklow, L.M.S. 10, A2.
Brinkworth, G.W.R., 9, G4.
Brinscall, L.M.S., 24, E2.
Brislington, G.W.R., 8, D1.
Bristol, G.W.R./L.M.S., L.M.S., •G.W.R., 8, C2.
*Britannia Bridge*, L.M.S., 19, D2.
Brithdir, G.W.R., 8, B4.
Briton Ferry, G.W.R., 7, B4.
•Briton Ferry Road, G.W.R., 7, B4.
Brixham, G.W.R., 2, D3.
Brixton, S.R., 5, B3.
•Brixton Road, G.W.R., 2, E5.
Brixworth, L.M.S., 10, A3.
Brize Norton & Bampton, G.W.R., 10, E5.
Broadbottom, *see* Mottram.
Broad Clyst, S.R., 2, B3.
Broadfield, L.M.S., 20, B1.
Broad Green, L.M.S., 20, C4.
Broadheath, L.M.S., 20, C2.
•Broadley, L.M.S., 20, A1.
Broadstairs, S.R., 6, B1.
Broadstone, S.R./S.D., 3, F5.
Broad Street, L.M.S., 5, A3.
Broadway, G.W.R., 9, C4.
•Brock, L.M.S., 24, D3.
Brockenhurst, S.R., 4, E4.
Brocketsbrae, L.M.S., 31, D1.
Brockford & Wetheringsett, L.N.E.R., 12, C4.
Brockholes, L.M.S., 21, F2.
Brocklesby, L.N.E.R., 22, E3.
Brocton, *see* Milford, L.M.S.
Brodie, L.M.S., 36, D3.
*Brodsworth Coll.*, L.N.E.R., 21, F4.
Bromborough, B.J., 20, C4.
Bromfield, S.H., 9, A1.
•Bromford Bridge, L.M.S., 15, G5.
Bromham & Rowde, G.W.R., 3, B5.
Bromley Cross, L.M.S., 20, A2.
Bromley North (Kent), S.R., 5, B4.
Bromley South (Kent), S.R., 5, B4.
Brompton, L.N.E.R., 28, G5.
Bromsgrove, L.M.S., 9, A4.
*Bromshall Jc.*, L.M.S./L.N.E.R., 15, D4.
Bromyard, G.W.R., 9, B2.
Bronwydd Arms, G.W.R., 13, G4.
Brookland Halt, S.R., 6, E4.
Brooklands (Ches.), M.S.J.A., 20, C1.
Brookman's Park, L.N.E.R., 11, G2.
Brooksby, L.M.S., 16, E3.
Brookwood, S.R., 5, C1.
Broom (Jc.), L.M.S., 9, B4.
Broome, L.M.S., 14, C1.
*Broomfield Jc.*, L.M.S./L.N.E.R., 37, C4.
Broomfleet, L.N.E.R., 22, E4.
Broomhill (Inverness), L.M.S., 36, F3.
Broomhill (North'd.), L.N.E.R., 32, G1.
Broomieknowe, L.N.E.R., 31, C4.
Broomielaw, L.N.E.R., 27, E4.
Brora, L.M.S., 39, G2.
Broseley, *see* Iron Bridge.
Brotton, L.N.E.R., 28, E3.
Brough, L.N.E.R., 22, E4.
Broughton (Lancs.), *see* Barton.
Broughton (Peebles), L.M.S., 31, E3.
Broughton & Bretton, L.M.S., 20, D4.
Broughton Astley, L.M.S., 16, G4.
Broughton-in-Furness, L.M.S., 24, A5.
Broughton Lane, L.N.E.R., 21, G4.
Broughty Ferry D.A., 37, E2.
Brownhills, L.M.S., 15, F4.
Broxbourne & Hoddesdon, L.N.E.R., 11, F3.
*Broxburn Oil Works*, L.N.E.R., 31, B3.
Broxton, L.M.S., 20, E3.
Brucklay, L.N.E.R., 38, D2
Brundall, L.N.E.R., 18, F2.
•Brunswick (L'pool), C.L.C., & L.M.S., 20, C4.
Brunswick St. (Goods), L.M.S., 15, B3.
Bruton, G.W.R., 3, C3.
Brymbo, G.W.R./L.M.S. & •L.N.E.R., 20, E4.
•Bryn (Glam.), G.W.R., 7, B5.
Bryn (Lancs.), L.M.S., 20, B3.
Brynamman, G.W.R., & L.M.S./G.W.R., 7, A4.
•Brynglas, Tal., 13, B5.
Bryngwyn Halt, G.W.R., 14, A2.
Brynkir, L.M.S., 19, F2.
Brynmawr, L.M.S./G.W.R. 8, A4.
Brynmenyn, G.W.R., 7, C5.
Bryn Teify, G.W.R., 13, F4.
Bubwith, L.N.E.R., 21, D5.
Buchanan St. (Glasgow), L.M.S., 30, C1.
Buchlyvie, L.N.E.R., 30, A1.
Buckden, L.M.S., 11, C2.
*See also* Offord.
Buckenham, L.N.E.R., 18, F2.
Buckfastleigh, G.W.R., 2, D4.
Buckhaven, L.N.E.R., 31, A4.
Buckhurst Hill, L.N.E.R., 5, A4.
Buckie, L.N.E.R., 36, C1.
Buckingham, L.M.S., 10, D3
Buckley, L.N.E.R., 20, D4.
Bucknall & Northwood, L.M.S., 15, C3.
Bucknell, L.M.S., 14, D1.
Buckpool, L.N.E.R., 38, C5.
Bucksburn, L.N.E.R., 38, F2.
*Buddon*, D.A., 37, E3.
Bude, S.R., 1, A4.
Budleigh Salterton, S.R., 2 C2.
Bugle, G.W.R., 1, D2.
Buildwas, G.W.R., 15, F2.
Builth Road, G.W.R. & L.M.S., 14, E3.
Builth Wells, G.W.R., 14, E3.
Bulford, S.R., 4, C5.
Bulford Camp, S.R., 4, C5.
Bullgill, L.M.S., 26, D3.
Bullo Pill (Goods), G.W.R., 9, E2.
Bulwell, L.M.S. & L.N.E.R. 16, C4.
Bulwell Forest, L.N.E.R., 16, C4.
Bunchrew, L.M.S., 36, E5.
Bungay, L.N.E.R., 12, A2.
Buntingford, L.N.E.R., 11, E3.
Burbage, *see* Grafton.
Burbage (Goods), G.W.R., A5.
Burdale, L.N.E.R., 22, B4.
Bures, L.N.E.R., 12, E5.
Burford Bridge, *see* Box Hill.
Burgess Hill, S.R., 5, E3.
Burgh, *see* Belton.
Burgh-by-Sands, L.N.E.R., 26, C1.
Burghclere, G.W.R., 4, B3.
•Burghead, L.M.S., 36, C2.
Burgh Heath, *see* Kingswood.
Burgh-le-Marsh, L.N.E.R., 17, B4.
Burlescombe, G.W.R., 8, G5.
Burley-in-Wharfedale, O.I., 21, D2.
Burleigh St. (Goods), L.N.E.R., 22, D3.
Burmarsh Road Halt, R.H.D.R., 6, E3.
Burnbank, L.N.E.R., 30, C1.
Burneside, L.M.S., 27, G1.
•Burngullow, G.W.R., 1, D2.
Burnham (Bucks), G.W.R., 5, A1.
Burnham Market, L.N.E.R., 18, D5.
Burnham-on-Crouch, L.N.E.R., 12, G5.
Burnham-on-Sea, S.D., 8, E3
Burnley, L.M.S., 24, D1.
Burnmouth, L.N.E.R., 29, C3.
Burnside, L.M.S., 30, C1.
Burnt House (Goods) L.N.E.R., 11, A3.
Burntisland, L.N.E.R., 31, B4.
Burnt Mill, L.N.E.R., 11, F3.
Burrelton, L.M.S., 34, E1.
Burringham (Goods), *see* Gunness.
•Burrington, G.W.R., 8, D2.
Burry Port, G.W.R., 7, B2.
*See also* Pembrey.
Burscough Bridge, L.M.S., 20, A3.
Burscough Jc., L.M.S., 20, B4.
Bursledon, S.R., 4, E3.
Burslem, L.M.S., 15, C3.
Burston, L.N.E.R., 12, B4.
Burstwick, *see* Rye Hill.
Burton Agnes, L.N.E.R., 22, B3.
Burton & Holme, L.M.S., 24, B3.
Burton Joyce, L.M.S., 16, C3.
*Burton Lane Jc.*, L.N.E.R., 21, C5.
Burton Latimer, L.M.S., 10, A2.
Burton Point, L.N.E.R., 20, D4.
Burton (on Trent), L.M.S. & •L.N.E.R., 15, D5.
Burton Salmon, L.N.E.R., 21, E4.
§Burwarton, G.W.R., 15, G2.
Burwell, L.N.E.R., 11, C4.
Bury, L.M.S., 20, B1.
Bury St. Edmunds, L.N.E.R., 12, C5.
Busby, L.M.S., 30, C1.
*Bushbury Jc.*, L.M.S./G.W.R., 15, F3.
Bushey & Oxhey, L.M.S., 11, G1.
Bush Hill Park, L.N.E.R., 11, G3.
•Bute Road (Cardiff), G.W.R., 8, C4.

Evershot, G.W.R., 3, E2.
Evesham, G.W.R. & L.M.S., 9, C4.
Ewell, S.R., 5, C3.
Ewesley, L.N.E.R., 27, A4. *See also* Fontburn.
Ewood Bridge, L.M.S., 20, A1.
Exeter, G.W.R/ S.R. & S.R., 2, B3.
Exhall, *see* Longford (Warwicks.).
Exminster, G.W.R., 2, B3.
Exmouth, S.R., 2, C2.
Eyarth, L.M.S., 19, E5.
Eydon Rd. Plat., L.N.E.R., 10, C4.
Eye (Hereford), *see* Berrington.
•Eye (Suffolk), L.N.E.R., 12, B4.
Eye Green, M.G.N., 17, F2.
Eyemouth, L.N.E.R., 32, C3.
Eynsford, S.R., 5, C5.
Eynsham, G.W.R., 10, E4.
Eythorne, E.K.R., 6, C2.

## F

•Facit, L.M.S., 20, A1.
Failsworth, L.M.S., 20, B1.
Fairbourne, G.W.R., 13, A5.
Fairford, G.W.R., 9, F5.
Fairhaven, *see* Ansdell.
Fairlie, L.M.S., 30, D4.
*Fairlie Branch*, L.M.S., 30, E2.
Fairlie Pier, L.M.S., 30, D4.
•Fairlop, L.N.E.R., 5, A4.
Fakenham, L.N.E.R. & M.G.N., 18, D5.
Falahill (Goods), L.N.E.R., 31, C5.
Falkirk, **L.N.E.R.**/L.M.S. & •L.M.S., 31, B2.
Falkirk (High), L.N.E.R. 31, B2.
Falkland Rd., L.N.E.R., 37, G1.
Fallowfield, L.N.E.R., 20, C1.
Fallside, L.M.S., 30, C1.
Falmer, S.R., 5, F3.
Falmouth, G.W.R., 1, F1.
Falstone, L.N.E.R., 27, A2.
Fambridge, L.N.E.R., 12, G5.
Fangfoss, L.N.E.R., 22, C5.
Faicet, *see* Yaxley.
Far Cotton (Goods), L.M.S., 10, B2.
Fareham, S.R., 4, E3.
Faringdon (Berks.), G.W.R., 10, F5.
Farington, L.M.S., 24, E3.
Farnborough, S.R., 4, B1.
Farncombe, S.R., 5, D1.
Farnell Rd., L.M.S. 37, C3.
Farnham, S.R., 4, C1.
Farningham Rd. & Sutton-at-Hone, S.R., 5, B5.
Farnley, L.M.S., 21, D3.
•Farnsfield, L.M.S., 16, B3.
Farnworth, C.L.C. & L.M.S., 20, C3.
Farnworth, L.M.S., 20, B2.
Farringdon (Hants.), S.R., 4, C2.
Farthinghoe, L.M.S., 10, C4.
Fauldhouse, L.M.S., 31, C2.
•Fauldhouse & Crofthead, L.N.E.R., 31, C2.
Faversham, S.R., 6, C4.
Fawkham, S.R., 5, B5.
Fawley (Hants.), S.R., 4, E3.
Fawley (Hereford), G.W.R., 9, D1.
Fay Gate, S.R., 5, D3.
Fazakerley, L.M.S., 20, B4.
Fearn, L.M.S., 36, B4.
Featherstone, L.M.S., 21, E4.
Featherstone Park, L.N.E.R., 27, C2.
Felin Fach, G.W.R., 13, E5.
*Felin Foel*, G.W.R., 7, B3.
Felin Fran, G.W.R., 7, B4.
Felin Hen Halt, L.M.S., 19, D2.
Felixstowe, L.N.E.R., 12, E3.
Felling, L.N.E.R., 28, C5.
Felmingham, M.G.N., 18, D3.
Felsted, L.N.E.R., 11, E5.
Feltham, S.R., 5, B2.
•Fenay Bridge & Lepton, L.M.S., 21, E2.
Fencehouses, L.N.E.R., 28, C5.
Fenchurch Street, L.M.S./•**L.N.E.R.**, 5, B4.
Fencote, G.W.R., 9, B1.
Feniscowles, L.M.S., 24, E2.
Fenn's Bank, G.W.R., 20, F3.
Fenny Bentley (Goods), L.M.S., 15, C5.
Fenny Compton, G.W.R., 10, B4.
Fenny Compton, L.M.S., 10, B5.
Fenny Stratford, L.M.S., 10, D2.
Fenton, L.M.S., 15, C3.
Fenton Manor, L.M.S., 15, C3.
Ferndale, G.W.R., 8, D5.
Fernhill Heath, **G.W.R.**/L.M.S, 9, B3.
Ferniegair (Goods), L.M.S., 31, D1.
Ferriby, L.N.E.R., 22, E4.
Ferry, M.G.N., 17, E3.
Ferrybridge, L.N.E.R., 21, E4.
Ferryhill, L.N.E.R., 28, D5.
*Ferryhill Jc.*, L.M.S./L.N.E.R., 38, G2.
Ferryside, G.W.R., 7, A2.
*Fersit Siding*, L.N.E.R., 33, B5.
Festiniog, G.W.R., 19, F3.
Ffairfach, G.W.R., 13, G5.
•Ffridd Gate, Corris, 14, B5.
Ffrith, W.M., 20, E5.
Fidlers Ferry, L.M.S., 20, C3.
Fighting Cocks (Goods), L.N.E.R., 28, F5.
Filey, L.N.E.R., 22, A3.
Filleigh, G.W.R., 7, F4.
Fillongley, *see* Arley, L.M.S.
Filton Jc., G.W.R., 8, C1.
Fimber, *see* Sledmere.
Finchley Central, •**L.N.E.R**/L.P.T.B., 5, A3.
Findochty, L.N.E.R., 38, C5.
•Finedon, L.M.S., 10, A2.
Finghall Lane, L.N.E.R., 27, G5.
Finmere, L.N.E.R., 10, D3.
Finningham, L.N.E.R., 12, C4.
Finningley, L.N.E.R., 21, F5.
Finsbury Park, L.N.E.R. & L.P.T.B., 5, A3.
Firsby, L.N.E.R., 17, B4.
Fishbourne Halt, S.R., 4, E1.
Fishergate Hill (Goods), L.M.S., 24, E3.
Fisherrow (Goods), L.N.E.R., 31, B4.
Fishersgate Halt, S.R., 5, F3.
Fishguard & Goodwick, G.W.R., 13, F1.
Fishguard Harbour, G.W.R., 13, F1.
Fish Ponds, L.M.S., 8, C1.
Fiskerton, L.M.S., 16, C3.
Fittleworth, S.R., 5, E1.
Five Mile House, L.N.E.R., 17, B1.
§Five Ways, L.M.S., 15, E4.
Fladbury, G.W.R., 9, C4.
Flamborough, L.N.E.R., 22, B3.
Flax Bourton, G.W.R., 8, D2.
•Flaxton, L.N.E.R., 21, B5.
Flecknoe, L.M.S., 10, B4.
Fledborough, L.N.E.R., 16 B2.
Fleet (Hants.), S.R., 4, B1.
Fleet (Lincs.), M.G.N., 17, E3.
Fleetwood, L.M.S., 24, C4.
Flemington, L.M.S., 31, C1.
Fletton (Goods), L.N.E.R., 11, A2.
Flimby, L.M.S., 26, D3.
Flint, L.M.S., 20, D5.
Flitwick, L.M.S., 10, D1.
Flixton, C.L.C., 20, C2.
Flordon, L.N.E.R., 12, A3.
Floriston, L.M.S., 26, B1.
•Flushdyke, L.N.E.R., 21, E3.
•Fochabers Town, L.M.S., 36, C1.
Fochriw, G.W.R., 8, A5.
•Fockerby, A.J., 22, E5.
*Fodderty Jc.*, L.M.S., 35, D5.
Foggathorpe, L.N.E.R., 22, D5.
Foleshill, L.M.S., 10, A5.
Folkestone, S.R., 6, D2.
Fontburn Halt & Ewesley Goods, L.N.E.R., 27, A4.
Forcett (Goods), L.N.E.R. 27, F5.
*Forcett Jc.*, L.N.E.R., 27, E5.
Ford (Devon), S.R., 1, D5.
,, (Sussex), S.R., 5, F1.
Ford Bridge, S.H., 9, B1.
•Ford & Crossgates (Salop), S.M., 14, A1.
Forden, G.W.R., 14, B2.
•Ford Green, L.M.S., 15, C3.
Fordham, L.N.E.R., 11, C4.
Fordingbridge, S.R., 4, E5.
Fordoun, L.M.S., 37, B4.
Foregate St. (Worcester), G.W.R., 9, B3.
Forest Gate, L.N.E.R., 5, A4.
Forest Hall, L.N.E.R., 27, B5.
•Forest Mill, L.N.E.R., 31, A2.
Forest Row, S.R., 5, D4.
Forfar, L.M.S., 37, D2.
Forgandenny, L.M.S., 34, F2.
Forge Valley, L.N.E.R. 22, A4.
Formby, L.M.S., 20, B4.
Forncett, L.N.E.R., 12, A3.
Forres, L.M.S., 36, D3.
•Forrest Field, L.N.E.R., 31, C1.
Forsinard, L.M.S., 39, E1.
§Fort Augustus, L.N.E.R., 35, G4.
Fort Brockhurst, S.R., 4, E3.
Forteviot, L.M.S., 34, F2.
•Fort George, L.M.S., 36, D4.
*Forth Bridge*, Forth Bridge Ry. Co., 31, B3.
*Fortissat Colliery*, L.N.E.R., 31, C1.
Fort Matilda, L.M.S., 30, B3.
Fortrose, L.M.S., 36, D5.
Fort William, L.N.E.R., 33, C3.
•Forty Hill, L.N.E.R., 11, G3.
•Foryd Pier (Rhyl), L.M.S., 19, C5.
Foss Cross, G.W.R., 9, E4.
Foss Islands (Goods), L.N.E.R., 21, C5.
Fotherby Halt, L.N.E.R., 22, G2.
Foulis, L.M.S., 36, C5.
Foulridge, L.M.S., 21, —
Foulsham, L.N.E.R., 18, E4.
Fountainhall Jc., L.N.E.R., 31, D5.
Four Ashes, L.M.S., 15, F3.
Four Crosses (Mont.), G.W.R., 14, A2.
Four Marks, *see* Medstead.
Four Oaks, L.M.S., 15, F5.
Fourstones, L.N.E.R., 27, B3.
Fowey, G.W.R., 1, D3.
Foxdale, I.M.R., 23, B2.
Foxfield, L.M.S., 24, A5.
Foxton, L.N.E.R., 11, D3.
Framlingham, L.N.E.R., 12, C3.
Frampton, *see* Grimstone.
*Frankley*, H.J., 9, A4.
Frankton, G.W.R., 20, F4.
Fransham, L.N.E.R., 18, E5.
Frant, S.R., 5, D5.
Fraserburgh, L.N.E.R., 38, C2.
Fratton, S.R., 4, E2.
Fremington, S.R., 7, F3.
French Drove & Gedney Hill, L.N.E.R., 17, F3.
Freshfield, L.M.S., 20, B4.
Freshford, G.W.R., 3, B3.
Freshwater (I.W.), S.R., 4, F4.
Friargate (Derby), L.N.E.R., 16, D5.
Friary (Plymouth), S.R., 1, D5.
Frickley, S.K., 21, F4.
Friday St. (Goods), L.M.S., 21, E2.
Friden (Goods), L.M.S., 15, B5.
•Friezland, L.M.S., 21, F1.
Frimley, S.R., 4, B1.
Frinton-on-Sea, L.N.E.R., 12, F3.
Friockheim, L.M.S., 37, D3.
Frisby, L.M.S., 16, E3.
Frittenden Rd., K.E.S.R., 6, D5.
Fritwell & Somerton, G.W.R., 10, D4.
Frizinghall, L.M.S., 21, D2.
•Frizington, L.M.S., 26, E3.
Frocester, L.M.S., 9, E3.
Frodingham, *see* Scunthorpe.
Frodsham, B.J., 20, D3.
Froghall, *see* Kingsley.
Frogmore, *see* Park Street.
Frome, G.W.R., 3, B3.
Frongoch, G.W.R., 19, F4.
Frosterley, L.N.E.R., 27, D4.
•Fryston, L.N.E.R., 21, E4.
Fulbar St. (Renfrew), L.M.S., 30, C2.
Fulbourne, L.N.E.R., 11, C4.
Fullerton, S.R., 4, C4.
Fulwell (Middx.), S.R., 5, B2.
Fulwell & Westbury (Bucks.), L.M.S., 10, D3.
Furness Abbey, L.M.S., 24, B5.
Furness Vale, L.M.S., 15, A4.
Furze Platt Halt, G.W.R., 10, G2.
•Fushiebridge, L.N.E.R., 30, C5.
Fyling Hall, L.N.E.R., 28, F1.
Fyvie, L.N.E.R., 38, E3.

## G

*Gadlys Jc.*, G.W.R., 8, B5.
Gaerwen, L.M.S., 19, D2.
Gagie, L.M.S., 37, E2.
Gailes, L.M.S., 30, E3.
Gailey, L.M.S., 15, E3.
Gainford, L.N.E.R., 27, E5.
Gainsborough, L.N.E.R., 22, G5.
§Gairlochy, L.N.E.R., 33, B4.
Gaisgill, L.N.E.R., 27, F2.
Galashiels, L.N.E.R., 31, E5.
Galligreaves St. (Goods) L.M.S., 24, E2.
•Gallions, L.N.E.R., 5, B4.
Galston, L.M.S., 30, E2.
Gamlingay, L.M.S., 11, D2.
•Ganton, L.N.E.R., 22, A4.
Gara Bridge, G.W.R., 2, D4.
Garelochhead, L.N.E.R., 31, A3.
Garforth, L.N.E.R., 21, D4.
Gargrave, L.M.S., 21, C1.
•Gargunnock, L.N.E.R., 30, A1.
•Garlieston, L.M.S., 25, D4.
Garmouth, L.N.E.R., 36, C1.
Garnant, G.W.R., 7, A4.
•Garnedd Wen, Corris, 14, A5.
Garnkirk, L.M.S., 30, C1.
Garrochburn (Goods), L.M.S., 30, E2.
Garsdale, L.M.S., 27, G2.
Garstang & Catterall, L.M.S., 24, D3.
•Garstang Town, L.M.S., 24 D3.
Garston, C.L.C. & •L.M.S., 20, C4.
Garswood, L.M.S., 20, B3.
Gartcosh, L.M.S., 30, C1.
Garth, L.M.S., 14, E4.
§*Garth & Van Road*, G.W.R., 14, C4.
Gartly, L.N.E.R., 38, F5.
Gartmore, L.N.E.R., 30, A2.
Gartness, L.N.E.R., 30, B2.
Garton, L.N.E.R., 22, C4.
§Gartsherrie, L.M.S., 30, C1.
Gartshore (Goods), L.N.E.R., 30, B1.
Garve, L.M.S., 35, D4.
*Gascoigne Wood Junction*, L.N.E.R., 21, D4.
*Gask Siding*, L.N.E.R., 31, A3.
*Gaswater Branch*, L.M.S., 30, F1.
Gateacre, C.L.C., 20, C4.
Gatehead, L.M.S., 30, E2.
Gatehouse-of-Fleet, L.M.S., 25, C5.
Gateshead, L.N.E.R., 27, C5.
Gateside, L.N.E.R., 34, F1.
Gathurst, L.M.S., 20, B3.
Gatwick Airport, S.R., 5, D3.
•Gatwick Racecourse, S.R., 5, D3.
Gayton Road, M.G.N., 17, E5.
Geddington, L.M.S., 16, G2.
Gedling, L.N.E.R., 16, C3.
Gedney, M.G.N., 17, E3.
Gedney Hill, *see* French Drove.
Geldeston, L.N.E.R., 12, A2.
*Gelly Tarw Jc.*, G.W.R., 8, A5.
Georgemas Jc., L.M.S., 39, C3.
Georgetown, L.M.S., 30, C2.
Gerrards Cross, G.W.R./L.N.E.R., 10, F1.
Gidea Park, L.N.E.R., 5, A5.
•Giffen, L.M.S., 30, D3.
Giffnock, L.M.S., 30, C2.
•Gifford, L.N.E.R., 32, C5.
Giggleswick, L.M.S., 24, B1.
Gildersome, L.N.E.R. & •L.M.S., 21, E3.
Gileston, G.W.R., 8, D5.
•Gilfach Goch, G.W.R., 8, B5.
Gilling, L.N.E.R., 21, B5.
Gillingham (Dorset), S.R., 3, D4.
Gillingham (Kent), S.R., 6, B5.
Gilmerton, L.N.E.R., 31, C4.
Gilmour Street (Paisley), L.M.S., 30, C2.
Gilnockie, L.N.E.R., 26, B1.
Gilsland, L.N.E.R., 27, B1.
Gilwern Halt, L.M.S., 8, A4.
Girvan, L.M.S., 30, G4.
Gisburn, L.M.S., 24, C1.
Glais, L.M.S., 7, B4.
Glaisdale, L.N.E.R., 28, F2.
Glamis, L.M.S., 37, D2.
Glanamman, G.W.R., 7, A4.
Glan Conway, L.M.S., 19, D4.
Glandyfi, G.W.R., 14, A5.
Glanrhyd Halt, V.T., 14, G5.
•Glanton, L.N.E.R., 32, F2.
Glan-yr-Afon Halt, G.W.R., 14, C4.
Glanyrafon, G.W.R., 20, G5.
•Glapwell, L.M.S., 16, B4.
Glasbury-on-Wye, L.M.S., 14, F2.
Glasgow, L.M.S. & L.N.E.R., 30, —.
Glassaugh, L.N.E.R., 38, C4.
Glassel, L.N.E.R., 37, A3.
§Glassford, L.M.S., 30, D1.
•Glasson Dock, L.M.S., 24, C3.
Glasterlaw, L.M.S., 37, D3.
Glastonbury & Street, S.D., 3, C2.
Glazebrook, C.L.C., 20, C2.
*Glazebrook Moss Jc.*, C.L.C./L.N.E.R., 20, C2.
Glazebury, L.M.S., 20, B2.
Glemsford, L.N.E.R., 12, D5.
Glenbarry, L.N.E.R., 38, D4.
Glenboig, L.M.S., 31, C1.
Glenbuck, L.M.S., 31, E1.
*Glenburnie Jc.*, L.N.E.R., 34, F1.
Glencarron Plat., L.M.S., 35, D2.
Glencarse, L.M.S., 34, F1.
Glencoe, *see* Ballachulish.
•Glencorse, L.N.E.R., 31, C4.
*Glencraig Coll.*, L.N.E.R., 31, A3.
Glendon & Rushton, L.M.S., 10, A2.
Gleneagles, L.M.S., 34, F2.
Glenfarg, L.N.E.R., 34, F1.
•Glenfield, L.M.S., 16, F4.
Glenfinnan, L.N.E.R., 33, B2.
Glengarnock, L.M.S., 30, D3.
Gleniffer (Goods), L.M.S., 30, C2.
Glenluce, L.M.S., 25, C3.
•Glenside, L.M.S., 30, F3.
Glenwhilly, L.M.S., 25, B3.
Glogue, G.W.R., 13, F3.
Glodwick Road (Oldham), L.M.S., 21, F1.
Glossop, L.N.E.R., 21, G1.
Gloucester, G.W.R. & L.M.S., 9, E3.
Glyn Abbey, G.W.R., 7, A2.
*Glyncorrwg Coll.*, G.W.R., 7, B5.
Glynde, S.R., 5, F4.
Glyndyfrdwy, G.W.R., 20, F5.
Glyn Neath, G.W.R., 7, A5.
Gnosall, L.M.S., 15, E3.
Goathland, L.N.E.R., 28, F2
Gobowen, G.W.R., 20, F4.
Godalming, S.R., 5, D1.
Godley, L.N.E.R., 21, G1.
Godmanchester, **L.N.E.R.**/L.M.S., 11, B2.
Godshill (I.W.), S.R., 4, G3.
Godstone, S.R., 5, D3.
Goff's Oak, *see* Cuffley.
•Gogar, L.N.E.R., 31, B3.
Golant, G.W.R., 1, D3.
Golborne, L.M.S. & L.N.E.R., 20, B3.
Golcar, L.M.S., 21, E2.
Golden Grove, L.M.S., 13, G5.
Golden Hill, *see* Newchapel.
§Golden Hill Plat., G.W.R., 7, D2.
Goldsborough, L.N.E.R., 21, C4.
•Golfa, W.L., 14, B2.
Gollanfield Jc., L.M.S., 36, D4.
Golspie, L.M.S., 36, A4.
Gomersal, L.M.S., 21, E2.
Gomshall & Shere, S.R., 5, D2.
Goodmayes, L.N.E.R., 5, A4.
Goodwick, *see* Fishguard.
Goole, **L.N.E.R.**/L.M.S., 22, E5.
•Goole Dks., **L.M.S.**/L.N.E.R., 22, E5.
Goostrey, L.M.S., 15, B3.
Gordon, L.N.E.R., 32, D5.
Gordon Hill, L.N.E.R., 11, G2.
Gorebridge, L.N.E.R., 31, C5.
Goring & Streatley, G.W.R., 10, G3.
Goring-by-Sea, S.R., 5, F2.
§Gorleston North, N.S.J., 18, F1.
Gorleston-on-Sea, N.S.J., 18, F1.
Gorseinon, L.M.S., 7, B3.
Gosberton, L.N.E.R., 17, D2.
•Gosford Green, L.M.S., 10, A5.
Gosport, S.R., 4, E2.
Goswick, L.N.E.R., 32, D2.
*Gotham*, L.N.E.R., 16, D4.
Gotherington, G.W.R., 9, D4.
Goudhurst, S.R., 6, D5.
Gourdon, L.N.E.R., 37, B4.
Gourock, L.M.S., 30, B3.
Govan, L.M.S., 30, C2.
Govilon, L.M.S., 8, A4.
Gowerton, L.M.S., 7, B3.
Goxhill, L.N.E.R., 22, E3.
Grafham, L.M.S., 11, C1.
Grafton & Burbage, G.W.R., 4, B5.
*Grafton Jc.*, G.W.R., 4, B5.
Grahamston, **L.N.E.R.**/L.M.S., 31, B2.
Grampound Road, G.W.R., 1, E2.
Grandtully, L.M.S., 34, D3.
Grane Rd. (Goods), L.M.S., 20, A1.
Grange, L.N.E.R., 38, D5.
Grange Court, G.W.R., 9, E2.
Grange Lane, L.N.E.R., 21, G3.
Grangemouth, **L.M.S.**/L.N.E.R., 31, B2.
Grange-over-Sands, L.M.S., 24, B3.
Grange Road, S.R., 5, D3.
Grangetown (Durham), L.N.E.R., 28, E4.
Grantham, L.N.E.R., 16, D1.
•Granton, L.M.S. & L.N.E.R., 31, B4.
Grantown-on-Spey, L.M.S. & L.N.E.R., 36, F3.
Grantshouse, L.N.E.R., 32, C4.
•Grassington & Threshfield, L.M.S., 21, B1.
•Grassmoor, L.N.E.R., 16, B5.
Grateley, S.R., 4, C5.
Gravelly Hill, L.M.S., 15, G5.
Graveney (Goods), S.R., 6, C3.
Gravesend Central, S.R., 5, B5.
Gravesend, West Street, S.R., 5, B5.
Grayrigg, L.M.S., 27, G1.
Grays, L.M.S., 5, B5.
§Great Alne, G.W.R., 9, B5.
Great Ayton, L.N.E.R., 28, F4.
Great Barr, L.M.S., 15, F4.
Great Bentley, L.N.E.R., 12, E4.
Great Bridge, G.W.R. & L.M.S., 15, F4.
Great Bridgeford, L.M.S., 15, D3.
Great Chesterford, L.N.E.R., 11, D4.
Great Coates, L.N.E.R., 22, F2.
Great Dalby, L.M.S./L.N.E.R., 16, E2.
Great Glen, L.M.S., 16, F3.
Great Grimsby, L.N.E.R., 22, F2.
Greatham, L.N.E.R., 28, E4.
Great Harwood, L.M.S., 24, D1.
•Great Haywood Halt, L.M.S., 15, E4.
Great Horton, L.N.E.R., 21, D2.
Great Linford, L.M.S., 10, C2.
Great Longstone, L.M.S., 15, B5.
Great Malvern, **G.W.R.**/L.M.S., 9, C3.
Great Missenden, L.N.E.R. L.P.T.B., 10, F2.
Great Ormesby, M.G.N., 18, E1.
Great Ponton, L.N.E.R., 16, D1.
Great Shefford, G.W.R., 4, A4.
Greatstone, R.H.D.R. & S.R., 6, E3.
Great Yarmouth, *see* Yarmouth.
Gree (Goods), L.M.S., 30, D2.
Greenan Castle (Goods), L.M.S., 30, F3.
Green Ayre (Lancaster), L.M.S., 24, B3.
Greenfield, L.M.S., 21, F1.
Greenford, G.W.R., 5, A2.
Greengairs (Goods), L.N.E.R. 31, C1.
Greenhead, L.N.E.R., 27, B2.
Greenhill, L.M.S., 31, B1.
Greenhithe, S.R., 5, B5.
Greenlaw, L.N.E.R., 32, D4.
Greenloaning, L.M.S., 34, G3.
Greenmount, L.M.S., 20, A1
Greenock, L.M.S., 30, B3.
•Greenodd, L.M.S., 24, A4.
Green Road, L.M.S., 24, A5.
Greenside (Pudsey), L.N.E.R., 21, D2.
*Green's Wharf*, L.M.S., 16, F5.
Greenwich, S.R., 5, B4.
Greetland, L.M.S., 21, E2.
*Greetwell Jc.*, L.N.E.R., 16, B1.
*Grendon Underwood Jc.*, L.N.E.R., 10, D3.
Gresford, G.W.R., 20, E4.
Gresley, L.M.S., 16, E5.
Gretna, L.M.S. & •L.N.E.R., 26, B1.
Gretna Green, L.M.S., 26, B1.
Gretton, L.M.S., 16, F1.
•Griffith's Crossing, L.M.S., 19, D2.
Griffithstown, *see* Panteg.
Grimes Hill, G.W.R., 9, A5.
*Grimethorpe Coll.*, L.M.S., 21, F4.
Grimoldby, L.N.E.R., 17, A3
•Grimsargh, L.M.S., 24, D2.
Grimsby, *see* Great Grimsby
Grimston, L.M.S., 16, E3.
Grimston Road, M.G.N., 17 E5.
Grimstone & Frampton G.W.R., 3, F3.
Grindleford, L.M.S., 16, A5.
•Grindley, L.N.E.R., 15, D4.
•Grinkle, L.N.E.R., 28, E3.
Gristhorpe, L.N.E.R., 22, A3
Groeslon, L.M.S., 19, E1.
Groombridge, S.R., 5, D5.
Grosmont, L.N.E.R., 28, F2
Grotton, L.M.S., 21, F1.
Grove Ferry, S.R., 6, C2.
*Grove Jc.*, S.R., 5, D5.
Grove Park, S.R., 5, B4.
Guard Bridge, L.N.E.R., 37 F2.
Guay, L.M.S., 34, D2.
Guestwick, M.G.N., 18, E4.
Guide Bridge, **L.N.E.R.** L.M.S. & L.M.S., 21, F1.
Guildford, S.R., 5, C1.
Guisborough, L.N.E.R., 28, E3.
Guiseley, **L.M.S.**/L.N.E.R., 21, D2.
•Gullane, L.N.E.R., 31, B5.
*Gunheath*, G.W.R., 1, D2.
Gunhouse Wharf (Goods), L.N.E.R., 22, F5.
Gunnersbury, **S.R.**/L.M.S./L.P.T.B., 5, B2.
Gunness & Burringham (Goods), L.N.E.R., 22, F5.
Gunnislake, S.R., 1, C5.
Gunton, L.N.E.R., 18, D3.
Gurnos (Goods), L.M.S., 7, A4.
Guthrie, L.M.S., 37, D3.
Guyhirne, L.N.E.R., 17, F3.
•Gwaun-cae-Gurwen, G.W.R., 7, A4.
Gwersyllt & Wheatsheaf, L.N.E.R., 20, E4.
Gwinear Road, G.W.R., 1, E4.
Gwyddelwern, L.M.S., 19, F5.
Gwys, L.M.S., 7, A4.

HABROUGH—INGATESTONE

## H

Habrough, L.N.E.R., 22, F3.
Hackbridge, S.R., 5, B3.
Hackney Downs, L.N.E.R., 5, A3.
Haddenham (Bucks.), G.W.R./L.N.E.R., 10, E3.
•Haddenham (Cambs.), L.N.E.R., 11, B3.
Haddington, L.N.E.R., 31, B5.
Haddsicoe, L.N.E.R., 18, F1.
Hadfield, L.N.E.R., 21, G1.
Hadham, L.N.E.R., 11, F3.
•Hadleigh, L.N.E.R., 12, D4.
Hadley, L.M.S., 15, E2.
Hadley Wood, L.N.E.R., 11, G2.
Hadlow Road, B.J., 20, D4.
Hadnall, L.M.S., 15, E1.
Hafod, see Johnstown.
Hagley, G.W.R., 9, A3.
Haigh, L.M.S., 21, F3.
Hailsham, S.R., 5, F5.
Hainton, see South Willingham.
Hairmyres, L.M.S., 30, D1.
•Halbeath, L.N.E.R., 31, A3.
Hale, C.L.C., 20, C2.
Halebank, L.M.S., 20, C3.
•Halesowen, G.W.R./L.M.S., 15, G4.
*Halesowen Basin*, G.W.R., 15, G4.
Halesworth, L.N.E.R., 12, B2.
Halewood, C.L.C., 20, C3.
Halifax, L.M.S. & L.N.E.R., 21, E2.
Halkirk, L.M.S., 39, C3.
Hallaton, L.M.S./L.N.E.R., 16, F2.
Hallatrow, G.W.R., 3, B2.
*Hallcraig*, L.M.S., 31, D1.
*Hall End Coll.*, L.M.S., 15 F5.
Hall Green, G.W.R., 9, A4.
Halling, S.R., 5, C5.
Hallington, L.N.E.R., 17, A3.
Halliwell (Goods), L.M.S., 20, B2.
Hall Road, L.M.S., 20, B4.
•Halmer End, L.M.S., 15, C3.
•Halsall, L.M.S., 20, B4.
Halstead (Essex), L.N.E.R., 11, E5.
Halton (Ches.), B.J., 20, D3.
Halton (Lancs.), L.M.S., 24, B3.
•Halton Holgate, L.N.E.R., 17, B3.
Haltwhistle L.N.E.R., 27, B2.
Halwill, S.R., 1, B5.
Hambleton, L.N.E.R., 21, D5.
Ham Bridge Halt, S.R., 5, F2
Hamilton, L.M.S. & L.N.E.R., 30, C1.
Hamilton Sq. (Birkenhead), Mer./L.M.S., 20, C4.
Hammersmith, L.P.T.B., 5, B3.
Hammerton, L.N.E.R., 21, C4.
Hammerwich, L.M.S., 15, F4.
Hampden Park, S.R., 5, F5.
Hampole, L.N.E.R., 21, F4.
Hampstead Norris, G.W.R., 4, A3.
Hampsthwaite, L.N.E.R., 21, C3.
Hampton, S.R., 5, B2.
Hampton Court, S.R., 5, B2.
Hampton-in-Arden, L.M.S., 9, A5.
Hampton Loade, G.W.R., 15, G2.
Hampton-on-Sea, see Herne Bay.
Hampton Wick, S.R., 5, B2.
Ham Street & Orlestone, S.R., 6, D4.
Hamworthy (Goods), S.R., 3, F5.
Hamworthy Jc., S.R., 3, F3.
Handborough, G.W.R., 10, E4.
Handforth, L.M.S., 15, A3.
Handsworth, G.W.R., 15, G4.
Hanley, L.M.S., 15, C3.
Hannington, G.W.R., 9, F5.
Hanwell & Elthorne, G.W., 5, B2.
Hanwood, S.W. 14 A1.
Happendon, L.M.S., 31, E2.
Hapton, L.M.S., 24, D1.
•Harborne, L.M.S., 15, G4.
Harburn, L.M.S., 31, C3.
Harbury, see Southam Rd.
Harby, see Doddington.
Harby & Stathern, L.M.S./L.N.E.R., 16, D2.
Hardengreen (Goods), L.N.E.R., 31, C4.
*Hardham Jc.*, S.R., 5, E1.
Hardingham, L N.E.R., 18, F4.
Hardwick Road (Goods), M.G.N., 17, E5.
Haresfield, L.M.S., 9, E3.
Hare Park, L.N.E.R., 21, E3.
Harker Parkhouse Halt, L.N.E.R., 26, C1.
Harlech, G.W.R., 19, F2.
Harleston, L.N.E.R., 12, B3.
Harling Road, L.N.E.R., 12, A4.
Harlington (Beds.), L.M.S., 10, D1.
Harlington (Middlesex), see Hayes.
Harlington (Yorks.), L.M.S., 21, F4.
Harlow, L.N.E.R., 11, F3.
Harmston, L.N.E.R., 16, B1.
Harold Wood, L.N.E.R., 5, A5.
Harpenden, L.M.S. & L.N.E.R., 11, F1.
Harperley, L.N.E.R., 27, D4.
•Harpur Hill, L.M.S., 15, B4.
Harrietsham, S.R., 6, C4.
Harrington, L.M.S., 26, E3.
Harringworth, L.M.S., 16, F1.
Harrogate, L.N.E.R., 21, C3.
Harrow & Wealdstone, L.M.S., 5, A2.
Harrow-on-the-Hill, L.N.E.R./L.P.T.B., 5, A2.
Harston, L.N.E.R., 11, D3.
Hart, L.N.E.R., 28, D4.
Hartfield, S.R., 5, D4.
Hartford, L.M.S. & C.L.C., 20, D2.
Hartington, L.M.S., 15, B5.
Hartlebury, G.W.R., 9, A3.
•Hartlepool, L.N.E.R., 28, D4.
Hartley, L.N.E.R., 28, B5.
Harton Road, G.W.R., 15, G1.
Hartwood, L.M.S., 31, C1.
Hartwood Hill, L.N.E.R., 31, C1.
Harvington, L.M.S., 9, C4.
Harwich, L.N.E.R., 12, E3.
Hasland (Goods), L.M.S., 16, B5.
Haslemere, S.R., 4, C1.
Haslingden, L.M.S., 24, E1.
•Hassall Green, L.M.S., 15, B3.
Hassendean, L.N.E.R., 32, F5.
*Hassockrigg Coll.*, L.N.E.R., 31, C2.
Hassocks, S.R., 5, F3.
•Hassop, L.M.S., 15, B5.
Hastings, S.R., 6, F5.
Haswell, L.N.E.R., 28, D5.
Hatch, G.W.R., 8, G3.
Hatch End, L.M.S.R., 5, A2.
Hatfield (Herts.), L.N.E.R., 11, F2.
Hatfield (Yorks.), see Stainforth.
Hatfield Moor (Goods), A.J., 21, F5.
Hatfield Peverel, L.N.E.R., 11, F5.
Hatherleigh, S.R., 2, A5.
Hathern, L.M.S., 16, E4.
Hathersage, L.M.S., 15, A5.
•Hatton (Aberdeen), L.N.E.R., 38, E1.
Hatton (Warwick), G.W.R., 9, B5.
Haughley, L.N.E.R., 12, C4.
Haughton, L.M.S., 15, E3.
Havant, S.R., 4, E2.
Havenhouse, L.N.E.R., 17, B4.
Haven Street (I.W.), S.R., 4, F3.
Haverfordwest, G.W.R., 7, C2.
Haverhill, L.N.E.R., 11, D5.
•Haverthwaite, L.M.S., 24, A4.
Haverton Hill, L.N.E.R., 28, E4.
Hawarden, L.N.E.R., 20, D4.
Hawarden Bridge, L.N.E.R., 20, D4.
Hawes, L.M.S./L.N.E.R., 27, G3.
Hawick, L.N.E.R., 32, F5.
Hawkesbury Lane, L.M.S., 16, G5.
Hawkhurst, S.R., 6, E5.
Haworth, L.M.S., 21, D1.
Hawkser, L.N.E.R., 28, F2.
Hawthornden, see Rosewell.
Haxby, L.N.E.R., 21, C5.
•Haxey, A.J., 22, F5.
Haxey & Epworth, L.N.E.R., 22, G5.
•Haxey Jc., A.J., 22, F5.
•Haxey Town, A.J., 22, F5.
Hay, L.M.S./G.W.R., 14, F2.
Hayburn Wyke, L.N.E.R., 28, G1.
Haydock, L.N.E.R., 20, B3.
Haydon Bridge, L.N.E.R., 27, B3.
Hayes (Kent), S.R., 5, C4.
Hayes & Harlington (Middx), G.W.R., 5. B2.
Hayfield, L.M.S./L.N.E.R., 15, A4.
Hayle, G.W.R., 1, E4.
Hayling Island, S.R., 4, E2.
Haymarket (Edinburgh), L.N.E.R., 31, B4.
Haywards Heath, S.R., 5, E3.
Haywood, L.M.S., 31, C2.
Hazel Grove, L.M.S., 15, A3.
•Hazelwell, L.M.S., 9, A4.
•Hazelwood, L.M.S., 16, C5.
Hazlehead Bridge, L.N.E.R., 21, F2.
Heacham, L.N.E.R., 17, D5.
Headcorn, S.R./K.E.S.R., 6, D5.
Headingley, L.N.E.R., 21, D3.
Heads Nook, L.N.E.R., 27, C1.
•Heads of Ayr, L.M.S., 30, F3.
Headstone Lane, L.M.S., 5, A2.
Healey House, L.M.S., 21, F2.
Healing, L.N.E.R., 22, F2.
•Heanor, L.M.S. & L.N.E.R., 16, C4.
Heap Bridge (Goods), L.M.S., 20, B1.
Heapey, L.M.S., 24, E2.
Heath, L.N.E.R., 16, B4.
•Heather & Ibstock, L.M.S., 16, E5.
Heathfield (Devon), G.W.R. 2, C4.
Heathfield (Sussex), S.R., 5, E5.
*Heath Jc.*, G.W.R., 8, C4.
Heathway, L.M.S./L.P.T.B., 5, A4.
Heatley & Warburton, L.M.S., 20, C2.
Heaton, L.N.E.R., 27, B5.
Heaton Chapel, L.M.S., 20, C1.
*Heaton Lodge Jc.*, L.M.S., 21, E2.
Heaton Mersey, L.M.S., 20, C1.
Heaton Norris, L.M.S., 20, C1.
Heaton Park, L.M.S., 20, B1.
Hebburn, L.N.E.R., 28, B5.
Hebden Bridge, L.M.S., 21, E1.
Heck, L.N.E.R., 21, E5.
Heckington, L.N.E.R., 17, C2.
Heckmondwike, L.M.S., 21, E2.
Heddon-on-the-Wall, L.N.E.R., 27, B5.
•Hedgeley, L.N.E.R., 32, F2.
Hednesford, L.M.S., 15, E4.
Hedon, L.N.E.R., 22, E3.
Heeley, L.M.S., 16, A5.
Heighington (Durham), L.N.E.R., 27, E5.
Heighington (Lincs.), see Branston.
Hele & Bradninch, G.W.R., 2, A3.
Helensburgh, L.N.E.R., 30, B3.
Hellaby (Goods), L.M.S./L.N.E.R., 21, G4.
Hellesdon, M.G.N., 18, F3.
Hellifield, L.M.S., 24, C1.
Hellingly, S.R., 5, F5.
Helmdon, L.M.S., 10, C3.
„ L.N.E.R., 10, C4.
Helmsdale, L.M.S., 39, F2.
Helmshore, L.M.S., 20, A1.
Helmsley, L.N.E.R., 21, A5.
Helpringham, L.N.E.R., 17, D1.
Helpston, L.M.S., 17, F1.
Helsby B.J. & •C.L.C., 20, D3.
Helston, G.W.R., 1, F5.
•Hemel Hempsted, L.M.S., 10, E5.
Hemel Hempsted & Boxmoor, L.M.S., 10, E5.
Hemingborough, L.N.E.R., 21, D5.
Hemsby, M.G.N., 18, E1.
Hemsworth, L.N.E.R., 21, F4.
Hemyock, G.W.R., 2, A2.
Henbury, G.W.R., 8, C2.
Hendford (Goods), G.W.R., 3, D2.
Hendon, L.M.S., 5, A3.
Henfield, S.R., 5, F2.
Hengoed, G.W.R., 8, B4.
Henham Halt, L.N.E.R., 11, E4.
•Heniarth, W.L., 14, B3.
Henley-in-Arden, G.W.R., 9, B5.
Henley-on-Thames, G.W.R., 10, G2.
Henllan, G.W.R., 13, F4.
Henlow, see Arlesey.
Henlow Camp, L.M.S., 11, E1.
Hensall, L.M.S./L.N.E.R., 21, E5.
*Hensall Jc.*, L.M.S./L.N.E.R., 21, E5.
Henstridge, S.D., 3, D3.
Henwick (Worcs.), G.W.R., 9, B3.
Hepscott, L.N.E.R., 27, A5.
Hereford, S.H., 9, C1.
Heriot, L.N.E.R., 31, C5.
Hermitage, G.W.R., 4, A3.
Herne Bay & Hampton-on-Sea, S.R., 6, B3.
Herne Hill, S.R., 5, B3.
Hersham, S.R., 5, C2.
Hertford, L.N.E.R., 11, F2.
Hertingfordbury, L.N.E.R., 11, F2.
Hesketh Bank, L.M.S., 24, E3.
Hesketh Park, L.M.S., 20, A4.
Hesleden, L.N.E.R., 28, D4.
Heslerton, L.N.E.R., 22, B4.
Hessay, L.N.E.R., 21, C4.
Hessle, L.N.E.R., 22, E4.
Hest Bank, L.M.S., 24, B3.
Heswall, B.J., 20, C5.
Heswall Hills, L.N.E.R., 20, C4.
Hethersett, L.N.E.R., 18, F3.
Hetton (Durham), L.N.E.R., 28, D5.
Hever, S.R., 5, D4.
Heversham, L.M.S., 24, A3.
Hexham, L.N.E.R., 27, B3.
Heybridge, see Maldon East.
Heyford, G.W.R., 10, D4.
Heysham, L.M.S., 24, C3.
Heytesbury, G.W.R., 3, C4.
Heywood, L.M.S., 20, B1.
Hibaldstow, see Scawby.
Hibel Road (Macclesfield), L.M.S., 15, A3.
*Hibel Road Jc.*, L.M.S./L.N.E.R., 15, A3.
•Hickleton, L.N.E.R., 21, F4.
Higham (Kent), S.R., 6, B5.
Higham (Suffolk), L.N.E.R., 11, C5.
Higham Ferrers, L.M.S., 10, A1.
Highams Park, L.N.E.R., 5, A4.
High Barnet, •L.N.E.R./L.P.T.B., 11, G2.
•High Blantyre, L.M.S., 30, C1.
Highbridge, G.W. & S.D., 8, E3.
High Brooms, S.R., 5, D5.
Highclere, G.W.R., 4, B3.
Higher Buxton, L.M.S., 15, A4.
Higher Poynton, L.M.S./L.N.E.R., 15, A4.
High Field, L.N.E.R., 22, D5.
Highgate, •L.N.E.R./L.P.T.B., 5, A3.
High Halden Road, K.E.S.R., 6, D4.
•High Harrington, L.M.S., 26, E3.
Highlandman, L.M.S., 34, F3.
High Lane, L.M.S./L.N.E.R., 15, A4.
Highley, G.W.R., 9, A2.
High Shields, L.N.E.R., 28, B5.
*High Peak Jc.*, L.M.S., 16, C5.
Hightown, L.M.S., 20, B4.
Highworth, L.M.S., 9, F5.
High Wycombe, G.W.R./L.N.E.R., 10, F2.
Hildenborough, S.R., 5, C5.
Hilgay, L.N.E.R., 11, A4.
Hill End, L.N.E.R., 11, F2.
Hillfoot, L.N.E.R., 30, B1.
Hillhouse (Lancs.), see Altcar.
Hillhouse (Yorks.), Goods, L.M.S., 21, E2.
*Hillhouse Jc.*, L.M.S./C.L.C., 20, B4.
Hillington, M.G.N., 17, E5.
•Hillside (Kincard.), L.N.E.R., 37, C4.
Hillside (Southport), L.M.S., 20, A4.
Hills Road (Goods), L.M.S., 11, C3.
*Hilton Jc.*, L.M.S./L.N.E.R., 34, F1.
Hilton House, L.M.S., 20, B2.
•Himley, G.W.R., 15, G3.
*Hincaster Jc.*, L.M.S., 24, A3.
*Hindpool*, L.M.S., 24, B5.
Hinckley, L.M.S., 16, F4.
Hinderwell, L.N.E.R., 28, E2.
Hindley, L.M.S. & L.N.E.R., 20, B2.
Hindley Green, L.M.S., 20, B2.
Hindlow, L.M.S., 15, B5.
Hindolvestone, M.G.N., 18, D4.
Hinton (Glos.), L.M.S., 9, C4.
Hinton (Northants.), see Woodford.
Hinton Admiral, S.R., 4, F5.
Hipperholme, L.M.S., 21, E2.
Hirwaun, G.W.R., 8, A5.
Histon, L.N.E.R./L.M.S., 11, C3.
Hitchin, L.N.E.R./L.M.S. & •L.M.S., 11, E2.
§Hixon Halt, L.M.S., 15, D4.
Hockham, see Wretham.
Hockley (Birmingham), G.W.R., 15, G4.
Hockley (Essex), L.N.E.R., 6, A5.
*Hodbarrow Siding*, L.M.S., 24, A5.
Hoddesdon, see Broxbourne.
Hoddlesden (Goods), L.M.S., 24, E1.
Hodnet, G.W.R., 15, D2.
Hoghton, L.M.S., 24, E2.
Holbeach, M.G.N., 17, E3.
Holbeck, L.N.E.R./L.M.S. & L.M.S., 21, D3.
Holborn Viaduct, S.R., 5, B3.
*Holbrook Colls.*, L.M.S. & L.N.E.R., 16, A4.
Holcombe Brook, L.M.S., 20, A1.
Hole, S.R., 1, A5.
Holehouse Jc., L.M.S., 30, F2.
*Holgate Jc.*, L.N.E.R., 21, C5.
Holkham, L.N.E.R., 18, C5.
Holland Arms, L.M.S., 19, D1.
Holland-on-Sea, see Clacton.
Holland Road, S.R., 5, F3.
Hollingbourne, S.R., 6, C5.
•Hollin Well, L.N.E.R., 16, C4.
Hollins (Goods), L.M.S., 24, E2.
Hollinwood, L.M.S., 20, B1.
Hollinswood (Goods), G.W.R., 15, E2.
Hollybush (Ayr), L.M.S., 30, F2.
Holly Bush (Mon.), L.M.S., 8, A4.
Holme (Hunts.), L.N.E.R., 11, A2.
•Holme (Lancs.), L.M.S., 24, E1.
Holme (West'd.), see Burton.
Holme Hale, L.N.E.R., 18, F5.
Holme Lacy, G.W.R., 9, C1.
Holme Moor, L.N.E.R., 22, D5.
Holmes, L.M.S., 21, G4.
Holmes Chapel, L.M.S., 15, B3.
Holmfield, L.M.S./L.N.E.R., 21, E2.
Holmfirth, L.M.S., 21, F2.
Holmsley, S.R., 4, E5.
Holmwood, S.R., 5, D2.
Holsworthy, S.R., 1, A4.
Holt (Norfolk), M.G.N., 18, D4.
•Holtby, L.N.E.R., 21, C5.
Holt Jc., G.W.R., 3, B4.
Holton Heath, S.R., 3, F4.
Holton-le-Clay, L.N.E.R., 22, F2.
Holton-le-Moor, L.N.E.R., 22, F3.
Holton Village Halt, L.N.E.R., 22, F2.
Holwell (Goods), L.M.S., 16, E3.
Holygate (Goods), L.N.E.R., 31, B3.
Holyhead, L.M.S., 19, B2.
Holytown, L.M.S., 31, C1.
Holywell (North'd.) Goods, L.N.E.R., 28, B5.
Holywell Jc., L.M.S., 20, D5.
Holywell Town, L.M.S., 20, D5.
Holywood, L.M.S., 26, A4.
Homersfield, L.N.E.R., 12, A3.
Honeybourne, G.W.R., 9, C5
Honing, M.G.N., 18, D2.
Honington, L.N.E.R., 16 C1.
Honiton, S.R., 2, A2.
Honley, L.M.S., 21, F2.
Hook, S.R., 4, B2.
•Hookagate, S.M., 15, E1.
Hook Norton, G.W.R., 10, D5.
Hoole, L.M.S., 24, E3.
Hooton, B.J., 20, D4.
Hope (Derbys), L.M.S., 15, A5.
Hope (Flint), L.M.S. & L.N.E.R., 20, E4.
Hope Village, L.N.E.R., 20, E4.
•Hopeman, L.M.S., 36, C2.
Hopperton, L.N.E.R., 21, C4.
Hopton Heath, L.M.S., 14, C1.
Hopton-on-Sea, N.S.J., 18, F1.
Horam, see Waldron.
Horbling, see Billingboro'.
Horbury & Ossett, L.M.S., 21, E3.
Horbury, Millfield Road, L.M.S., 21, E3.
*See also* Ossett, L.N.E.R.
Horden, L.N.E.R., 28, D4.
•Horeb, G.W.R., 7, A3.
Horham, L.N.E.R., 12, B3.
Horley, S.R., 5, D3.
Hornby, L.M.S., 24, B2.
Horncastle, L.N.E.R., 17, B2.
Hornchurch, L.M.S./L.P.T.B., 5, A5.
Horninglow, L.M.S./•L.N.E.R., 15, D5.
Horninglow (Goods), L.N.E.R., 16, E5.
Hornsea, L.N.E.R., 22, C2.
Hornsea Bridge, L.N.E.R. 22, C3.
Horrabridge, G.W.R., 1, C5.
Horringford (I.W.), S.R., 4, F3.
*Horrocksford*, L.M.S., 24, D1.
Horsebridge, S.R., 4, D4.
Horsehay, G.W.R., 15, F2.
Horsforth, L.N.E.R., 21, D3.
Horsham, S.R., 5, E2.
Horsley, S.R., 5, C2.
Horsmonden, S.R., 5, D5.
Horsted Keynes, S.R., 5, E4.
Horton-in-Ribblesdale, L.M.S., 24, B1.
Horton Park, L.N.E.R., 21, D2.
Horwich, L.M.S., 20, B2.
Hoscar, L.M.S., 20, B3.
Hose, see Long Clawson.
Hothfield, S.R., 6, D4.
Hougham, L.N.E.R., 16, C2
Hough Green, C.L.C., 20, C3.
Hounslow, L.P.T.B. & S.R., 5, B2.
Houston & Crosslee, L.M.S., 30, C2.
Hove, S.R., 5, F3.
•Hovingham Spa, L.N.E.R., 21, B5.
Howden Clough, L.N.E.R., 21, E3.
Howdon-on-Tyne, L.N.E.R., 28, B5.
Howe Bridge, L.M.S., 20, B2.
How Mill, L.N.E.R., 27, C1.
Howsham, L.N.E.R., 22, F3.
Howwood, L.M.S., 30, C2.
Hoy Halt, L.M.S., 39, C3.
Hoylake, L.M.S., 20, C5.
Hoyland, see Elsecar.
Hoyland Common, see Wentworth.
Hubbert's Bridge, L.N.E.R., 17, D2.
Hucknall, L.M.S. & L.N.E.R. 16, C4.
*Hucknall Coll.*, L.N.E.R., 16, B4.
Huddersfield, L.M.S., 21, E2.
•Hugglescote, L.M.S., 16, E4.
Hull, L.N.E.R., 22, E3.
Hullavington, G.W.R., 9, G3.
*Humber Rd. Jc.*, L.N.E.R., 22, E3.
Humberstone, L.N.E.R., 16, F3.
Humberstone Road, L.M.S., 16, F3.
•Humbie, L.N.E.R., 31, C5.
Humshaugh, L.N.E.R., 27, B3.
Huncoat, L.M.S., 24, D1.
Hundred End, L.M.S., 24, E3.
Hungerford, G.W.R., 4, A4.
Hunmanby, L.N.E.R., 22, B3.
•Hunnington, H.J., 9, A4.
Hunslet, L.M.S. & •L.N.E.R. 21, D3.
Hunstanton, L.N.E.R., 17, D5.
Huntingdon East, L.N.E.R., L.M.S., 11, B2.
Huntingdon Nth., L.N.E.R., 11, B2.
Huntly, L.N.E.R., 38, E5.
Hunt's Cross, C.L.C., 20, C4.
Hunwick, L.N.E.R., 27, D5.
Hurdlow, L.M.S., 15, B5.
Hurlford, L.M.S., 30, E2.
Hurstbourne, S.R., 4, B4.
*Hurst Green Jc.*, S.R., 5, C4.
•Hurworth Burn, L.N.E.R., 28, D5.
•Huskisson (L'pool), C.L.C., 20, C4.
Husthwaite Gate, L.N.E.R., 21, B4.
Hutton (Essex), see Shenfield.
Hutton (Lancs.), see New Longton.
Hutton Cranswick, L.N.E.R., 22, C4.
Hutton Gate, L.N.E.R., 28, E3.
•Huttons Ambo, L.N.E.R., 22, B5.
Huyton, L.M.S., 20, C4.
Huyton Quarry, L.M.S., 20, C3.
Hyde, L.M.S./L.N.E.R., 21, G1.
Hyde Jc., L.M.S./L.N.E.R., 21, G1.
Hykeham, L.M.S., 16, B2.
Hylton, L.N.E.R., 28, C5.
Hythe (Essex), L.N.E.R., 12, E4.
Hythe (Hants.), S.R., 4, E4.
Hythe (Kent), S.R. & R.H.D.R., 6, D3.

## I

Ibrox, L.M.S., 30, C2.
Ibstock, see Heather.
Ickenham, see West Ruislip.
Ide, G.W.R., 2, B3.
•Idle, L.N.E.R., 21, D2.
•Idridgehay, L.M.S., 16, C5.
Ifield, S.R., 5, D3.
•Ilderton, L.N.E.R., 32, E2.
Ilford, L.N.E.R., 5, A4.
Ilfracombe, S.R., 7, E3.
Ilkeston, L.M.S. & L.N.E.R. 16, C4.
Ilkley, O.J., 20, C2.
Ilminster, G.W.R., 8 G3.
Immingham, L.N.E.R., 22, E3.
Immingham Dock, L.N.E.R. 22, E2.
Ince (Lancs.), L.M.S., 20, B3.
*See also* Lower Ince.
Ince & Elton, B.J., 20, D3.
Inchcoonans (Goods), L.M.S., 34, E1.
Inches, L.M.S., 31, E1.
•Inchgreen, L.M.S., 30, B3.
Inchture, L.M.S., 37, E1.
Ingarsby, L.N.E.R., 16, F3.
Ingatestone, L.N.E.R., 11, G4.

PINCHINTHORPE—SALE

inchinthorpe, L.N.E.R., 28, F4.
nged Halt, G.W.R., 7, A2.
nhoe S.R , 2, B3.
nkhill, L.N.E.R., 16, A4.
nmore, L.M.S., 25, A3.
nner, L.N.E.R./L.P.T.B., 5, A2.
nwherry, L.M.S., 25, A3.
nxton, L.N.E.R. & *L.M.S., 16, C4.
pe Gate, L.M.S., 15, C2.
*rbright Jc.*, S.R., 5, C1.
rton, L.M.S., 9, C3.
tcaple, L.N.E.R., 38, E3.
tlochry, L.M.S., 34, C3.
tlurg, L.N.E.R., 38, E2.
tmedden, L.N.E.R., 38, F3.
tney, *see* Long Sutton.
tsea, L.M.S., 6, A5.
'itsford & Brampton, L.M.S., 10, B3.
ttenweem, L.N.E.R. 37, G3.
ttington, L.N.E.R., 28, D5.
tts Hill, L.M.S., 15, C3.
ains, L.N.E.R., 31, C1.
aidy, L.N.E.R., 38, D3.
*lank Lane Jc.*, L.N.E.R./L.M.S., 20, B3.
ashetts, L.N.E.R., 27, A2.
as Marl, G.W.R., 7, B4.
as Power, G.W.R. & L.N.E.R., 20, E4.
awsworth, L.N.E.R., 27, C5.
ealey Road, S.W., 14, B1.
ean, L.M.S., 31, A1.
*lean Pits*, L.M.S., 31, A1.
easington, L.M.S., 24, E2.
easley, L.M.S. & L.N.E.R., 16, B4.
eck, L.M.S., 15, F4.
essey, L.N.E.R., 27, B5.
ockton, L.M.S., 35, E1.
odder Lane, L.M.S., 20, B2.
uckley, S.R., 6, D4.
umley, C.L.C., 20, D2.
umpton (Cumb.), L.M.S., 27, D1.
umpton (Sussex), S.R., 5, F3.
*umpton Jc.*, L.M.S., 24, A4.
umstead, S.R., 5, B4.
umtree, L.M.S., 16, D3.
ym Bridge Platform, G.W.R., 2, D5.
ymouth, G.W.R. & S.R., 1, D5.
ympton, G.W.R., 2, D5.
ymstock, **S.R.**/*G.W.R., 1, D5.
ocklington, L.N.E.R., 22, C5.
okesdown, S.R., 4, F5.
olegate, S.R., 5, F5.
olesworth, L.M.S., 16, F5.
ollington, *see* Snaith, L.N.E.R.
*lkemmet Weighs*, L.N.E.R., 31, C2.
llokshaws, L.M.S., 30, C1.
olmont, L.N.E.R., 31, B2.
olsham, S.D., 3, C2.
olton, L.N.E.R., 31, C4.
mathorn Halt, L.N.E.R., 31, C4.
onder's End, L.N.E.R., 11, G3.
*oneil Jc.*, L.M.S., 31, E1.
ond St. (Sheffield) Goods, L.M.S., 16, A5.
nfeigh, L.M.S., 31, E2.
ntardawe, **L.M.S.**/G.W.R., 7, A4.
ntardulais, G.W.R./L.M.S., 7, A3.
ontdolgoch, G.W.R., 14, B3.
ontefract, L. M. S. & L.N.E.R., 21, E4.
onteland, L.N.E.R., 27, B5.
ontesbury, S.W., 14, B1.
onthenry, G.W.R., 7, A3.
onthir, G.W.R., 8, B3.
ontllanfraith, G.W.R. & L.M.S., 8, B4.
ont Llanio, G.W.R., 13, E5.
ontlliw, G.W.R., 7, B3.
ontlottyn, G.W.R., 8, A4.
ntnewydd, G.W.R., 8, B3.
ntnewynydd, G.W.R., 8 B3.
ntrhydyfen, G.W.R., 7, B5.
ntrhythallt, L.M.S., 19, D2.
ntrilas, G.W.R., 14, G1.
ntsarn, G.W.R./L.M.S., 8, B5.
ntsticill Jc., G.W.R., 8, A5.
ntyates, G.W.R., 7, A3.
ntyberem, G.W.R., 7, A3.
ntycymmer, G.W.R., 7, B5.
nt-y-pant, L.M.S., 19, E3.
ntypool, G.W.R., 8, B3.
ntypool Road, G.W.R., 8, B3.
ntypridd, G.W.R., 8, B5.
ntyrhyll, G.W.R., 7, B5.
ol (– in – Wharfedale), L.N.E.R., 21, D3.
ole, **S.R.**/S.D., 3, F5.
ol Quay, G.W.R., 14, A2.
ppleton, L.N.E.R., 21, C5.

Portbury, G.W.R., 8, C2.
Portchester, S.R., 4, E2.
*Port Clarence, L.N.E.R., 28, E4.
Port Dinorwic, L.M.S., 19, D2.
Port Elphinstone (Goods), L.N.E.R., 38, F3.
Port Erin, I.M.R., 23, C1.
Portesham, G.W.R., 3, F2.
Portessie, L.N.E.R., 38, C5.
Port Glasgow, L.M.S., 30, B3.
Port Gordon, L.N.E.R., 38, C5.
Porth (Glam.), G.W.R., 8, B5.
Porthcawl, G.W.R., 7, C5.
Porthywaen, G.W.R., 20, G5.
Port Isaac Road, S.R., 1, C3.
Portishead, G.W.R., 8, C2.
Portknockie, L.N.E.R., 38, C5.
Portland, G.W.R./S.R., 3, G3.
Portlethen, L.M.S., 37, A5.
Portmadoc, G.W.R., 19, F2.
Portobello, L.N.E.R., 31, B4.
Port of Menteith, L.N.E.R., 30, A1.
Porton, S.R., 4, C5.
Portpatrick, L.M.S., 25, C1.
Port St. Mary, I.M.R., 23, C1.
Portskewett, G.W.R., 8, B2.
Portslade & West Hove, S.R., 5, F3.
Portsmouth (Yorks.), L.M.S., 20, A1.
Portsmouth & Southsea, S.R., 4, E2.
Portsmouth Arms, S.R., 7, G4.
Portsmouth Harbour, S.R., 4, E2.
Port Soderick, I.M.R., 23, C2.
Portsoy, L.N.E.R., 38, C4.
Port Sunlight, B.J., 20, C4.
Port Talbot, G.W.R., 7, B4.
Port Victoria, S.R., 6, B4.
Postland, L.N.E.R., 17, E3.
Potterhanworth, L.N.E.R., 17, B1.
Potter Heigham, M. G. N., 18, E2.
*Potterhill, L.M.S., 30, C2.
*Potterick Carr. Jc.*, L.N.E.R./S.Y., 21, F5.
Potters Bar, L.N.E.R., 11, G2.
Potto, L.N.E.R., 28, F4.
Potton, L.M.S., 11, D2.
Poulton (Lancs.), L.M.S., 24, D4.
Poundon, *see* Marsh Gibbon.
Powerstock, G.W.R., 3, F2.
Poynton, L.M.S., 15, A3.
Praze, G.W.R., 1, E5.
Prees, L.M.S., 15, D1.
*Preesall, L.M.S., 24, C4.
Prescot, L.M.S., 20, C3.
Prestatyn, L.M.S., 19, C5.
Prestbury, L.M.S., 15, A3.
Presteign, G.W.R., 14, D2.
Presthope, G.W.R., 15, F2.
Preston, L.M.S., 24, E3.
Preston Brook, L.M.S., 20, C3.
Preston Jc., L.M.S., 24, E2.
Prestonpans, L.N.E.R., 31, B5.
Preston Park, S.R., 5, F3.
Preston Road, L.M.S., 20, C4.
Preston St. (Whitehaven) Goods, L.M.S., 26, E4.
Prestwich, L.M.S., 20, B1.
Prestwick, L.M.S., 30, E3.
Priestfield, G.W.R., 15, F4.
*Prince of Wales Dock* (Workington), L.M.S., 26, E3.
Princes End, G.W.R., 15, F4.
Princes Pier (Greenock), L.M.S., 30, B3.
Princes Risborough, G.W.R./L.N.E.R., 10, F2.
Princes St. (Edinburgh), L.M.S., 30, B4.
Princes St. (Perth), L.M.S., 34, F1.
Princetown, G.W.R., 2, C5.
Priory (Dover), S.R., 6, D2.
Prittlewell, L.N.E.R., 6, A4.
Privett, S.R., 4, D2.
Probus & Ladock Plat., G.W.R., 1, E2.
Promenade (Morecambe), L.M.S., 24, B3.
Prudhoe, L.N.E.R., 27, B4.
Pudsey, L.N.E.R., 21, D3.
Pulborough, S.R., 5, E2.
Pulford (Goods), G.W.R., 20, E4.
Pulham Market, L.N.E.R., 12, B3.
Pulham St. Mary, L.N.E.R., 12, B3.
*Puncheston, G.W.R., 13, F1.
Purfleet, L.M.S., 5, B5.
Purley, S.R., 5, C3.
Purley Oaks, S.R., 5, C3.
Purton, G.W.R., 9, F4.
Putney, S.R., 5, B3.
Puxton & Worle, G.W.R., 8, D3.
§*Pwllglas & Trefeglwys*, G.W.R., 14, C4.

Pwllheli, G.W.R., 19, F1.
Pye Bridge, L.M.S., 16, C4.
Pye Hill & Somercotes, L.N.E.R., 16, C4.
*Pye Wipe Jc.*, L.N.E.R., 16, B1.
Pyle, G.W.R., 7, C5.
Pylle, S.D., 3, C2.

## Q

Quainton Rd., L.N.E.R./L.P.T.B., 10, E3.
Quaker's Drove (Goods), L.N.E.R., 11, A3.
Quaker's Yard, G.W.R., 8, B5.
*Quarter, L.M.S., 31, D1.
Queenborough, S.R., 6, B4.
Queens Road (Sheffield) Goods, L.M.S., 16, A5.
Queen Street (Glasgow), L.N.E.R., 30, C1.
Queen St. (Cardiff), G.W.R., 8, C4.
Queensbury, L.N.E.R., 21 D2.
Queensferry, L.M.S., 20, D4.
Quintrell Downs Platform, G.W.R., 1, D1.
Quorn & Woodhouse, L.N.E.R., 16, E4.
*See also* Barrow-on-Soar.
Quy, L.N.E.R., 11, C4.

## R

Racks, L.M.S., 26, B3.
Radcliffe, L.M.S., 20, B1.
*See also* Black Lane.
Radcliffe Bridge, L.M.S., 20, B2.
Radcliffe-on-Trent, L.N.E.R., 16, D3.
Radford, L.M.S., 16, D4.
Radlett, L.M.S., 11, G2.
Radley, G.W.R., 10, F4.
Radstock, G.W.R. & S.D., 3, B3.
Radway Green, L.M.S., 15, C3.
Radyr, G.W.R., 8, C4.
Raglan, G.W.R., 8, A3.
Rainford Jc., L.M.S., 20, B3.
Rainford Village, L.M.S., 20, B3.
Rainham (Essex), L.M.S., 5, A4.
Rainham (Kent), S.R., 6, B5.
Rainhill, L.M.S., 20, C3.
Rainworth, *see* Blidworth.
Ramsbottom, L.M.S., 20, A1.
*Ramsden Dock, L.M.S., 24, B5.
Ramsey, I.M.R. & M.E., 23, A3.
*Ramsey East, L.N.E.R. 11, B2.
*Ramsey North, L.N.E.R., 11, B2.
Ramsgate, S.R., 6, B1.
Rankinston, L.M.S., 30, F2.
Rannoch, L.N.E.R., 33, D5.
Ranskill, L.N.E.R., 16, A3.
Raskelf, L.N.E.R., 21, B4.
*Ratby, L.M.S., 16, F4.
*Ratgoed Quarry*, Corris, 14, A5.
Rathen, L.N.E.R., 38, C2.
Ratho, L.N.E.R., 31, B3.
Rauceby, L.N.E.R., 17, C1.
Raunds, L.M.S., 10, A1.
§Ravelrig Halt, L.M.S., 31, C3.
Ravenglass, L.M.S. & R.E.R., 26, G3.
Ravenscar, L.N.E.R., 28, F1.
*Ravenscraig, L.M.S., 30, B3.
Ravensthorpe, L.M.S., 21, E3.
Ravenstonedale, L.N.E.R., 27, F2.
*Ravenstone Wood Jc.*, L.M.S., 10, B2.
*Ravenswood Jc.*, L.N.E.R., 32, E5.
Rawcliffe, L.M.S., 21, E5.
*See also* Airmyn.
Rawtenstall, L.M.S., 20, A1.
*Rawyards, L.N.E.R., 31, C1.
*Raydon Wood, L.N.E.R., 12, D4.
Rayleigh, L.N.E.R., 6, A5.
Rayne, L.N.E.R., 11, E5.
Raynes Park, S.R., 5, B3.
Raynham Park, M.G.N., 18, D5.
Reading, G.W.R. & S.R., 4, A2.
Reading West, G.W.R., 4, A2.
Rearsby, L.M.S., 16, E3.
*Redbourn, L.M.S., 11, F1.
Redbridge, S.R., 4, E4.
Redbrook-on-Wye, G.W.R., 8, A2.
Redcar, L.N.E.R., 28, E3.
Redcar East, L.N.E.R., 28, E3.
Redcastle, L.M.S., 36, D5.
Redding (Goods), L.N.E.R., 31, B2.
Reddish, L.M.S. & L.N.E.R., 21, G1.
Redditch, L.M.S., 9, B4.
Redheugh (Goods), L.N.E.R., 27, C5.

Redhill, S.R., 5, C3.
*Red Hill Jc.* (Hereford), G.W.R./L.M.S., 9, C1.
§*Red House*, G.W.R., 14, C4.
Redland, G.W.R./L.M.S., 8, C2.
Redmarshall, L.N.E.R., 28, E5.
Redmile, L.M.S./L.N.E.R., 16, D2.
Redmire, L.N.E.R., 27, G4.
Rednal & W. Felton, G.W.R. 20, G4.
*Red Post Jc.*, S.R./G.W.R., 4, C4.
Red Rock, L.M.S., 20, B3.
Redruth, G.W.R., 1, E5.
Redwharf Bay & Benllech, L.M.S., 19, C2.
Reedham (Norfolk), L.N.E.R., 18, F2.
*Reedness, A J., 22, E5.
Reedsmouth, L.N.E.R., 27, A3.
Reepham (Lincs.), L.N.E.R., 17, B1.
Reepham (Norf'k.), L.N.E.R., 18, E4.
*See also* Whitwell, M.G.N.
Reigate, S.R., 5, C3.
Renfrew, L.M.S., 30, C2.
Renishaw, *see* Eckington.
Renton, L.M.S./L.N.E.R., 30, B3.
Repton & Willington, L.M.S., 16, D5.
Resolven, G.W.R., 7, B5.
Reston, L.N.E.R., 32, C3.
Retford, L.N.E.R., 16, A3.
Rhayader, G.W.R., 14, D4.
Rhewl, L.M.S., 19, E5.
Rhiwderin, G.W.R., 8, C4.
*Rhiwfron, V.R., 14, C5.
Rhoose, G.W.R., 8, D5.
*Rhos (Denbigh), G.W.R., 20, F5.
Rhosgoch, L.M.S., 19, C1.
Rhosneigr, L.M.S., 19, B2.
*Rhostyllen, G.W.R., 20, E4.
Rhu, L.N.E.R., 30, B3.
Rhuddlan, L.M.S., 19, D5.
Rhydowen, G.W.R., 13, F3.
Rhydymwyn, L.M.S., 20, D5.
*Rhydyronen, Tal., 13, B5.
Rhyl, L.M.S., 19, C5.
Rhymney, G.W.R., 8, A4.
Rhymney Bridge, G.W.R./L.M.S., 8, A5.
Ribblehead, L.M.S., 24, A1.
Riccall, L.N.E.R., 21, D5.
*Riccarton & Craigie, L.M.S., 30, E2.
Riccarton Jc., L.N.E.R., 32, G5.
Richmond (Surrey), **S.R.**/L.M.S./L.P.T.B., 5, B2.
Richmond (Yorks.), L.N.E.R., 27, F5.
Rickmansworth, L.N.E.R./L.P.T.B. & L.M.S., 5, A2.
Riddings, L.N.E.R., 26, B1.
Riddlesdown, S.R., 5, C3.
Ridgmont, L.M.S., 10, C1.
Riding Mill, L.N.E.R., 27, C4.
*Rigg, L.M.S., 26, B2.
*Rillington, L.N.E.R., 22, B5.
Rimington, L.M.S., 24, C1.
Ringley Rd., L.M.S., 20, B1.
Ringstead & Addington, L.M.S., 10, A1.
Ringwood, S.R., 4, E5.
*Ripley, L.M.S., 16, C5.
Ripley Valley, L.N.E.R., 21, C3.
Ripon, L.N.E.R., 21, B3.
*Rippingale, L.N.E.R., 17, D1.
Ripple, L.M.S., 9, C3.
*Ripponden, L.M.S., 21, E1.
Risby, *see* Saxham.
Risca, **G.W.R.**/L.M.S., 8, B4.
Rishton, L.M.S., 24, D1.
*Rishworth, L.M.S., 21, E1.
Roade, L.M.S., 10, C2.
Roath (Goods), G.W.R., 8, C4.
Robertsbridge, S.R., 6, E5.
*Robin Hood, L.N.E.R., 21, E3.
Robin Hood's Bay, L.N.E.R., 28, F1.
Roby, L.M.S., 20, C4.
Rocester, L.M.S., 15, D5.
Rochdale, L.M.S., 20, A1.
Roche, G.W.R., 1, D2.
Rochester, S.R., 6, B5.
Rochford, L.N.E.R., 6, A4.
Rockcliffe, L.M.S., 26, C1.
Rock Ferry, B.J./Mer., 20, C4.
Rockingham, L.M.S., 16, F2.
Rodmarton, G.W.R., 9, F3.
Rodmell Halt, *see* Southease.
Rodwell, G.W.R./S.R., 3, G3.
Rogart, L.M.S., 36, A5.
Rogate, S.R., 4, D1.
Rogerstone, G.W.R., 8, B4.
Rollesby, *see* Martham.
Rolleston Jc., L.M.S., 16, C2.
Rolleston-on-Dove, **L.M.S.**/*L.N.E.R., 15, D5.
Rollright Halt, G.W.R., 10, D5.
Rolvenden, K.E.S.R., 6, E4.
Ronaldkirk, L.N.E.R., 27, E4.
Roman Bridge, L.M.S., 19, E3.

§Roman Road, (Woodnesborough), E.K.R., 6, C2.
*Rome Street Jc.* (Carlisle), L.M.S./L.N.E.R., 26, C1.
Romford, L.N.E.R. & L.M.S., 5, A4.
Romiley, L.M.S./L.N.E.R., 21, G1.
Romsey, S.R., 4, D4.
Rookery, L.M.S., 20, B3.
Rookery Bridge (Goods), L.M.S., 15, B2.
Roose, L.M.S., 24, B4.
Ropley, S.R., 4, C2.
*Rosebush, G.W.R., 13, F2.
Rose Grove, L.M.S., 24, D1.
Rose Hill, L.M.S./L.N.E.R., 21, G1.
*Rosehill Jc.*, L.M.S., 26, E3.
Rosemill (Goods), L.M.S., 37, E2.
Rosemount, L.M.S., 34, D1.
Rosewell & Hawthornden, L.N.E.R., 31, C4.
*Roskear*, G.W.R., 1, E5.
*Roslin, L.N.E.R., 31, C4.
Rossett, G.W.R., 20, E4.
Rossington, L.N.E.R., 20, F5.
Rosslyn Castle, L.N.E.R., 31, C4.
Rosslynlee, L.N.E.R., 31, C4.
Ross-on-Wye, G.W.R., 9, D1.
Rothbury, L.N.E.R., 32, G2.
Rotherfield & Mark Cross, S.R., 5, E5.
Rotherham, L.M.S. & L.N.E.R., 21, G4.
Rotherham Road, L.N.E.R., 21, G4.
*Rotherwas Jc.* (Hereford), G.W.R./L.M.S., 9, C1.
Rothes, L.N.E.R., 36, D1.
Rothiemay, L.N.E.R., 38, D5.
Rothie Norman, L.N.E.R., 38, E3.
Rothley, L.N.E.R., 16, E4.
Rothwell (Northants.), *see* Desborough.
*Rothwell (Yorks.), L.N.E.R., 21, E3.
Rough Castle (Goods), L.N.E.R., 31, B1.
*Roughton Rd. Jc.*, L.N.E.R./N.S.J., 18, D3.
Round Oak, G.W.R., 15, G3.
Rowde, *see* Bromham.
Rowden Mill, G.W.R., 9, B2.
Rowfant, S.R., 5, D3.
Rowland's Castle, S.R., 4, E2.
Rowlands Gill, L.N.E.R., 27, C5.
*Rowley, L.N.E.R., 27, C4.
Rowley Regis, G.W.R., 15, G4.
*Rowrah, L.M.S., 26, E3.
Rowsley, L.M.S., 16, B5.
Roxburgh, L.N.E.R., 32, E4.
Roy Bridge, L.N.E.R., 33, B4.
Roydon, L.N.E.R., 11, F3.
Royston (Herts.), L.N.E.R., 11, D3.
Royston & Notton, L.M.S., 21, F3.
*See also* Notton.
Royton, L.M.S., 21, F1.
Royton Jc., L.M.S., 21, F1.
Ruabon, G.W.R., 20, F4.
*Rubery, H.J., 9, A4.
Ruddington, L.N.E.R., 16, D3.
Rudgwick, S.R., 5, E2.
Rudyard Lake, L.M.S., 15, B4.
Rufford, L.M.S., 20, A3.
Rugby, L.M.S. & L.N.E.R., 10, A4.
Rugeley, L.M.S., 15, E4.
Rugeley Town, L.M.S., 15, E4.
Ruislip, L.P.T.B., 5, A2.
Rumbling Bridge, L.N.E.R., 34, G2.
Rumworth, L.M.S., 20, B2.
Runcorn, L.M.S., 20, C3.
*Runton West Jc.*, M.G.N./N.S.J., 18, D3.
Rushbury, G.W.R., 15, G1.
Rushcliffe Plat., L.N.E.R., 16, D4.
Rushden, L.M.S., 10, B1.
Rushey Platt (Goods), G.W.R., 9, G5.
Rushton (Northants.), *see* Glendon.
Rushton (Staffs.), L.M.S., 15, B4.
Ruskington, L.N.E.R., 17, C1.
Ruswarp, L.N.E.R., 28, F2.
Rutherford, L.N.E.R., 32, E5.
Rutherglen, L.M.S., 30, C1.
Ruthin, L.M.S., 19, E5.
Ruthven Road, L.M.S., 34, E2.
Ruthwell, L.M.S., 26, B3.
Rutland Street (Swansea), Mum. R., 7, B4.
Ryburgh, L.N.E.R., 18, E5.
Ryde (I.W.), S.R., 4, F3.
Rye, S.R. & § R.C.T., 6, E4.
*Ryeford, L.M.S., 9, E3.
Rye Hill & Burstwick, L.N.E.R., 22, E2.
Rye House, L.N.E.R., 11, F3.

Ryhall, L.N.E.R., 17, F1.
Ryhill, *see* Wintersett.
Ryhope, L.N.E.R., 28, C5.
Ryhope East, L.N.E.R., 28, C5.
*Rylstone, L.M.S., 21, C1.
*Ryston, L.N.E.R., 17, F4.
Ryton, L.N.E.R., 27, B5.

## S

Saddleworth, L.M.S., 21, F1.
Saffron Walden, L.N.E.R., 11, D4.
St. Agnes, G.W.R., 1, E1.
St. Albans, L.M.S. & L.N.E.R., 11, F1.
St. Andrews, L.N.E.R., 37, F2.
St. Andrew's (Derby) Goods, L.M.S., 16, D5.
St. Andrews Road, G.W.R., 8, C2.
St. Annes-on-the-Sea, L.M.S., 24, E4.
St. Anne's Park, G.W.R., 8, C1.
*St. Ann's Well, L.N.E.R., 16, C3.
St. Asaph, L.M.S., 19, D5.
St. Athan, G.W.R., 8, D5.
St. Austell, G.W.R., 1, D2.
St. Bees, L.M.S., 26, F4.
*St. Blazey, G.W.R., 1, D3.
St. Boswells, L.N.E.R., 32, E5.
St. Botolph's, L.N.E.R., 12, E4.
St. Briavels, G.W.R., 8, A1.
St. Budeaux, S.R., 1, D5.
St. Budeaux Plat., G.W.R., 1, D5.
*St. Catherine's Jc.*, L.M.S./S.Y., 21, F5.
St. Clears, G.W.R., 7, A1.
St. Columb Road, G.W.R., 1 D2.
St. Combs, L.N.E.R., 38, C1.
St. Cyrus, L.N.E.R., 37, C4.
St. David's (Exeter), **G.W.R.**/S.R., 2, B3.
*St. Dennis Jc.*, G.W.R., 1, D2.
St. Denys, **S.R.**/G.W.R., 4, E4.
St. Devereux, G.W.R., 14, F1.
St. Dunstans, L.N.E.R., 21, D2.
St. Enoch (Glasgow), L.M.S. 31, C1.
St. Erth, G.W.R., 1, E4.
St. Fagans, G.W.R., 8, C4.
St. Fillans, L.M.S., 34, F4.
St. Fort, L.N.E.R., 37, E2.
St. Germains, I.M.R., 23, B2.
St. Germans, G.W.R., 1, D4.
St. Harmons, G.W.R., 14, D4.
St. Helens (I.W.), S.R., 4, F2.
St. Helens (Lancs.), L.M.S & L.N.E.R., 20, C3.
St. Helens Jc., L.M.S., 20, C3.
St. Ives (Cornwall), G.W.R., 1, E4.
St. Ives (Hunts.), **L.N.E.R.**/L.M.S., 11, B2.
St. James (Chelt'm.), G.W.R. 9, D4.
St. James (Paisley), L.M.S., 30, C2.
St. James Deeping, L.N.E.R., 17, F2.
St. John's (Bedford), L.M.S., 11, D1.
St. John's (I.O.M.), I.M.R., 23, B2.
St. John's Chapel, L.N.E.R. 27, D3.
St. John's Rd., (I.W.), S.R., 4, F3.
St. Kew Highway, S.R., 1, C3.
St. Keyne, G.W.R., 1, D4.
St. Lawrence (I.W.), S.R., 4, G3.
St. Leonards, S.R., 6, F5.
St. Luke's, L.M.S., 20, A4.
St. Margaret's (Herts.), L.N.E.R., 11, F3.
St. Margaret's (Middx.), S.R., 5, B2.
St. Marnock's (Goods) L.M.S., 30, E2.
St. Mary Cray, S.R., 5, B4.
St. Mary's (Goods), *see* Dumfries.
*St. Mary's (Hunts.), L.N.E.R., 11, A2.
St. Mary's Bay, R.H.D.R., 6, E3.
St. Michael's, C.L.C., 20, C4.
St. Monance, L.N.E.R., 37, G3.
St. Neots, L.N.E.R., 11, C2.
St. Olave's, L.N.E.R., 18, F1.
St. Pancras, L.M.S., 5, A2.
St. Paul's, (Halifax), L.M.S./L.N.E.R., 21, E2.
St. Peter's, L.N.E.R., 27, B5.
St. Philip's (Bristol), L.M.S., 8, C2.
St. Thomas (Exeter), G.W.R., 2, B3.
St. Thomas (Swansea) L.M.S., 7, B4.
*St. Vigean's Jc.*, D.A., L.M.S., L.N.E.R., 37, D3.
Sale, M.S.J.A., 20, C1.

etton (Derbys.), L.M.S., 16, B5.
etton & Clay Mills (Staffs.), L.M.S., 16, D5.
*etton Jc.*, L.M.S., 16, D5.
ichen, L.N.E.R., 38, C2.
ines, L.M.S./L.N.E.R., 15, A4.
ome Ferry, L.M.S., 35, E1.
ood, S.R., 6, B5.
oud, G.W.R. & §L.M.S., 9, E3.
ian, L.M.S., 34, C3.
ibbins, L.M.S., 20, A1.
idley & Astwood Bank, L.M.S., 9, B4.
irmer, L.N.E.R., 11, D5.
irminster Newton, S.D., 3, E3.
irry, S.R., 6, C3.
irton, L.N.E.R., 16, A2.
itton (Goods), L.N.E.R., 21, D4.
val, L.M.S., 15, A3.
ckley, G.W.R., 9, B2.
dbury (Middlesex), *see* Wembley.
dbury (Staffs.), L.M.S./ L.N.E.R., 15, D5.
dbury (Suffolk), L.N.E.R., 12, D5.
dby Bridge, I.M.R., 23, A3.
dby Glen, I.M.R., 23, A3.
ly, G.W.R., 8, D4.
mmer Lane, L.N.E.R., 21, F3.
mmerseat, L.M.S., 20, A1.
mmerston, L.N.E.R., 30, B1.
mmit (Beattock) Goods, L.M.S., 31, F2.
nbury, S.R., 5, B2.
nderland, L.N.E.R., 28, C5.
ndridge Park, S.R., 5, B4.
nilaws, L.N.E.R., 32, D4.
nningdale, S.R., 5, B1.
nnymeads, S.R., 5, B1.
nnyside (Coatbridge), L.N.E.R., 31, C1.
rbiton, S.R., 5, B2.
rfleet, L.N.E.R., 17, D2.
tton (Cambs.), L.N.E.R., 11, B3.
tton (Notts.), *see* Barnby Moor.
tton (Surrey), S.R., 5, C3.
tton-at-Hone, *see* Farningham Road.
tton Bingham, S.R., 3, E2.
tton Bridge, M.G.N., 17, E4.
tton Coldfield, L.M.S., 15, F5.
tton-in-Ashfield, L.M.S. & L.N.E.R., 16, B4.
tton Jc., L.M.S., 16, B4.
tton Oak, L.M.S., 20, C3.
tton-on-Hull, L.N.E.R., 22, D3.
tton-on-Sea, L.N.E.R., 17, A4.
tton Park, L.M.S., 15, F5.
tton Scotney, G.W.R., 4, C3.
adlincote, L.M.S., 16, E5.
affham, L.N.E.R., 18, F5.
affhamprior, L.N.E.R., 11, E4.
ainsthorpe, L.N.E.R., 18, F3.
alecliffe, *see* Chestfield Halt.
alwell, L.N.E.R., 27, C5.
anage, S.R., 3, G5.
anbourne, L.M.S., 10, D2.
anley, S.R., 5, B4.
annington, L.M.S., 16, E5.
ansea, G.W.R., L.M.S. & Mum. R., 7, B4.
ansea Bay, L.M.S., 7, B4.
an Village, G.W.R., 15, F4.
anwick, S.R., 4, E3.
arkestone, *see* Chellaston.
avesey, L.N.E.R./L.M.S., 11, C3.
ay, S.R., 4, F4.
aythling, S.R./G.W.R., 4, D4.
imbridge, G.W.R., 7, F4.
nderby, L.M.S., 16, B2.
ndon, G.W.R., 9, G5.
ne, L.N.E.R., 22, D3.
ineshead, L.N.E.R., 17, D2.
*inlees Branch*, L.M.S., 30, D3.
inton (Lancs.), L.M.S., 20, B1.
inton (Yorks.), L.M.S. & L.N.E.R., 21, F4.
*thland Siding*, L.N.E.R., 16, E4.
xehouse, L.N.E.R., 21, E5.
*kes Jc.*, L.N.E.R., 16, A2.
fean, W.L., 14, B2.
nington, L.M.S., 31, E2.
monds Yat, G.W.R., 9, E1.
ston, L.M.S., 16, E3.

† The C.L.C. works into this joint station

## T

Tadcaster, L.N.E.R., 21, D4.
Tadworth & Walton-on-Hill, S.R., 5, C3.
Taffs Well, G.W.R., 8, C4.
Tain, L.M.S., 36, B4.
Takeley, L.N.E.R., 11, F4.
Talacre, L.M.S., 19, C5.
Talerddig, G.W.R., 14, B4.
Talgarth, G.W.R./L.M.S., 14, F3.
Talley Road, V.T., 13, G5.
Tallington, L.N.E.R., 17, F1.
Talsarn Plat., G.W.R., 13, E5.
Talsarnau, G.W.R., 19, F2.
Talybont-on-Usk, G.W.R., 14, G3.
Tal-y-Cafn & Eglwysbach, L.M.S., 19, D3.
Talyllyn Jc., G.W.R./ L.M.S., 14, G3.
Talywain, *see* Abersychan.
Tamerton Foliot, S.R., 1, D5.
Tamworth, L.M.S., 15, F5.
•Tanfield, L.N.E.R., 21, A3.
†Tanhouse Lane, L.N.E.R./ L.M.S., 20, C3.
Tankerton, *see* Whitstable.
Tannadice, L.M.S., 37, C2.
Tanshelf, L.M.S., 21, E4.
Taplow, G.W.R., 5, B1.
Tarbet, *see* Arrochar.
•Tarbolton, L.M.S., 30, E2.
Tarff, L.M.S., 26, C5.
Tarset, L.N.E.R., 27, A3.
Tattenhall, L.M.S., 20, E3.
Tattenhall Road, L.M.S., 20, E3.
Tattenham Corner, S.R., 5, C3.
Tattershall, L.N.E.R., 17, C2.
Taunton, G.W.R., 8, F4.
Tavistock, G.W.R. & S.R., 1, C5.
Tay Bridge (Dundee) L.N.E.R., 37, E2.
Taynuilt, L.M.S., 33, E3.
Tayport, L.N.E.R., 35, E4.
Tean, L.M.S., 15, D4.
Tebay, L.M.S./L.N.E.R., 27, F1.
Teddington, S.R., 5, B2.
Teigngrace, G.W.R., 2, C4.
Teignmouth, G.W.R., 2, C3.
Templecombe, S.R./S.D. & S.D., 3, D3.
Temple Hirst, L.N.E.R., 21, E5.
Temple Meads (Bristol), G.W.R./L.M.S., 8, C2.
Temple Sowerby, L.N.E.R., 27, E1.
Templeton, G.W.R., 7, C3.
Tempsford, L.N.E.R., 11, C2.
Tenbury Wells, G.W.R./ L.M.S., 9, A1.
Tenby, G.W.R., 7, D3.
Tenterden St. Michael's Halt, K.E.S.R., 6, D4.
Tenterden Town, K.E.S.R., 6, E4.
Tern Hill, G.W.R., 15, D2.
Terrington, M.G.N., 17, E4.
Teston Crossing Halt, S.R., 6, C5.
Tetbury, G.W.R., 9, F3.
•Tettenhall, G.W.R., 15, F3.
•Teversall, L.M.S. & L.N.E.R., 16, B4.
Tewkesbury, L.M.S., 9, D3.
Teynham, S.R., 6, C4.
Thame, G.W.R., 10, E3.
Thames Ditton, S.R., 5, B2.
•Thames Haven, L.M.S., 6, B5.
*Thames Haven Jc.*, L.M.S., 5, B5.
Thankerton, L.M.S., 31, E2.
Thatcham, G.W.R., 4, A3.
Thatto Heath, L.M.S., 20, C3.
Thaxted, L.N.E.R., 11, E4.
Thealby, *see* Winterton.
Theale, G.W.R., 4, A2.
Theddingworth, L.M.S., 16, G3.
Theddlethorpe, L.N.E.R., 17, A4.
Thelwall, L.M.S., 20, C2.
The Mound Jc., L.M.S., 36, A4.
The Oaks, L.M.S., 20, B2.
•Theobalds Grove, L.N.E.R., 11, G3.
Thetford, L.N.E.R., 12, B5.
Thetford Bridge, L.N.E.R., 12, B5.
Theydon Bois, L.N.E.R., 8, G3.
*Thingley Jc.*, G.W.R., 3, A4.
Thirsk, L.N.E.R., 21, A4.
Thongs Bridge, L.M.S., 21, F2.
•Thorganby, D.V.L., 21, D5.
Thorington, L.N.E.R., 12, E4.
Thornaby, L.N.E.R., 28, E4.
•Thornbury, L.M.S., 9, F2.
Thorndon, *see* Aspall.
Thorne, L.N.E.R., 21, E5.
Thorner, L.N.E.R., 21, D4.
Thorney, M.G.N., 17, F2.
Thorney & Kingsbury Halt, G.W.R., 3, D1.
Thorneyburn, L.N.E.R., 27, A2.
•Thorneywood, L.N.E.R., 16, C3.
Thornfalcon, G.W.R., 8, F3.
Thornhill (Dumfries), L.M.S., 31, G2.
Thornhill (Yorks.), L.M.S., 21, E3.
Thornielee, L.N.E.R., 31, E5.
Thornley, L.N.E.R., 28, D4.
*Thornley Coll.*, L.N.E.R., 28, D5.
Thornliebank, L.M.S., 30, C1.
Thornton (Ches.), *see* Stanlow.
Thornton (Lancs.), L.M.S., 24, D4.
Thornton (Yorks.), L.N.E.R., 21, D2.
Thornton Abbey, L.N.E.R., 22, E3.
Thornton Dale, L.N.E.R., 22, A5.
Thorntonhall, L.M.S., 30, D1.
Thornton-in-Craven, L.M.S., 21, C1.
Thornton Jc., L.N.E.R., 31, A4.
Thorp Arch, L.N.E.R., 21, C4.
Thorpe (Northants.), L.M.S., 11, B1.
Thorpe (Norwich), L.N.E.R., 18, F3.
Thorpe Bay, L.M.S., 6, A4.
Thorpe Cloud, L.M.S., 15, C5.
Thorpe Culvert, L.N.E.R., 17, B4.
Thorpe Gates (Goods), L.N.E.R., 21, D5.
•Thorpe-in-Balne, L.N.E.R., 21, F5.
Thorpe-le-Soken, L.N.E.R., 12, F3.
Thorpeness, L.N.E.R., 12, C2.
Thorpe-on-the-Hill, L.M.S., 16, B1.
•Thorpe Thewles, L.N.E.R., 28, E5.
Thorverton, G.W.R., 2, A3.
Thrapston, L.M.S., 10, A1.
Three Bridges, S.R., 5, D3.
Three Cocks Jc., G.W.R./ L.M.S., 14, F2.
Three Counties, L.N.E.R., 11, E2.
*Three Horse Shoes Siding* (Cambs.), L.N.E.R., 11, A3.
Threlkeld, L.M.S., 26, E1.
Threshfield, *see* Grassington.
Throsk, L.M.S., 31, A1.
•Thrumster, L.M.S., 39, D4.
Thrumpton (Goods), L.N.E.R., 16, A3.
Thurcroft (Goods), L.M.S./ L.N.E.R., 21, G4.
Thurgarton, L.M.S., 16, C3.
*Thurgoland*, L.N.E.R., 21, F3.
Thurlby, L.N.E.R., 17, E1.
Thurnley & Scraptoft, L.N.E.R., 16, F3.
Thurnham, *see* Bearsted.
Thursford, M.G.N., 18, D4.
Thurso, L.M.S., 39, C3.
Thurstaston, L.M.S., 20, C5.
Thurston, L.N.E.R., 12, C5.
Thuxton, L.N.E.R., 18, F4.
Tibbermuir, L.M.S., 34, E2.
Tibshelf, L.N.E.R. & •L.M.S., 16, B4.
•Tickhill & Wadworth, S.Y., 21, G5.
Tiddington, G.W.R., 10, E3.
Tidenham, G.W.R., 8, B2.
Tidworth, G.W.R., 4, B5.
Tilbury, L.M.S., 5, B5.
Tile Hill, L.M.S., 10, A5.
Tilehurst, G.W.R., 4, A2.
Tillicoultry L.N.E.R., 31, A2.
Tillietudlem, L.M.S., 31, D1.
Tillyfourie, L.N.E.R., 38, F4.
Tillynaught, L.N.E.R., 38, C4.
Tilton, L.M.S./L.N.E.R., 16, F2.
Timberland, *see* Scopwick.
Timperley, M.S.J.A., 20, C1.
Tingley, L.N.E.R., 21, E3.
Tinsley, L.N.E.R., 21, G4.
Tintern, G.W.R., 8, B2.
Tipton, G.W.R. & L.M.S., 15, F4.
Tipton St. John's, S.R., 2, B2.
Tiptree, L.N.E.R., 12, F5.
*Tir Pentwys Coll.*, G.W.R., 8, B4.
Tir Phil, G.W.R., 8, A4.
Tirydail, G.W.R./L.M.S., 7, A4.
Tisbury, S.R., 3, D4.
Tissington, L.M.S., 15, C5.
Tisted, S.R., 4, C2.
Titley, G.W.R., 14, E2.
Tiverton, G.W.R., 2, A3.
Tiverton Jc., G.W.R., 2, A2.
Tivetshall, L.N.E.R., 12, A3.
Tochieneal, L.N.E.R., 38, C5.
Toddington, G.W.R., 9, D4.
Todmorden, L.M.S., 21, E1.
•Tod Point, L.N.E.R., 28, E4.
Toft & Kingston (Goods), L.M.S., 11, C3.
*Tolcarn Jc.*, G.W.R., 1, D1.
Toller, G.W.R., 3, E2.
Tollerton, L.N.E.R., 21, B4.
Tollesbury, L.N.E.R., 12, F5.
Tolleshunt D'Arcy, L.N.E.R., 12, F5.
Tomatin, L.M.S., 36, E4.
Tonbridge, S.R., 5, D5.
Tondu, G.W.R., 7, C5.
Tonfanau, G.W.R., 13, B5.
•Tonge & Bredon, L.M.S., 16, E5.
•Tongham, S.R., 4, B1.
Tonyrefail, G.W.R., 8, B5.
Tooting, S.R., 5, B3.
Topcliffe, L.N.E.R., 21, A4.
Topsham, S.R., 2, B3.
Torksey, L.N.E.R., 16, A2.
Torpantau, G.W.R., 8, A5.
Torphins, L.N.E.R., 38, G4.
Torquay, G.W.R., 2, D3.
Torrance, L.N.E.R., 30, B1.
Torre, G.W.R., 2, D3.
Torrington, S.R., 7, G3.
•Torryburn, L.N.E.R., 30, B2.
Torver, L.M.S., 26, G2.
Totley, *see* Dore.
Totnes, G.W.R., 2, D4.
Tottenham, L.N.E.R., 5, A3.
Totteridge, •L.N.E.R./ L.P.T.B., 5, A3.
Tottington, L.M.S., 20, A1.
Totton, S.R., 4, E4.
Towcester, L.M.S., 10, C3.
Tower Hill, S.R., 1, B5.
Towiemore Halt, L.N.E.R., 38, D5.
Tow Law, L.N.E.R., 27, D4.
Towneley, L.M.S., 24, D1.
Town Green, L.M.S., 20, B4.
*Townhill Jc.*, L.N.E.R., 31, A3.
Towyn, G.W.R. & Tal., 13, B5.
Trabboch, L.M.S., 30, F2.
Trafford Park, C.L.C., 20, C1.
Tram Inn, G.W.R., 9, D1.
•Tranent, L.N.E.R., 31, B5.
Trawscoed, G.W.R., 13, D5.
Trawsfynydd, G.W.R., 19, F3.
Treborth, L.M.S., 19, D2.
Tredegar, L.M.S., 8, A4.
Treeton, L.M.S., 21, G4.
Trefeglwys, *see* Pwllglas.
Trefeinon, G.W.R./L.M.S., 14, F3.
Trefnant, L.M.S., 19, D5.
Treforest, G.W.R., 8, B5.
Trefriw, *see* Llanrwst.
Tregaron, G.W.R., 14, E5.
Tregarth, L.M.S., 19, D2.
Trehafod, G.W.R., 8, B5.
Treherbert, G.W.R., 7, B5.
Trench Crossing, L.M.S., 15, E2.
Trenholme Bar, L.N.E.R., 28, F4.
Trent, L.M.S., 16, D4.
Trentham, L.M.S., 15, D3.
Trentham Gardens, L.M.S., 15, D3.
Treorchy, G.W.R., 8, B5.
Tresmeer, S.R., 1, B4.
Trethomas, G.W.R., 8, B4.
Trevil, L.M.S., 7, A4.
Trevor, G.W.R., 20, F5.
§*Trewythan*, G.W.R., 14, C4.
Trimdon, L.N.E.R., 28, D5.
Trimingham, N.S.J., 18, D2.
Trimley, L.N.E.R., 12, E3.
Trimsaran (Goods), G.W.R., 7, A3.
Trimsaran Rd., G.W.R., 7, A2.
Tring, L.M.S., 10, E1.
Troedyrhiw, G.W.R., 8, B5.
Troedyrhiew Garth, G.W.R., 7, B5.
Troon, L.M.S., 30, E3.
Troutbeck, L.M.S., 26, E1.
Trowbridge, G.W.R., 3, B4.
Trowell, L.M.S., 16, C4.
•Trowse (Norwich), L.N.E.R., 18, F3.
Troy (Monmouth), G.W.R., 8, A1.
Truro, G.W.R., 1, E1.
Trusham, G.W.R., 2, C3.
Truthall Platform, G.W.R., 1, F5.
Tub's Hill (Sevenoaks), S.R., 5, C4.
Tullibardine, L.M.S., 34, F3.
Tulloch, L.N.E.R., 33, B5.
Tulse Hill, S.R., 5, B3.
•Tumble, G.W.R., 7, A3.
Tumby Woodside, L.N.E.R., 17, C2.
Tunbridge Wells, S.R., 5, D5.
Tunstall, L.M.S., 15, C3.
•Turnberry, L.M.S., 30, G4.
Turnchapel, S.R., 1, D5.
•Turnhouse, L.N.E.R., 31, B3.
Turriff, L.N.E.R., 38, D3.
Turton, L.M.S., 20, A2.
Turvey, L.M.S., 10, C1.
Tutbury, L.M.S./•L.N.E.R., 15, D5.
Tuxford, L.N.E.R., 16, B2.
Twechar, L.N.E.R., 30, B1.
Tweedmouth, L.N.E.R., 32, D2.
Twenty, M.G.N., 17, E2.
Twickenham, S.R., 5, B2.
Twizell, L.N.E.R., 32, D3.
Twyford, G.W.R., 4, A1.
Twywell, L.M.S., 10, A1.
*Tycoch Jc.*, G.W.R., 7, A2.
Ty Croes, L.M.S., 19, D1.
Tydd, M.G.N., 17, E3.
Tyldesley, L.M.S., 20, B2.
Tylorstown, G.W.R., 8, B5.
Tylwch, G.W.R., 14, C4.
Tyndrum, L.M.S. & L.N.E.R., 33, E5.
Tyne Dock, L.N.E.R., 28, B5.
Tynehead, L.N.E.R., 31, C5.
Tynemouth, L.N.E.R., 28, B5.
Tyseley, G.W.R., 15, G5.
•Tytherington, L.M.S., 9, F2.

## U

Uckfield, S.R., 5, E4.
Uddingston, L.M.S., 30, C1.
Udny, L.N.E.R., 38, E2.
Uffculme, G.W.R., 2, A2.
Uffington (Berks.), G.W.R., 10, F5.
Uffington & Barnack, L.M.S., 17, F1.
•Ulbster, L.M.S., 39, E4.
Ulceby, L.N.E.R., 22, E3.
Ulleskelf, L.N.E.R., 21, D4.
Ullesthorpe, L.M.S., 16, G4.
Ulting, *see* Langford.
Ulverston, L.M.S., 24, A4.
Umberleigh, S.R., 7, F3.
Union Mills, I.M.R., 23, B2.
Unstone, L.M.S., 16, A5.
Uphall, L.N.E.R., 31, B3.
Uphill, *see* Bleadon.
Upholland, L.M.S., 20, B3.
Uplawmoor, L.N.E.R., 30, D2.
Upminster, L.M.S./L.P.T.B., 5, A5.
Upminster Bridge, L.M.S./ L.P.T.B., 5, A5.
Upper Bank, L.M.S., 7, B4.
Upper Batley, L.N.E.R., 21, E3.
Upper Broughton, L.M.S., 16, D3.
Upper Greenock, L.M.S., 30, B3.
Upper Jc. Goods (Greenhill), L.N.E.R., 31, B1.
•Upper Lydbrook, S.V.Y., 9, E1.
•Uppermill, L.M.S., 21, F1
Upper Pontnewydd, G.W.R., 8, B3.
Upper Port Glasgow (Goods), L.M.S., 30, B3.
Upper Warlingham, S.R., 5, C3.
Uppingham, L.M.S., 16, F2.
Upton (Ches.), L.N.E.R., 20, C5.
Upton & Blewbury, G.W.R., 10, F4.
•Upton (Yorks.), L.N.E.R., 21, E4.
Upton Magna, G.W.R./ L.M.S., 15, E1.
Upton-on-Severn, L.M.S., 9, C3.
•Upwell, W.U.T., 17, F4.
Upwey, G.W.R., 3, F3.
Upwey Jc., G.W.R., 3, F3.
Urmston, C.L.C., 20, C2.
Urquhart, L.N.E.R., 36, C1.
Ushaw Moor, L.N.E.R., 27, D5.
Usk, G.W.R., 8, B3.
Usselby, *see* Claxby.
Usworth, L.N.E.R., 28, C5.
Utterby Halt, L.N.E.R., 22, G2.
Uttoxeter, L.M.S./•L.N.E.R., 15, D5.
Uxbridge, G.W.R. & L.P.T.B., 5, A2.

## V

Valley, L.M.S., 19, B2.
Van Road, *see* Garth, G.W.R.
Vauxhall (Gt. Yarmouth), L.N.E.R., 18, F1.
*Vauxhall Fish Mkt.*, L.N.E.R. /M.G.N., 18, F1.
Velvet Hall, L.N.E.R., 32, D3.
Venn Cross, G.W.R., 8, F5.
Ventnor (I.W.), S.R., 4, G3.
Ventnor West (I.W.), S.R., 4, G3.
Verney Jc., L.M.S./•L.N.E.R. /•L.P.T.B., 10, D3.
Verwood, S.R., 3, E5.
Victoria (London), S.R. & L.P.T.B., 5, B3.
Victoria (M'chester.), L.M.S. 20, B1.
Victoria (Mon.), G.W.R., 8, A4.
Victoria (Norwich) Goods, L.N.E.R., 18, F3.
Victoria (Nott'm.), L.N.E.R., 16, C4.
Victoria (Sheffield), L.N.E.R., 21, G3.
Victoria (Swansea), L.M.S., 7, B4.
Victoria Docks, L.N.E.R., 5, B4.
Vine Street (Uxbridge), G.W.R., 5, A2.
Virginia Water, S.R., 5, B1.
Vobster (Goods), G.W.R., 3, B3.
•Vowchurch, G.W.R., 14 F1.

## W

Wadborough, L.M.S., 9, C3.
Waddington, L.N.E.R., 16 B1.
Waddon, S.R., 5, C3.
Wadebridge, S.R., 1, C2.
Wadhurst, S.R., 5, E5.
Wadsley Bridge, L.N.E.R. 21, G3.
Wadworth, *see* Tickhill.
•Waenavon, L.M.S., 8, A4.
Wainfleet, L.N.E.R., 17, C4.
Wakefield, L.M.S. & L.N.E.R., 21, E3.
Wakerley & Barrowden, L.M.S., 16, F1.
Wakes Colne, *see* Chappel.
Walcot, G.W.R./L.M.S., 15, E1.
Waldron & Horam, S.R., 5, E5.
Waleswood, L.N.E.R., 16, A4.
Walkden, L.M.S., 20, B2.
Walker, L.N.E.R., 28, B5.
Walkerburn, L.N.E.R., 30, E5.
Walker Gate, L.N.E.R., 28, B5.
Walkeringham, L.N.E.R., 22, G5.
Wall, L.N.E.R., 27, B3.
Wallasey, L.M.S., 20, C4.
Wall Grange, L.M.S., 15, C4.
Wallingfen, L.N.E.R., 22, D5.
Wallingford, G.W.R., 10, F3.
Wallington, S.R., 5, C3.
Wallsend, L.N.E.R., 28, B5.
Walmer, S.R., 6, C1.
Walpole, M.G.N., 17, E4.
Walsall, L.M.S., 15, F4.
•Walsall Wood, L.M.S., 15, F4.
Walsden, L.M.S., 21, E1.
Walsingham, L.N.E.R., 18, D5.
Waltham, L.N.E.R., 22, F2.
Waltham Cross & Abbey, L.N.E.R., 11, G3.
•Waltham-on-the-Wold, L.N.E.R., 16, D2.
Walton (Derby), *see* Barton.
Walton (Northants.), L.M.S., 17, F2.
Walton (& Anfield) (Lancs.), L.M.S., 20, C4.
Walton-on-Hill, *see* Tadworth.
Walton-on-Thames, S.R., 5, C2.
Walton-on-the-Naze, L.N.E.R., 12, E3.
Wamphray, L.M.S., 26, A3.
Wanborough, S.R., 5, C1.
Wansford, L.M.S., 11, A1.
Wanstrow, G.W.R., 3, C3.
Wantage Road, G.W.R., 10, F5.
Wappenham, L.M.S., 10, C3.
*Wapping Wharf* (Bristol), G.W.R., 8, C2.
Warblington Halt, S.R., 4, E2.
•Warboys, L.N.E.R., 11, B2.
Warburton, *see* Heatley.
Warcop, L.N.E.R., 27, E2.
Wardhouse, L.N.E.R., 38, E4.
•Wardleworth, L.M.S., 20, A1.
Ware, L.N.E.R., 11, F3.
Wareham, S.R., 3, F4.
Wargrave, G.W.R., 10, G2.
Wark, L.N.E.R., 27, B3.
Warkworth, L.N.E.R., 32, F1.
Warley, *see* Brentwood.
Warlingham, S.R., 5, C3.
Warminster, G.W.R., 3, C4.
Warmley, L.M.S., 8, C1.
Warmsworth (Goods), L.N.E.R., 21, F5.
Warnham, S.R., 5, D2.
*Warren Hill Jc.*, L.N.E.R., 11, C4.
Warrington, L.M.S. & C.L.C., 20, C2.
Warrior Sq. (St. Leonards), S.R., 6, F5.
Warsop, L.N.E.R., 16, B4.
Warthill, L.N.E.R., 21, C5.
Wartle, L.N.E.R., 38, E3.
Warwick, G.W.R., 10, B5.
Warwick (Milverton), L.M.S., 10, B5.
Washford, G.W.R., 8, E5.
Washington, L.N.E.R., 28, C5.
Waskerley (Goods), L.N.E.R., 27, D4.
Wassand, L.N.E.R., 22, D3.
Watchet, G.W.R., 8, E5.
•Watchingwell (I.W.), S.R., 4, F3.
Waterbeach, L.N.E.R., 11 C3.
•Waterfall, I.M.R., 23, B2.

---

† The C.L.C. works into Widnes Joint Station.

Printed by Ian Allan Printing Ltd at their works at Coombelands in Runnymede, England